Creating Equality at Home

Creating Equality at Home tells the fascinating stories of 25 couples around the world whose everyday decisions about sharing the housework and childcare – from who cooks the food, washes the dishes, and helps with homework, to who cuts back on paid work – all add up to a gender revolution. From North and South America to Europe, Asia, and Australia, these couples tell a story of similarity despite vast cultural differences. By rejecting the prescription that men's identities are determined by paid work and women's by motherhood, the couples show that men can put family first and are as capable of nurturing as women, and that women can pursue careers as seriously as their husbands do – bringing profound rewards for men, women, marriage, and children. Working couples with children will discover that equality is possible and exists right now.

Francine M. Deutsch, author of *Halving It All: How Equally Shared Parenting Works* (1999), is Emerita Professor of Psychology at Mount Holyoke College, USA. She has published extensively on issues of gender justice. She and her husband equally shared the care of their son.

Ruth A. Gaunt, Associate Professor at the University of Lincoln, UK, previously held a tenured senior lectureship at Bar Ilan University, Israel, and prestigious fellowships at both Harvard University, USA, and the University of Cambridge, UK. Her published research focuses on the social psychology of gender and families. She and her husband have three children and share childcare equally.

Advance Praise for *Creating Equality at Home*

"This is an impressive work, both for its scope of research and for its optimism that equality at a household level is possible. The stories provide much-needed nuance to the lives of couples who 'undo gender,' and how women, men, and children benefit from equal sharing."

Gary Barker, President and CEO, Promundo, USA, and co-author of
State of the World's Fathers

"It is the most compelling and inspirational book about involved fathering to appear in decades. Not only are the couples' stories illuminated with sensitivity to cultural and political differences, but personal struggles and intergenerational tensions are expertly discussed. This is the best book on family labor-sharing."

Scott Coltrane, sociologist, Senior Vice President, University of Oregon, USA, and author of Gender and Families

"The authors successfully solve the puzzle of how couples can resist the dominant gender norms surrounding them. This fascinating book demonstrates that, beyond cultural and institutional differences, fathers benefit from equality as much as mothers when they contribute in tandem with their partner to shape a new and fairer world."

Jeanne Fagnani, Emeritus Senior Research Fellow in Sociology, University of Paris-Sorbonne, France, and co-author of Fathers and Mothers

"We have been given an exceptionally comprehensive account of how heterosexual couples throughout the globe endeavor to create domestic equality. The stories demonstrate how, under the right social conditions, partners can overcome barriers to forge equal relationships. It is an indispensable guide for dismantling the outdated norms and structures that support gender inequality."

Kathleen Gerson, Professor of Sociology and Collegiate Professor of Arts and Science, New York University, USA

"This is a fascinating book, providing riveting stories that show how couples around the world become resisters and 'undo gender.' Other books explain inequality, while this important book explains equality and how it can be accomplished. Couples attempting to reconcile work and family, seasoned activists and scholars, graduates and undergraduates should read it."

Naomi Gerstel, Distinguished University Professor, University of Massachusetts, USA, and co-author of Unequal Time

"This book is a perfect blend of scholarly analysis and compelling personal stories of couples who have bucked gender norms to create equality in their homes. From twenty-two countries across the globe, these men and women provide road maps for undoing gender, and make a powerful case for the tremendous rewards that follow from embracing equality."

Ronnie Janoff-Bulman, Professor Emerita of Psychological and Brain Sciences, University of Massachusetts, USA, and author of Shattered Assumptions

"This is the collection I have been waiting for. The editors bring together a brilliant group of scholars from around the world to share stories of equal-sharing couples in twenty-two countries. They provide a wonderful journey through 60/60 parenting in Israel, dismantling housewifization in Indonesia, flying toward equality in Honduras, and more."

Gayle Kaufman, Nancy and Erwin Maddrey Professor of Sociology, Davidson College, USA, and author of Superdads

"This creative book analyzes the sharing process established by couples from different cultures. Based on international comparisons, it highlights the benefits of egalitarian couples who fairly split domestic tasks. It is a truly amazing book for mapping out a household's journey toward gender equality!"

Hélène Périvier, economist, Director of the Programme de Recherche et d'Enseignement de Savoirs sur le Genre (PRESAGE), and co-author of Le Deuxième Âge de l'émancipation

"This innovative book demonstrates, using interviews from twenty-two countries, how couples undo gender, by describing a typical day in their lives. I would recommend the book for every family (and to academics researching families) to become happy in their own way."

Andrea Pető, Professor, Central European University, Hungary, and co-editor of Gendered Wars, Gendered Memories

"While gender inequality at home seems intractable, this study shows that equal sharing is possible and a common methodology across cases reveals the conditions under which it happens. With vivid qualitative data and an engaging writing, this book is a superb teaching resource as well as a must-have for researchers."

Juliet Schor, Professor of Sociology, Boston College, USA, and author of After the Gig

"Here is a book with a mission. Its goal is to inject some optimism into debates that focus on the persistence of 'traditional' gender roles in house-work and childcare. It's an uplifting account and an informative read."

Jacqueline Scott, Emerita Professor of Empirical Sociology, University of Cambridge, UK

"For anyone interested in relationships or gender, this unique compilation of case studies on gender resisters is a must-read. The authors show what gender resisters share, regardless of nationality, and convincingly demon-strate how equality is achieved, as well as the benefits it affords for both women and men."

Janice M. Steil, Professor Emeritus of Psychology, Adelphi University, USA, and author of Marital Equality

EDITED BY
FRANCINE M. DEUTSCH
RUTH A. GAUNT

CREATING EQUALITY AT HOME

How 25 Couples Around the World Share Housework and Childcare

CAMBRIDGE
UNIVERSITY PRESS

CAMBRIDGE
UNIVERSITY PRESS

University Printing House, Cambridge CB2 8BS, United Kingdom

One Liberty Plaza, 20th Floor, New York, NY 10006, USA

477 Williamstown Road, Port Melbourne, VIC 3207, Australia

314–321, 3rd Floor, Plot 3, Splendor Forum, Jasola District Centre,
New Delhi – 110025, India

79 Anson Road, #06–04/06, Singapore 079906

Cambridge University Press is part of the University of Cambridge.

It furthers the University's mission by disseminating knowledge in the pursuit of
education, learning, and research at the highest international levels of excellence.

www.cambridge.org
Information on this title: www.cambridge.org/9781108497886
DOI: 10.1017/9781108597319

First published 2020

Printed in the United Kingdom by TJ International Ltd. Padstow Cornwall

A catalogue record for this publication is available from the British Library.

Library of Congress Cataloging-in-Publication Data
NAMES: Deutsch, Francine, 1948– author. | Gaunt, Ruth A., 1969– author.
TITLE: Creating equality at home : how 25 couples around the world share housework
and childcare / Francine M. Deutsch, Mount Holyoke College, Massachusetts,
Ruth A. Gaunt, University of Lincoln.
DESCRIPTION: 1st Edition. | New York : Cambridge University Press, 2020. |
Includes index.
IDENTIFIERS: LCCN 2019038858 (print) | LCCN 2019038859 (ebook) |
ISBN 9781108497886 (hardback) | ISBN 9781108708845 (paperback) |
ISBN 9781108597319 (epub)
SUBJECTS: LCSH: Sex discrimination against women. | Women's rights. | Women–Violence
against–Prevention. | Women–Education–Law and legislation.
CLASSIFICATION: LCC HQ1237 .D488 2020 (print) | LCC HQ1237 (ebook) |
DDC 305.42–dc23
LC record available at https://lccn.loc.gov/2019038858
LC ebook record available at https://lccn.loc.gov/2019038859

ISBN 978-1-108-49788-6 Hardback
ISBN 978-1-108-70884-5 Paperback

To Jerry and Doram
Our Equally Sharing Husbands

Contents

List of Contributors   *page* xiii
Acknowledgments   xvii
Development and Gender Equality in Participating Countries   xxiii

SETTING THE STAGE

1   Introduction   1
    Francine M. Deutsch and Ruth A. Gaunt

2   Past and Current Research   8
    Francine M. Deutsch and Ruth A. Gaunt

CONSCIOUSLY CREATING EQUALITY

3   Israel   29
    Ruth A. Gaunt

4   Honduras   43
    Erin Murphy-Graham

5   Montenegro   55
    Milena Račeta Stojanović

6   Switzerland   69
    Julia C. Nentwich, Stefanie Schälin, and Wiebke Tennhoff

7   Sweden   80
    Linda Haas and Leslie Stanley-Stevens

VIOLATING SOCIAL NORMS

8   Indonesia   93
    Siti Kusujiarti

9   Croatia   107
    Lynette Šikić-Mićanović

10 Bhutan   121
    Dolma Choden Roder and Tashi Choden

11 Hungary   134
    Judit Takács

12 USA: Southern California   147
    Alicia Márquez

PRIORITIZING FAMILY

13 USA: New England   161
    Francine M. Deutsch

14 Brazil   181
    Maria Auxiliadora Dessen and Cláudio V. Torres

15 Australia   195
    Judy Rose and Janeen Baxter

16 Singapore   206
    Karen Mui-Teng Quek and Carmen Knudson-Martin

DRAWING ON LESSONS FROM FAMILIES OF ORIGIN

17 Austria   221
    Sabine Buchebner-Ferstl and Mariam Irene Tazi-Preve

18 Turkey   236
    Cagla Diner

19 Czech Republic   247
    Hana Maříková

20 People's Republic of China   270
    Yifei Shen Translated by Jiayi Qian

21 Slovenia   281
    Živa Humer and Metka Kuhar

USING GOVERNMENT POLICIES

22 Iceland   295
    Ingólfur V. Gíslason

23 Germany   307
    Anna Dechant, Harald Rost, and Florian Schulz

24 United Kingdom   317
    Oriel Sullivan

25 Portugal 331
Karin Wall, Vanessa Cunha, and Sofia Marinho

WHAT WE HAVE LEARNED

26 Undoing Gender: Different Cultures, Similar Stories 345
Francine M. Deutsch and Ruth A. Gaunt

27 Conclusion: The Paths to Equality 366
Francine M. Deutsch, Ruth A. Gaunt, and
Madison E. Richards

Index 395

Contributors

Janeen Baxter
Institute for Social Science Research, The University of Queensland, Australia

Sabine Buchebner-Ferstl
Austrian Institute for Family Studies, University of Vienna

Tashi Choden
ZIJI Consultancy, Bhutan

Vanessa Cunha
Institute of Social Sciences, University of Lisbon, Portugal

Anna Dechant
Federal Institute for Population Research, Germany

Maria Auxiliadora Dessen
University of Brasília and Catholic University of Salvador, Brazil

Cagla Diner
Kadir Has University, Turkey and Institute for Advanced Study in the Humanities, Germany

Ingólfur V. Gíslason
Faculty of Sociology, Anthropology and Folkloristics, University of Iceland

Linda Haas
Indiana University at Indianapolis, USA

Živa Humer
The Peace Institute, Institute for Contemporary Social and Political Studies, Slovenia

Carmen Knudson-Martin
Lewis and Clark Graduate School of Education and Counseling, USA

Metka Kuhar
Faculty of Social Sciences, University of Ljubljana, Slovenia

Siti Kusujiarti
Department of Sociology and Anthropology, Warren Wilson College, USA

Sofia Marinho
Institute of Social Sciences, University of Lisbon, Portugal

Alicia Márquez
Cochella Valley Unified School District, USA

Hana Maříková
Institute of Sociology of the Czech Academy of Sciences, Czech Republic

Erin Murphy-Graham
Graduate School of Education, University of California, Berkeley, USA

Julia C. Nentwich
Research Institute for Organizational Psychology, University of St. Gallen, Switzerland

Jiayi Qian
IQVIA, People's Republic of China

Karen Mui-Teng Quek
Marriage and Family Therapy Program, Biola University, USA

Madison E. Richards
The University of Pennsylvania School of Dental Medicine, USA

Dolma Choden Roder
Royal Thimphu College, Bhutan

Judy Rose
Faculty of Arts, Education, and Law, Griffith University, Australia

Harald Rost
State Institute for Family Research at the University of Bamberg, Germany

Stefanie Schälin
Institute for Gender Studies, University of Basel, Switzerland

Florian Schulz
State Institute for Family Research at the University of Bamberg, Germany

Yifei Shen
School of Social Development and Public Policy, Fudan University, People's Republic of China

Leslie Stanley-Stevens[†]
College of Liberal and Fine Arts, Tarleton State University, USA

Milena Račeta Stojanović
Podgorica, Montenegro

Oriel Sullivan
Department of Social Science, University College London, United Kingdom

Lynette Šikić-Mićanović
Institute of Social Sciences Ivo Pilar, Croatia

Judit Takács
Centre for Social Sciences, Hungarian Academy of Sciences

Mariam Irene Tazi-Preve
Department of Political Science, University of Central Florida, USA

Wiebke Tennhoff
Research Institute for Organizational Psychology, University of St. Gallen, Switzerland

Cláudio V. Torres
Institute of Psychology, University of Brasília, Brazil

Karin Wall
Institute of Social Sciences, University of Lisbon

Acknowledgments

This project was conceived more than a decade ago. With no funding, and just the hope/belief that, if illuminated, stories of couples around the world would provide clues to how gender equality at home could be achieved, I (Fran) was fortunate to recruit scholars to participate. I knew none of them personally before the project began. Ruth and I are extremely grateful to these social scientists who represent multiple disciplines and 22 countries. We are honored by the involvement of this impressive group of scholars: for the trust they showed by signing on to this vision, for their hard work, their analytic insights, their tolerance for our endless requests, their patience, and their commitment to gender justice.

This book couldn't exist without our international collection of 25 equally sharing couples who generously opened their homes and their hearts to tell their stories. We offer them our heartfelt thanks.

In the course of this long project, lives began and ended. We welcomed a number of babies who were born to our authors. Tragically, Leslie Stanley-Stevens was diagnosed with pancreatic cancer and died less than a year later at age 55. We mourn her loss. Leslie had stepped in to rescue our Sweden chapter when the original Swedish partner backed out. Not satisfied to conduct an interview by phone from the USA, she volunteered to go to Sweden to do it on-site. When she got sick and couldn't continue, Linda Haas agreed to join the project and finish the chapter, so Sweden was rescued again.

Friends and colleagues who live very busy lives nonetheless took time to comment on the chapters I co-authored with Ruth. The insightful comments of Naomi Gerstel, Vanessa Cunha, Oriel Sullivan, and

Maureen Perry-Jenkins led to many interesting conversations between Ruth and me, forcing us to qualify and clarify our ideas, and to pay attention to ideas we might have ignored. Ronnie Janoff-Bulman gave us critical advice about how to re-organize the concluding chapters. Virginia Brabender reminded these two social psychologists that personality matters too. Elizabeth Hay and Hedda Orkin weighed in on which cases might persuade a publisher to endorse the book, and Gail Robinson provided editing advice on those chapters.

Two grammar gurus, Robert Zussman and Robert Shilkret, saved us from many grammatically incorrect pitfalls. Bill Sweet helped with German translations of statistical information on Austria and Switzerland. Rocio Ramirez translated Spanish interviews. Jessica Salvatore consulted on current social psychological literature.

Cambridge University Press has been the perfect home for this book. Janka Romero possesses a rare combination of reassuring calmness and conscientious attention to myriad publishing issues and details, which make it a joy to work with her. Her quick, comprehensive, and intelligent responses to all of my emails from the very first one rightly signaled that she would be the ideal editor for us. Emily Watton, her editorial assistant, juggled all of the pieces that brought this publication together with great aplomb, perhaps answering more questions than any previous author had asked. Many thanks to Adam Hooper for his efficient handling of the production side, and to Deborah Hey, copyeditor extraordinaire, whose work simply amazed us.

Fran's work on this project was supported by a faculty grant and a faculty fellowship from Mount Holyoke College and an ACE-Sloan Capstone award for "Global Project in Family Work." Ruth's work on this project was supported by a research grant from Bar-Ilan University and a Marie Curie Intra-European Fellowship from the European Union. The map illustrations were substantially modified by N. Stahl from the vector globe image by Erin Dill. The license can be accessed from: https://creativecommons.org/licenses/by/3.0/us/legalcode.

A Personal Note from Fran

When I did the research for *Halving it All*, I was struck by how couples who ostensibly believed in gender equality were derailed from practicing it because they clung to essentialist ideas that women were fundamentally different from men. They believed that a father could not provide the nurturance that we usually associate with mothers. Equal sharers, however, held no such belief and showed every day that fathers can care as well as mothers. At the time, I thought, "I wish someone would do some quantitative research on this topic." Lo and behold, in 2007, I discovered Ruth Gaunt's article in *Sex Roles* doing exactly that. I got in touch with her and to my delight she agreed to participate in my fledgling project. She helped me refine the methodology, identified her own couple in Israel, skillfully interviewed them, and wrote a case chapter. When I read her terrific chapter on Netta and Gadi, I asked her to co-edit the book. She demurred at first, modestly citing her status as a non-native speaker, but then she agreed. Her incisive intellect and succinct, engaging writing style meant both astute editing and perceptive analyses. Our collaboration could not have been more rewarding; every chapter in the book is better because of her contributions. Ruth is an extraordinary scholar and just as extraordinary a human being. Although I had the intuition that she would be a great partner, I had no idea how great. Our years of work together were filled with thought-provoking discussions about the nature and bases of equality at home. We didn't always agree. When we disagreed, I was usually convinced that she was right, but if I didn't relent and she deferred, she was gracious and undefensive, even when she wasn't convinced. Ruth is one of the most honest and caring people I have ever known. Little did I know when sending out that email that the collaboration that began by serendipity would develop into a cherished friendship.

Work and family have become a mantra that reflects their inextricable link. I've often thought that friendship and work are linked in my life as well. Both a friend and colleague, Naomi Gerstel's work continues to inspire and teach me. My closest friends have supported me in so many ways that make it possible to face the ups and downs of professional and personal life. They have encouraged me, teased me for being a workaholic (making me laugh at my workaholic self), and celebrated my successes. Virginia Brabender, Beth Hay, Hedda Orkin, Cindy Cohen, Andrea Ayvazian, Naomi Gerstel, Barbara Burns, Judy Kroll, Robert Zussman, Stephen Slatin, and Lynn Posner Rice have my gratitude for always being there. I am especially grateful to Lynn for our many spontaneous coffee dates during which she spent endless hours listening to tales of the travails and triumphs of this multi-year project.

It was a thrill to work with my friend of many decades, renowned illustrator, Nancy Stahl, who generously donated an abundance of her time to create maps to my specifications as illustrations for the case chapters.

Mount Holyoke College, my professional home for over 30 years, is filled with brilliant students, staff, and colleagues who contributed to *Creating Equality at Home*. My amazing colleagues in Psychology and Education create the kind of environment where scholarship can thrive: inspiring with examples, honoring each person's intellectual pursuits, and taking time out to recharge with the laughter of lobby lunches. The incomparable Janet Crosby, administrative assistant for the department, is the glue who holds it all together. She is a wizard at accomplishing any task laid before her, from finding obscure information and negotiating with administrators, to providing a calming word when the frustrations of academic life become too much. Audrey Hildebrandt, Phuong Ta, and Elizabeth Nelson served as invaluable research assistants: finding information, conducting screening interviews, and coding. Madison Richards's superb contributions as my undergraduate research assistant at Mount Holyoke College rose to the level of joint authorship of our concluding chapter. The LITS help desk, led by the outstanding Aimee DeGrenier, was a lifesaver in the many computer crises encountered by this reluctant Luddite. Jim Burke managed our project website. Displaying a tolerance that might have strained the patience of a saint, he never complained about my repetitive questions about our group email.

My impressive feminist colleagues Marie-Thérèse Letablier, Hélène Périvier, and Jeanne Fagnani created a second intellectual home for me in Paris. And finally, I discovered a peaceful retreat in Luang Prabang where Souksaikham Sengsavang's welcoming guest house, Ssen Mekong, was the perfect place to complete the final editing of the book and escape the New England winter.

In the midst of this project, I was diagnosed with an aggressive form of breast cancer that made me doubt that I would make it to the end. The expert and compassionate care I received from the medical team at Massachusetts General Hospital saved my life. I am indebted to Jerry Younger, my oncologist, Barbara Smith, my surgeon, Alphonse Taghian, my radiation oncologist, and to my primary care nurse, Elisabeth Costigan, for reaching this day. I am also grateful to Mark Breibart and Sheryl White for their loving hospitality while I underwent treatment.

Jerry Epstein, my economist husband of 34 years, has equally shared family work with me from the outset (except that his exclusive responsibility for dishes and laundry might now tip the scales toward him). I often think of research that shows that men's success is due to women who stand behind them, freeing them from the chores of everyday life so they can concentrate on their careers. Instead, Jerry and I stand alongside each other. I cannot imagine my life without his love, support, and inspiration. I certainly would not have been able to complete this project without his help. Shared parenting with him has been and continues to be one of life's greatest adventures.

Eli Epstein-Deutsch, our precious child, has now grown up into an impressive young adult. A talented writer himself, I often called him for advice about wording and to get his feedback on chapters while working on the book. His intelligence, empathy, humor, and perceptiveness still seem miraculous to me. I am thankful for his existence every single day.

A Personal Note from Ruth

Over the 12 years of working on this project I was fortunate to receive help and support from numerous people. I am grateful to the many colleagues, students, and research assistants who helped me along the way, and would like to extend special thanks to Or Anabi for conducting dozens of screening interviews; to my dedicated language editor Esther Singer for going over everything I wrote for so many years; to my dear friends and colleagues Orly Benjamin and Orna Sasson-Levy for enduring my constant complaining and helping me develop my thinking on gender; and to Jacqueline Scott for stimulating discussions of the gendered division of work and care. I also warmly thank my colleagues at the University of Lincoln and especially Fenja Ziegler and Susan Chipchase who opened their home to me when I needed a home away from home.

I am ever grateful for the love and support of my parents, Rachel and Nathan Pessach, whose 64 years of marriage (and counting) taught me what I see as one of the solid bases of equal sharing: putting the family first. Their devotion, loving relationship, and teamwork have always been something to aspire to.

I owe the most to my life partner and best friend since teenage years, Doram Gaunt, who constantly challenges my thoughts, questions every convention, and engages me in endless discussions about absolutely everything. For him, staying home for the first two years with each of our three children while juggling work from home and night shifts seemed like the obvious thing to do. Without his continued support and encouragement none of this would have happened.

My children, Amitai, Lily, and Boaz, have given me the privilege of raising them and being part of their lives, and motivated me to set an example and show them that it is, in fact, possible to have it all. Seven-year-old Boaz once asked me, "Did you know, Mum, that in some families it is the mother who does the cooking?" His obliviousness to gender norms made me proud and filled me with hope that one day, when our children and their peers read this book, they will think, "Seriously? That's so outdated!"

And finally, my sincere thanks go to Francine Deutsch. Accidentally running into her "Husbands at Home" paper 20 years ago, while I was a young postdoc working in a completely different field, was a turning point in my research career. Fran's work opened up a whole new world for me and has been a source of inspiration since then. I was over the moon when one summer evening 12 years ago, completely out of the blue, I received an email from her inviting me to collaborate on this global project. I am forever grateful for her friendship and for the opportunity to join her in this wonderful journey with equally sharing couples around the world.

Participating Countries	HDI ranks[1][2]	GDII ranks[1][3]	CEDEW year of ratification[4]
Australia	3	23	1983
Austria	20	13	1982
Bhutan	134	117	1981
Brazil	79	94	1984
China	86	36	1980
Croatia	46	29	1992
Czech Republic	27	29	1993
Germany	5	14	1985
Honduras	133	109	1983
Hungary	45	54	1980
Iceland	6	9	1985
Indonesia	116	104	1984
Israel	22	21	1991
Montenegro	50	32	2006
Portugal	41	19	1980
Singapore	9	12	1995
Slovenia	25	7	1992
Sweden	7	3	1980
Switzerland	2	1	1997
Turkey	64	69	1985
United Kingdom	14	25	1986
United States	13	41	Not ratified

[1] Human Development Indices and Indicators: 2018 Statistical Update. Human Development Report Office, United Nations Development Programme. Retrieved from: www.hdr.undp.org. License: https://creativecommons.org/licenses/by/3.0/igo/legalcode.

[2] The Human Development Index (HDI) is a composite based on life expectancy, education, and income per capita. A rank of "1" indicates the highest human development.

[3] Gender Inequality Index (GII) is a composite based on reproductive health (e.g., maternal mortality), political empowerment (i.e., percentage of parliamentary seats), education, labor market participation. A "1" indicates the most gender-equal country.

[4] The CEDEW is the Convention of the Elimination of all Forms of Discrimination Against Women treaty adopted by the United Nations General Assembly and ratified by 189 states. From Convention on the Elimination of All Forms of Discrimination Against Women by UN Women, ©2018, United Nations. Reprinted with the permission of the United Nations.

I

Introduction

Francine M. Deutsch and Ruth A. Gaunt

Gender is changing. Men's and women's lives are converging in many ways. Globally, there has been a dramatic increase in women's legal rights since the mid-20th century when the Convention on the Elimination of All Forms of Discrimination against Women (CEDAW) was adopted by the United Nations. Following suit, legislation throughout the world now reflects the increasing consensus that women should have the same political and social rights as men, and should be free of harmful practices such as domestic violence, genital cutting, and early marriage. Girls now are as likely as boys to go to primary school in 117 out of 187 countries, and overall, around the world today, young women are even more likely than young men to attend universities. Fertility rates have fallen dramatically, from 5 births per woman in 1960 to 2.5 in 2008, which means a decrease in maternal death and more time for women to improve their economic standing (World Bank, 2012). During the same period, women entered the labor force in increasing numbers all over the world. In the overwhelming majority of countries, women's labor force participation rate increased between 1980 and 2016, although men's participation rate is still higher than women's in every country (Ortiz-Ospina & Tzvetkova, 2017).

While women's lives have changed dramatically in the public sphere, numerous studies around the globe document the persistence of gender inequality at home. After spending a day at the workplace, women are often burdened by a second shift at home, a situation that Arlie Hochschild (1989) has dubbed "the stalled revolution." True, in many countries today, it is no longer a shock to see men diapering a baby or washing the dishes. Over the past few decades, men have been increasing their contributions to domestic labor and women have been reducing theirs, easing the disproportionate burden on women. Interestingly, at least in Europe, some of the more conservative countries (e.g., Italy, Spain) have shown the biggest leaps, albeit they are still behind the most egalitarian countries (e.g., Sweden, Finland) (Altintas & Sullivan, 2017).

Despite these accounts of the decreasing gender gap, women still do more childcare and housework than men in every country studied in the world (Adams & Trost, 2005; Camilleri-Cassar, 2017; Galey, 2007; Habib, Nuwayhid, & Yeretzian, 2006; Knudsen & Wærness, 2008; Moon & Shin, 2018; Ortiz-Ospina & Tzvetkova, 2017; Simister, 2013; Simulja, Wulandari, & Wulansari, 2014; Teerawichitchainan, Knodel, Vu, & Vu, 2010; Torosyan, Gerber, & Gonalons-Pons, 2016; Treas & Tai, 2016; United Nations Development Program in Montenegro, 2012).[1] Even in tiny Vanatinai, an island in the South Pacific touted as the most egalitarian place on earth, men hunt the wild boar, which confers status, while women sweep up pigshit (Wilford, 1994). Moreover, there is some evidence that in the most egalitarian countries the gap between men and women is no longer decreasing (Altintas & Sullivan, 2017).

Paradoxically, even in the most unlikely contexts couples can and do choose equality. *Creating Equality at Home* tells the real-life stories of heterosexual couples in 22 countries who are bucking the tide and equally sharing the work of the home. The 22 countries represent 5 continents, different levels of development, and are predominantly Muslim, Christian, Buddhist, or Jewish. Among the countries included are the UN's top-ranked gender egalitarian country, as well as a country that ranks 117 out of 189 countries (United Nations Development Programme, 2018). Despite the vast cultural diversity, the book tells a story of similarity rather than difference. In all cases, from Brazil to Bhutan, from Iceland to Indonesia, men and women are undoing gender on a daily basis, having

---

[1] The countries referenced in these citations include: Albania, Algeria, Argentina, Australia, Austria, Bangladesh, Belgium, Benin, Bhutan, Brazil, Bulgaria, Cambodia, Cameroon, Canada, Chad, Chile, China, Colombia, Croatia, Cuba, Cyprus, Czech Republic, Denmark, Ecuador, Egypt, Estonia, Finland, France, Georgia, Germany, Ghana, Guatemala, Honduras, Hungary, Iceland, India, Indonesia, Ireland, Indonesia, Israel, Italy, Japan, Kazakhstan, Kenya, Latvia, Lebanon, Lithuania, Macedonia, Madagascar, Mali, Malta, Mexico, Mongolia, Montenegro, Netherlands, New Zealand, Nigeria, Nicaragua, Norway, Pakistan, Peru, Philippines, Poland, Portugal, Romania, Russia, Serbia, Slovakia, Slovenia, South Africa, South Korea, Spain, Sweden, Switzerland, Tanzania, Thailand, Turkey, Uganda, United Kingdom, and the United States. For a number of these countries there are multiple studies confirming the inequality. To save space, they are not cited here because they merely confirm the findings already cited.

to contend with the social costs of doing so, but also reaping its rewards. *Creating Equality at Home* is a story of gender resisters. These are couples who refuse to simply enact the norms that surround them. Defying constraints, finding structural loopholes, or taking advantage of equality-friendly policies, through their own agency these couples find ways to forge revolutionary ways of living.

Why It Matters

For both women and men, this new kind of family can be liberating. Women increase their power by having an equal chance to succeed in the paid work force. Gender inequality is a self-perpetuating system that is driven by the gendered division of labor. When women specialize in domestic work, while men focus on breadwinning/career, husbands' jobs give them more economic power, which translates into more time in the labor force and less contribution to the work at home. As women take on more domestic labor, they invest less in career, which results in lower wages and less of the nonmaterial rewards of achievement and public recognition as well as less power in and outside the family (Chafetz, 1988; Noonan, 2001). These dynamics are buttressed by ideologies perpetuated by men that tout women's superior nurturing abilities, and by a "rhetoric of choice," which in a world of pressure and constraint pushing them toward gendered roles, women claim to be freely choosing those roles (Stone, 2007).

It is not simply power that is at issue, though. By sharing the work of the home, both men and women access the opportunity to develop key capacities within themselves, opportunities that Nussbaum (2011) has argued are central to the quality of human life. Theories that focus on power emphasize that women are victims of constraining gendered roles, but men's capabilities are stunted as well by the constraints of masculinity (Elliott, 2016). By sharing childcare men are able to develop as nurturers and experience the kind of closeness with their children that is typically reserved for mothers. Moreover, the shared breadwinning that is enabled by shared domestic labor could potentially give men (at least in more economically privileged families) more freedom to pursue the work of their choice, even if it is not well compensated financially.

The Research Literature

Creating Equality addresses questions raised in the research literature. Is it necessary for women to have a high income or at least high relative to their husbands to achieve equal sharing? How do husbands and wives decide on how to allot time to paid and family work? What drives the equal sharers' deployment of free time to childcare and housework? To what extent does explicit nontraditional gender ideology underwrite equality? Are other beliefs, such as the rejection of essentialism, key to creating equality? How are a country's policies addressed at the couple level? In egalitarian countries, do couples explicitly acknowledge the ways in which structural factors help them? How do couples in less gender equality-friendly countries get around the lack of supportive policies and cultures?

Creating Equality shows how couples undo gender. At the core, the undoing gender perspective assumes human agency. The structural and ideological context in which families live can push them toward or away from equality, but where couples end up depends on how they interpret and respond to those contexts. Gendered norms are strong forces that shape everyday life. We don't dispute that men and women are accountable to those norms and often suffer disapproval or worse if they don't live up to them. However, norms can be thwarted. How equal sharers resist and undo gender to create equality unfolds in *Creating Equality at Home*.

The Case Studies

Twenty-three chapters include 25 case studies of equally sharing couples from 22 different countries. (Two chapters represent the United States, and two chapters include two contrasting cases.) Each chapter includes: 1) the everyday life of the couple, the "who does what" of equality; 2) the history of how equality was developed in their family; 3) the ways in which paid work and family are integrated; and 4) an analysis of the factors that facilitate and impede the couple's efforts to share equally.

A typical day in the life of each couple is described: the nuts and bolts of who gets breakfast together for the kids, takes them to school, puts them to bed, wakes up with a crying child at night, who cleans up, who makes sure everyone has clean laundry. Parenting entails more than chores, however, so the relationships between parents and children are also described: who comforts, who plays. In these descriptions, equality emerges in different ways that vary in the extent to which couples undo gender. The history examines whether equality was an agreed-upon principle adopted from the outset. Did negotiations over time promote a more egalitarian life or did circumstances conspire to push a given couple in an egalitarian direction? Careers are then considered. In what ways do couples subvert the typical pattern that women cut back while men forge ahead? How are schedules managed to allow for sharing? The analysis then takes a careful look at the forces that operate for each couple. What allows them to undo powerful gendered norms? What is the role of families of origin, their social worlds, their jobs/careers, their country's family policies, and their beliefs about gender? Finally, to help the reader put the couple in context, in addition to the case description and analysis, each country chapter offers a description of the demographics, the typical division of household labor, and the family policy in that country.

Organization of the Chapters

After the introduction, a chapter will review extant theories and research on domestic labor and will describe how our global study was conducted. The 23 case study chapters that follow will be presented in five groups. Each group highlights a different aspect of equal sharing: how couples consciously create equality; resist social norms; prioritize family; draw on lessons from families of origin; and use government policies. Although all of the chapters have information that bears on each of these aspects, this structure emphasizes that creating equality and the factors that facilitate it operate similarly in the diverse cultures represented in our research. We start with Israel, Honduras, Montenegro, Switzerland, and Sweden to illustrate couples who consciously translate egalitarian principles into equally sharing practice. The second group (Indonesia, Croatia, Bhutan, Hungary, and USA: California) provide examples of couples who thwart gendered social norms, despite criticism. The third group (USA: New England, Brazil, Australia, and Singapore) illustrates the prioritization of family. In the fourth group (Austria, Turkey, Czech Republic, People's Republic of China, and Slovenia), family of origin provides models and anti-models for equal sharing. The fifth group comprises Iceland, Germany, the United Kingdom, and Portugal, where couples took advantage of government leave policies that promoted paternal care. Finally, we bring the insights across countries together with two concluding chapters: a chapter describing the key aspects of undoing gender, the "how" of equality; and a chapter analyzing the factors that facilitate the undoing of gender, the "why" of equality.

References

Adams, B. N. & Trost, J. (eds.) (2005). *Handbook of World Families*. Thousand Oaks, CA: Sage Publications.

Altintas, E. & Sullivan, O. (2017). Trends in Fathers' Contribution to Housework and Childcare under Different Welfare Policy Regimes. *Social Politics*, 24(1), 81–108.

Camilleri-Cassar, F. (2017). About Time: Gender Equality in Malta's Working-Time Regime. *Social Policy and Society*, 16(4), 561–575.

Chafetz, J. S. (1988). The Gender Division of Labor and the Reproduction of Female Disadvantage: Toward an Integrated Theory. *Journal of Family Issues*, 9(1), 108–131.

Elliott, K. (2016). Caring Masculinities: Theorizing an Emerging Concept. *Men and Masculinities*, 19(3), 240–259.

Galey, K. (2007). *Patterns of Time Use and Happiness in Bhutan: Is there a Relationship Between the Two?* Institute of Developing Economies, Japan External Trade Organization VRF Series No. 432. Retrieved from: www.ide.go.jp/library/English/Publish/Download/Vrf/pdf/432.pdf

Habib, R. R., Nuwayhid, I. A., & Yeretzian, J. S. (2006). Paid Work and Domestic Labor in Disadvantaged Communities on the Outskirts of Beirut, Lebanon. *Sex Roles*, 55(5–6), 321–329.

Hochschild, A. R. (1989). *Second Shift: Working Families and the Revolution at Home*. New York, NY: Viking.

Knudsen, K., & Wærness K. (2008). National Context and Spouses' Housework in 34 Countries. *European Sociological Review*, 24(1), 97–113.

Moon, S. H., & Shin, J. (2018). The Return of Superman? Individual and Organizational Predictors of Men's Housework in South Korea. *Journal of Family Issues*, 39(1), 180–208.

Noonan, M. C. (2001). The Impact of Domestic Work on Men's and Women's Wages. *Journal of Marriage and Family*, 63(4), 1134–1145.

Nussbaum, M. C. (2011). *Creating Capabilities: The Human Development Approach*. Cambridge, MA: Harvard University Press.

Ortiz-Ospina, E., & Tzvetkova, S. (October 16, 2017). Working Women: Key Facts and Trends in Female Labor Force Participation. Our World in Data Blogpost. Retrieved from: https://ourworldindata.org/female-labor-force-participation-key-facts.

Simister, J. (2013). Is Men's Share of Housework Reduced by "Gender Deviance Neutralization"? Evidence from Seven Countries. *Journal of Comparative Family Studies*, 44(3), 311–325.

Simulja, J., Wulandari, E. H., & Wulansari, S. A. (2014). Gender Inequality and the Division of Household Labor: A Comparative Study of Middle-Class, Working Married Men and Women in Japan and Indonesia. *Makara Hubs-Asia*, 18(2), 109–126.

Stone, P. (2007). The Rhetoric and Reality Of "Opting Out." *Contexts*, 6(4), 14–19.

Teerawichitchainan, B., Knodel, J. E., Vu, M. L., & Vu, T. H. (2010). The Gender Division of Household Labor in Vietnam: Cohort Trends and Regional Variations." *Journal of Comparative Family Studies*, 41(1): 57–85.

Torosyan, K., Gerber, T. P., & Gonalons-Pons, P. (2016). Migration, Household Tasks, and Gender: Evidence from the Republic of Georgia. *International Migration Review*, 50(2), 445–474.

Treas, J. & Tai, T. (2016). Gender Inequality in Housework across 20 European Nations: Lessons from Gender Stratification Theories. *Sex Roles*, 74(11–12), 495–511.

United Nations Development Programme (2018). Human Development Indices and Indicators: 2018 Statistical Update. Retrieved from: www.hdr.undp.org.

United Nations Development Program in Montenegro, Government of Montenegro Ministry of Justice, EU Delegation to Montenegro, (2012). Women in Politics, p. 81. Retrieved from: www.me.undp.org/content/montenegro/en/home/library/social_inclusion/WomenPolitics.html.

Wilford, J. N. (March 29, 1994). Sexes Equal on South Sea Island. *New York Times*, SEC,PG:COL: C, 1:1 Retrieved from:. www.nytimes.com/1994/03/29/science/sexes-equal-on-south-sea-isle.html?pagewanted=all.

World Bank (2012). *World Development Report: Gender Equality and Development*. Retrieved from: http://siteresources.worldbank.org/INTWDR2012/Resources/7778105-1299699968583/7786210-1315936222006/chapter-1.pdf.

2

Past and Current Research

Francine M. Deutsch and Ruth A. Gaunt

Theories of Domestic Labor

A vast literature has tried to explain why women do the majority of domestic labor. Five theoretical approaches have dominated. These include relative resources, time availability, gender ideology, national context, and "doing gender." Each will be described and reviewed in turn. In contrast to all of this work, *Creating Equality at Home* will focus on how couples create equality by undoing gender in their everyday interactions.

Relative Resources

The relative resources approach argues that couples divide household labor according to the resources they contribute. Although hypothetically resources could be money, status, or education, most empirical work on relative resources focuses on the relative incomes of husbands and wives. The greater the relative income of a spouse, the less household labor s/he will do. Two conflicting theoretical positions underlie this prediction. The first, argued by Becker (1991), is that it is simply good economic sense for the well-being of the family for the person with the greatest potential for earning to specialize in market work, while the other spouse specializes in domestic labor. He assumes that women have a comparative advantage in child-rearing, whereas men, because of their greater investment in market work, have an advantage in that domain. Becker has been widely criticized by feminist scholars because of his assumption that the family operates as a cooperative unit in which everyone benefits from the specialization entailed in the unequal division of domestic labor (England & Folbre, 2005; Ferber, 2008). In contrast, the second approach, which is sometimes called the bargaining approach, assumes that no one wants to do housework and childcare, so the person with the greater income has more clout to get out of it. Women end up doing more domestic labor simply because they tend to make less money than men.

Several multi-country studies have provided support for the relative resources theory (Aassve, Fuochi, & Mencarini, 2014; Davis & Greenstein, 2004; Fahlén, 2016; Geist, 2005; Knudsen & Wærness, 2008). In Fahlén's 10-country European study (2016), however, the increasing share of husbands' domestic labor was mostly due to their wives' spending less time on housework, rather than on their doing more. In contrast, a Swedish study showed that women with higher relative incomes did have a relatively more equal division of housework, but only because their husbands increased their contributions. In that study, the women's housework hours were unaffected (Evertsson & Nermo, 2007). Finally, in Davis and Greenstein's study (2004), only men's reports showed the equalizing effects of women's greater relative resources.

Several researchers have critiqued the relative resources approach by showing that once women's incomes exceed their husband's, rather than diminishing their share of labor, their share increases (Brines, 1994; Greenstein, 2000; Bittman, England, Sayer, Folbre, & Mateson, 2003). They interpreted this curvilinear relationship as illustrating gender deviance neutralization. When women out-earn their husbands it violates gender norms; to compensate and reassert the gender order, either women increase their household labor, men decrease theirs, or both. However, these findings have either failed to replicate (Evertsson & Nermo, 2007; Kan, 2008; Sullivan & Gershuny, 2016), have been dismissed as trivial (England, 2011), or have been debunked as statistical artifacts (Gupta, 2007; Sullivan, 2011). Moreover, presumably, unemployment poses the strongest threat to masculine identity, yet several studies show that men do more domestic labor when unemployed (Fahlén, 2016; Gough & Killewald, 2011; Kamo, 1988). Nonetheless, recent studies in more traditional cultures, such as Australia, Taiwan, Romania, and India, have shown evidence consistent with gender deviance neutralization (Aassve et al., 2014; Baxter & Hewitt, 2013; Luke, Xu, & Thampi, 2014).

Gupta (2007) has proposed and provided evidence that women's absolute, rather than their relative incomes, reduce their hours of housework, thereby reducing their share. Even so, his "autonomy hypothesis," implying that with more income women are freer to do what they want without having to bargain over domestic labor with their husbands, is consistent with the notion that money talks. He does not provide evidence of the mechanism by which greater income leads to less housework for women, but speculates that they could be using the income to outsource domestic work, or they might feel freer to loosen up on household standards.

A rigorous cross-sectional and longitudinal study in Britain took a broader approach to resources, which included human capital factors (Sullivan & Gershuny, 2016). Based on a composite measure of education, job experience, and status, it showed the importance of women's absolute level of human capital for both women's and men's hours in housework. Although husbands' and wives' relative human capital did reveal the predicted effects, women's absolute level had a much bigger impact on their housework hours. The more resources women had, the less time they spent on cleaning, cooking, and laundry. For men, although relative resources was technically the stronger predictor, men's incomes had little impact. Overall, both spouses seemed to adjust their housework contributions based on the resources available to wives (Sullivan & Gershuny, 2016).

However, there are limits to the absolute income effect in the USA. In both cross-sectional and longitudinal data of couples who were both employed full-time, as low-income women's earnings increased, their housework hours decreased a lot, but at the higher end of the income spectrum, further increases in income had little effect. The resulting non-linear relationship did not mean that women were compensating by doing more housework. They did not do more than other women, but still did a lot of housework, despite their financial contributions to the family (Killewald & Gough, 2010). Some work cannot be outsourced.

Although the relative resources theory was formulated to predict both housework and childcare, most of the research refers only to housework. When childcare is included, relative income is less associated with childcare than with housework (Deutsch, Lussier, & Servis, 1993; Kan & Gershuny, 2010; Mannino & Deutsch, 2007). Therefore, this theoretical approach may tell us something about how husbands and wives divide housework, but it doesn't tell us much about childcare nor how couples can achieve equality. The inequality in housework persists no matter how high women's incomes or no matter what their income is compared to their husband's (Evertsson & Nermo, 2007; Greenstein, 2000; Killewald & Gough, 2010). In *Creating Equality at Home* we will examine the role that income plays among equal sharers. Is equal income a necessary (although clearly not a sufficient) condition for achieving equality? Do women in equally sharing couples tend to have exceptionally high incomes?

Time Availability

The time availability hypothesis argues that domestic labor will be divided based on who is available to provide it. Time is assumed to be available when the individual is not working for pay. This approach is sometimes called the demand/response model because the time devoted to domestic labor is both a function of what is needed and a spouse's capability of responding. The major predictions are that spouses' time in domestic labor will be negatively related to their own employment hours and positively related to their spouses' hours (Shelton & John, 1996).

The time availability perspective has received robust support. With respect to housework, across countries as diverse as Austria, Norway, France, and Rumania, when women are employed full-time they do a smaller share, whereas full-time employment for husbands means a greater share for wives (Aassve et al., 2014). Baxter and Hewitt (2013) documented that every hour of women's paid work in Australia translated to 7 fewer minutes devoted to housework. Similarly, in Sweden (Evertsson, 2014), Korea, Japan, and Taiwan (Kim, 2013), as wives' employment hours increased, their housework hours decreased, whereas as their partners' employment hours increased, their housework hours increased. In urban China, the more hours wives worked for pay, the more time their husbands spent on housework on weekdays (Zhang, 2017). Several multi-country studies also showed that overall, women's time in the labor force reduced the time they spent on housework (Geist, 2005; Knudson & Wærness, 2008; Treas & Tai, 2016).

Turning to childcare, although some evidence supports time availability, the picture is more mixed. In her multi-country study, Hook (2006) found that men with children do more housework and childcare as their wives' paid work hours increase. Similar associations between mothers' paid work hours and fathers' share of childcare were found in the UK (Gaunt & Scott, 2014), Sweden (Evertsson, 2014), and Israel (Gaunt, 2005, 2018). Studies have also shown that fathers' paid work hours reduced their time with children (e.g. Gaunt & Scott, 2014; Maume, 2011) or their share of specific childcare tasks such as diapering (e.g. DeMaris, Mahoney, & Pargament, 2011; Gaunt, 2005; Gaunt & Scott,

2014). A time-use study in Canada showed that for both mothers and fathers, paid work hours reduced time with children, whereas spouses' paid work hours increased time (Buchanan, 2016). Nonetheless, in general, the effects are small. For example, dads who work 50+ hours per week spend only 1 hour less per week on childcare than those with more standard work hours.

The implication of the time availability hypothesis is that if only women and men spent equal time on paid labor, equality at home would be achieved. We know, however, that although women's time in paid labor may reduce their time in domestic labor, and reduce their share, wives still do more than husbands when they spend equal hours in the labor force (Bittman et al., 2003). The domestic labor gap remains even when women's time in paid work exceeds their husbands' (Fahlén, 2016; Shelton, 2000). Moreover, the time availability hypothesis begs the question of how time was allocated to begin with. Why do women and men spend their time differently?

By considering what goes on inside the family, *Creating Equality at Home* aims to illuminate decisions about the allocation of time, including how much time each spouse spends in the workforce. Moreover, we investigate how time is spent outside of paid work and whether equality in the division of domestic labor also means equal time for leisure pursuits for men and women.

Gender Ideology

The gender ideology hypothesis argues that the division of household labor and childcare reflects husbands' and wives' beliefs about appropriate roles for men and women. Couples with traditional beliefs are expected to have a less equal division of labor than those with nontraditional beliefs (Shelton & John, 1996). Gender ideology is measured via research participants' agreement with statements such as, "A man's job is to earn money; a woman's job is to look after the home and family" (i.e., traditional). "When husband and wife both work full-time, they should share housework and childcare equally" (i.e., nontraditional). Strong support for the importance of gender ideology has been obtained in the domestic labor literature. However, the relative impact of men's and women's ideologies differs across studies, and the effects differ for housework and childcare.

In a classic study based on 1988 US data, Greenstein (1996) found that men did the highest percentage of household labor when both they and their wives shared a nontraditional gender ideology. Egalitarian men married to traditional women did not do a greater share of domestic labor than their more traditional counterparts. Kamo (1988) found that both men's and women's nontraditional ideology reduced the gender gap in housework, but men's ideology had the bigger impact. When their ideologies conflicted, the ideology of the person with the greater power in the relationship prevailed. Gender ideology has been shown to be strongly associated with sharing in both western and eastern Europe (Aassve et al., 2014). Likewise, Fuwa's (2004) 22-country study, which included cultures as diverse as Bulgarian, Japanese, New Zealander, Norwegian, and American, showed a reduction in the gender gap in housework associated with nontraditional gender ideologies of both men and women. As relative shares of tasks become more equal, however, it is not always clear whether the reduction in the gap is due to women's doing less household labor or men's doing more. In one study of Israeli and German women, their hours of housework were reduced when they endorsed nontraditional gender ideology (Lewin-Epstein, Stier, & Braun, 2006). Presumably, their share would then be reduced regardless of whether or not their husbands changed their behavior. Finally, although Kan (2008) confirmed gender ideology effects on the housework gap, that did not override the effects of relative resources in her British sample.

Gender ideology may matter even more for childcare than for housework (e.g., Deutsch et al., 1993). Infant care, in particular, may be influenced by what mothers and fathers think is appropriate for men. In two Israeli studies, both mothers' and fathers' gender ideologies predicted their share of specific childcare tasks, as well as the mothers' time with infants, but not the fathers' time (Gaunt, 2006, 2018). McGill (2014) found that American fathers who worked 50 or more hours per week but endorsed the "new fatherhood," which extols the equal importance of mothers and fathers, took as much responsibility for children and did as much caregiving and playing as fathers who worked more standard hours. In Korea, however, nontraditional gender ideology only predicted paternal involvement for men who do not work long hours for pay. Dads who worked more than 60 hours per week did little childcare regardless of their gender attitudes (Moon & Shin, 2018). Finally, not surprisingly, mothers' gender attitudes have been particularly important in shaping their husband's involvement in childcare because gatekeeping by mothers (i.e., acting to limit paternal involvement with children) is strongly associated with traditional gender ideology (Kulik & Tsoref, 2010).

Gender ideology certainly matters. Nonetheless, there is ample evidence that a nontraditional ideology does not in and of itself give rise to gender equality in household labor. Couples who espouse equality may be more equal than other couples on average, but women in those families are still doing more of the work at home. Other attitudes and circumstances may take precedence over the belief that men and women should have equal rights and responsibilities. For example, essentialism, the belief that women are inherently more suited to caregiving, may butt up against the notion that fathers and mothers should share care (Gaunt, 2006).

Creating Equality at Home examines the ideologies expressed by the equally sharing couples. To what extent do explicitly feminist ideas underlie their division of labor? Beyond a general belief in nontraditional roles for men and women, how important is the rejection of essentialist notions to the establishment of equality in families? What helps couples put their egalitarian ideas into practice?

National Context

The approaches we have discussed thus far operate at the individual or couple level. The degree of inequality between husband and wife stems from their characteristics as a couple (relative income) or as individuals within a couple (absolute incomes, time in paid work, gender ideology). Researchers have turned to national context to examine cultural beliefs and practices and government policies that shape the ways couples share housework and childcare. In addition, they examine how characteristics of countries (e.g., the overall level of gender equality) influence the strength of women's resources, their time in the work force, and spouses' gender ideologies in equalizing the gender gap in domestic labor.

The more egalitarian gender ideology held on average in a country, the more equally couples in that country share domestic tasks, regardless of their personal circumstances or beliefs (Fahlén, 2016). Likewise, the higher the overall gender equality of a nation, the more equally tasks are divided between husbands and wives (Fuwa, 2004; Knudsen & Wærness, 2008). In more gender-equal countries women's hours of household work are reduced (Knudsen & Wærness, 2008; van der Lippe, 2010) and couples' gender ideologies have stronger effects (Fuwa, 2004). Diefenach (2002) divided countries into egalitarian, traditional, and transitional (i.e., in between) and found that the impact of relative resources was strongest in the transitional group. However, Knudsen and Wærness

(2008) found that more gender-equal countries showed the strongest equalizing effect of relative resources.

Countries differ with respect to policies that may influence the division of labor in couples. One approach to understanding these effects has been to categorize and compare countries that represent different welfare regimes, such as social-democratic (i.e., the Nordic countries), liberal (e.g., USA, UK, Australia), and conservative (e.g., Italy, Germany). Geist (2005) adopted this approach to categorize 10 developed countries and showed that social-democratic countries had the most egalitarian divisions of housework and the conservative countries the least, controlling for the relative incomes, gender ideologies, and paid work hours in couples. Although overall, relative income, gender ideology, and time availability were associated with the division of labor, in conservative regimes the gender ideologies of husbands and wives didn't matter, but women's paid work hours had a stronger equalizing effect than in the other regimes. Altintas and Sullivan (2017) used a similar classification to examine changes over time and found that Nordic countries have changed the most over a 50-year period, corporatist countries (e.g., France, Slovenia) the least, southern countries (e.g., Italy, Spain) are moving to catch up, and liberal countries are polarizing, increasing the differences in the contributions among men.

Hook and Wolfe (2012) adopted this approach to examine men's involvement in parenting, including physical care, one-to-one interactions with children, and time alone with them. They identified four countries to represent the three welfare regimes: Norway (social-democratic); USA and UK (liberal); Germany (conservative). As predicted, Norwegian fathers did the most physical care of children; German fathers did the least. American and British fathers were the most responsive to women's paid work hours. British fathers who had days off during the week were especially likely to spend time interacting with children and time alone with them.

Several problems plague the regime approach. First, researchers have not been consistent in identifying countries that fit particular categories. Although the Nordic countries are consistently named as the representatives of the social-democratic group, and the USA and UK consistently represent the liberal regimes, there is more discrepancy in countries named as conservative, which makes it difficult to have confidence in the findings. Geist (2005), for example, included Italy, Japan, and Austria as representatives of conservative countries. Her finding that women's paid work hours had a stronger effect in equalizing household tasks in conservative countries than in the other regimes was not replicated by van der Lippe (2010), but she used Belgium, Germany, and the Netherlands as examples of conservative countries.

In addition, as Cooke (2010) points out, specific policies matter. Countries within the same regimes often have very different policies. For example, Australia and the USA are both classified as liberal, but although Australia has strong anti-discrimination policies vis-à-vis the workforce, other policies encourage families to adopt a male breadwinner/female part-timer model. The USA, in contrast, has little in the way of family policy and less access to part-time work than Australia. Moreover, policies within countries can have contradictory effects. Long parental leaves and access to part-time work, for example, can discourage sharing by prompting women to stay out of the workforce or reduce their time in it, whereas public childcare as well as strong anti-discrimination policies may encourage women to be employed full-time and thereby increase sharing at home (Cooke, 2010; Geist & Cohen, 2011; Hook, 2006). In Sweden, the push for longer earmarked leaves for fathers, which would promote equality, is at odds with Swedish initiative to promote a longer period of breastfeeding (Ellingsæter, 2010).

Studies that include multiple countries without classifying them according to regime are useful for examining the impact of specific policies. For example, Fuwa and Cohen (2007) showed that the absence of discriminatory policies, such as forbidding women to work night shifts, carry heavy loads, or work underground, was related to a more equal division of household labor. Moreover, relative resources had a bigger impact on equalizing housework in countries that did not have gender discriminatory labor practices (Fuwa & Cohen, 2007). However, affirmative action policies and the availability of public childcare did not affect the division of household labor. Hook (2006) also reported that men's time in housework and childcare were lessened by a country's long parental leaves, but were increased when the country provided exclusive paternal leave.

Pfau-Effinger (2010) argues that policies, however, do not tell the whole story because the interactions between culture and policy have to be taken into account. For example, although Norway and Denmark have high availability of public childcare, mothers often don't take advantage of it to pursue full-time employment. In Nordic countries the disapproval of hiring household help may discourage women from full-time employment, and thus shape the division of labor between husband and wife.

Hook (2010) drew on time-use research on married parents in 19 European countries to study how work cultures as well as leave and public childcare policies shaped the time husbands and wives spent cooking, arguing that cooking was particularly important because it was relatively inflexible routine work. Work culture seems more important than actual hours in predicting a man's cooking time. In high work-hour cultures men worked an average of 50 hours per week as compared to 37 hours per week in low work-hour cultures. Hook discovered that a man who worked a 10-hour day in a short work-hours culture spent as much time cooking as a man who worked a 5-hour day in a long work-hours culture. Moreover, echoing previous studies, she found that long parental leaves were associated with greater time cooking for women and less for men, but the availability of parental leave for men and public childcare only decreased women's cooking time.

In an earlier study, Hook (2006) showed that the national level of women's employment influenced men's unpaid work. The higher the percentage of married women who were employed, the more unpaid labor men did, regardless of the paid work configuration in their own family.

No matter how friendly policies or cultural norms are to gender equality, it is the ongoing interactions within couples that determine how and when those policies and norms will be applied. One thing is indisputable across all multi-country studies of gender attitudes, regime differences, policy effects, and work cultures: gender trumps everything. Women in all countries studied do more housework and childcare than men, regardless of a country's egalitarian philosophy, family-friendly policies, or social-democratic organization.

Gender Construction

The "doing gender" approach was developed to explain why inequality in domestic work persists in the face of dramatic increases in women's employment, their incomes, and changes in gender attitudes. Berk (1985) argued that housework produces more than a clean house; it produces gender. Women and men are differentiated by their differing contributions to the household. West and Zimmerman (1987) built on this idea in their classic article, "Doing Gender." They argued that gender is created in social interactions for which men and women are always and everywhere held accountable to gendered norms. People act knowing that they will be judged for being suitably womanly women or manly men.

The standards for appropriate masculinity and femininity vary from culture to culture but exist everywhere (West & Zimmerman, 1987). Although the husbands of tea pluckers in India would help with some typically female chores, they would only rarely do clothes washing, which was considered inherently feminine. The unusual men who washed their own clothes hid it from other people (Luke et al., 2014). Anderson (2017) showed that in the Ukraine the gendered treatment of money was used to create the image that men were the breadwinners, even when their incomes were meager. Women's incomes were treated as merely supplemental. For example, men's incomes were used to buy physical objects whereas women's were used for consumable products. Clearly, the gender neutral assumptions of the relative resources hypothesis would not hold in that context.

An interesting study conducted in Poland found that when men were given false feedback that they had low testosterone levels, they were less likely to endorse sharing of housework and childcare (Kosakowska-Berezecka, Korzeniewska, & Kaczorowska, 2016). Presumably to shore up their masculinity in the face of threat, they denigrated the feminine realm of domestic work. In Poland, a man who is too involved with his family will be looked down on and considered incompetent, whereas father involvement is praised in Norway. Interestingly, Polish men who migrate to Norway do more domestic labor than their counterparts back in Poland, suggesting that gendered behavior is responsive to changing norms (Kosakowska-Berezecka et al., 2016).

The centrality of gender is highlighted at a key moment in the life of a couple: the birth of a first child. It is well established that the transition to parenthood has a traditionalizing effect in the family (Fox, 2009; Grunow, Schulz, & Blossfeld, 2012; Starbuck & Lundy, 2016). From the earliest days of parenting, women take on the mental work accompanying the baby care. Some of that worrying is simply required for infant care, such as remembering to get diapers. However, Walzer (1996) argues that "thinking about the baby" is also part and parcel of living up to the gendered expectations of being a good mother. Mothers worry.

Gendered expectations push women to feel responsible for the care of children, men for breadwinning. After the birth of a child, women's allocation of time shifts much more toward the home and children than do men's (Kühhirt, 2012). Couples then make critical decisions, which are gendered, about how to structure the balance of family and work life and thus set up the conditions that shape the division of labor over time. Men continue to prioritize paid work, whereas women prioritize care. The greater the number of children and the younger the children, the more central are men's work identity and the less central are women's (Gaunt & Scott, 2017). Women tend to scale back on their jobs/careers, turning to part-time work, less demanding jobs, or more flexible jobs, or take time out of the labor force (Becker & Moen, 1999; Lyonette & Crompton, 2015). Women are more likely to negotiate with their employers for reduced hours or flex-time, and when men do ask for flex-time, they sometimes hide that it is for family care (Young & Schieman, 2018). Even within couples with two high-status careers, including two-physician couples, it is women who adjust or reduce their careers (Hardill, 2004; Hinze, 2000). As women's careers fade, their work at home expands.

Paid work remains central to men after fatherhood. Gender ideology is lacking as a theory for the division of domestic labor because it doesn't address the gendered identity issues that men face (Petts, Shafer, & Essig, 2018). Gaunt (2018) found, for example, that when paid work was central to men's identity, they did less housework and childcare. Hegemonic masculinity norms are at odds with involved fatherhood. Not only are achievement and earning essential components of hegemonic masculinity, many of the characteristics of a nurturing parent clash with masculine mandates to restrict emotionality, avoid anything feminine, be tough, aggressive, and detached from relationships. Calls for the "new fatherhood," which demands nurturance and engagement with children, are at direct odds with hegemonic masculinity. In fact, men who endorsed masculinity norms were less involved with their children and more likely to use harsh discipline, which was partially explained by their rejecting the new fatherhood ideals (Petts et al., 2018). Even men who reject the emotional constriction of hegemonic masculinity and happily embrace the nurturing as part of their identity may still be as invested in their job/ career performance as any traditional man (Deutsch, 1999).

There is ample evidence that gender shapes both resources and time. Even when support for time availability is obtained, for example, women's time is not deployed the same way as men's. For example, both men and women may do more housework when they are unemployed, but the increase for women is greater than for men, at least in Canada, the United Kingdom, France, and Germany (Gough & Killewald, 2011; Sayer, 2010). Underlining the paramount role of gender, women and men who work full-time and have equal salaries still show a gender gap in domestic labor. Resources may confer power, but they don't confer as much power on women as on men (Davis & Greenstein, 2013). "Women cannot easily buy their way to equality with men when it comes to household labor responsibilities" (Killewald & Gough, 2010, p. 101). Gender accounts for more than any other factor in the distribution of household labor.

The "doing gender" approach was a brilliant breakthrough which countered prevailing static notions of gender as being either biological or socialized in childhood. Instead, West and Zimmerman (1987) argued that gender had to be constantly reproduced. However, the flaw in this theory was their contention that both behaviors that conformed and those that violated gendered norms are instances of "doing gender" because the actors would be judged by gender standards in either case. By failing to differentiate between behaviors that conform and those that resist, we effectively render resistance invisible. Thus the "doing gender" theory does not recognize the possibility of equality. Nonetheless, West and Zimmerman's focus on the interactional level of analysis can be brought to bear on acts of resistance that undo gender (i.e., reduce the difference between men and women) (Deutsch, 2007).

Undoing Gender

Instead of doing gender, the equal sharers we studied undo gender (Deutsch, 2007)! Perhaps not always perfectly or completely, but their struggles show that it is possible to live less gendered lives.[1] Our focus on the interactional level of analysis illuminates the couples' acts of resistance that undo gender. In *Creating Equality*, the undoing gender approach means that we focus on couples' negotiations, acts, conflicts, and decisions, which often defy the pressure to conform to gendered norms. Previous studies on topics as diverse as housework, work on an oil rig, breakdancing, leisure, and public versus private fathering, have already shown the utility of this approach (Domínguez-Folgueras, Jurado-Guerrero, Botía-Morillas, & Amigot-Leache, 2017; Ely & Meyerson, 2010; Langnes & Fasting, 2017; Shaw, 2001; Shows & Gerstel, 2009). This undoing gender frame will undergird the analysis of the equally sharing case studies by showing how couples' everyday lives challenge gender norms. We demonstrate how the ongoing acts and decisions that

---

[1] When couples violate gendered behavioral norms, they challenge gender itself: the notion that humans can be categorized into two mutually exclusive groups. Our work reinforces recent arguments made by scholars of transgender identity that refute the gender binary (Tate, Ben Hagai, & Crosby, 2019).

comprise the interactions of husbands and wives with each other and their children can add up to equality.

How We Did the *Creating Equality* Research

Recruitment of Scholars

Creating Equality at Home began with the recruitment of family scholars. The first editor contacted feminist researchers who studied family issues in countries around the globe, and invited them to participate in the project. Each researcher would be responsible for his/her own expenses. There was no restriction on discipline, and thus, the collaborators recruited include social psychologists, sociologists, and anthropologists. They were identified through searches in the literature on housework, gender, and childcare, so in almost all cases had previously published in English-language journals. Researchers in 22 countries agreed to participate and completed all parts of the project. In a number of cases, the scholars originally contacted took on co-authors. In all, 36 social scientists were involved in the research for the book.

The Protocol

The researchers responsible for each country were instructed to recruit an equally sharing couple to interview. The criteria were that the heterosexual married or cohabiting couple were native language speakers, had at least one child aged 10 or younger, that both husband and wife were employed, and that neither were professors or university academics. Same-sex couples were not included because they do not have an intractable history of inequality in domestic labor. Freed of the male/female dynamics that underwrite the inequality between husbands and wives, same-sex couples hold more egalitarian ideals and practice more egalitarian divisions of domestic labor than do heterosexual couples (Rostosky & Riggle, 2017).

Once the researchers identified a potential couple, they were to administer a screening interview, usually by telephone, to husband and wife separately, which assessed their overall view of how household chores and childcare were divided, and then asked how 30 tasks were divided, on a 5-point scale ranging from (1) almost always done by my spouse to (5) almost always done by me, with (3) as the indicator of equality. The tasks included routine housework, such as laundry, cooking, and cleaning, and a range of childcare tasks, such as putting children to bed, feeding, playing/reading, getting up at night with them, comforting, and sick care. To be considered equal, couples had to agree that it was, and the division of tasks overall had to be consistent with their assessment. Researchers consulted with the editors to verify that the division of labor was equal. In a few cases, the equally sharing couple was chosen from other research projects that had revealed their equal sharing (e.g., Germany), in which case they did not complete the screening interview.

The second phase entailed a face-to-face interview with each member of the couple. The interview included questions asking them to describe a typical day in the life of their family, the history of how they came to share chores and childcare, how they currently share, conflicts in how they handled domestic labor, similarities and differences in their relationships with their children, and whether they believed that men and women were equally capable of caring for children. Participants were asked about their jobs: how much time each put into paid work, how much each was paid, whose job got priority, how each of them felt about their work, and how paid work and family affected each other. Families of origin were also explored in the interviews: the extent to which their own parents followed gendered roles, and how they felt about the roles they witnessed growing up. They were asked about praise and criticism they received for their nontraditional lives, and about whether there were government or employer programs or benefits that helped them share equally. Finally, couples were asked why they thought they were different from other families.

The interviews were audio-taped, transcribed, and translated. The transcripts were then "discussed" with the editors with the goal of identifying the factors that seemed to be operating to facilitate the couple's equality. After those discussions, drafts of the chapters were written and revised.

The Analyses

Initially, as indicated above, a within-case analysis was conducted. Based on close readings of the transcripts, the researchers and editors proposed and discussed the reasons that lay behind the couples' equality. Occasionally, researchers went back to the couple to clarify questions raised by these discussions. Evidence from the interviews was marshaled to support interpretations and a consensus was reached for that case.

Subsequently, a cross-case analysis was conducted. The transcripts were read and reread multiple times. Using Nvivo, a qualitative software package, to facilitate the qualitative analysis, the first editor and a research assistant identified themes and developed codes, which were then refined as needed. The research assistant did the initial coding, which was then verified by the first editor with input from the second editor, altering the codes to capture the significant themes uncovered. This approach reflects the principles and practices identified by Tesch's (1990) summary of the methods of major qualitative researchers. Among qualitative approaches it is best characterized as thematic analysis (Braun & Clarke, 2006). In addition, a number of variables in the transcripts were coded quantitatively (e.g., who had the greater income), and analyzed via SPSS, a statistical software package.

Ethical Issues

The most important ethical issue we faced was to protect the privacy and confidentiality of the participants. To that end, all names used in the book are pseudonyms, and any identifying characteristics have been disguised with a comparable substitute.

Addressing the Literature

Creating Equality at Home goes beyond the standard social psychological theories (i.e., relative resources, time availability, and gender ideology) designed to account for the distribution of household labor between men and women. While there is evidence that women's contributions to the household income, their limited time for domestic work, and husbands' and wives' egalitarian beliefs contribute to a relatively more egalitarian household, the key word here is "relative." Even when women earn pay equal to their husbands, work as many hours in the labor force, and share a nontraditional gender ideology with their husbands, on average they still cook, clean, and change more diapers than their husbands do. We aim to understand not simply families where the gender gap is reduced, but families in which it disappears: equally sharing families.

References

Aassve, A., Fuochi, G., & Mencarini, L. (2014). Desperate Housework, Relative Resources, Time Availability, Economic Dependency, and Gender Ideology across Europe. *Journal of Family Issues, 35*(8), 1000–1022.

Altintas, E. & Sullivan, O. (2017). Trends in Fathers' Contribution to Housework and Childcare under Different Welfare Policy Regimes. *Social Politics*, 24(1), 81–108.

Anderson, N. (2017). To Provide and Protect: Gendering Money in Ukrainian Households, *Gender and Society*, 31(3), 359–382.

Baxter, J. & Hewitt, B. (2013). Negotiating Domestic Labor: Women's Earnings and Housework Time in Australia. *Feminist Economics*, 19(1), 29–53.

Becker, G. S. (1991). *A Treatise on the Family*. Cambridge, MA: Harvard University Press.

Becker, P. E. & Moen, P. (1999). Scaling Back: Dual-earner Couples' Work-Family Strategies. *Journal of Marriage and the Family*, 61(4), 995–1007.

Berk, S. F. (1985). *The Gender Factory: The Apportionment of Work in American Households*. New York: Plenum.

Bittman, M., England, L., Sayer, L., Folbre, N., & Mateson, G. (2003). When Does Gender Trump Money? Bargaining and Time in Household Work. *American Journal of Sociology*, 109(1), 186–114.

Braun, V. & Clarke, V. (2006). Using Thematic Analysis in Psychology. *Qualitative Research in Psychology*, 3(2), 77–101.

Brines, J. (1994). Economic Dependency, Gender, and the Division of Labor at Home. *American Journal of Sociology*, 100(3), 652–688.

Buchanan, T. (2016). Counterfactual Analysis of the Gender Gap in Parenting Time: Explained and Unexplained Variances at Different Stages of Parenting. *Journal of Comparative Family Studies*, 47(2), 95–112.

Cooke, L. P. (2010). The Politics of Housework. In J. Treas and S. Drobnič (eds.) *Dividing the Domestic: Men, Women, and Household Work* (pp. 59–78). Stanford, CA: Stanford University Press.

Davis, S. N. & Greenstein, T. N. (2004). Cross-National Variations in the Division of Household Labor. *Journal of Marriage and Family*, 66(5), 1260–1271.

Davis, S. N. & Greenstein, T. N. (2013). Why Study Housework? Cleaning as a Window into Power in Couples. *Journal of Family Theory & Review*, 5(2), 63–71.

DeMaris, A., Mahoney, A., & Pargament, K. I. (2011). Doing the Scut Work of Infant Care: Does Religiousness Encourage Father Involvement? *Journal of Marriage and Family*, 73(2), 354–368.

Deutsch, F. M. (1999). *Halving it All: How Equally Shared Parenting Works*. Cambridge, MA: Harvard University Press.

Deutsch, F. M. (2007). Undoing Gender. *Gender and Society*, 21(1), 106–127.

Deutsch, F. M., Lussier, J., & Servis, L. S. (1993). Husbands at Home: The Predictors of Paternal Participation in Childcare and Housework. *Journal of Personality and Social Psychology*, 65(6), 1154–1166.

Diefenbach, H. (2002). Gender Ideologies, Relative Resources, and the Division of Housework in Intimate Relationships: A Test of Hyman Rodman's Theory of Resources in Cultural Context. *International Journal of Comparative Sociology*, 43(1), 45–64.

Domínguez-Folgueras, M., Jurado-Guerrero, T., Botía-Morillas, C., & Amigot-Leache, P. (2017). 'The House Belongs to Both': Undoing the Gendered Division of Housework, *Community, Work & Family*, 20(4), 424–443.

Ellingsæter, A. L. (2010). Feminist Policies and Feminist Conflicts: Daddy's Care or Mother's Milk? In J. Scott, R. Crompton, & C. Lyonette (eds.) *Gender Inequalities in the 21st Century* (pp. 257–274). Cheltenham: Edward Elgar.

Ely, R. J. & Meyerson, D. E. (2010). An Organizational Approach to Undoing Gender: The Unlikely Case of Offshore Oil Platforms. *Research in Organizational Behavior, 30*, 3–34.

England, P. (2011). Missing the Big Picture and Making Much Ado About Almost Nothing: Recent Scholarship on Gender and Household Work. *Journal of Family Theory and Review, 3*(1), 23–26.

England, P. & Folbre, N. (2005). Gender and Economic Sociology. In N. J. Smelser & R. Swedberg (eds.) *The Handbook of Economic Sociology* (pp. 627–649). Princeton University Press.

Evertsson, M. (2014). Gender Ideology and the Sharing of Housework and Childcare in Sweden, *Journal of Family Issues, 35*(7), 927–949.

Evertsson, M. & Nermo, M. (2007). Changing Resources and the Division of Housework: A Longitudinal Study of Swedish Couples. *European Sociological Review, 23*(4), 455–470.

Fahlén, S. (2016). Equality at Home – A Question of Career? Housework Norms and Policies in European Perspective. *Demographic Research, 35,* 1411–1440.

Ferber, M. A. (2008). A Feminist Critique of the Neoclassical Theory of the Family. In K. S. Moe (ed.) *Women, Family, and Work: Writings on the Economics of Gender* (pp. 9–24). Malden, MA: Blackwell.

Fox, B. (2009). *When Couples Become Parents: The Creation of Gender in the Transition to Parenthood.* Toronto: University of Toronto Press.

Fuwa, M. (2004). Macro-level Gender Inequality and the Division of Household Labor in 22 Countries. *American Sociological Review, 69*(6), 751–767.

Fuwa, M. & Cohen, P. N. (2007). Housework and Social Policy. *Social Science Research, 36*(2), 512–530.

Gaunt, R. (2005). Value Priorities as a Determinant of Paternal and Maternal Involvement in Child Care. *Journal of Marriage and Family, 67*(3), 643–655.

Gaunt, R. (2006). Biological Essentialism, Gender Ideologies, and Role Attitudes: What Determines Parents' Involvement in Child Care. *Sex Roles, 55*(7), 523–533.

Gaunt, R. (2018). [Men's Identities and Involvement in Housework and Childcare.] Unpublished raw data.

Gaunt, R. & Scott, J. (2014). Parents' Involvement in Child Care: Do Parental and Work Identities Matter? *Psychology of Women Quarterly, 38*(4), 475–489.

Gaunt, R. & Scott, J. (2017). Gender Differences in Identities and their Socio-Structural Correlates: How Gendered Lives Shape Parental and Work Identities. *Journal of Family Issues, 38*(13), 1852–1877.

Geist, C. (2005). The Welfare State and the Home: Regime Differences in the Domestic Division of Labour. *European Sociological Review, 21*(1), 23–41.

Geist, C. & Cohen, P. N. (2011). Headed Toward Equality? Housework Change in Comparative Perspective. *Journal of Marriage and Family, 73*(4), 832–844.

Gough, M. & Killewald, A. (2011). Unemployment in Families: The Case of Housework. *Journal of Marriage and Family*, 73(5), 1085–1100.

Greenstein, T. N. (1996). Husbands' Participation in Domestic Labor: Interactive Effects of Wives' and Husbands' Gender Ideologies. *Journal of Marriage and Family*, 58(3), 585–595.

Greenstein T. N. (2000). Economic Dependence, Gender, and the Division of Labor in the Home: A Replication and Extension. *Journal of Marriage and Family*, 62(2) 322–335.

Grunow, D., Schulz, F., & Blossfeld, H. (2012). What Determines Change in Housework Over the Course of Marriage? *International Sociology*, 27(3), 289–307.

Gupta, S. (2007). Autonomy, Dependence or Display? The Relationship Between Married Women's Earnings and Housework. *Journal of Marriage and Family*, 69(2), 399–417.

Hardill, I., (2004). Juggling Work and Home in a Post-Industrial World: Case Studies of Dual Career Households. *Hagar*, 5(1), pp. 39–52.

Hinze, S. W. (2000). Inside Medical Marriages: The Effect of Gender on Income. *Work and Occupations*, 27(4), 464–499.

Hook, J. L. (2006). Care in Context: Men's Unpaid Work in 20 Countries, 1965–2003. *American Sociological Review*, 71(4), 639–660.

Hook, J. L. (2010). Gender Inequality in the Welfare State: Sex Segregation in Housework, 1965–2003. *American Journal of Sociology*, 115(5), 1480–1523.

Hook, J. L. & Wolfe, C. M. (2012). New Fathers? Residential Fathers' Time with Children in Four Countries, *Journal of Family Issues*, 33(4), 415–450.

Kamo, Y. (1988). Determinants of Household Division of Labor: Resources, Power, and Ideology, *Journal of Family Issues*, 9(2), 177–200.

Kan, M. Y. (2008). Does Gender Trump Money? Housework Hours of Husbands and Wives in Britain. *Work, Employment, and Society*, 22(1), 45–66.

Kan, M. Y. & Gershuny, J. (2010). Gender Segregation and Bargaining in Domestic Labour: Evidence from Longitudinal Time Use Data. In J. Scott, R. Crompton, & C. Lyonette (eds.) *Gender Inequalities in the 21st Century: New Barriers and Continuing Constraints* (pp. 153–173). Cheltenham: Edward Elgar.

Killewald, A. & Gough, M. (2010). Money Isn't Everything: Wives' Earnings and Housework Time. *Social Science Research*, 39(6), 987–1003.

Kim, Y. M. (2013). Dependence on Family Ties and Household Division of Labor in Korea, Japan and Taiwan. *Asian Journal of Women's Studies*, 19(2), 7–35.

Knudsen, K. & Wærness K. (2008). National Context and Spouses' Housework in 34 Countries. *European Sociological Review*, 24(1), 97–113.

Kosakowska-Berezecka, N., Korzeniewska, L., & Kaczorowska, M. (2016). Sharing Housework Can Be Healthy. *Health Psychology Report*, 4(3), 189–201.

Kühhirt, M. (2012). Childbirth and the Long-Term Division of Labour within Couples: How Do Substitution, Bargaining Power and Norms Affect Parents' Time Allocation in West Germany? *European Sociological Review*, 28(5), 565–582.

Kulik, L. & Tsoref, H. (2010). The Entrance to the Maternal Garden: Environmental and Personal Variables that Explain Maternal Gatekeeping. *Journal of Gender Studies*, 19(3), 263–277.

Langnes, T. F. & Fasting, K. (2017). Gender Constructions in Breaking. *Sport in Society*, 20(11), 1596–1611.

Lewin-Epstein, N., Stier, H., & Braun, M. (2006). The Division of Household Labor in Germany and Israel. *Journal of Marriage and Family*, 68(5), 1147–1164.

Luke, N., Xu, H., & Thampi, B. V. (2014). Husbands' Participation in Housework and Child Care in India, *Journal of Marriage and Family*, 76(3), 620–637.

Lyonette, C. & Crompton, R. (2015). Sharing the Load? Partners' Relative Earnings and the Domestic Division of Labor. *Work, Employment, and Society*, 29(1), 23–40.

Mannino, C. A. & Deutsch, F. M. (2007). Changing the Division of Household Labor: A Negotiated Process Between Partners. *Sex Roles*, 56(5–6), 309–324.

Maume, D. J. (2011). Reconsidering the Temporal Increase in Fathers' Time with Children. *Journal of Family and Economic Issues*, 32(3), 411–423.

McGill, B. S. (2014). Navigating New Norms of Involved Fatherhood: Employment, Fathering Attitudes, and Father Involvement. *Journal of Family Issues*, 35(8), 1089–1106.

Moon, S. H. & Shin, J. (2018). THE Return of superman? Individual and Organizational Predictors of Men's Housework in South Korea. *Journal of Family Issues*, 39(1), 180–208.

Petts, R. J., Shafer, K. M., & Essig, L. (2018). Does Adherence to Masculine Norms Shape Fathering Behavior? *Journal of Marriage and Family*, 80(3), 704–720.

Pfau-Effinger, B. (2010). Cultural and Institutional Contexts. In J. Treas and S. Drobnič (eds.) *Dividing the Domestic: Men, Women, and Household Work* (pp. 125–146). Stanford University Press.

Rostosky, S. S. & Riggle, E. D. (2017). Same-Sex Couple Relationship Strengths: A Review and Synthesis of the Empirical Literature (2000–2016). *Psychology of Sexual Orientation and Gender Diversity*, 4(1), 1–13.

Sayer, L. C. (2010). Trends in Housework. In J. Treas and S. Drobnič (eds.) *Dividing the Domestic: Men, Women, and Household Work* (pp. 19–38). Stanford University Press.

Shaw, S. M. (2001). Conceptualizing Resistance: Women's Leisure as Political Practice. *Journal of Leisure Research*, 33(2), 186–201.

Shelton, B. A. (2000). Understanding the Distribution of Housework Between Husbands and Wives. In L. Waite, C. Bachrach, M. Hindin, E. Thomson, & A. Thornton (eds.) *Ties that Bind: Perspectives on Marriage and Cohabitation* (pp. 242–355), Hawthorne, NY: Aldine de Gruyter.

Shelton, B. A. & John, D. (1996). The Division of Household Labor. *Annual Review of Sociology*, 22, 299–322.

Shows, C. & Gerstel, N. (2009). Fathering, Class, and Gender: A Comparison of Physicians and Emergency Medical Technicians. *Gender and Society*, 23(2), 161–187.

Starbuck, G. H. & Lundy, K. S. (2016). *Families in Context: Sociological Perspectives*. Abington: Routledge.

Sullivan, O. (2011). An End to Gender Display through the Performance of Housework? A Review and Reassessment of the Quantitative Literature Using Insights from the Qualitative Literature. *Journal of Family Theory and Review*, 3(1), 1–13.

Sullivan, O. & Gershuny, J. (2016). Change in Spousal Human Capital and Housework: A Longitudinal Analysis. *European Sociological Review*, 32(6), 864–880.

Tate, C. C., Ben Hagai, E., & Crosby, F. J. (2019). *Undoing the Gender Binary*. Manuscript submitted for publication.

Tesch, R. (1990). *Qualitative Research: Analysis Types and Software Tools*. New York: Falmer.

Treas, J. & Tai, T. (2016). Gender Inequality in Housework across 20 European Nations: Lessons from Gender Stratification Theories. *Sex Roles*, 74(11–12), 495–511.

van der Lippe, T. (2010). Women's Employment and Housework. In J. Treas and S. Drobnič (eds.) *Dividing the Domestic: Men, Women, and Household Work* (pp. 41–58). Stanford University Press.

Walzer, S. (1996). Thinking About the Baby: Gender and Divisions of Infant Care. *Social Problems*, 43(2), 219–234.

West, C. & Zimmerman, D. (1987). Doing Gender. *Gender and Society*, 1(2), 125–151.

Young, M. & Schieman, S. (2018). Scaling Back and Finding Flexibility: Gender Differences in Parents' Strategies to Manage Work–Family Conflict. *Journal of Marriage and Family*, 80(1) 99–118.

Zhang, Z. (2017). Division of Housework in Transitional Urban China. *Chinese Sociological Review*, 49(3), 263–291.

3

Israel

Ruth A. Gaunt

In many respects, Netta[1] and Gadi are no different from many other middle-class Jewish Israeli couples who choose to raise their children in a rural environment away from the hustle and bustle of the city. Like most Israeli couples, they both work full-time jobs and their children, 4-year-old Aya and 2-year-old Adam, attend daycare until 4:00 p.m. Netta and Gadi's child-centered approach is also typically Israeli, which gives their children considerable freedom and autonomy. What makes Netta and Gadi unique is the way they share childcare and housework. While everywhere around them wives pick up the children from daycare and do most of the housework and childcare, and husbands work longer paid hours, Gadi and Netta have chosen differently.

"Exhausted in a Fair Way"

Netta and Gadi met at the university and moved in together during their graduate studies. A few years later, when they were expecting their second child, Adam, Gadi was offered a job as an applied researcher in an institution located in Kibbutz Revivim – a small rural community in the Negev desert. They decided to accept the offer and relocate. Adam was born the same week. Netta took him and Aya to her parents for 3 days, "I packed our stuff by myself and we moved," Gadi recalls. They now live a short walking distance from both their jobs and their children's daycare.

Their division of childcare is, as Netta puts it, "fixed but constantly changing." Although Netta drops the children off in the mornings and Gadi picks them up in the afternoon, their activities with their children the

---

[1] The names of the participants in all chapters are pseudonyms. In some cases, details of their lives (e.g., places of residence) were disguised to protect their anonymity.

rest of the time are flexible and "divided in terms of what suits each best," Gadi says. He cites that morning as an example:

> Well ... I was up all night because I had some work to do, so ... Aya woke up relatively late, at 6:30. I greeted her, I let her watch a movie on the computer while I dressed her, brushed her teeth, combed her hair, and yes, she was caught up in the movie so I didn't need to chase her ... and then, when Adam wakes up, it's much simpler. You don't need to do his hair, just change him and dress him and he is ready.

And was that a typical morning? "It all depends," Netta says. "Gadi often works at night and then he is still awake when the kids wake up. And then he doesn't wake me up, he simply does whatever needs to be done." "But there are times," Gadi adds, "when I don't sleep properly for several days, and I'm tired in the morning, and then Netta gets up and does it. Last week, for example, she did it twice."

Founded as a Jewish state, the State of Israel has been involved in armed conflict with the Palestinians and the neighboring Arab states since its establishment in 1948. Of its 9 million citizens, 74% are Jews and 21% are Palestinian Arabs, the majority of whom are Muslim (85%) (Israel Central Bureau of Statistics [ICBS], 2017; 2019). Israel is a densely populated and very urbanized country. Over 90% of its population lives in urban areas (ICBS, 2017). Israel formally grants women equality with respect to legal, economic, and political rights. Nevertheless, a unique combination of demographic, economic, and religious forces has contributed to the gender and family norms that differ from those in other developed countries. Since the early 1950s, the Israeli state has promoted high fertility rates alongside the integration of women into the workforce (Izraeli, 1992). These policies were aimed to achieve a Jewish majority, and to ensure a labor force sufficiently large to develop the economy as part of Israel's nation-building project. Women earn two-thirds of what men earn, but that is partially accounted for by their shorter paid work hours (45 vs. 37, respectively) (ICBS, 2018). Even while working full-time, women are concentrated in sectors where they often finish working in the afternoon and can then return home to care for children (Frenkel, 2008).

These state policies, combined with the dominance of Jewish religious tradition and the massive waves of immigration from North African and Asian countries, resulted in a society that is family oriented, child-centered and strongly pro-natalist (Katz & Lavee, 2005). Parenthood is the predominant normative requirement and Israeli women have more children than women in other developed countries (an average of 3.1 compared to 1.7 in the OECD countries) (Mandel & Birgier, 2016). Childlessness is rare and divorce rates are relatively low (Remennick, 2000; Nahir, 2016; Yeshua-Katz, 2019). Childlessness, full-time delegation of care, and stay-at-home motherhood are all socially frowned upon (Frenkel, 2008), and the dual-earner family pattern is the most common in Israel. Over 80% of Jewish Israeli mothers are in the labor force (ICBS, 2018).

These high employment rates are supported by government policies and the availability of public and private childcare services. Subsidized centers that provide full daycare for babies and toddlers from the age of 3 months are widespread, and nearly all 3-year-old Jewish children attend either private or state-supported nursery schools (Israel National Council for the Child, 2015). It is common and socially acceptable for Israeli women to return to full-time employment after their 14 weeks of paid maternity (Katz & Lavee, 2005). Despite their extensive participation in the workforce, Israeli women continue to perform the lion's share of family work. Recent studies reported that women did at least 7 weekly hours more than men of care and housework in about 75% of Israeli couples (DeRose et al., 2019) and all the cooking and laundry in more than 60% of the couples (Mandel & Birgier, 2016).

At around 7:00 a.m., Netta takes the children to daycare on her way to work. Although the route itself is only a few minutes on foot, dropping them off takes closer to an hour as each child gets some individual attention, play time, or "reading a story or two" before saying goodbye.

Gadi picks up the children at 4:00 p.m., but they rarely head back home. Instead, Netta joins them and they go to the playground, meet friends, or spend the afternoon in the kibbutz swimming pool during the long summer months. Gadi explains that because of the desert climate, "most families are like 'let's rush back to the air-conditioned house and stay there until the sun goes down, and then we can go out again.' But with us it's different, both Netta and I love the heat, so we stay outside and do things."

In the evening they come back home for supper, and then Gadi bathes the children while Netta washes the dishes. Netta reads a bedtime story and tucks them into bed. "But recently he felt he had enough with bathing them so we swapped," she says. "So he washed the dishes and read the stories. But usually he bathes them and I'm in charge of the dishes and stories."

The evenings are devoted to reading, watching movies together, or taking turns going to exercise classes. They usually stay up until midnight, although once in a while each of them feels worn-out and "collapses on the bed" straight after the children are tucked into theirs.

Flexible division characterizes the way they respond to their children's calls at night as well. "Many times I'm still awake or already awake, and I go," Gadi explains. "But if both of us are asleep, many times Netta goes. It's simply the one who is more conscious."

They both believe that their relationships with the children are equally close. "My daughter does her job testing her limits and all that stuff," Netta says:

> but she frequently tells me, "Mommy you are sweet" or "Mommy I love you." On the other hand, of course there are days when Aya fights with me, and then she wants "Daddy, only Daddy," and the reverse, after she fights with him, "Only Mommy, only Mommy," so I guess it's the same.

When facing dilemmas regarding the children's education, Netta and Gadi have long discussions which eventually lead to a joint decision. "We don't argue at all, about anything," Netta says, and mentions a recent example:

> We're having bedwetting problems with our daughter, so we had a rather stormy – discussion; I don't know how to define it, not an argument but simply a misunderstanding. He tried to tell me something, and I tried to tell him, but we were unsuccessful over and over, until finally, after a long time trying to clarify the issue, we finally were able to explain to one another what we meant and to reach some kind of decision … But we are very flexible, we re-assess the situation all the time: every day, every hour, whenever there is a need.

Do they ever experience conflicts over who does what with the children? Both of them deny that: "No, I don't remember us saying to each other, 'I did this yesterday, now it's your turn,'" Gadi says. "And what about one of you just feeling unfairly exhausted?" "Not unfairly," Gadi responds. "The kids definitely let us feel exhausted, but in a fair way."

"Things that Suit Us More"

Gadi and Netta are not keen on housework. When asked who does the cleaning, both gave the same response, "Well, as you can see – no one does." Nevertheless, their house does look nice and tidy. Gadi says, "I can't tell you who does it more. Actually Netta is more aware of cleanliness than I am, I mean I can tolerate a lot more mess than she can. Both of us aren't too enthusiastic, but when it is necessary, I do it or she does it."

They specialize more in the division of cooking and washing; each of them does what the other dislikes most. During the week, the children eat in the daycare; the only "real cooking" is done on the weekend. Netta usually cooks the meat and Gadi prepares rice and salad. "Let's say Netta doesn't like frying, so I do frying," Gadi adds. When it comes to laundry, Netta washes, Gadi hangs it up and takes it down, and Netta folds and puts the clean clothes away. Gadi explains:

> Look, there are things that suit us more, so, for example, I hate loading up the dishwasher – I dislike dealing with all those little things, and the cups and all that. I can do it. I do it when the sink is overflowing and I get annoyed, then I do it. But first I wait for Netta to do it. On the other hand, Netta doesn't like hanging up the laundry, so when I'm away on reserve duty for three days, I come home to four loads of laundry [laughs] – "Please hang everything up now." It's not that she can't do it, she just doesn't want to.

Netta claims more responsibility for the management and planning around the children's activities. Bringing a change of clothes and diapers to daycare, a flower wreath for the Shavuot holiday, or a white shirt for Passover – "I'm the one who takes care of these kinds of things." On the other hand, "Gadi knows exactly what's needed in the afternoon backpack and whether there's enough," Netta says. "I have no idea. I go out with the kids and forget the backpack, and then find out I don't have any of the things they need. Gadi always takes it everywhere he goes."

"Not Very Much into Our Careers"

Because they live and work in a small Kibbutz, no time is wasted on commuting or traffic. Gadi's job is more flexible and enables him to respond to midday calls from the daycare, "Let's say they call from daycare to say that they've run out of diapers, or we didn't bring the pacifier, right? Someone has to go and bring those things, so I do it."

Gadi likes his job as a researcher and feels that it suits him well. It is professionally fulfilling and he enjoys the considerable autonomy. When the pressure is on to complete a project for a deadline, he rarely stays longer hours at the office. Instead, he maintains the daily afternoon routine with the children, and starts working again after they are asleep.

> Let's say there is something I have to submit, and I wasn't able to finish it on time, so many times . . . I leave it, go away, spend time with the family, and then later I return to it. It's not like "first I'll finish my work and only afterwards I'll talk to the family," not with me.

If he works late at night, he can sleep in the morning when the children are off to daycare.

At the time of the interview, Netta's job was less satisfying. She was working full-time in an administrative position in the kibbutz, and earned significantly less than Gadi. However, both of them described her job as a temporary solution, and said she was looking for a more challenging job. Indeed, one year later, she had already switched to a management position related to her background as an ecologist, and was very satisfied with this better-paying and professionally rewarding job.

Although both Gadi and Netta are highly educated, their joint income at the time of the interview was slightly below average, and their careers were not given high priority. Netta explained:

> Because both of us, I think, are people who are not very much into money and not very much into our careers; we can devote time to the family in peace and arrange our lives so that we can be a family. Supporting the family financially, staying late at work, advancing our careers – all these are secondary, and are not particularly important.

"It's Not Mine – It's Ours!"

Netta and Gadi's equal sharing goes back to the very beginning of their lives as a couple. Netta came up with the idea to move in together after she graduated and had to leave the student dorm. Gadi said, "yes," and they started sharing an apartment and all the housework involved. Although they were doing everything together – shopping, cleaning, cooking – Netta was unhappy about the division of labor. "At some point I think I felt that I was doing more than him. Not that I was actually doing more, but that the responsibility for getting things done was mine . . . It's not as if he didn't do, but I had to tell him 'do.'"

Netta's discontent did not last long because she soon got into action:

> So I told him, "Listen, this house is not just mine, it's ours. The chore is not mine and the responsibility is not mine, it's also yours. Look around and take

responsibility whenever you see something that needs to be done." And that's it; since that day on, "it's not just mine."

This rule of shared responsibility was then put into practice: "Afterwards, you know, there are things we already agreed on: how we would clean the house, 'I'll do these things and you do those,' and after a long time when we'd had enough of it we'd switch – I'll do your things and you do mine."

A History of Juggling

Netta and Gadi shared the care of their first baby equally. When Aya was born, Gadi worked mainly from home on his postdoctoral research job, and Netta took a 4-month maternity leave from her work as a research technician. As the baby demanded 24-hour care, they decided to split the job between them so that Gadi was in charge of the nights, and Netta had the days. Netta explains:

> She had lots of gas, she used to make noises all the time, 24 hours a day, so it's impossible to sleep next to a thing like that, which makes noises all the time. And you had to actually turn her over every 20 minutes ... so we used to take turns. She slept in the living room next to him, and I was in my room, trying to sleep as much as I could.

Breastfeeding, however, had to be done day and night, so it was Gadi's job to bring the baby to Netta for feeding and to respond to any other needs during his night shift.

After the first 4 months, Netta went back to her job, and Gadi took care of Aya at home while doing his research. Usually Israeli women return to full-time employment after birth, as paid maternity leave only covers 3 months, and one income is not enough. So Netta's colleagues were not surprised to see her there. "If there was any reaction at work it was like, 'so why didn't you come back right after 3 months, why only now?'" she laughs.

Combining a full-time job with breastfeeding was tricky, though. They both vividly remember the ordeal they went through when Netta had to go on a 2-week fieldwork project, which involved "ensnaring gerbils at night" and sleeping out in the field.

> So I traveled to do my stuff and he would come with her all the way from our home to the research site, just so that I could nurse her. He'd sleep there with her all night, then he would drive back home in the morning. At noon I'd come home, nurse her, return to work in the afternoon, and then he would drive

down again in the afternoon. That's the way it was for those 2 weeks ... he was actually chasing me back and forth, back and forth, every day ... it seemed completely natural to me. Today I think that I was nuts.

Although exhausting, this struggle to combine a full-time job with breast-feeding lasted for a short period of time, since Aya soon started to eat solid food, and could do with just morning and evening nursing. Gadi's struggle to combine his own full-time job with caring for the baby was more prolonged and just as demanding.

His research job also included fieldwork: he had to travel to Tel Aviv and obtain samples of insects from people's backyards:

So I used to take Aya with me to Tel Aviv and I had no problem being with her for entire days. I used to prepare a pack with chopped food that I cooked. I'd leave with bags packed to the brim, and we'd be off – we would walk the streets for an entire day, and when we'd get back, she'd already be asleep.

Surprisingly, Gadi reports that carrying a baby helped him:

We'd approach people, knock on their doors ... I would stop an old lady who normally would have slammed the door in my face, [but] since I had my baby, the woman would ask me "What do you want?" I'd tell her about the study and everything, and she would say, "no problem" and "what an adorable baby" [imitates the woman], and it was great!

Nevertheless, working from home and writing research reports while caring for the baby became more and more challenging as Aya got older and demanded more attention. "She slept less and less and had demands," Netta recalls. "She did not agree to just lie there on the floor with her toys and be quiet; she wanted to go outside and take a walk, and she did not let him do anything else." As time went by, Gadi was less able to do his work, which made him "more and more irritable and jumpy because he felt that he wasn't doing what he was paid to do." "I became extremely irritable," Gadi confirms. "I told Netta, 'I have no problems raising Aya, it's fun, and I have no problems doing my post-doc. But doing both together – that's tough.' Sometimes the pressure was really tough."

So by the age of 1, baby Aya started attending daycare in a nearby kibbutz. Gadi would pick her up in the afternoon and "roam all over the kibbutz till it got dark or even after, or sometimes we'd go to the swimming pool or the cowsheds. We'd go on hikes and Aya would show me what they did in daycare that day."

The division of labor changed considerably one year later, when their second child, Adam, was born. Gadi got a job offer which posed a difficult dilemma for the family: taking the job meant they had to move, and Netta would have to give up her own job:

> It was a difficult decision, because I had a really good job that I liked very much, but ... I realized that I had got to a point where I had started to feel that I had enough of it ... so I said, "OK, this is a one-time opportunity for him to get a job in his profession, and for me – I can do anything."

So Netta quit her job and the family moved. For one year, Netta stayed at home with baby Adam. After the first year, she found a job. With both of them employed again, their division of childcare returned to being equal.

Rejecting Gender-Based Abilities

Gadi and Netta's views, priorities, and personalities combine to produce their equal sharing. Above all, it is obvious that their division of labor reflects a conscious, purposeful choice, guided by their egalitarian ideologies. Gadi opposes "the idea that just because you are a man or a woman, you are imprisoned in a specific role."

Both of them reject essentialist beliefs in women's inherent and naturally superior caring abilities. When asked whether there is a difference in the abilities of men and women to take care of children, Netta responded that "there are tons of differences between men and women but those differences don't testify to abilities, but to different approaches." When asked specifically about caring for young babies, Netta seemed surprised, "But why should they be less able to care for little babies? No, no way. There is a difference in the way they care but not in the ability to care," she concluded.

Likewise, Gadi said,

> The differences are more individual than gender-based. Of course there are things that are more difficult for men to do than women, right? Nursing for example; bottle-feeding is different than breastfeeding. And maybe it is more instinctive for men to horse around with the children in the Gymboree than women. Still, it depends on the individual: I mean there are women who like horsing around with their kids and men who are couch-potatoes.

Nevertheless, egalitarian ideologies and rejection of essentialist beliefs in themselves are not sufficient to produce an egalitarian division of labor. In Gadi and Netta's case, these ideologies have been translated into practice by Netta's assertiveness, her use of "reverse gatekeeping" strategies, and Gadi's interest and willingness to take on his share.

Netta's Share of Equal Sharing: "Because I Said So"

Many women who hold egalitarian views are nevertheless reluctant to give up their advantaged position as the more knowledgeable and skillful parent. Such women may encourage their husbands' participation yet maintain overall responsibility by setting standards and supervising the husband's involvement in childcare (Gaunt, 2008). This gatekeeping enables women to preserve an important source of authority, autonomy, and self-esteem.

Unlike many women, Netta's identity is not caught up in her maternal role. She deliberately distances herself from the prescribed normative images of motherhood as a natural, intuitive, and irreplaceable role. During the interview, Netta took every opportunity to declare her non-conformity, sometimes provocatively. For example, when describing her decision to have children, she challenged the notion of women's biological clock and natural desire for a child:

> I'll tell you something: I had kids because I was bored with my life. It's not because I'm some great fan of kids, actually I can't stand kids, but I said – enough. Up to now I've done a lot: I studied, found a job, worked a few years, figured things out, got married – enough. Now I'm ready for the next stage, otherwise my life was really boring.

Presenting her choice as a way to fight boredom, she also rejects the normative expectation that women like children. "From someone who couldn't stand children, I turned into someone who loves her own children, with limited tolerance toward other children." Finally, when asked from whom does she think she learned to take care of children, her response was, "I didn't learn. Who said I learned?"

Not only does Netta give up the privileges attached to maternal expertise and authority, she goes further to encourage Gadi's seniority as the knowledgeable parent. Gadi admits he reads parenting guides "a thousand times more than her" and recalls that when she got pregnant "she used to tell me, 'I don't feel like reading all this nonsense; you read and tell me.' So I read it all more or less, and since then I continue to read birth and parenting forums on the internet."

Netta seems happy to foster her secondary status in this respect. Recanting her earlier teasing comment, she acknowledged. "I've learned a lot, I didn't know how to be a parent, and I'm growing all the time. Gadi helps me; he knows better than I do," she says repeatedly. "In my opinion he knows more than me, he has a clearer direction and vision that guides him." Netta seems to deliberately remain ignorant of certain minor childcare tasks, "Only he knows how to braid hair. No, the truth is that when he was away for a week on reserve duty and I had to do it, so I learned during that week how to braid hair. But why should I bother if he's there?"

Finally, Netta's assertive approach was key to creating an equal division. "As I told you earlier, I said, 'take responsibility. Look around you and see what needs to be done and do it, don't wait for me to look around and tell you what to do'."

Netta's assertiveness must have been inspired when, as a teenager, she witnessed the dramatic effects of her mother's assertiveness. As a child, both of her parents worked at their jobs until around 4:00 p.m., and their division at home was not strictly traditional. Her father was in charge of "taking us to the pool and sometimes playing with us in the afternoons . . . and baths were always his job, always, from the first to last day we needed someone to do it for us." However, her mother did most of the housework and childcare, and her father "used to sit while she warmed up the food and served it to him."

After 20 years of sole responsibility for cooking, washing, and cleaning:

> one day my mother said, "enough is enough." Out of the blue, she said, "I'm fed up, that's it." And from then on, my father underwent a total changeover: he does the dishes, tidies up the house and folds the laundry, and all those things that he had never done for years, he suddenly started doing.

Presumably, observing her parents' transformation contributed to Netta's vision of genuinely shared responsibility and the feasibility of a real change, as well as to her feelings of entitlement:

> I think that most men avoid taking the responsibility; they wait to be given tasks to do. It's not that they can't do the tasks, it's not that they don't do the tasks, it's that they don't take responsibility for deciding what task to perform and when to perform it.

"And why is it different with you?"

> It's different because I said so. I simply addressed the issue. You know what, it's not even a matter of lack of will; it's a matter of lack of awareness. The minute you're aware that you're not doing something then you can bring it to your attention and do it.

Gadi's Share of Equal Sharing: "My Decision To Do It Was Substantial"

It takes two to tango, and Netta's egalitarianism and assertiveness alone would not have resulted in equal sharing without Gadi's interest in sharing childcare. "Yes, it interests me," Gadi admits. "I read a lot about parenthood, about childcare. My mother was a social worker who worked with at-risk children, so I was familiar with many issues in this field." Gadi had also had some childcare experience before becoming a parent:

> When I had just finished my army service, I traveled abroad to relatives of mine and stayed with them for a few months, where I took care of their son who was about a year old ... I think that I am drawn to – and also have some ability in – educating and raising children,

he confesses, and Netta agrees: "His advice is often better than the things that I carry out or know."

Like Netta, Gadi's family of origin maintained a relatively traditional division, but not strictly so. His mother was employed and did most of the housework and childcare, and his father worked longer paid hours, "but on Saturdays he used to take us on hikes. It was the three of us: me, and my brother, and my father." His father was also in charge of cleaning, "He didn't work on Friday; he would stay home and clean the house; that was his job."

Gadi's inherent interest in child-rearing, together with his family-centered approach, has led him to prioritize the family over his career. From taking care of his baby while working from home to leaving his job in the afternoon and then catching up late at night, Gadi consciously chooses equal sharing. "I'm fairly convinced that my decision to do it was crucial, that is, if I had decided differently, then we wouldn't share in this way."

Creating the Circumstances

One could argue that Gadi and Netta enjoy special circumstances that enable them to share equally. Indeed, Gadi attributes their division of childcare partly to their employment conditions:

> When Netta had a set job and my work was flexible, I took on more. When the reverse was true, and I had work that was less flexible and I had to invest a lot, at least at the beginning, and Netta was more flexible – then she took on more.

Although flexible employment conditions certainly help equal sharing, in Gadi and Netta's case these are a consequence, rather than a cause, of their life choices. Most full-time researchers would not choose to take care of their babies even if their job enabled them to work from home, or leave the office at 4:00 p.m. when they are expected to work longer hours.

Moreover, with their slightly-below-average family income, Gadi and Netta maintain a very modest standard of living. Yet, when asked whether he would take an offer for a similar but better-paying job involving longer work hours, Gadi's response was "only if I had to." He decisively explained why he would turn down a higher salary, "Our ideal is to be together with the children. If you want to continue living like a bachelor even when you have a family you can do that, it's considered legitimate, I meet people like that. But why would I?"

60/60 Parenting

Although they were interviewed separately, when asked what percentage of childcare each of them does, both Netta and Gadi responded, "Each of us does 60%." Mathematically incorrect, they both insisted, "That's the right answer!" Netta volunteered to explain:

> Each of us does just enough to subjectively feel that he or she is doing a little more than the other, and then it's a sure thing that we are quite the same. This is an idea we once picked up from friends of ours, and since then we've been living according to this rule.

"For us," she concludes, "it works like magic."

References

DeRose, L. F., Goldscheider, F., Brito, J. E., Salazar-Arango, A., Corcuera, P., Corcuera, P. J., & Gas-Aixendri, M. (2019). Are Children Barriers to the Gender Revolution? International Comparison. *European Journal of Population*. Retrieved from: https://doi.org/10.1007/s10680-018-09515-8.

Frenkel, M. (2008). Reprogramming Femininity? The Construction of Gender Identities in the Israeli Hi-Tech Industry Between Global and Local Gender Orders. *Gender, Work & Organization, 15*(4), 352–374.

Gaunt, R. (2008). Maternal Gatekeeping: Antecedents and Consequences. *Journal of Family Issues, 29*, 373–395.

Israel Central Bureau of Statistics (2017). *Israel in Figures 2016. Population*. Retrieved from: www.cbs.gov.il/he/publications/DocLib/isr_in_n/isr_in_n16e.pdf.

Israel Central Bureau of Statistics (2018). *Women and Men 2016*. Retrieved from: www.cbs.gov.il/he/Statistical/statist166_h.pdf.

Israel Central Bureau of Statistics (2019). *Population of Israel on the Eve of 2019*. Retrieved from: www.cbs.gov.il/he/mediarelease/DocLib/2018/394/11_18_394b.pdf.

Israel National Council for the Child (2015). *The State of Young Children in Israel 2015*. https://bernardvanleer.org/app/uploads/2016/03/The-State-of-Young-Children-in-Israel-2015_hi-res.pdf.

Izraeli, D. N. (1992). *Culture, Policy, and Women in Dual-Earner Families in Israel*. Thousand Oaks, CA: Sage Publications, Inc.

Katz, R. & Lavee, Y. (2005). Families in Israel. In B. N. Adams & J. Trost (eds.). *Handbook of World Families* (pp. 486–506). Thousand Oaks, CA: Sage.

Mandel, H. & Birgier, D. P. (2016). The Gender Revolution in Israel: Progress and Stagnation. In N. Khattab, S. Miaari, & H. Stier (eds.) *Socioeconomic Inequality in Israel* (pp. 153–184). New York: Palgrave Macmillan.

Nahir, Shlomo (2016, August) *Total Divorce Rate in Israel*. Poster presented at European Population Conference, Mainz, Germany.

Remennick, L. (2000). Childless in the Land of Imperative Motherhood: Stigma and Coping Among Infertile Israeli Women. *Sex Roles*, 43(11–12), 821–841.

Yeshua-Katz, D. (2019). Blame or Shame: The Search for Online Support and Stigma Origin Among Israeli Childless Women. *Mass Communication and Society*, 22(1), 117–138.

4

Honduras

Erin Murphy-Graham

"Yesterday, because I didn't work, it was my turn. If I'm not home, he is the one who does it . . . and when there's no school we spontaneously do chores. We don't have to say you have to do it . . . Doing things comes from him and from me too." "Spontaneity" is the term that Angelica used to explain how she and her partner, Robinson, get through the chores of their daily lives. While one of them prepares breakfast, the other makes sure that the children are ready for school. Later, whoever gets home first cooks and serves lunch, and usually they both spend their afternoons with the children. They have three children, a 5-year-old daughter, Angie, and two sons: Lenin, aged 8, and Leo, aged 13.

Angelica and Robinson are an outlier couple, a rare exception to the norms in Honduras that dictate *la mujer es de la casa y el hombre es de la calle* [a woman's place is at home and a man's in the street]. They live in a small concrete home in *Ciudad España*, a planned community in Tegucigalpa, the Honduran capital, established after Hurricane Mitch destroyed large, makeshift settlements in Tegucigalpa.

Honduras is one of the poorest countries in the western hemisphere and, as of 2016, had the second highest homicide rate in the world (United Nations Office on Drugs and Crime, n.d.). Increasingly the favored gateway of drug traffickers moving product from the Andes to the United States, Honduras is the site of a major US counter-narcotics intervention, and it has received an enormous influx of American military and antidrug support over the past few years. Much of the American military support centers on a region known as La Mosquitia, or the Mosquito Coast, which is an area of sparsely populated jungle and savannah that is only accessible by inland waterway and light aircraft. This is where Robinson grew up and, until 2 years ago, worked as a teacher in a village school. Robinson belongs to an ethnic minority group, the Miskito, the namesake of the region, and he considers the language, Miskitu, to be his mother tongue.

Angelica also moved to Tegucigalpa from a rural part of Honduras, near the southern city of Choluteca. Her father tragically drowned when Angelica was just 3 years old. She explained, "My dad was a teacher, too. He had to cross a river to get to school, and that's how he drowned." The seventh of eight children, Angelica has memories of her siblings helping to care for and raise her. When she was 15 years old, Angelica and her mother moved to Tegucigalpa so that she could study in a teacher-training high school, an *escuela normal*.

From these humble beginnings, Angelica and Robinson have created a home environment that challenges the traditional gender division of labor in Honduras and exemplifies the rewards of shared parenting.

Honduras is the second poorest country in Central America, with 66% of people living below the poverty line, almost a third of whom live in conditions of extreme poverty (World Bank, 2018b). Honduras has a total population of approximately 9 million people. Almost half (43%) live in rural areas (Central Intelligence Agency, 2019) where poverty is prevalent, mostly for the majority of indigenous and Afro-Honduran people, who represent approximately 7% of the population. Catholicism (37%) and Evangelism (39%) are the dominant religions (Latinobarómetro, 2018).

Rampant crime and violence, the lack of employment opportunities, and low agricultural productivity underlie the persistent poverty in the country. Honduras has the highest rate of income inequality in Latin America (World Bank, 2018b). Violence and lack of opportunity have led thousands of migrants to join caravans walking through Central America and Mexico to seek asylum in the US (Borger, 2018).

In Honduras, female labor force participation is 51% compared to 86% of their male counterparts (World Bank, 2018a). Gender discrimination in employment is legally forbidden in Honduras (World Bank Group, 2018). Nevertheless, women earn only 53% of what men earn (Statistica, 2017).

Honduran women are entitled to a paid maternity leave for a period of 12 weeks (Globalization Partners, n.d.), but parental and paternity leave do not exist. The law also stipulates 1-hour paid breaks for nursing mothers, as well as childcare subsidies (Soto, 2011). However, given that a significant proportion of female work is precarious, that labor informality is the norm, and that many employers do not comply with labor law, these policies benefit a small proportion of women (García & Oliveira, 2011). As of 2017, 43% of the children starting at age 3 were enrolled in preprimary education (World Bank, 2019).

Honduran women's participation in the labor market has not elicited a proportional participation of men in household labor and childcare. On average, with no children under 6 years old, women spent 3:07 hours on domestic labor, compared to the 1:34 hours spent by men, whereas with young children, women spent 4:25 hours to men's 1:52 hours (Agenda de las Mujeres, 2010). When employment, childcare, and housework are considered together, women's workweeks exceed men's (García & Oliveira, 2011).

"I Have To Complement Her, and She Has To Complement Me"

Angelica and Robinson agree that they shared the work of parenting equally. However, when asked for a precise estimate of his contribution, Robinson said that he does roughly 60%, whereas she said 50%. At the time of our interview, Robinson was enrolled in an online master's program, which meant he was home more than Angelica, who was employed at the local preschool as a teacher. His flexible schedule and ability to work from home for his master's degree means that this year he is doing slightly more housework and cooking than he has done in the past. He explained:

> There are days when I am in charge of doing the house chores because I am at home. Yesterday I had to do it because I was there and that is our arrangement. I woke up at 5 a.m. to cook breakfast for everyone; I cleaned up the house, made lunch, dinner, and left everything in order.

On the days that Angelica isn't at her job, she often completes these tasks, although they each follow their preferences. For example, Robinson has developed an interest in cooking. Angelica laughed and explained, "Sometimes I cook, but he cooks more!" However, Robinson does not like cleaning. Angelica said that he normally only cleans when she is not around, or they assign this chore to the older kids, Leo and Lenin. When the time comes for laundry, they take turns doing it. If one of the children becomes sick, they often both take him/her to the doctor. Putting the children to bed is also a shared task. Robinson explained, "I do it or she does it. If she sleeps first because she is tired and I'm still working on the computer doing homework, then I make the decision of when to send the children to bed." Likewise, they try to equally attend to administrative tasks like managing school enrollment, although some-times those jobs fall through the cracks. Robinson explained that they had been very busy when they were supposed to enroll the kids in school:

> She didn't know the date and neither did I. When we realized it, Lenin had missed enrollment, and . . . her [Angelica's] mother had to go do it, my mother-in-law. And then I had to run to school to see if Lenin's enrollment was due, and it was! . . . So we both divide. If she's busy, if I'm busy, we both share.

Recently, Robinson has been spending more time helping the children with their schoolwork. Angelica explained, "With their homework, for example, he knows English, I don't, so he gets more involved with their English homework." Likewise, through his online studies, he has become increasingly comfortable using the desktop computer that sits in the family's small living room. Angelica explained, "The computer, he knows more than me, I hardly do, so he helps them with their homework . . . he gets more involved with that." Their 5-year-old daughter, Angie, particu-larly enjoys working on the computer. During one of our interviews, Angie sat at the desk, typing out the alphabet. When she got to "P," the lights flickered and the power went off. Angie sighed, accustomed to the frequent power outages. When asked to recall a specific time that one of the children was upset, and who they turned to for help, Angelica reported that little Angie often got upset when the power went off. "Well, it's like when they get sad because maybe the lights went off and they couldn't keep playing with the computer . . . So to distract them we go to the park, something like that, we would all go for a walk."

Screen time has become a parenting challenge for Robinson and Angel-ica. Robinson tries to make sure the children do not spend too much time in front of the television or the computer. He felt strongly about this, and so began to manage the time that the children spent with these devices. He told Angelica that they had to "take care of them, and not just let them spend their time in front of the television or the computer for hours without our attention." Likewise, he wanted to make sure that they used the computer in ways that would help their learning, "so that we can introduce things that would really help with their studies, not just playing on the computer but turning their work on the computer into something productive."

The degree of sharing that Angelica and Robinson have is so uncommon that it is often seen as a "curiosity." For example, Robinson said that when close friends were visiting, they were surprised to see him cook, which had even prompted playful complaints from women to their husbands for not being more like Robinson. Angelica explained that her own brothers are not as involved as Robinson, and that sometimes her sisters-in-law have commented that they wished their husbands could be more like him. When asked how people react to the way they share the housework and childcare, Angelica said:

> You know, they have congratulated us at church ... The women congratulate us. They tell me, "I wish I could have a husband like yours" ... I imagine that maybe it doesn't work like that with them ... They have congratulated us, and they also have congratulated him for being a good husband.

Learning To Build Equality with Balance

Angelica and Robinson met when they were both studying for their undergraduate degrees at the National Pedagogical University in Tegucigalpa. At first, they were just friends and classmates. Independently, both discontinued their studies for a brief period. Angelica became involved with a man, the father of her oldest son, whom she describes, "Very *machista*, he was never at home, only outside ... we were together for a short time, I didn't like it. That's why we ended it. He was a womanizer." As a teenager, Robinson fathered two daughters who are now teenagers. His relationship with their mother did not last. She eventually moved out of the region, leaving Robinson responsible for their two daughters, who are currently living with Robinson's mother in La Mosquitia. Angelica commented that they had both learned a great deal from their previous relationships, helping them better understand what they wanted from a partner.

Five years after discontinuing their university studies, coincidentally, they both re-enrolled and became romantically involved. Robinson explained, "With time, I started noticing her and started to visit her." On one occasion, Angelica told Robinson that she would like to offer him something to eat, but he said that better yet, he would cook for her and her family. "I went to the kitchen and started cooking and all. She told me that she didn't know what to do, how to cook for me. So I told her, 'I'll do it and you can learn, so just come and talk with me while I cook.'" Angelica, who never learned to cook, was impressed by Robinson's culinary skills and impressed that, as a man, he knew how to cook at all. As he explained, "This was something new to her, it seemed as if she hadn't seen that behavior before," and according to him, was part of what brought them together as a couple. He would routinely bring groceries and they would cook together, "We kept getting to know each other more and then we decided to get together."

After finishing their degrees, they both got jobs as teachers, but Robinson's post required him to return to La Mosquitia to work in a village school. Angelica began teaching at the preschool where she now works in *Ciudad España*, which meant that they lived apart; Robinson could only come and stay during school vacations or holidays. The airfare from La Mosquitia to Tegucigalpa costs "more than a roundtrip ticket to Miami!"

After some time, Angelica became pregnant with their son, Lenin, and she explained that it was really then that they became a formal couple, although, like many Honduran couples, they are not legally married. Living apart was challenging for Angelica and, during Robinson's long absences, her mother helped her with childcare and housework, "Back then I practically did more things because he wasn't there, but on vacations it was half and half, 50-50." Over time they both grew tired of living apart. When their second child was born, they tried to find a way to live in the city together. Angelica said, "Well, we need each other, and the children also. I felt lonely, and I always told him that I didn't want to be alone. 'When are you coming home?' And the children [would say this] too." He also missed the children.

Around this time, they both took advantage of an opportunity to apply for a scholarship for an online master's program in education. Angelica was rejected. She confessed her disappointment, "Well, a little sad at the beginning, but ... Because I always want to be at the same level as him, so maybe [I felt] not jealousy but that it was a little unjust."

Robinson's job was considered a hardship post by the government so it paid well, more than Angelica's job in the city. Although they were reluctant to have him give up his teaching post and the salary that they depended on, in La Mosquitia internet service is available only through cell phone modems, which would have made it difficult for him to do an online program there. Coupled with their desire to reside together, Robinson decided to quit his teaching position and go live with Angelica and the children, continuing his online studies. They hoped that he would be able to find a teaching job near *Ciudad España*. However, getting a job was more difficult than they had imagined. Angelica explained, "Here in Honduras getting a teaching position is very politicized ... if you don't have someone to help you, even though you have all the credentials, it doesn't count." For Angelica, the decision for Robinson to quit his job caused some stress, but she believed that they are better off, "I think economically we didn't do well because of that. It was a mistake economically speaking, but emotionally we are better, so it evens out. That's how I see it."

"What Matters Is What Is on the Inside": Angelica, the Free Thinker

Angelica is now the primary breadwinner for her family, which also makes the couple an outlier in Honduras. Because they did not have any savings, nor did they have a joint bank account, if Robinson needed money, he had to ask her for cash, a concrete example of their nontraditionally gendered roles. Angelica explained that although she and Robinson did not fight over finances, they both felt the strain of relying on one income, "There is the tension of him not having a job; this is what worries us right now, that he doesn't have a job because my salary is not enough. We are always short on cash. So that tension is there from his part too." Yet despite the financial challenges of the past year, they were not considering the possibility of living apart. They were still optimistic that he would find employment. Angelica maintained an upbeat perspective.

Angelica rejects both the cultural expectation that a man should provide for his family and the equally strong cultural beliefs that a woman should take care of the household by cooking, cleaning, and taking care of children. According to her, there is no difference between men and women in their ability to take care of children. She claimed, "It must be because I've seen it in my home. I don't see any differences; it's the same thing." She rejects a gendered role for herself; since the beginning she was drawn to Robinson because of this, "I liked this, and that is why I am with him."

Angelica's ability to resist cultural expectations is also evident in her willingness to partner with a man from an ethnic minority. When asked if Angelica had ever been criticized for being with a Miskito, she recalled that once a cousin asked her how she could be with Robinson, "Don't you find him ugly?" Angelica explained that what matters to her is how a person acts and how they are on the inside. She thinks for herself, and tries not to be influenced by the comments and expectations of others.

While Angelica is generally quite successful in her efforts to counter gender expectations, she struggles with one aspect of her relationship with Robinson. Perhaps influenced by her previous relationship as well as dominant social norms about men as womanizers who will cheat on their spouses when given the opportunity, Angelica sometimes feels uncomfortable if she does not know how Robinson is spending his time. "For me it is still hard . . . not knowing where he is all the time." However, she and Robinson discussed the need to trust each other and to actively resist the stereotype of men as cheating *machistas*. Robinson says:

> Each one must try to build a balance. At the same time, we must not trap each other. We both have to have that freedom, because the commitment is within each of us. If I am away . . . that doesn't mean that I have total freedom outside of my house to do what I want. So the two must try to blend properly to be able to have that type of freedom and not smother each other.

While they are able to distribute work equally, Angelica's description of her struggle over not always knowing Robinson's whereabouts illustrates that challenging gendered norms requires both the physical effort of changing behavior, as well as mental energy for resisting sexist thinking. Angelica's personality, which she described as relaxed and flexible, "easygoing," seems a good match with Robinson's, which is more certain, strong, and unwavering in his beliefs.

Renouncing Patriarchal Behavior: Robinson the Deep Thinker

For Robinson, sharing the tasks of the household was the manifestation of deeply rooted ideological beliefs that reject patriarchy. When asked if he was satisfied with the current division of labor in his household, he replied that he was "not part of patriarchal behavior." He takes credit for bringing new ideas to Angelica:

> I am the one who had the initiative of bringing in the idea that in a couple's life, the woman doesn't have to be the one who does everything in the house, that the man also has to share that responsibility. He has to contribute in taking care of the children, cooking and serving food, doing the laundry, cleaning the house, mopping.

Robinson emphasized that his co-parenting was learned. He explained that his grandmother, with whom he lived growing up, may have been influenced by indigenous belief systems that did not see God as male or society as patriarchal, "She was a very, very, special woman." Robinson's family raised him to think differently. Perhaps more importantly, they taught him the skills required to translate these ideological beliefs into actions: how to cook, to clean, to wash clothes, to iron. He explained that both of his parents taught him and his siblings by example, "If my mother was occupied, then my father was taking care of us, or if my mother could not prepare dinner, my father immediately made dinner." He believed that growing up in that household has socialized him and his siblings and shaped their attitudes, "I grew up in an environment of mutual support and I think that has influenced us to have the same attitude." He credits his family of origin for teaching him not to wait for Angelica to do things for him.

In addition to being socialized in a more equal environment, his educational opportunities also shaped his attitudes and behaviors. He worked as a research assistant for a professor who was investigating Honduran gender norms. This experience allowed him to link his own beliefs and life experiences to scholarly work on gender and society. In our interview, words uncommon in everyday talk in his neighborhood, such as "patriarchy," "patriarchal ideologies," and "subordinate" rolled off his tongue, and he incorporated his analysis of society and the family in an intellectually rich and clear manner. In particular, he critiqued the common social arrangement in Honduras where, if both individuals are employed, the woman hires a maid to "take care of her husband." Robinson mimicked what women say, "I can get a house worker so she can take care of my husband because I'm working and at the same time taking care of the house. I'm getting tired, I can't do it!" Instead, Robinson believed that a couple should share the work, "That [hiring help] would not be necessary if we complement each other. From the perspective of a shared social life, breaking the barriers that have been set on us by patriarchal ideologies. And everything would work better!"

Robinson demonstrated a sophisticated ability for social critique. He articulates his rich understanding of many of the issues feminist scholars write about, and an endorsement of a feminist future:

> In our Latin culture *machismo* is very rooted, even mothers induce it from home. They say, "Son, you will not marry a woman with children," even though they are themselves single mothers! So there are a lot of contradictions ... Culture is shaped by this way of thinking, which is based on patriarchal culture. But if ... culture changed and if we built a more equitable society, because equal participation of women should not only be within the house, that participation which begins in the house should also expand outside the house. Their power to make decisions outside the house ... society will be strengthened ... and changes would be more sustainable ... In the case of the United States which is a country that we all know, but where

development is not that solid, because the complementing part, which are the women, don't have equal strength with men.

He is motivated to create a new kind of family, "The family is ... a social institution that must be managed ... I try to do this because I don't want my daughter to go through that type of life, and to be with a man who is a *machista* ... try to build a respectful and equal relationship."

Angelica did not enter the relationship with the same exposure to scholarly feminist ideas. Because her father died when she was so young, her mother did everything with the help of her siblings. Robinson's approach, he explained, "was strange to her but it was normal in my house. So I started to teach her that she doesn't have to subordinate to the whims of a man ... Even if we separate, you should never ever subordinate to a husband. Try to be independent! Try to be equitable." In his words, he has been "teaching" her that things can be different, that things can be shared. He provided the concrete example of cooking, and how he was teaching her how to cook so that they can be better balanced in that domain, so she could "be at 50% with me." He explains:

> I liked the food to be well prepared, so when I noticed that she had a weakness in that aspect, I practically assumed all the responsibility. And now she is learning. She always looks to me when she makes a certain food, asking me what to use and what the ingredients are.

Concluding Thoughts: Airplane Ride Toward Equality

For Angelica and Robinson, communication has been key for their success as a couple, particularly in terms of how they parent their children. When tensions arise, they discuss things calmly, and according to Angelica, "never had a strong argument with fighting and shouting. Never." For Robinson, "If there is not a fluent and reliable communication between home members, if there is no communication at all, it is very hard to understand and work out the differences." Angelica echoed him when she explained, "I think communication is important, communicating and saying what I like and what I don't like ... He knows what I don't like and I know what he doesn't like."

One recent source of tension was how they structure the children's time at home. Robinson believed that they should regulate the kids' activities more, and he discussed the importance of trying to guide their older son, Leo, in the difficult and "confusing" period of adolescence. He invokes the experience he gained by parenting his older daughters. He was very young when they were born, and assumed a "great responsibility" when their mother moved away. Thus, he is "more aware of everything" as a parent, "That ... very strong responsibility at a very early age ... helped me to be more attentive with children." Likewise, his own socialization in a family with two involved parents also shaped his views about how to care for his children. "I think it's my father and my mother's way of life, that we are very caring with children ... so I'm more attentive of everyone, so any complaint, any attention, any type of affection, they seek me, so it's like the kids know already who to come to first."

Angelica grew up with a single mother who was taking care of eight children, and probably had large stretches of unsupervised time. As a result, she was somewhat more relaxed and, in Robinson's estimation, "inattentive." He described this tendency as a personality "flaw" and urged her to become more involved as a parent. Robinson commented, "She is a little more unaware, like a more, let's say a more libertarian mother, and I am someone who likes to take care of the details and correct anything in time." He added, "I don't want her to be neglecting. If we neglect we'll end up affecting them [the children] with a future that may not be appropriate. And also the house, all the harmony in coexistence could be affected, so I always complain about that."

Ironically, although Robinson articulates a clear stance against patriarchy and participates fully in the work of the household, he seems to take a position of authority: making demands, levying criticisms, and "teaching" Angelica, which can sound condescending. There is some risk that by assuming the role of leader in their relationship, he is retaining male privilege.

Robinson and Angelica bring different personalities and different experiences to their relationship. He is a scholar who has a precise social critique he can incorporate into everyday conversation. She is a freethinker, willing to follow her own instincts and defy social expectations. They are both preoccupied by the financial difficulties of his current unemployment, but they are not willing to separate their family for economic reasons.

Robinson used the metaphor of an airplane to explain his position on why equal sharing was so important:

> A couple can work better if they complement each other in their relationship ... The two need to bring balance as the two wings of a plane: if a wing is broken, logically the plane will then fall. That's what happens in a couple's relationship when one doesn't try to be part of the two wings, then everything is pulled downward. This means a potential total split in the future, and I always tell her that we don't have to go to that extreme, that we must try to build the two wings with equity, so we can both fly in balance.

References

Agenda de las Mujeres, Fondo de Desarrollo de las Naciones Unidad para la Mujer, Instituto Nacional de Estadistica Honduras (2010). *Programa agenda económica de las mujeres. Boletín uso del tiempo en Honduras* [Women's Economic Agenda Program: Use of Time in Honduras.] (Gráfico 3, Trabajo Doméstico según presencia de menores de 6 años en el hogar) Retrieved from: www.gemlac.org/attachments/article/340/8.%20Boletin%20Modulo %20Uso%20del%20Tiempo_Honduras_2010.pdf.

Borger, J. (December 19, 2018). Fleeing a Hell the US Helped Create: Why Central Americans Journey North. *The Guardian.* Retrieved from: www.theguardian.com/us-news/2018/dec/19/central-america-migrants-us-foreign-policy.

Central Intelligence Agency (2019). Honduras. *The World Factbook.* Retrieved from: www.cia.gov/library/publications/the-world-factbook/geos/ho.html.

García, B. & Oliveira, O. 2011. Family Changes and Public Policies in Latin America. *Annual Review of Sociology, 37,* 593–611.

Globalization Partners (n.d.) *Maternity/Paternity Leave in Honduras.* Retrieved from: www.globalization-partners.com/globalpedia/honduras-employer-of-record/.

Latinobarómetro (2018). *El Papa Francisco y La Religión en Chile y América Latina.* [Pope Francis and Religion in Chile and Latin America] Retrieved from: www.cooperativa.cl/noticias/site/artic/20180112/asocfile/ 20180112124342/f00006494_religion_chile_america_latina_2017.pdf.

Soto, M. G. (2011). *Country Gender Profile: Honduras. Final Report.* Japan International Cooperation Agency. Retrieved from: www.jica.go.jp/english/ our_work/thematic_issues/gender/background/pdf/e1ohon.pdf.

Statistica (2017). *Labor Market Gender Gap Index in Honduras in 2017, by Category.* Retrieved from: www.statista.com/statistics/803807/honduras-gender-gap-labor-market-category/.

United Nations Office on Drugs and Crime (n.d.). *Intentional Homicide Victims.* Retrieved from: https://dataunodc.un.org/crime/intentional-homicide-victims.

World Bank (2018a). *Honduras: Labor Force Participation by Sex.* Retrieved from: http://datatopics.worldbank.org/gender/country/honduras.

World Bank (2018b). *The World Bank in Honduras: Overview.* Retrieved from: www.worldbank.org/en/country/honduras/overview.

World Bank (2019). *School Enrollment, Preprimary.* Retrieved from: https://data .worldbank.org/indicator/se.pre.enrr.

World Bank Group (2018). *Women, Business and the Law 2018.* Washington, DC: The World Bank. Retrieved from: http://documents.worldbank.org/curated/en/ 926401524803880673/pdf/125804-PUB-REPLACEMENT-PUBLIC.pdf.

5

Montenegro

Milena Račeta Stojanović[1]

Montenegro is famous for its high mountains and wild beauty. The beautiful landscapes once had an important role in Montenegrin history – they were natural boundaries able to protect the country from invaders, but also from foreign influences. One could argue that Montenegrins still resist those influences. Despite the gender revolution around the world, Montenegrin society remains deeply patriarchal and conservative, but not completely.

Maja and Luka are a young couple living on their own terms. They have two small sons, 5-year-old Nikola and 3-year-old Bogdan. They are both employed full-time and live in her family house in the capital along with her grandparents. Their sons spend their day in a daycare center until 4 p.m. and after that it's family time together. Unlike most families in Montenegro where mothers do housework and raise children while their husbands read the newspaper and watch TV with friends, Maja and Luka have achieved equality in the division of family labor.

"I Dress One Child; He Dresses the Other One"

Maja reports, "My husband and my younger son get up first in the morning, and they are usually already drinking milk when I and my older son are waking up. Then, I dress one child, he dresses the other one, and we dress ourselves, and into the car." They leave their children at the kindergarten, then Luka drives Maja to work, and finally, he arrives at his office. She finishes her job before he does. Sometimes she picks up the children, sometimes he does. They usually go straight home where they spend time in their back yard. Some days neighbors stop by to socialize,

[1] Milena Račeta Stojanović is an independent researcher.

other days Luka and Maja sit and play with the children, or they go upstairs to visit Maja's grandparents or they go for a walk. In the evening, Maja reports:

> Usually one of us bathes one child; the other bathes the other one. We take them to bed; Luka reads them a bedtime story; and all four of us lay together because we all sleep together. Then, either I talk with Nikola about his day, since he likes to talk in bed, or I leave the room and Luka stays to cuddle with them. Then they all fall asleep and Luka wakes up an hour or two later.

The Republic of Montenegro has a population of only 629,212 inhabitants (World Population Review, 2019). Montenegro's ethnic structure is diverse, consisting of 45% Montenegrins, 29% Serbs, 9% Bosnians, 5% Albanians, and 7% of other nationalities (5% didn't want to declare). Although the census only reports 1% of the population as Roma, civil organizations estimate that they make up almost 3% (Roma Education Fund, 2015). The population of Montenegro includes Orthodox Christians (72%), Muslims (19%), Catholics (3%), and other religions (2%). One percent identify as atheists and the remaining 3% do not declare any religion (Statistical Office of Montenegro [MONSTAT], n.d.).

The percentage of employed women is 39.4% compared to 50.5% for men (MONSTAT, 2017). Although discrimination against women is forbidden by law, women in Montenegro are, on average, paid 16.1% less then their male counterparts. Women tend to be employed in sectors that are less well paid, even though, on average, they have higher educational levels than men (Avlijaš, Ivanović, Vladisavljević, & Vujić, 2013).

The majority of households in Montenegro (87%) are family households (MONSTAT, 2013a). Married couples and cohabiting couples with children under 25 years old represent the most common type of family household (50.7%). Couples without children represent 20.7%, 11% are couples with adult children, 8.4% are lone parents with children under 25, and

9.3% are lone parents with adult children (MONSTAT, 2013b). Although no data is available for the percentage of dual-earner couples, in two-thirds of Montenegrin families, men contribute more than women to the total family income (UNDP Montenegro, 2012).

Montenegrin law allows 365 days of full paid parental leave for a working mother, which must begin at least 28 days and can begin up to 45 days before her due date. Fathers can use parental leave instead of their female partners but they rarely do (Evropski pokret u Crnoj Gori, 2011). In 2013, only about 1% of Montenegrins using paid parental leave were fathers (Đukanović, 2014). Although, in theory, the law protects working fathers and mothers from losing their jobs if they take advantage of these policies, the law is only fully enforced in the public sector, especially during periods of economic instability.

Married Montenegrin women spend on average 4.5 hours per day on housework and childcare as compared to the 1.5 hours spent by men. Moreover, 96% of people who admit doing no family work are men (UNDP Montenegro, 2012).

Public early childhood and preschool education is available in Montenegro from birth to 6 years old. Fifteen percent of children from birth to 3 years old are enrolled in crèches, while 52% of children age 3 to 6 attend preschool. Private institutions account for only 3.3% of enrolled children. Enrollment is highly related to socioeconomic status. Sixty-six percent of children of the richest families are enrolled, whereas only 7% of the poorest families are. It is also highly related to the level of development of the municipality (Prica, Čolić, & Baronijan, 2014). Only 18.5% of Roma children attend (Roma Education Fund, 2015).

The evenings are often devoted to watching TV together or surfing the internet. Luka sometimes works while Maja writes her blog. They also might do some chores, like cooking the lunch for the next day or cleaning the house. "We would put the laundry out to dry together. I'm the one who usually prepares the lunch for the next day. During that [time] Luka cleans the bathroom or washes the floors ... We pick up the toys. There are Lego cubes all over our house." They are usually awake until midnight. Luka is up even later because of his habit of falling asleep with the boys when tucking them into bed.

On weekends Maja enjoys sleeping in. Luka explains, "She likes to sleep a lot ... I wake up with the children. I don't mind that. I like those morning moments with them." Their weekends are devoted to children, and catching up with family and friends. As Luka observes:

On weekends we both really try to spend as much time as possible with the children, and we do some housework in between playing with them. Also, sometimes I spend more time with the children on weekends than Maja if she stayed with them the whole past week, due to their having a cold or something similar.

One of their favorite weekend leisure activities is going to the movies with Nikola. Since Bogdan is still too small for that, one of them takes Nikola and the other stays with Bogdan. They take turns, "We are all into movies, so the one who's going with him is always happy!" Luka explains.

Typically, each takes care of one of the two children and then they switch. Because Bogdan is younger, he requires more hands-on care. Maja points out, "I know we are equal because Bogdan is still small, and these duties can be very boring for us, so it's actually like, 'I bathed/fed/whatever Bogdan last time, now it's your turn,' and we both use that sentence."

Maja and Luka see themselves as permissive and loving parents. Maja reports, "The children are very attached to us; we are all very close as a family. Maybe they are even less independent than other children their age; for example, they both sleep with us." Luka admits, "I used to say that I would spank spoiled children who make scenes; now, when my spoiled children are making scenes I don't even raise my voice."

Nonetheless, there are differences between them. Maja reports, "They ask me more when they need a playmate or when they want to talk about something that troubles them, and Luka is more into cuddling, tickling, fooling around with them." Luka concurs, "Nikola likes to come to me when he needs a hug, or to kiss him, to tell him I love him, and he goes to her to share some of his fears or hopes." Maja points out, "Maybe I only talk more about emotions, but he loves them as much as I do and they feel that ... They are definitely equally attached to both of us. I think kids perceive us as a couple, not as two individuals."

Luka explains how they recently handled a problem with Nikola's jealousy:

> Nikola commented that I surely love Bogdan more than him ... and that is something we are trying to fix right now – through that physical contact, because that's what he wants – me kissing and hugging him. So what I do differently now: I cuddle more with Nikola; I spend more time with Nikola. If they are both asking for my attention at the same time, I sometimes take one and sometimes the other one, while before I would turn to younger Bogdan, almost always, just because he is younger and louder. Or when we go to bed, since we all sleep together, I lay down next to Nikola.

They share the mental work of parenting. Maja is on top of school activities:

> My Luka would absolutely forget that they are going to the pool tomorrow with the kindergarten and they need swimming suits and sunscreen ... I'm the manager of kindergarten-related activities ... but we are equal about other activities: buying clothes or shoes for the children. For example, he often says, "Let's go to the mall to buy a jacket for Nikola," and I had the same thought while I was at work.

Luka also reports that he decides on when the children should go to the doctor because Maja overreacts to their illnesses. After discussion, he makes the appointments and takes them, although she goes along sometimes. On the other hand, Luka says, "Children's birthday parties are Maja's thing."

Luka believes that the disputes they have as parents stem from their paid work lives, "I don't think that we fight because we're not satisfied with ourselves, but [because of] ... stress from work, too much work, fatigue ... It's mainly related to work." He explains:

> When I am yelling at the kids because I am nervous about something else, or when my wife overreacts when Nikola won't eat. Also, it bothers her if someone calls me in regard to work when I am with the kids. I would say that these are the most common fights we have ... We are very open to each other, so our disputes don't last forever. Actually, in my opinion, the key is that we both understand the perspective of the other one: I really understand her frustration ... on the other hand, I think she must relax a bit more ... When I'm, let's say, yelling at the kids, she is completely right to get angry at me, because I don't want to be that kind of father, and she knows that ... but still, I'm only human, and so is she.

Although happy with their division of childcare responsibilities, Maja laments that they do not have more help from extended family, as do many young Montenegrin couples, who often live with their parents and other family members. Although her grandparents live in the same apartment building and have loving relationships with the children, they do not take significant caregiving roles.

"To Be Honest, Neither of Us Is Obsessive about Cleaning"

Everything in its place at every moment – that is not how Luka and Maja see their home and housework. Luka explains, "To be honest, neither of us is obsessive about cleaning, so sometimes the house really needs cleaning, but we don't care ... In other cases, one of us notices something that needs to be done, and one of us does that ... Nowadays, we never argue about house duties. It's somehow a routine."

There are some duties that are typically done by just one of them. Luka reports:

> I wash the floors; she almost never does that ... I wash the floors, and clean the bathroom, since I'm physically stronger, so I can wash harder ... We're equal in vacuuming, I think. But I never dust. She does that, and she picks up toys after the children and does a lot of that everyday cleaning, you know, putting things in their right place. But it's only me ironing. I iron only my shirts, and we don't iron anything else.

All the kitchen chores are shared. Luka says, "We're equal in cleaning the kitchen, cleaning the dishes, and there is no particular rule about who does what. If I see some dirty dishes, I'll clean them; if she sees some mess in the kitchen, she'll clean."

Maja adds:

> When it comes to cooking ... he enjoys cooking during the weekend; he prepares meat and stuff. During the workweek, I'm the one who usually cooks lunch ... basically, now we are pretty equal even when it comes to cooking meals, which is something that I did more in the past ... Luka needs much more time when he cooks because he enjoys the process. He plays with spices etc., while I cook just because we need to have something to eat.

As for laundry, they both hang out the wet clothes, but Maja folds them, since he hates doing that. Also, she jokes:

> He really can do and actually does everything, except for one thing ... the washing machine. I'm the one who fills the machine, pours the detergent in, starts the machine. Once, when I was away on some seminar, he called me on the phone to ask me how to start a washing machine ... He doesn't have a similar "problem" with the dishwasher, he uses it very often.

She laughs.

Two Stressful Jobs

Maja and Luka are both full-time employees with permanent contracts. Luka is a lawyer in a private law company; Maja is a psychologist working for the state in the area of social welfare. They agree that their jobs are equally respected, but Luka explains why his career takes priority:

> Because it brings in more money. I stay to work overtime and I do not take sick leave. My wife works in the public sector and when the kids are sick ... she has

the right to take the sick leave. I mean, I have that right too, but since I work in private sector, that would heavily influence my future career. That is not the case in public sector.

Although he earns more, her paychecks are always on time and his aren't. Maja points out, moreover, that if she had a more lucrative job, they would have to spend money on outside help since she would have "fewer opportunities to stay at home."

Maja feels ambivalent about her job. She loved her previous position within the same institution, where she worked with abandoned children, but she doesn't like her current position working on divorces. She describes her job as stressful, hard, with little, if any, personal satisfaction. Maja also reveals that if she didn't have children, she would be more ambitious and take on freelance work with an NGO to supplement her regular job.

Luka describes his paid work as "demanding, stressful, but rewarding." He works 50 to 60 hours per week and admits, "I am often still at work in my mind when I arrive home, and they call me on weekends and holidays." Although Maja reports that "since the children are here, Luka . . . sees himself as more responsible for providing," neither of them wants Luka to work more and earn more. Luka recalls:

> I refused to be relocated into another office to earn more, although I had that opportunity. Because my current employment gives me enough freedom to take the day off, be home on time, and spend a lot of time with the family. I didn't do that, and I think it was a good decision from a family perspective.

He tries to fit work around the family. Maja recalls one particular event when she persuaded him to stay in the office longer and finish a job rather than come home and work the whole night, "but" she says, "it didn't work out for him, he was miserable because he didn't see the children the whole day."

"Why Should I Tell You? ... It's the Same Household"

Maja and Luka met while finishing their studies. At the time, she lived in Belgrade, Serbia, where she studied, and he lived in her hometown, Podgorica, the capital of Montenegro. Even before they had children and got married, they decided that she should move to Podgorica where they would both have better job prospects and would be close to both of their families. They both think it was a good decision, despite having given up Belgrade's cultural scene. Maja had dreamed of becoming a writer and the move to Podgorica meant losing the opportunities for young writers in the capital. She still writes and publishes a blog.

After moving in together, Maja says:

> I remember telling him often, at the beginning of our relationship, that he shouldn't wait for somebody to clean the kitchen, but he should do that himself. I wanted him to understand that he shouldn't take for granted that I'll be the one who cleans the table after lunch, while he reads a newspaper ... I wanted him to see that we both could clean the table, as well as relax after a meal, and he got it very quickly. He sometimes used to say, "Maja, please, tell me what to do," and I would reply, "Why should I tell you, when you know it yourself, it's the same household?"

When Maja became pregnant, Luka was working in an NGO with flexible work hours and she was working as a psychologist in the public sector. Just before the birth of their first son, Nikola, he got an offer to start working for a law firm, which meant less flexibility and possibly longer hours. Maja recalls:

> At the time ... we didn't see that decision from a family perspective, it was more a decision to support him to fulfill his true potential and be the lawyer he wanted to ... So, yes, those were some decisions that, at the end, influenced how much time he would have for the family.

Luka took that job and his career has progressed ever since. Just a few months before their first son was born, Maja also advanced in her career, signing a permanent employment contract. Since she worked for the state, she could use her maternity leave without fear that she might lose the job, which is uncommon in the private sector, despite the law ostensibly protecting leave-takers. So when their first son, Nikola, was born, Maja stayed at home with him.

She reports that Luka was "very involved" from the start, "bathing them, changing diapers, putting them to sleep. He did all that on his own. I didn't have to remind him of his responsibilities." Maja describes what happened when Luka arrived home:

> He would take the baby in his arms the moment he came from work, or I would sometimes wait until he finished his lunch and would give him the baby then. I used that time either to do something around the house that I couldn't do with the baby – and these activities seemed like a vacation to me at the time, or just to have a break – meaning to surf the internet for an hour, half an hour while he was in charge of the baby. For example, if a baby needed diaper changing he would do that ... Then, when we put the children to bed, we would split duties, so he would take the laundry to dry while I'd be cleaning the dishes. He would wash the floor, and I would dust. Back then, we mainly cleaned the house in the evening.

She recalls how differently they reacted to the challenges of caring for a newborn, "When our first son was born, he didn't sleep all night and I was very frustrated and angry. Basically, I acted like a man usually acts when there is a newborn in the house. Unlike me, he was very patient ... 'It's normal; he's just a baby.'"

She adds:

> Luka was always more mature than I am, he was much better prepared for children, he always knew that he wanted to have children, and he is very unselfish. He knows how to put others' needs first ... Luka can control himself a lot better than me when children are screaming or spilling food on the floor, he's like, "It's ok, they're just kids."

Soon Maja was pregnant with Bogdan, their second baby, and took a pregnancy leave, followed by another year-long parental leave. However, during that leave she attended a 3-year course for family therapy to learn more and to keep connected to her job.

Luka then took care of the children during weekends and on weekday evenings when she needed to study for exams or to attend lectures. From Luka's perspective, these were just "minor adjustments," similar to his attitude toward waking up with their sons at night after Maja stopped breastfeeding.

After their younger son, Bogdan, celebrated his first birthday, Maja went back to work. She sometimes questioned whether she should be employed but concluded, "It's important that children grow up with a mother who is more than a housewife, waiting for others to come home; it's good for them to see me work, try hard, and earn money." She also thought it would be good for her children to have other influences besides her.

Nonetheless, the transition back to paid work was hard for her:

> I was panicking about two things – washing the laundry and preparing the lunch for the next day. Luka was always very relaxed about that, and thought that could wait, but I was pressuring him like, "Come on, come and help me! I won't finish on time!" so he would come. Yes, I think we had conflicts about that ... I was very worried how I would achieve everything now, when I am working, when it was barely achieved when I was at home the whole day. There are too many things to be done, too much laundry, too much food that needs to be prepared, too many toys to be cleaned. But now I see he had a point, and I got over that panic. Back then, I was under pressure to finish everything I could before they fell asleep, ... but then I realized that Luka does that perfectly in the morning, plus he is relaxed.

So how did they resolve this conflict? She answers:

> I think I have changed; I have changed my perspective. I simply don't have that "must" feeling – there must be a lunch for tomorrow, laundry must be finished

right now, we must clean the house or everything will fall apart. Yes, I have changed. I am more relaxed now and it feels good.

More recently, Luka was called upon to assume even more responsibility for childcare. Maja's father, who lived with them, died unexpectedly, and Maja just couldn't cope with her grief. Soon after his death, she took a sick leave from her job and stayed at home. During that period, which lasted for several months, Luka took care of all of the everyday duties. Luka says, "She really needed that time ... I'm referring to her father's death, she took that very hard, and I understand she needs more time to recover."

"My Father [Did] Virtually Nothing, Nothing!"

Maja's grandparents had a large role in raising her and her brother. She describes her father as a man focused on his job and thus not very involved in their childhood. Later, she realized that his devotion to his job was also for the good of the family. Her mother spent little time in paid labor and did everything around the house. Maja recalls:

> She was always in the kitchen; she didn't have so much interaction with us ... psychological stuff – well, it's like she even didn't know that exists. She even told us once, "My job was to keep you children clean and fed, I didn't go to school for mothers, I didn't know what more should I do."

Neither Maja nor her brother did any of the housework. As a teenager, Maja started to notice that her mother wasn't happy with her role. "I was about 15 when I realized that my mother became more and more upset about her housewife duties ... for example, I would ask her to spread jam on bread for my breakfast, and she was angry because of that."

Although her parents were not role models for her nontraditional life, her grandparents were. Her hardworking maternal grandmother built a house for the family with her own two hands, and still managed to take care of several grandchildren at the same time with love and patience. She says of her paternal grandfather, who was perhaps her most significant influence, "He was always walking with us, feeding us, changing our clothes or diapers, bathing us, measuring our temperature with grandma when we were ill." She emphasizes his unusual nurturing character. "It's really unbelievable for a man in Montenegro, especially that age. He is a person who never puts his own needs first. It's a quality I rarely see in men and my grandpa, my husband, and also my deceased uncle ... all have." Tearing up, she recounts how her grandfather helped her through a tough adolescence, "that feeling that I was loved, and that was the feeling my grandpa had for me ... that love is the only thing that can save a person. I really believe that even now."

Luka describes his family life growing up:

> It's a total disaster! My mother does everything; she always did and still does, my father virtually nothing, nothing! It's not even like the archetypal family; it was much more drastic ... he barely participated in our life as a father! He was present, but like he wasn't ... My mother was a parent, a worker, an advice giver, and my father was an unemployed, gloomy, distant figure where everyone was happy when he was not at home.

His father was neither involved in housework nor building emotional relationships with Luka and his brother. Clearly, Luka's father represents an anti-role model for him, but Luka is also critical of his mother, "I know I won't be passive, distant, and disconnected from family life and family member's needs as my father is, but my mother isn't to be admired, either! Yes, she did everything and raised us both, but she never stood up against that ... she made so many bad choices."

However, he did find some positive role models. Luka's voice is filled with admiration when he describes what he learned from Maja's father and grandfather:

> It's their commitment to family life, commitment to children. Maja's father spoiled our children, in a good way. I am thankful for that. Maja's grandfather spoiled her and he adores our kids. He is always there for them, and he really puts effort, no matter how old he is now ... They put family first, and that's what I learned from them. Children are cherished, and that's the way things should be.

"It's Different Because I'm One Loudmouthed Feminist"

When asked why she and Luka have constructed their family so differently than others, Maja answers, "It's different because I'm one loudmouthed feminist." Growing up, she never imagined that she and her brother should have different roles in life. Maja remembers how she felt the first time she heard some statements claiming that women were less worthy than men or should work more, "It didn't make sense to me, it had no logic."

However, she lives in a social context that does not support gender equality. When her mother died, for example, her neighbors thought that she should now cook for her father and her brother. Luka and Maja acknowledge that things have changed in their generation and they do have friends who share, like the father Maja observed washing the vomit-soaked blanket of his child. However, Maja asserts that sharing is not typical:

> Since it is rare here to have a husband ... who is as involved in family life and raising the children, others see him as wonderful, extraordinary, while women who do all that are seen as "normal" by others because they are expected to be good mothers and devoted wives. So sometimes Luka criticizes me, "Don't insist so much on that, since everybody says that I am an ideal of a father and husband!"

Maja goes on to explain that she didn't change Luka. She intentionally chose a husband who would share equally, "I didn't take my husband and make someone else from him, but it's because I would never marry someone who is not like that ... While we were still dating, I saw that I could have a fair relationship and fair life with this man." But, in fact, in the beginning of their relationship, by communicating clearly and effectively that he was as responsible for housework as she, she resisted his initial efforts to put her in charge of housework.

Nonetheless, despite her feminism, Maja could potentially undermine their sharing by overseeing his care. She quotes Luka's complaints, "We let you sleep longer during the weekends and we do everything just fine, even without you, but still when you wake up, you have all these questions, 'Did they have their tea? Did they eat some fruit and honey?'" She justifies the questions by asserting that sometimes he does forget. However, she sees his point when he criticizes her micro-managing his emotional relationships with the children:

> My husband often tells me, "You ... interfere in our communication while we are doing just fine solving things on our own. You ... tell me, 'Ask him this; ask him that' ... and there is really no need for that." ... Maybe he is right; maybe I should give him more space regarding these issues.

Luka's high-powered job also could have been an obstacle to equality. Luka, however, limits his career striving. By turning down a job opportunity and refusing overtime and freelance work, by consigning his extra hours of work to when his children are asleep, and by taking over on the weekends, Luka ensures his position as an equally sharing father.

Despite Maja's interference and his career, Luka is undaunted. When it comes to childcare, Luka's stance is every bit as nontraditional as Maja's. Both believe that there are no differences in men's and women's capability to care for children. Luka says, "I wanted to be a father who is always there for his children, who is involved in their life, as opposite of distant."

Still, while Maja adamantly refuses a traditional gendered division of labor with regard to housework, Luka does not, "I think that I am not anti-traditional, I am just flexible, and that's why the things are like they are. I mean, I wouldn't mind if she would want to do everything around the house, but this way is fine with me, too."

The equality that Luka and Maja have constructed grows out of their commitment to put family at the center of their lives. Luka reveals, "I needed someone who is as committed to family and children as I am." Maja recalls her grandfather when she says, "I knew I needed someone who would love me and my children like that for the rest of my life."

References

Avlijaš, S., Ivanović, N., Vladisavljević, M., & Vujić, S. (2013). *Gender Pay Gap in the Western Balkan Countries: Evidence from Serbia, Montenegro and Macedonia*. FREN-Foundation for the Advancement of Economics. Retrieved from: www.fren.org.rs/sites/default/files/Gender%20pay%20gap%20in%20the%20Western%20balkan%20countries.pdf.

Đukanović, A. (June 6, 2014). Porodiljsko koristi 111 Crnogoraca [111 Montenegrin men are using maternity leave]. *Dnevne Novine*. Retrieved from: https://issuu.com/dnevne-novine/docs/dnevne_16._jun_2014.

Evropski pokret u Crnoj Gori. (2011). *Socio-ekonomski položaj žena u Crnoj Gori* [Socioeconomic Position of Women in Montenegro]. Podgorica: Evropski pokret u Crnoj Gori and IPSOS. Retrieved from: www.emim.org/images/publikacije/socio-ekonomski_polozaj_zena_u_crnoj_gori.pdf.

Prica, I., Čolić, L., & Baronijan, H. (2014). *A Study on Investigating in Early Childhood Education in Montenegro*. Podgorica: UNICEF Montenegro. Retrieved from: www.unicef.org/montenegro/sites/unicef.org.montenegro/files/2019-01/A study on investing in early childhood education in Montenegro.pdf.

Roma Education Fund (2015). *Advancing the Education of Roma in Montenegro REF Country Assessment – 2015*. Retrieved from: www.romaeducationfund.org/publications/studies-policy-documents/country-assessments/.

Statistical Office of Montenegro (2013a). *Households and Families in Montenegro, Census 2011*. Retrieved from: www.monstat.org/userfiles/file/popis2011/saopstenje/domac%20i%20porodice%20,%20en-za%20sajt.pdf.

Statistical Office of Montenegro (2013b). *Structure of Families in Montenegro, Census of Population, Households and Dwellings in Montenegro 2011* (Table 1, Families by composition, Census 2011). Retrieved from: www.monstat.org/userfiles/file/popis2011/saopstenje/Structure%20of%20family%202020.pdf.

Statistical Office of Montenegro (2017). *Labour Force Survey 2016*. Retrieved from: www.monstat.org/userfiles/file/ars/2016/ARS%20-%20Godisnje%20 saopstenje,%202016.pdf.

Statistical Office of Montenegro (n.d.). *2011 Census Data*. (Table CG1 Population by age and ethnicity). Retrieved from: www.monstat.org/eng/page.php? id=393&pageid=57.

UNDP Montenegro, Government of Montenegro Ministry of Justice, & EU Delegation to Montenegro, (2012). *Survey about Attitudes towards Women in Politics in Montenegro*. Retrieved from: www.me.undp.org/content/monte negro/en/home/library/social_inclusion/WomenPolitics.html.

World Population Review (2019). *2019 World Population by Country*. Retrieved from: http://worldpopulationreview.com/.

6

Switzerland

Julia C. Nentwich, Stefanie Schälin, and
Wiebke Tennhoff

Martin and Judith's house in a small village in German-speaking Switzerland was easy to find. Decorated with colorful Tibetan prayer flags, it can be seen from far away, even on a gray and rainy afternoon in April. Judith and Martin welcomed us and introduced us to their children Paul (6) and Lisa (4) who were playing in the big eat-in kitchen. The colorful furniture and the children's toys created a warm and cozy atmosphere.

Equality is at the heart of Judith and Martin's life formula. A memo lying on the living room table spelled it out: "leitmotif: sharing 3+3+1." Both are employed 3 days a week, are at home with the kids 3 days, and spend 1 day together as a family. Judith is a 45-year-old teacher at the local primary school. She spends 2 days at school teaching and preparing her lessons and 1 day running a local arts and crafts store, where she works on weekends. Fifty-three-year-old Martin works 3 days a week as a social worker at a vocational school, providing counseling for pupils, parents, and supervisors. Martin earns a bit more money than Judith, but since Judith makes extra money from an apartment that she rents out, they both contribute 50% of the family's income.

Paul attends compulsory kindergarten for 3½ hours in the mornings and, after a lunch break at home, for another 2 hours on 2 afternoons. Four-year-old Lisa is at home and will start kindergarten after the summer holidays. Judith and Martin deliberately decided not to send Lisa to the village's nursery to avoid an overly structured program, and to avoid the high cost of the privately run nursery. One day of childcare is covered by an "honorary granny" who volunteers in their home.

With their '3+3+1' model, Martin and Judith are unique in the Swiss context. Their model differs from the two most common family forms: the neotraditional 1.5 job family with a full-time employed father and a part-time employed mother, and the traditional male-breadwinner family. Although mothers often work part-time for pay, fathers do not (Witzig, 2017).

In Switzerland, with about 8 million inhabitants, four official languages are spoken, including German (63%), French (23%), Italian (8%), and Rhaeto-Romance (0.5%). In addition, 3 to 5% speak English, Portuguese, or Albanian. The majority of Swiss are Christians (68%) (37% Roman Catholic, 25% Protestant Reformed, and 6% other Christians); 5% are Muslims, while 23% do not belong to any religion (Federal Chancellery, 2019).

Women won the right to vote in national elections in 1971. In one canton, however, women could not vote in local elections until 1990 (Voegeli, 2015).

The labor force participation rate for women over 15 is 62.8% versus 74.5% for men (World Bank, 2018). Discrimination against women at the workplace is illegal, but women earn 19.6% less than men (Swiss Federal Statistics Office [SFSO], 2019a).

Couples with children represent 28% of households (Swiss Federal Statistical Office, 2019c). About a quarter (23.3%) of Swiss families with the youngest child under 3 years old fit the traditional breadwinner model, whereas families with a full-time working father and a part-time working mother account for almost half of families (47.8%). Families in which husband and wife work comparable hours in paid labor include 11.5% in which both parents work full-time and 9% in which both parents work part-time (SFSO, 2019b).

Mothers benefit from a 14-week maternity leave, 8 weeks of which are mandatory, with a reimbursement of 80% of their income. There is no paternity leave or any other support for fathers. Some collective agreements provide for additional benefits (Valarino & Nedi, 2018).

Swiss society is still organized around the assumption of the male breadwinner and caregiving mother. In 75% of families, women are responsible for the housework (Witzig, 2017). Women with children under 6 years old spend 57.8 hours per week in childcare and housework and 13.9 hours in paid work, while men spend only 32.7 hours in childcare and housework and 37.6 hours in paid work (SFSO, 2017a).

This gender imbalance is also promoted by the lack of school schedules and available childcare that would support dual-earning families. There are no public full-time schools, and no public childcare system exists. Nurseries in Switzerland are mostly privately run. Over half (57%) of the households with children under 13 use childcare services, although more often in non-institutionalized ways (relatives or child-minders), and mainly on only 1 or 2 days per week (SFSO, 2017b).

Clarity about Responsibilities

Martin and Judith belong to the small but growing group of equal sharers in Switzerland (Bürgisser, 2017). Their sharing model dictates that the partner who is at home is responsible for all the daily routine tasks, as well as for the spontaneous activities that arise with small children. The partner at home prepares meals, does the shopping and cleaning, plays with the kids, comforts them, gets Paul to kindergarten, and picks him up. Thus, to them, equality means being responsible for the same number of hours.

Judith and Martin also equally share the infrequent duties, such as attending the kindergarten's parents' evening, by taking turns. They keep track of who attended the last meeting in a special folder with other kindergarten-related information. Being clear about responsibilities facilitates their equal sharing.

Judith and Martin's work lives intersect with their family lives differently. Judith spends her lunch break at home on workdays because her school is close by. Martin, in contrast, commutes 2 hours to and from his job, and is absent on those days from 6:30 a.m. until 6:30 p.m. He thinks her "on-off" scheme is more stressful than his long, but uninterrupted workdays away from home. The separation of paid and family work seems like an advantage to him, "I can fully devote myself to the work that I am doing at a certain moment. For me, this is easy to organize because I can separate them fairly easy or better organize them. It works out quite well."

Most of the everyday responsibilities (i.e., cooking, shopping, cleaning, and childcare) are shared by taking turns, but a different logic prevails for doing the laundry (Judith) and taking care of the garden and the three rabbits (Martin), which are assigned according to skills and interests. Judith explains:

> Well, I am not capable of mowing the lawn [laughs] and I don't enjoy Martin doing the laundry. The washhouse – that's more my piece of cake. Martin is a trained gardener; he enjoys watering the lettuce in the evening outside.

Martin concurs that Judith wants no responsibility for the garden and the rabbits:

> She said, "If you and the kids want animals, then it is the three of you that have to take care of them." She is drawing a firm line here. Also in the garden, she does those things she likes, like picking the flowers or harvesting vegetables, but nothing else.

Specific skills and interests are also the guiding principle for who changes the car tires and gets gas (Judith), and who creates a photo album or arranges the next meeting with friends (Martin). Responsibilities are also allocated by gender homogeneity. Whereas Martin took his son to the doctor when he needed a minor testicular surgery, Judith would feel responsible for issues concerning her daughter's genital hygiene. Judith has usually gotten up at night with children because she is easier to wake up. However, when the children are sick, Martin camps out at night close to their beds. Martin describes what happens:

> When the kids are sick, your sleep time decreases rather quickly. And when they puke the whole night, you will not sleep at all and still, the next morning, everything starts all over again, and it doesn't matter if this is at home or at work, you somehow cope with it.

A third logic of how they allocate family work is based on essentialist ideas of motherhood that are prevalent in German-speaking countries (Witzig & Nentwich, 2016). Despite their egalitarian ideals, Martin explains that his being less protective than Judith stems from the "different roles that mothers and fathers have," and Judith stresses that kids "automatically" ask for their mother when they are in need of emotional comfort. Especially when it comes to the emotional needs of her daughter, Judith describes herself as a bit more competent, and that, as members of the same sex with similar needs, she has insight into her daughter's feelings:

> Well, this morning Lisa was in a very bad mood; she was still a bit tired. Martin kept telling her, "Come on, get up now, do this and do that," and she got more and more upset. Then I said, "Come on, give her a break!" After a while she

called for me, "Mummy!" [in a childlike voice]. It worked. I believe that I am better in realizing that … I realize with Lisa that you have to sometimes leave her for a moment; she will recover. That's what he is not that good at. Maybe I am better in understanding the girl here, because I also need my breaks from time to time.

Apart from these exceptions, however, their idea of equal sharing relies on a fixed schedule that regulates who is responsible for the day. They both believe that if one takes equal sharing seriously, one needs to establish strong structures, a "model" or "system" to translate their ideals into practice. For Judith and Martin, the explicit division of responsibility orients both them and the children. For instance, Judith regularly works in her shop on Saturday mornings. Even after she returns home around lunchtime, Saturdays are Martin's days to be responsible and Judith does not interfere. Although their approach might sound strict, both of them recall negative experiences when they were not clear about their arrangements. Martin reports that the hardest days are those when they are both at home, but haven't agreed on who is responsible, which leads to chaos and confusion, "Then we drive each other nuts, and the kids realize that and then, then it is all a mess and there is no orientation for anybody."

Martin and Judith's sharing also relies on long-term planning. Martin explains how he organizes his paid work hours around Judith's fairly inflexible schedule:

I take the idea of equal sharing always as the basic principle. I do my planning on a half-year basis, of course, after talking to my wife … She is less flexible than I am, but usually she has her plan ready, the dates when she has to be present, and then I can organize around that. Actually, I can decide on my workdays fairly flexibly if I do it in time.

Their schedule is rather inflexible. Although both of them tout the importance of their careful long-term planning, Judith also sees the downside, that it does not allow for spontaneous activities. She envies a friend who can say, "Well, the weather is nice today, and I have two kids here at home. Now we will go out."

Judith is quite happy, however, that both her job and Martin's provide generous "holidays" when they can be more flexible. They are allowed to work overtime during school weeks so they can take days off during the 14 weeks of school holidays. Martin, for instance, regularly works 60% while holding a 50% contract. Holidays serve as islands of free time and allow them to engage in activities that don't fit in normal workweeks. Otherwise, Judith admits, her schedule would be rather squeezed.

Nonetheless, even during their holidays they stick to their system of assigning responsibilities on a day-to-day basis, trying to avoid unclear responsibilities.

Judith and Martin closely observe their everyday practices and reflect on them in terms of equality or inequality. For example, although in theory Martin follows a clear on-off scheme, Judith still feels that his job interferes too often with family life. She complains:

> He gets many phone calls, and if he is on the phone, he forgets the children … Yes, ok, maybe it is an emergency, eventually somebody commits suicide or something else, or somebody quits the professional training, of course, but – it's enough if you ask me!

Martin admits there is a problem with these work–life spillovers:

> I am on my phone too often, or at the computer, and leave the kids to themselves too often. Oftentimes I do recognize that myself; sometimes my wife has to tell me. Or sometimes the kids tell me too, "Dad, you are on the phone again. You are always on the phone; that is annoying!" Sometimes I don't change that immediately, but I am open to those changes, and I do implement that too, yes.

Managing these situations is one of the challenges to their ideal of sharing, making it necessary to renegotiate and talk.

Becoming Equal in the Light of Difference

Although becoming parents has enriched their lives, Martin and Judith also have had very tough times. Their first daughter, Nina, was born with severe health problems that caused her death at age 2. Because the hospital required traveling to a different city quite some distance away, not only were they emotionally stressed by having a seriously ill child, but they also faced relentless daily hassles. They eventually had to move to be closer to their daughter.

Martin's experiences have changed his feelings toward active fatherhood. At first he chafed at the constraints of his new role "because my world became quite small. Life was like this: small children, a small world." Now, he loves the direct and immediate way of the kids. Watching his children growing up has affected him profoundly. When he was young, he was always in need of a "kick," engaging in extreme sports and physically demanding work. But now he enjoys the "adventure of having a family" and the dialogue with his children and his wife. In reframing his experience, Martin manages to narrate his life as an "adventurer":

I do like this way of life, this adventure, the adventure of having a family ... I have been an adventurer, I am an adventurer, and I will stay an adventurer [laughs]. No matter if it is paid work or if it is family work, it is strenuous and I am very tired in the evening.

Both Judith and Martin point out differences in their parenting styles. Judith recounts how Martin once arranged a "boy's day" for his son, inviting his friends over for some wild and tumble play, playing tag, and having a barbecue. That would be unthinkable for Judith. She comments:

I think parents should be the parents ... Martin would rather be the friend as well, or the buddy. But I think both ways are all right, and they appreciate both. I don't let them tie me to a tree; I just don't do this, and he would of course. Yes, there are different perspectives to this and, yes, I am the mother and I want them to be fine.

Judith is also the stricter parent:

I am also the one insisting, "If you can deposit your shoes properly [at home], you can also do this at school. Then everybody is happy and you yourself as well." This is a basic principle that we try to be strict about. Learn the rules quickly because, if you know the rules, you have more latitude later on.

Martin employs the metaphor of Judith "being more the mother" to explain her protecting the children from potentially harmful and painful learning experiences. He invokes gender differences between them:

As a man, I do dare to do more with the kids. I am not less protective; I simply have a different kind of role. I think that is really important, that mother and father do have two different kind of roles. I really think they need both poles whether they are girls or boys.

They are convinced that being clear about which parent is responsible is helpful in managing their differences and avoiding conflict. Sharing the family work by having one parent taking the initiative and one staying more in the background serves as a reliable system for both of them.

Maintaining Equality Is Hard Work

Why would a couple in Switzerland want to be equal sharers? Despite some reforms and improvements with regard to gender equality, today Swiss society is still organized around the assumption of the male bread-winner, the caregiving mother, and the traditional nuclear family (Nentwich, 2008; Witzig & Nentwich, 2016). For instance, the Swiss school system relies on mothers being at home during lunchtime and in the afternoons; there is no public childcare system for children under 4. The tax system often discriminates against dual incomes, and part-time employment is the norm for women while men are employed full-time (Girardin, Bühlmann, Hanappi, LeGoff, & Valarino, 2016).

The traditional family is something that "just happens" (Maihofer & König, 2004), and reflects what is perceived as the natural gender order. Equally shared parenthood, in contrast, demands effort. It requires new ways of sharing work, and must transform parents' gendered identities as mothers and fathers (König, 2012; Nentwich, 2008). This entails ongoing negotiation, communication, and conflict. As Martin emphasizes, "Men and women were given a mouth to talk with," and they should make use of this gift to communicate their needs. Martin and Judith regularly engage in micro-strategies that allow them to counteract any tendency toward unequal sharing. For example, both of them currently feel they have too little time for themselves. Martin believes it is important to revive friendships that he has let lapse due to his family responsibilities. So he has just started going out in the evenings to meet his friends. However, Judith thinks that he has been going out too often. Although she admits that she does enjoy staying home, on a recent week, when Martin went out three times, and Judith didn't even make it to her weekly Pilates lesson, she was angry:

> This is when I hit the roof, "Now I have had enough with you going out!" He understands my feeling immediately, yes, we don't have to argue about these things. Like last week, we didn't have a discussion about this, that's for sure. That's my time and that's a pre-arranged matter.

Judith's expressing her anger directly about missing out on personal time or being left alone too often in the evenings mitigates against their reverting to inequality. "We don't have to argue about these things" means that they don't have to discuss the rights and wrongs here but directly take action and try to re-establish an equal share of time for themselves. Putting the "leitmotif: sharing!" into practice means finding solutions that suit them both. In this case, not only would Martin stay at home more often, but Judith would arrange time with a good friend. Equal sharing is negotiated, not only in the details of everyday lives, but in their outcomes. Martin emphasizes the importance of being tolerant of the partner's needs and sensitive to each other's limits.

"Just Buying Things" Was Not Enough

For Judith and Martin, having a family is a life project that has profoundly changed them. Martin states that although they already had a house and could afford everything, "just buying things" did not provide meaning to their lives. Spending money for their family to see their children grow up and develop their personalities, however, he considers as an investment in the future. Fatherhood has enriched his life:

> My attitude towards reproductive work, this has changed very much. Today I know that this is precious work, work that is not compensated for in terms of money, that you only get fairly little recognition for in society. It was good for me as a man to have this experience, [to see] what it means, really means, to experience this. It is self-sacrifice it is, if kids are small, it is a lot of self-sacrifice I believe. But on the other hand, you win out, because I am in a relationship with growing up humans and they are even my children. I watch them: how they feel joy, how they get angry about something, how they get stubborn, how they get attention, become loving, and that is the benefit.

Both Martin and Judith point out that their decision to equally share demands that they earn less money than they otherwise could. Being frugal is the premise for their way of working and living. Judith and Martin make light of the disadvantages. They are proud of living their moral values and investing in the next generation. Judith criticizes the prevalence of overly materialistic lifestyles and people who always want more. She continually asks herself, "Do we need this? Is this what we want? There are great gadgets [points to an iPhone lying on the table, joint laughter]. But, – really?" She adds, "We only have half of a car. We don't have a TV, and we only go on vacations for about, pfff, 5 days per year. We don't wear designer clothes [laughs]; we eat from our own garden." They prioritize time for their children over spending a lot of money.

Family over Career

For Martin and Judith, it has always been "pretty clear" that if they had children, they would both continue their jobs and work part-time. As older parents, they both already had their careers on track. Having occupations that don't rely on hierarchical career paths also helped. Moreover, both of their professions are female dominated with opportunities for part-time work. Nevertheless, their conscious choice of part-time employment means turning down other career opportunities, as Judith explains:

> In one year, my colleague will be retired. Then I could do much more teaching – so really get more lessons, but I don't know if I want to. And with Martin, he was still interested in something else for his profession, but realized that he then has to work irregularly and has subsequently canceled. So I think he is happy at the moment, because then he just knows what he is in for at home – what he can and must perform, yes.

Martin's willingness to compromise his career has been strongly affected by his early biography. After having had a serious sports accident that resulted in several fractures, Martin found himself to be a "broken man." Doctors advised him to stop working full-time and work part-time instead. This crisis propelled him to change his life. Although he was raised by parents with a traditional gender-based division of labor, he always thought that "there needs to be something more." As a consequence, he started to engage in the men's emancipation movement and discovered different family models and roles for men:

> For me, the idea of "leitmotif sharing" developed quite early after the accident, after this rupture in my biography. I was 30 then; now I am 53. It is a story that grew out of this. It is not somehow a quick fix idea, but something that really stabilized my life.

Martin asserts that it is not only a matter of personal affinities, however. He advocates for more men to engage in discussions about sharing family and paid work, "It is a question of priorities and values ... when I say the leitmotif is sharing, then I have to do something for it, and sometimes one even has to fight for it." Martin would love to see more Swiss couples become equal sharers.

Their story of equal sharing contains all its joyful moments on the one hand, but also its difficulties, conflicts, and constraints on the other. Martin sums up that their "leitmotif sharing" simply puts into practice ordinary fundamental human needs: the longing both to become mothers and fathers and to be involved and active at professional work.

References

Bürgisser, M. (2017). *Partnerschaftliche Rollenteilung – ein Erfolgsmodell.* [Sharing Equally: A Succesful Model]. Bern: Hep-Verlag.

Federal Chancellery (2019). *The Swiss Confederation – A Brief Guide 2019.* Retrieved from: www.bk.admin.ch/bk/en/home/dokumentation/the-swiss-confederation–a-brief-guide.html.

Girardin, N., Bühlmann, F., Hanappi, D., LeGoff, J.-M., & Valarino, I. (2016). The Transition to Parenthood in Switzerland: Between Institutional Constraints and Gender Ideologies. In D. Grunow & M. Evertsson (eds.). *Couples' Transitions to Parenthood: Analysing Gender and Work in Europe* (pp. 146–170). Cheltenham: Edward Elgar.

König, T. (2012). *Familie heißt Arbeit teilen: Transformationen der symbolischen Geschlechterordnung* [Family Means to Share Work: Transformations of the Symbolic Gender Order]. Konstanz: UVK Verlagsgesellschaft.

Maihofer, A. & König, T. (2004). „Es hat sich so ergeben" : Praktische Normen familialer Arbeitsteilung. ["It's Turned Out Like This": The Practical Norms of Dividing Labor in Families.] *Familiendynamik: interdisziplinäre Zeitschrift für systemorientierte Praxis und Forschung*, 29(3), 209–232.

Nentwich, J. C. (2008). New Fathers and Mothers as Gender Trouble Makers? Exploring Discursive Constructions of Heterosexual Parenthood and their Subversive Potential. *Feminism and Psychology, 18*(2), 207–230.

Swiss Federal Statistical Office (2017a). *Durchschnittlicher Aufwand für Erwerbsarbeit, Haus- und Familienarbeit und Freiwilligenarbeit nach Geschlecht und Familiensituation.* [Average expenditure for employment, domestic and family work and voluntary work according to gender and family situation.] Retrieved from: www.bfs.admin.ch/bfs/de/home/statistiken/wirtschaftliche-soziale-situation-bevoelkerung/gleichstellung-frau-mann/vereinbarkeit-beruf-familie/belastung-erwerbsarbeit-familienarbeit-freiwilligenarbeit.assetdetail.2922604.html.

Swiss Federal Statistical Office (2017b). *Familien in der Schweiz. Statistischer Bericht 2017.* [Families in Switzerland. Statistical Report 2017.] Neuchâtel: Swiss Federal Statistical Office. Retrieved from: www.bfs.admin.ch/bfs/en/home/statistics/catalogues-databases/publications.assetdetail.2347880.html.

Swiss Federal Statistical Office (2019a). *Analysis of the Pay Gap Between Women and Men.* Retrieved from: www.bfs.admin.ch/bfs/en/home/statistics/work-income.gnpdetail.2018-0606.html.

Swiss Federal Statistical Office (2019b). *Erwerbsmodelle bei Paaren mit und ohne Kind(er) im Haushalt, 2017.* [Employment Models in Couple Households.] Retrieved from: www.bfs.admin.ch/bfs/en/home/statistics/economic-social-situation-population/gender-equality/balancing-work-family/employment-couple-housholds.assetdetail.5106170.html.

Swiss Federal Statistical Office (2019c). *Private Households by Household Type.* Retrieved from: www.bfs.admin.ch/bfs/en/home.assetdetail.7486195.html.

Valarino, I. & Nedi, R. (2018). Switzerland Country Note. In S. Blum, A. Koslowski, A. Macht, & P. Moss (eds.) *International review of leave policies and research 2018* (pp. 411–422). Retrieved from: www.leavenetwork.org/lp_and_r_reports/.

Voegeli, Y. (2015). Frauenstimmrecht [Women's Suffrage]. *Historisches Lexikon der Schweiz.* Retrieved from: www.hls-dhs-dss.ch/textes/d/D10380.php.

Witzig, V. (2017). Forschungsstand zur egalitären Rollenteilung [The State of Research on Egalitarian Division of Roles]. In M. Bürgisser (ed.) *Partnerschaftliche Rollenteilung – ein Erfolgsmodell* (pp. 85–101). Bern: Hep-Verlag.

Witzig, V. & Nentwich, J. (2016). Neue Väter, alte Mütter? Elternschaft zwischen Egalität und Unterschiedlichkeit. [New Fathers, Old Mothers? Parenthood Between Equality and Difference.] *Journal für Psychologie, 24*(1), 191–224.

World Bank (2018). *Labor Force Participation Rate Female/Male (% of population ages 15+).* Retrieved from: https://data.worldbank.org/indicator/SL.TLF.CACT.FE.NE.ZS and https://data.worldbank.org/indicator/SL.TLF.CACT.MA.ZS.

7

Sweden[1]

Linda Haas and Leslie Stanley-Stevens[†]

Like many well-off middle-class dual-career couples in Stockholm, Mikael and Elisabet hold white-collar, professional jobs and earn enough for two cars, a suburban detached house, and a vacation home. They were together for 12 years before they had children, and like many Swedes, they only married after their first child was born. They now have two children, 14-month-old Lars, and 3-year-old Sven. Sven attends government-subsidized preschool.

"We Are Trying To Be as Equal as Possible"

Mikael and Elisabet differ from the majority of Swedish couples. Although most Swedish fathers (90%) take advantage of government-provided paid parental leave, Mikael has used more than half of all of the couple's leave, a pattern that is very uncommon (Duvander & Haas, 2018). Mikael said, "We are trying to be as equal as possible. I mean ... we have [both] been home with the kids, [but] I've been home with the kids more than she has."

At the time of the interview, Mikael was home on parental leave, having already been home for 8 months. Elisabet acknowledged, "Right

[1] The interviews were conducted by Leslie Stanley-Stevens (deceased). The research was supported by Tarleton State University, part of the Texas A&M University System. Special thanks to Patrick Prewit for typing the interview transcriptions. Leslie died after completing a first draft of the chapter. We are grateful to Christopher Stanley-Stevens, her husband, for assisting us in bringing the chapter to publication.

now he takes the bigger part during the week." She reported on how their typical day begins:

> I wake up first. I get up pretty early around five thirty, six. I try to be quiet … I make myself ready, and around six thirtyish Sven wakes up and normally he is allowed to watch iPad … I normally pick up or take out the laundry. Clean out the cat litter … I wake Mikael up and I go to work.

Sweden has 10.2 million residents. Immigration, especially by asylum seekers, has led to considerable ethnic diversity: 24% of residents aged 25 to 64 are foreign-born or children of two foreign-born parents (Statistics Sweden [SCB], 2019). Although 64% of Swedes belong to the Evangelical Lutheran Church (mainly because citizens were automatic members until 2000), Sweden is highly secular, with only 8% attending services regularly (Swedish Institute, 2018a). Couples with children represent 20% of Swedish households (Eurostat, 2018).

Eighty percent of women aged 20 to 64 were employed in 2017, compared to 84% of men in the same age group. However, 23% of women were in part-time jobs compared to only 9% of men (SCB, 2018b). Overall, 83% of mothers are in the labor force (Rubery & Figuiredo, 2018), but 40% of mothers of children under 6 are in part-time work (SCB, 2018a). The gender wage gap for full-time workers in 2016 was 12% (SCB, 2018c).

Parents are entitled to 16 months of paid parental leave per child, 13 months at 80% or more of wages. To encourage fathers to take leave, 3 months are set aside for them and cannot be transferred to mothers (Duvander & Haas, 2018). Preschool is available to all children starting at age 1. Eighty percent of children aged 1 to 5 are enrolled in formal childcare (Swedish Institute, 2018b).

In 2011, when the last national time-use study was conducted, mothers on average spent 57 minutes more in unpaid household work per day than fathers, and 28 more minutes per day in childcare (Hagqvist, Nordenmark, Perez, Aleman, & Gådin, K., 2017).

Mikael continued the story:

> She leaves before seven ... Normally I get up before she leaves and I start
> making breakfast for the kids and we eat breakfast and then we brush our teeth
> and get ready for daycare. I ... leave Sven at the daycare center at nine ... They
> have something called an "Open Preschool" ... you meet other parents
> and you play ... So normally [Lars and I] go there ... Then we go home for
> lunch and he sleeps for about ... an hour and a half. We have some afternoon
> snack ... and then I go pick up Sven at three at the latest. We go home and start
> making dinner. Elisabet comes home at six, six thirty and we eat. The kids take
> a bath and at 7:30 p.m. they go to bed.

On weekday evenings, between Elizabet's return home and the children's bedtime, she often takes on more childcare. For example, although
they often both bathe the children, Mikael reported, "Elisabet might take
care of some of the kid stuff while I ... take care of the dishes." Elisabet
agreed, "When I come home I try to take care of the kids as much as
possible. Not just to relieve him, but also for my own sake since I have
been apart from them during the day." On the weekends, Mikael added,
"I even step back a little bit and just let her be more with the kids – it's
kind of a nice relief sometimes." Elisabet makes a point, however, that
every night they each put one of the children to bed, alternating which
one. The parents also share coping with the children's difficulties getting
to sleep. Mikael reported:

> She usually brings home her work and she works at night. So I think a little
> more often I ... go and try to put them back to sleep, but she helps and we try
> to ... make it equal, you know. But it depends, like sometimes if I'm doing
> something or watching something then she takes them.

Since Elisabet stopped breastfeeding Lars, the parents have practiced co-
sleeping arrangements, with each parent sleeping with a child in a separate
bed. They also try to maintain equality by taking deliberate steps to establish
both parents as problem solvers and disciplinarians. Elisabet reported:

> When we have a conflict with the kids or we try to correct something, we try to
> make it that the first person who starts it or has the confrontation with the kid
> is to finish the conversation or finish the correction ... We have been trying not
> to ... undermine each other.

"She Is Always Thinking about Things Ahead of Time"

Despite their efforts, some of the couple's behavior reflects gendered
norms. Like a traditional father, Mikael is stricter than Elisabet. "I don't

enjoy when you're spoiled a lot so I'm trying to be more strict. They are more restricted in what they get and Elisabet is more generous in that sense." Elisabet reported that Mikael was also more playful and, according to Sven, more "goofy" than she is. Mikael expresses less concern than Elisabet about the children's safety. "I think she is more ... worried that they might get hurt in some ways, and I'm more laid back about that kind of stuff ... not, of course, when it's really dangerous, but we have different views on what's really dangerous." Moreover, they argue because she thinks he is too impatient and he thinks she gives in too much.

Mikael also reported that Elisabet seemed to connect more emotionally with their children:

> Elisabet of course is a ... little more of an emotional person ... They come and hug me as much as they do her, but ... even [though] I've been home more than she has, there are still a lot of Mommy feelings going on ... They kind of like to cuddle more sometimes with Mommy than me ... Yeah, when she comes home they just want to be with her, because they have missed her during the day, but it's also because she's a comforting person, you know ... If they get hurt and we were standing next to each other I would be 100% sure they would run to Mommy.

However, on reflection, Mikael adds that he is only talking about Sven. Lars, he says, "is very into me right now and it's all Daddy ... When he gets hurt he actually wants to come to me." Elisabet praised Mikael's increased openness, "When we met he was kind of closed up with his feelings. Now he is open with his feelings, which I think is great, and he talks to the kids and the way he is with the kids – the physical, kissing and hugging is super important to me so I feel really good about his fathering."

Like other Swedish women, Elisabet took on more responsibility for managing and planning (Haas & Hwang, 2013). Mikael confessed:

> That is where she is much better than me. So she does 80% of that and she is always thinking about things ahead of time ... you know what clothes we need to bring for the kids, what time we are going to be there and here ... umm keeping track of stuff. Yeah, the management ... she is good at that. That's what she does at work too – manages.

He admits that he does not step up, but also blames her personality:

> She feels that she needs to keep control of everything at all times because I don't do it ... I don't know if I can ... I try to work on it, but ... it just gets solved sometimes so I don't have to worry about it ... I think, "Well you pack a little too much, you know. You think ahead a little too much." ... And I think it's stress for her and it's in her personality.

Elisabet concurred that she did 80% of child management, "I'm more of a control freak ... I really need to plan stuff and organize it for my own sake." However, she also criticized Mikael's approach, "He really has to work on his memory [laughing]. He really has to start remembering things because before it was just us. If we forgot buying food or something ... we pretty much managed, but ... you can't forget buying diapers."

Mikael indicated that because he was home full-time, he was responsible for "all of the household stuff ... like cleaning, vacuuming, and cooking dinner ... I am on the floor wiping the floor four times a day. Every meal you have to like go and pick everything up and they spill a lot. So there are a lot of paper towels going."

Surprisingly then, Mikael claimed they divided housework, "pretty equally," while Elisabet estimated "60/40 my advantage." Elisabet's chores seemed more time-consuming than Mikael's. They agreed that she tidied up around the house more than he did, and that she did most of the laundry.

Mikael defended his assertion of a 50/50 division by citing his work on traditionally male tasks, "I do other stuff like cutting the grass or taking care of the cars." He also took credit for keeping track of their spending, "Yeah, it's just different kind of housework." Elisabet, however, downplayed those contributions. Although she acknowledged that he was better than she at repairs and painting, she claimed that they shared yard work and that someone else did the car care.

"He Knew I Was a Feminist"

Even before marriage and children Elisabet and Mikael explicitly committed themselves to creating an equal relationship. Elisabet was the initiator, spurred on by her reaction to her parents' traditional marriage, her interest in feminism, her commitment to a career, and her negative judgment of friends' adopting traditional lifestyles. She explained:

> My parents have a very traditional relationship or marriage. My mother takes care of the household. She has been raising the [four] kids and my dad has been the breadwinner making a lot of money ... I think he would see himself as a patriarch in our family ... my whole youth I was looking for something to explain how the world worked ... When I grew up, I felt that there was something wrong with the system. Some ... systematic discrimination ... When I came into college I started to take women's studies classes, which ... [explained] why I felt like something was wrong.

Mikael appeared to share her feminist values:

> I wanted [Mikael] to have the same values as me, and of course he wasn't as
> into the theory that I was or into academic women's studies, but I think he
> could also see the discrimination ... we have really talked about the ground
> values and the way we wanted to become parents and the way we wanted to
> live together. He knew I was a feminist, and I think if you asked him he would
> say he is a feminist.

She was worried about the traditionalizing effects of having children, but
Mikael convinced her that he planned to be an involved father. She
explained:

> For me it was really important, because I saw my friends that ... I thought were
> more liberal ended up in very traditional roles, especially the men who ...
> weren't home with their kids at all ... I was very scared of becoming one of the
> traditional families or traditional in the sense that the mother is supposed to ...
> take the sole or main responsibility of the kids and the house and everything.
> I had a career ... which made me realize that we needed to talk about how we
> were going to manage when we had a kid. Mikael said from the start that "I
> want to split the parental leave in half," which I was very happy about, and
> I think that was a precondition for me to think about having a child.

Mikael explained how sharing parental leave met both of their
needs, "She always wanted to go back to work and I wanted to come
home and take care of the kids so I'd get to know them when they're
small. It's ... important to me that it's not just 'Mommy, Mommy,
Mommy' all the time, but Daddy can be good too." With both children, Mikael took on childcare responsibilities from the outset, "When
she was breastfeeding, wake up, tried to relieve her, and put them to
bed when they were screaming. I think we were trying to be equal
about that."

"It Wasn't that Easy that We Could Just Split it in Half"

When it came to housework, equality was difficult to achieve. Elisabet
confided, "I guess if you ask us how ... we get from having this perfect
theory of how we are going to split everything ... It wasn't that easy that
we could just split it in half." Different standards got in the way.

They clashed over her expectations for "how clean the home was
supposed to be, how much laundry was okay to have in the basket."
She said, "I really needed to change the way I looked at order and
cleanliness." The difficulties started while Elisabet was home on leave:

For me it was, "Okay I have to stay home for 8 months, but you can't expect me to do all of the housework, all of the laundry, the yard work and all, everything, with a child." So it was important for me that my work was the child and all of the rest needed to be split in half, and I think he had the same values.

But once she was home with Sven, she felt the responsibility for having the house picked up and clean when Mikael got home, "If you were home 8 hours a day ... it's much easier for you to start the laundry or clean or make food ... But I was pretty stressed when he came home, and he said, 'I don't expect that, you need to change the way you think.'"

Over time, Elisabet learned to lower her standards. Nevertheless, she still tidied up more and did the laundry. Conflicts persist with moderately intense weekly arguments. She reported, "We had different preferences [about] how to clean and when to clean and how often we are going to clean." To reduce conflict, they pay for a food service that delivers menus and food to their home, sparing them meal planning and shopping, and for housekeepers who come every other week for 4 hours, subsidized by the Swedish government.

"She Works a Lot"

Elisabet is a high-level manager of a public transit authority, with several divisions and hundreds of employees for whom she is responsible. She works about 50 to 60 hours a week, including time at home after the children are asleep. She is very committed to her high-powered job and career. Mikael reported, "She needs to do everything perfectly ... She has meetings all day, and she doesn't feel like she has time to do what she needs to do, so she normally opens up her laptop and sits for a couple of hours during the night every day. So she works a lot."

Her earnings were substantially higher than Mikael's, but she disagreed that this made her more of the family breadwinner or gave her more power, "We are trying to make equal decisions about the money." And although Elisabet's career was important, she did make a career sacrifice when Sven was around a year old to protect their family life. She reported, "I had two job offers. One of them ... a lot of traveling [was] involved, traveling outside Sweden, which I didn't take just because of the traveling. I got another job that was more fun probably, and I said 'no.'"

Mikael, when not on parental leave, is a software engineer, who, as he explained, was responsible for projects, not people. He worked full-time (40 hours), and only occasionally did work at home. Mikael reported, "I enjoy working a lot ... so I like my job a lot." Nonetheless, he looked forward to a more challenging job once he returned from leave: "I am in a process to see if I'm going to switch jobs, [a] ... development talk with my supervisor about what I'm going to do when I come back, and that sounds exciting too."

"I Understand Her Job Is Really Important to Her"

Both indicated that her job was more important than his. Elisabet made more money than Mikael did, and at first she implied that her superior earnings was the reason. But knowing that she would never accept that reason if he were earning more, she retreated, "I don't think that the money issue is that important. Since I have a lot of people reporting to me I guess ... I feel awful when I say it ... I feel like my work is a little more important ... Mine is a little more prestigious."

Mikael invoked how much she cared about her job to explain why it was more important, "I'm trying to support her working because ... I understand her job is really important to her." He had turned down a job offer in Florida because it would mean his wife would have to give up her career in Sweden.

Despite her career investment, however, Elisabet isn't always happy with the travel required by her job, "I didn't think I would feel so bad leaving them for a night or two, but it does. It's really hard sometimes." She and Mikael agreed about the difficulties of combining paid work and family life:

> He told me when he was working and I was at home with the two kids that you had a bad conscience all the time. "[If] you are at work, you have a bad conscience, and if you are at home you have a bad conscience just because you are not at work," and I think we experience the same feelings about that.

Nonetheless, Elisabet was basically happy with the balance in her life. She explained how having children had positively affected her work life:

> I had no limits working. I could work a lot of hours. I had nothing keeping me from really digging into work. Now, I feel more vulnerable because ... something else is taking my energy, my time and focus, which is a good thing for me ... My kids give me a safe and solid base to stand on. I think they affected me to become a better work person, to be a better professional, to be a better director.

Elisabet also asserted the benefits of her work life to her family:

> I try to be a good role model for my kids ... That you can ... do things that you
> really enjoy and you can be good at something and dedicated to something ...
> I think it's good that their Mommy's working. I think I'm a better role model.
> I feel better about myself and I feel good working. So I think they have a
> happier Mommy when I'm working.

Overall, Mikael reported less work–family conflict than Elisabet, perhaps because he reported more flexibility at his workplace:

> They rely on you doing your work the best way you can. They don't count
> you've been in the office for 40 hours ... so it's a lot of flexibility ... It's a little
> easier for me to take off from work than Elisabet ... She has a bigger
> responsibility ... less flexibility because she's in a lot of meetings ... She is
> going to have a tougher time ... putting everything aside if somebody gets sick
> and you have to come home and pick them up.

Mikael expressed concern that his flexibility would mean that he would
always be responsible for sick children, "My fear is that I'm going to be
the one, but we have talked about it and ... we might even make a
schedule: if something happens this day and it's you, or if something
happens that day, it's me."

Swedish parents with preschool-aged children can reduce their employment hours to 80% (at reduced pay). Elisabet was wary of this option for
herself, "Sometimes they say in Sweden, 'It's a typical women's trap.' They
just say you only work 80%, but no one is taking off 20% of your
workload, which ... just makes that you ... do the same amount of work
and you earn less." Mikael added, "Neither of us are really interested in the
idea of doing that." Elisabet admitted, however, that she wished that
Mikael would return to his job at 80% time, "I don't think he wants to,
but I would like it if he worked less." They were considering other ways of
managing. Mikael thought that after his leave, they may call on a family
member to come "a day or two and get the kids from daycare a little earlier
and maybe give them a sandwich or something so that when we come home
it's a little easier." Elisabet also offered the possibility of hiring a nanny.

"Elisabet Is Very Pro-Equality and I Am the Same"

In Sweden, there has been a longstanding political consensus that men
and women should be equal, with the same opportunities, rights, and
responsibilities in employment and parenting (Government Offices of
Sweden, 2009). Couples are encouraged to conform to the dual-earner/

dual-caregiver model of family life, which is seen as promoting child well-being and economic productivity as well as gender equality (Lundqvist, 2012). They are helped by social benefits such as paid parental leave, highly subsidized childcare, and the right to reduced paid work hours.

Elisabet and Mikael fit the dual-earner/dual-caregiver model promoted by the government; both seemed committed to child-rearing and domestic work, as well as to paid employment. However, this couple differs from most Swedish couples in three respects, which puts them further on the road to equality. First, both partners described themselves as ideologically predisposed to an egalitarian marriage. Among young Swedes, 73% of women and 66% of men support gender equality in marriage (Oláh, & Gähler, 2014). Second, Mikael had taken more than half of the couple's parental leave, which is very uncommon. Although the majority of Swedish fathers take parental leave, on average, they take only 27% of the leave days (Duvander & Haas, 2018). Third, Elisabet worked full-time at a high-level administrative job. Although 60% of mothers of young children are employed full-time, about 40% are employed at "long" part-time jobs of 30 hours a week (SCB, 2018a). In addition, Elisabet earns more than 60% of the family income, giving her more power than the average Swedish woman who earns only 27% of family income (Nieuwenhuis, van der Kolk, & Need, 2017). For his part, Mikael was not stuck like other Swedish men in the "male model of work," with long hours and little flexibility (Haas & Hwang, 2016).

Elisabet invoked Swedish culture and politics when explaining her belief in equality, "If I talk about Northern Europe, we talk about the equality between people in theory . . . We have in the UN declaration that everyone has the same value. I think it is just the matter of transcending into practice and turning it into real life." The Swedish zeitgeist probably informed her anti-essentialist views that gendered behavior stemmed from different experiences rather than biology:

> When we grow up, and I talk about Sweden only, I think girls are . . . taking more responsibilities in the family . . . We are used to taking care of kids and . . . perhaps [then] it is easier for us to take care of a family . . . But I think that men have the same ability as a person, as a human being, loving and caring and being a very good role model.

Although Mikael still believed in some biological differences, he agreed that "everyone can take care of kids."

Despite the ostensible Swedish support for gender equality, Elisabet detected veiled criticism of her involvement in her career. Mikael, however, felt part of a larger community of involved fathers, "If you go to the open preschool like there . . . could be nine fathers and one mother there. So a lot of people are doing the same thing we are doing . . . so it felt kind of normal."

Their reasons for creating equality stemmed from their personal backgrounds as well. Elisabet advocated feminism because she disliked her parents' traditional marriage, took women's studies courses in college, and disliked seeing her friends fall into traditional roles after they became parents. Mikael's pro-equality stance developed into a more feminist consciousness under Elisabet's influence. He chose to take so much parental leave because he had a strong personal interest in involved fatherhood, and wanted to accommodate Elisabet's desire to return to her career. Elisabet's involvement in full-time employment reflected the importance of a job that required long hours but that gave her a great deal of personal satisfaction, status, and income.

This couple's experience, however, suggests that some traditional expectations and cultural norms for women and men can be difficult to change, even in a supportive social setting. Elisabet, despite working more than full-time while Mikael was home on leave, still did the laundry, picked up more, and took overall responsibility for planning and management. Mikael retained some traditionally male tasks. Some tasks were no longer even up for negotiation. They admitted to arguments over cleaning and solved them by hiring housecleaning help. Sweden now offers generous tax breaks for such help. In some contexts, this choice might be criticized as shifting domestic work to low-paid women workers. In Sweden, however, domestic workers have higher pay than in other countries and eligibility for welfare state benefits (Bowman & Cole, 2014).

Elisabet admits that they have not completely achieved their ideal. While she criticizes Mikael for not taking enough responsibility, she also confesses her own tendency to take over:

> I think that we're not perfect. We have our issues and differences. We believe in equality and we try not to just call that's a nice word in our family. We really try to transcend that into practice but it takes a lot of work. Sometimes I really have to shake myself and say, "Elisabet, you're not supposed to take care of that. You have to leave it." Because sometimes I think that it is better that I do it. It goes quick and I know how to do it . . . I really have to work with myself and say, "It's his responsibility, but it's not the same way that you like to do the dishes or . . . exactly the way you like it clean." So it's been working with myself too.

Overall, Elisabet is happy with the family she has created with Mikael, "We . . . share the same values . . . and that also makes him a good role model I think for our children and it makes him a very good partner to me." Their shared values benefit Mikael as well, as he says, "Elisabet is very pro-equality and I am the same ... I have the same idea ... There shouldn't really be a difference in how much we take care of the household or the kids. I want to be as big part of their lives than [sic] she is ... for me it's a privilege, something I want to do."

References

Bowman, J. & Cole, A. (2014). Cleaning the 'People's Home': The Politics of the Domestic Service Market in Sweden. *Gender, Work and Organization*, 21(2), 187–204.

Duvander, A.-Z. & Haas, L. (2018). Sweden Country Note. In S. Blum, A. Koslowski, A. Macht, & P. Moss (eds.) *International Review of Leave Policies and Research 2018* (pp. 401–410). Retrieved from: www .leavenetwork.org/lp_and_r_reports/.

Eurostat (2018). *Private Households by Household Composition, 2017.* Retrieved from: https://ec.europa.eu/eurostat/statistics-explained/images/5/ 5f/Private_households_by_household_composition%2C_2017_%28%25_ of_private_households%29_final.png.

Government Offices of Sweden. (2009). *The Swedish Government's Gender Equality Policy*. Stockholm: Ministry of Integration & Gender Equality.

Haas, L. & Hwang, C. P. (2013). Fatherhood and Social Policy in Scandinavia. In D. W. Schwalb, B. J. Shwalb, & M. E. Lamb (eds.) *Fathers in Cultural Context* (pp. 303–331). New York: Routledge.

Haas, L. & Hwang, C. P. (2016). "It's About Time!": Company Support for Fathers' Entitlement to Reduced Work Hours in Sweden." *Social Politics*, 23(1), 142–167.

Hägvist, E., Nordenmark, M., Perez, G., Aleman, S., & Gådin, K. (2017). Parental Leave Policies and Time Use for Mothers and Fathers: A Case Study of Spain and Sweden. *Society, Health & Vulnerability* , 8(1), 1–11.

Lundqvist, Å. (2012). The Gender Equal Father? (Welfare) Politics of Masculinity in Sweden 1960–2010. In P. McDonald & E. Jeanes (eds.), *Men, Wage Work and Family* (pp. 34–50). London: Routledge.

Nieuwenhuis, R., van der Kolk, H., & Need, A. (2017). Women's Earnings and Household Inequality in OECD Countries, 1973–2013. *Acta Sociologica*, 60(1), 3–20.

Oláh, L. and Gähler, M. (2014). Gender Equality Perceptions, Division of Paid and Unpaid Work, and Partnership Dissolution in Sweden. *Social Forces*, 93(2), 571–594.

Rubery, J. & Figueiredo, H. (2018). Gender, Equality and Social Policy. In S. Shaver (ed.), *Handbook of Gender and Social Policy* (pp. 129–152). Cheltenham: Edward Elgar Publishing.

Statistics Sweden (2018a). *Women and Men in Sweden 2018: Facts and Figures.* (Employed parents aged 20–64 with children at home, by number of

children, the youngest child's age, and length of working time, 2017) (p. 60).
Örebro: Statistics Sweden. Retrieved from: www.scb.se/contentassets/
4550eaae793b46309da2aad796972cca/le0201_2017b18_br_x10br1801eng
.pdf.

Statistics Sweden (2018b). *Women and Men in Sweden 2018: Facts and Figures.*
(Population aged 20–64 in and not in the labour force 2017) (p. 53). Örebro:
Statistics Sweden. Retrieved from: www.scb.se/contentassets/4550eaae79
3b46309da2aad796972cca/le0201_2017b18_br_x10br1801eng.pdf.

Statistics Sweden (2018c). *Women and Men in Sweden 2018: Facts and Figures.*
(Women's pay as a percentage of men's by sector, 1994–2016) (p. 80).
Örebro: Statistics Sweden. Retrieved from: www.scb.se/contentassets/4550
eaae793b46309da2aad796972cca/le0201_2017b18_br_x10br1801eng.pdf.

Statistics Sweden (2019). *Summary of Population Statistics 1960–2018.* Retrieved
from: www.scb.se/en/finding-statistics/statistics-by-subject-area/population/
population-composition/population-statistics/pong/tables-and-graphs/yearly-
statistics–the-whole-country/summary-of-population-statistics/.

Swedish Institute (2018a). *Fundamentals of Religion in Sweden.* Stockholm:
Swedish Institute. Retrieved from: https://sweden.se/society/10-fundamentals-
of-religion-in-sweden/.

Swedish Institute (2018b). *Preschool – A Place to Grow.* Stockholm: Swedish
Institute. Retrieved from: https://sweden.se/society/play-is-key-in-preschool/.

8

Indonesia

Siti Kusujiarti

Budi and his wife, Tuti, live in a rural village located around 15 miles from the district capital in Yogyakarta province, Indonesia, with their two children, an 8-year-old boy and a 5-month-old baby daughter. Javanese norms dictate that husbands should be older than their wives to reinforce their authority as leaders of the family. But Budi, at 38, is only a year older than Tuti. They are both high school teachers and Budi is also an assistant principal. Many of the people in this village work in the agricultural sector, but some occupations in the formal sector, including teaching and government jobs, are quite common. Based on their professions and as college graduates, Budi and Tuti are considered middle class. They live in a relatively modern three-bedroom brick house. The road in front of their house is paved, unlike others in the village. Chickens wander around the yard outside. Rice fields surround the village, and cows and goats graze nearby. Like other Javanese couples, they live close to their parents, and are intensely devoted to family life.

Islam has significant influence on people's daily lives in Indonesia, including their family relations. Javanese families typically have a very clear gendered division of labor: the husband as the head of the household represents his family publicly; women are mostly responsible for the domestic sphere and for socializing children. Their roles as mothers and wives are pivotal for their identities (Tickamyer & Kusujiarti, 2012). Although Budi and Tuti are Muslims, contrary to the stereotypical patriarchal family in predominantly Muslim countries, they demonstrate equal and democratic gender relations. They may look like other Javanese couples and others may perceive Budi as the formal head of the household, but this couple is unique because they equally share household chores and childcare responsibilities.

The Republic of Indonesia with a population of over 268 million people is the fourth most populous nation in the world, after China, India, and the USA (World Population Review, 2019). The population is very diverse, composed of more than 300 ethnic and linguistic groups. The Javanese, mostly living in the densely populated island of Java, are the largest ethnic group, comprising around 40% of the total population. Sundanese, Malay, and Batak are the next three largest ethnic populations with 15.5%, 3.7%, and 3.6%, respectively (based on 2010 estimates) (Central Intelligence Agency, 2019). The Indonesian government recognizes six official religions: Islam, Protestantism, Catholicism, Hinduism, Buddhism, and Confucianism. Islam comprises the largest population with 87.18%, which makes Indonesia the country with the largest Muslim population in the world (Indonesia Census Bureau, 2010).

For the population 15 years or older, women's labor force participation is 50.7%, whereas it is 81.8% for men (United Nations Development Programme [UNDP], 2018). However, these statistics may underrepresent women's labor because many females work in the informal sector and consider it part of their domestic labor (Tickamyer and Kusujiarti, 2012). On average, women earn half of what men earn (UNDP, 2018).

The Indonesian Constitution ensures all citizens equal rights. Women have equal rights to vote, to work, and to obtain political positions. Nonetheless, the Marriage Act of 1974 stipulates that the legal age of marriage is 16 years for women and 19 years for men. The Marriage Act also legitimates men as the heads of households and also allows Muslim men to be polygamous under certain conditions, such as having an infertile wife (Soewondo, 1977). Early marriage is still prevalent, especially in rural areas. Between 2010 and 2017, 14% of married women aged 20 to 24 married before 18 years old (UNICEF, 2018).

Fifty-nine percent of the male population 10 years old or older are married, 38% are single, 1% are divorced, and 2% are widowed. Of women, 60% are married, 28% are single, 2% are divorced, and 9.6% are widowed (Indonesian Census Bureau, 2012). Women are stigmatized by divorce.

Indonesian law mandates 3 months paid maternity leave for women and at least half of the leave must be taken after the delivery (Angloinfo Indonesia, n.d.). This law, however, generally only applies to those who work in the formal sector, including government institutions and big businesses, while most of those working in the informal sector are not covered. A recent law entitles male civil servants to a 1-month leave when their wives give birth, which replaces the 2-day paid leave they were granted previously ("One-month paternity leave," 2018).

Even when women work outside the home, they do the majority of household labor, childcare, and elder care. However, one study of Indonesian dual-earner couples found that in 53%, household labor and childcare was also performed by extended family members or a paid worker. The responsibility for the remaining work fell to wives (Simulja, Wulandari, & Wulansari, 2014). In fact, the marriage law indicates that wives are responsible for caring for the household (Soewondo, 1977).

"When My Wife Was Nursing the Baby, I Was the One Who Would Place the Baby in the Right Position"

Budi and Tuti met when they were both in college. At first they were just friends, but not long after Tuti broke up with a previous boyfriend, Budi approached her, and after a short courtship, she agreed to marry him.

The couple lived with Budi's parents during the first 3 years of their marriage, a common practice among younger Javanese couples. The parents provide support for the new couple and socialize them into family life. Although today younger couples increasingly try to establish their own household as soon as they can and move to a new place (neo-local), Javanese families tend to be patrilocal (close to the husband's family) (Tickamyer & Kusujiarti, 2012).

Tuti got pregnant with their first child not long after their marriage. For the first month after the child was born, they moved in with Tuti's parents because she needed help to learn how to take care of the baby, and she felt more comfortable asking for help from her own parents, especially her mother, than from Budi's parents. When they stayed with Tuti's parents, Budi immediately started to get involved in taking care of the baby, despite some occasional criticism from his in-laws. He reports:

Oh yes, I did everything. For example, when my wife was nursing the baby, I was the one who would place the baby in the right position so that the baby can reach the nipple and my wife can nurse well, because it was quite challenging, especially when the baby was crying. My wife was panicking, so I had to do it to make sure that the baby was well fed. I get involved in everything since the children were born. On one occasion, my in-laws criticized the way I held the baby because I put the head on my right arm. They told me not to do it, I have to put the head on my left arm because only a dead body can be put on our right arm. I did not know or believe that; it's just the belief system.

Back living with Budi's parents, both Budi and Tuti did less housework than they do now, as Tuti describes, "It was my husband's mother who cooked and did most of the household chores. I was just helping her, so the changes took place gradually." Budi concurred, "To be honest, I did less at that time since my mother did a lot of work for us. She helped a lot in taking care of our child."

Javanese society is very hierarchical (Mulder, 1992), so parents have significant power over their adult children. While the couple was living with Budi's parents, they did not have much authority in the household. Budi reported a significant change to an equitable division of labor when they moved out of his parents' house:

> We have done this since we have had our own house. But the change went automatically. We did not have any intentional discussion or plan to change it; we just feel that everything is our responsibility now. We are together in this situation and we also want to enjoy this life and house together.

"There Is No Strict and Clear Division of Labor; We Just Help Each Other"

Both Tuti and Budi agreed that there were no fixed or definite rules on who should do what in their family; their main goal is to get the job done together. Budi reports:

> We always help each other. For example, when my wife is cooking, I am doing the laundry or cleaning the house. If my wife does the laundry, I cook the rice ... If I see my wife is busy doing something, I will also do some other things; my wife does the same thing.

Tuti emphasized, "The main principle that my husband and I hold is that we do this flexibly, we just have to keep adjusting whenever we need to do so." The notion that they have to work together to get the job done reflects the Javanese concept of *gotong-royong* or mutual or reciprocal assistance (Bowen, 1986). Budi's description captures this spirit, "There is no strict and clear division of labor; we just help each other." The sense of belonging, understanding, and commitment are the basis of reciprocity in this family. Neither Budi or Tuti felt comfortable using the word "division" in the context of family labor because this word implies rigid separation, while for them flexibility, cooperation, and fluidity are keys to getting things done. Despite some recurring patterns, each is open to doing anything needed, which enables them to defy gendered expectations for the division of household labor. Budi asserted, "We don't divide the chores; we look at the chores as joint responsibilities."

Tuti echoes Budi:

> We don't have clear division of labor. Whoever has time and can do it, then we just do it. For example, when I am cooking and the children are fine then my husband does laundry. But if the baby is crying and wants to be held, then my husband will hold or take care of the baby while I am cooking, or vice versa.

A Typical Day

Islam shapes their daily routine. There are five obligatory praying times during the day. Since there is always a loudspeaker from the nearby mosque, this call for prayer also reminds them of their daily responsibilities and creates a predictable routine.

Their daily routine starts early in the morning and like many other dual-income couples with children, their mornings are very hectic. Tuti is awake by 3:30 a.m. and does most of the cooking early in the day, although Budi will pitch in and cook too if Tuti sleeps a bit later. Budi usually rises and does his morning prayer around 4:30 a.m. He explained, "After that, my wife and I do chores and take care of the children from 4:30 a.m. until 6:30 a.m., and then we get ready for work." Tuti usually tends to the baby while Budi helps his son bathe and gives him breakfast. Tuti gets their son's book, pens, pencils, and snacks ready for school. Budi and his son leave home first; Budi drops his son off at his school on the way to work. Tuti leaves the house a little bit later, since her school is closer to their home.

When the couple is working, a household helper, a neighbor they know quite well, takes care of the baby, including washing her clothes and diapers and ironing them. Although it is usually Budi's job to do the rest of the laundry and put it out to dry, when he is pressed for time, the helper assists with that. She arrives around 6:30 a.m., before the couple go to their jobs, and leaves after they come home. To give the helper time to pray and eat at noon, Budi's mother, who lives next door, comes and helps take care of the baby for an hour or so. The couple also hires another person who comes twice a week to iron their clothes. Household chores are quite time-consuming because most of the work is done manually, but hiring helpers is usually affordable for couples like Budi and Tuti who live in a rural area where it is easy to find domestic workers.

School and work hours are adjusted to enable people to perform their religious obligations. Most schools are dismissed around 1:00 to 1:30 p.m., which allows people to perform the second prayer of the day. Budi and Tuti are usually home before 2:30 in the afternoon. Tuti usually comes home around 30 minutes earlier than Budi. Budi picks up their son from school unless he has a meeting or other obligation, in which case Tuti or one of her parents will pick him up. Budi and the second grade son typically eat their lunch at their schools, but Tuti usually has lunch at home, which consists of the leftovers from breakfast. The family only cooks once a day in the morning, so dinner consists of leftovers as well. If they need additional food, they usually buy something from the nearby food stalls.

Once they are at home, the couple works together, as Budi describes:

> After work we do chores and take care of the children again. It is hard to differentiate the chores and caring for children. In many cases we do them simultaneously, such as cleaning the house while making sure that the oldest child is doing homework. My wife and I usually do different chores at the same time, such as she is washing dishes and I am sweeping the floor, or I am cooking while she is feeding the baby.

Budi helps their son bathe and assists him with homework, while Tuti gives the baby an afternoon bath. Budi usually also cleans the house and sweeps the yard or does laundry, while Tuti washes most of the dishes, but leaves the glasses for Budi to do because she does not like that task. Their son usually watches TV or plays at a friend's house while his parents are busy doing housework. If he is watching TV, Budi and Tuti may leave the baby with him while they do the chores.

After the third prayer around 3:00 p.m. until 5:00 p.m., when they have finished the housework, the family spends time together watching TV or talking, although occasionally Tuti goes to her parents' house or spends time with women in the neighborhood, leaving Budi with the children. Sometimes Budi takes the children out for a walk around the neighborhood.

Around 5:00 p.m. Budi helps his father, who is in a wheelchair, out to the porch. The entire family spends the next hour together until the next prayer time and dinner. After praying and having dinner, Tuti makes sure that their son has everything needed for school the following day, and

Budi helps him study. Tuti tends to the baby's needs and usually goes to sleep around 8:00 p.m. if she does not have extra work from her job. After tucking their son into bed, Budi sometimes watches more TV or does some job-related work.

If the children wake up in the middle of the night, Budi and Tuti share taking care of them. Budi said, "Usually my wife will take the baby and then she will ask me to prepare the bottle and make the milk [formula], so both of us are awake. If it's our son who wakes up, I usually help him to get back to sleep."

Budi and Tuti both mentioned that even though they both are very involved in caring for the children, Budi spends more time caring for their son, while Tuti spends more time taking care of the girl. Despite this division along gender lines, they try to be flexible. Tuti points out, "If my husband comes home first, he will take care of the baby first."

Tuti sometimes feels that her son prefers his dad and is closer to him, which upsets her:

> At one point . . . I was so sad and cried because my son did not want me to tuck him into bed; he only wanted his dad to do it. This is because I tend not to talk much; I cannot imitate bird sounds or other animal sounds that make my son happy, while my husband is good at doing that so my son enjoys spending time with him.

She added,

> My son also studies and does homework with my husband; my husband is more patient in dealing with him . . . When my son does something wrong, my husband can talk with him patiently, whereas I tend to sound like I am angry. So my son does not like the way I reprimand him . . . In terms of emotional support, my husband does more.

Budi also mentioned, "I tend to allow the children to do what they want; my wife tends to say 'no.' Sometimes my wife says that I am too lenient. I am trying to be supportive." Again, Budi defies cultural expectations. Fathers in Javanese society are expected to demand respect, to be stricter, and to have less of an emotional tie with children than mothers (Tickamyer & Kusujiarti, 2012). Likewise, Tuti's role with the school is unusual. She says, "I deal with stuff connected to my son's school. For example, if there is a parent–teacher meeting, I am the one who comes." The school is considered a public space, and thus it is usually the husband who would represent the family there.

Other tasks, such as doing grocery shopping, taking care of sick children and getting them to the doctor, deciding about their schools, and managing their social activities, the couple does these together. Budi says, "Nobody actually manages things here . . . We are here in the family together and we do things together. That's our principle." The only exception is shopping for clothes or going to the traditional market. Tuti exclusively does these highly gendered activities. Budi explains that although it's fine for him to do grocery shopping since the space is considered as gender neutral, the traditional market is different:

> I don't feel comfortable going to the traditional market by myself. If I am there to take my wife, then it's okay. However, people will look at me awkwardly if I am there by myself, since most of the traders there are women and we have to haggle or bargain with them. It's hard for men to do that. It is okay if I am there with my children.

The traditional market is perceived as women's space, despite an increasing number of men traders in more urban areas (Brenner, 1998). The market is also a social space where local women exchange information, joke, or tell news or gossip with each other. Bargaining is more than negotiating price; it enables the trader and buyer to get to know each other. Some public spaces for men and women in Javanese rural areas are segregated based on gender, and it is not culturally appropriate for a person from one gender to intrude upon the space allocated to the other.

"I Am Happy When I Am with My Family. That's Who I Am"

Budi and Tuti prioritize their family, especially their children; neither is primarily career oriented. Because they are both teachers, obtaining more education would usually mean a promotion and an increase in salary, but neither of them is currently interested in getting more education, although Tuti hopes that Budi will get a master's degree sometime in the future. Going back to school would mean being busier and having less time for the family life they value. Budi explains, "I am happy when I am with my family, that's who I am. When I go far away from my family for a few days because of my job, I always think and miss my family, I always want to be with them, I am the happiest when I am with them."

Although both Budi and Tuti are high school teachers, Budi has a higher income than his wife because of his additional position as an assistant principal. Tuti reported, "He sometimes makes extra money from honoraria from various activities." Nonetheless, Tuti emphasized that although her husband makes more money, "I think my husband's job and my job have equal value and prestige."

Budi has a harder time juggling work and family than does Tuti, partly because as an assistant principal he has more work and responsibilities. Sometimes Budi has had to bring work home, and either lose family time or stay up very late to work after the children go to sleep. Because of his commitment to the family, Budi indicated that although he had been offered a position as a school principal, after consulting with his wife, he politely declined the offer. He explained:

> It is very demanding to be a school principal; they have to be at school from early morning until the end of the day. They are the first to come and the last to leave the school. Also, it's hard to make everybody happy. People always talk of bad things about principals. I don't want people to talk badly about me.

Recently he redoubled his efforts to spend more time with his family, "After work, I try to focus on my family ... I no longer bring any work home so I can spend more time with my children."

Tuti explained that she does not experience much work–family conflict, "I think that my family is more important than my job; however, I don't think that my responsibilities to my family hinder my ability to do my job. I try to do my best in the job as well." Nonetheless, she too has made adjustments to spend more time with the family. Tuti recently transferred to a school located closer to her house so that she can leave for her job a little bit later and come home earlier. Notably, that change did not compromise the quality of her work life. She mentions that her new school is better than her old one with students who perform better academically and challenge her more. Not only does she enjoy the work, but the job is ideal in terms of compensation, hours, and flexibility.

Their extended family and paid workers also help them juggle their responsibilities. Tuti says, "If I have extra or emergency work, we ask my mother-in-law to watch the children or sometimes ask the household helper to stay longer."

Musyawarah: A Consensus-Based Decision-Making Process

The couple uses *musyawarah* in making family decisions. It is a decision-making process in which all parties involved have to work together to adjust their positions or viewpoints and listen to each other to reach general agreement or consensus. Sometimes those who have contrasting or contradictory standpoints need to create a conceptual synthesis to reach the agreement (Koentjaraningrat, 1967). The practice of *musyawarah* is commonly used in the context of Javanese society in both the state and the family. When asked about the decision-making in their family, Budi mentioned, "We use *musyawarah* and both of us are involved in the process." This method of decision-making enables them to respect each other's viewpoints, to air differences, and to arrive at a consensus. Tuti's voice, for example, was quite important in making the decision to hire a domestic worker to assist them in doing childcare and housework. Budi described what happened:

> At first my mother wanted to take care of the children when we are at work, since she lives next door. However, my wife did not agree with this idea since if my mother does that, my wife won't have any say in how the children should be treated and . . . if she does not agree with what my mom does, she won't be able to say it to my mother. So we decided to hire a nanny, and if my mom wants to come and help take care of the children, she can do that on her free time.

Thus, Budi was willing to follow Tuti's lead to enable her to maintain her independence in child-rearing. The situation was quite delicate because they had to tell Budi's mom carefully to avoid offending her. As a compromise, they proposed that grandma could provide childcare when she wants to, but not be burdened with childcare as an obligation. The open communication and mutual understanding between Budi and Tuti helped resolve this issue.

Moreover, Budi's making more money than Tuti does not mean that he controls financial decisions. As is common in Javanese families, Tuti holds the family's purse strings (Tickamyer & Kusujiarti, 2012). She explained, "My husband gives me all of his salary so that I can manage the money for our household." However, typically in Javanese families, the husband, as the head of the household, retains power in financial decision-making while the wife just implements the decisions (Tickamyer & Kusujiarti, 2012); Tuti and Budi defy this traditional model. Tuti makes decisions on spending and does not report to her husband. She says, "My husband makes more money; you can call him the primary income earner. I manage all of the money. He does not even know how I spend the money. I give my orphan nephews and my parents some money every month from my salary." Notably, she spoke about her power openly, whereas some Javanese women would not want to reveal this dynamic to save their husband's face.

Defying Housewifization and *Bapakism* (Father Knows Best)

Budi and Tuti achieve equality by refusing to follow the prescribed gendered norms. Their behavior is atypical for Javanese couples who usually uphold the strong cultural belief that men and women need to fulfill their *kodrat* or predestined obligations and characteristics. Men and women are perceived as having different *kodrat* and the expression of these differences permeates Javanese gender relations (Tickamyer & Kusujiarti, 2012). The belief in *kodrat* reflects an essentialist view of gender differences. By rejecting those beliefs, Budi and Tuti manage to maintain more flexible gender perceptions and practices. When Budi was asked whether men and women are different, he focused on the experiences that shape a person's behavior rather than on gender:

> I think this depends on the person's characteristics and experience, not so much on the gender. For example, many people would take their younger children to my parents' house when I was a child. This way, I am used to taking care of the children, so I don't see this as a woman's job or that women are better in taking care of the children. In essence, if men and women understand each other well, they will see that there is no real difference between them ... Past experience influences our characteristics. Also, I think in general, women tend to use their emotions more while men tend to use their logical reasoning because of what they tend to do in their daily lives, but again this depends on their experience. I tend to use my logical reasoning because I am a math teacher; a man who is a social science teacher may think differently.

Even when Budi mentions that women tend to be more emotional than men, he points out that this was due to their daily experiences. He does not essentialize the difference.

This couple's non-essentialist view on gender also helps them defy the gender ideology that prescribes women's main role as housewife and mother. This ideology has been called "housewifization" (Mies, Bennholdt-Thomsen, & von Werlhof, 1988) or "state *Ibuism*" (ibu is mother) (Suryakusuma, 1996). Since part of a woman's *kodrat* is to be a housewife and mother, these two roles define her womanhood, and other roles become secondary. The Javanese commonly assume that women's careers or jobs may interfere with their duties as wives and mothers, that they may become overly absorbed in their work, causing them to neglect their family (Tickamyer & Kusujiarti, 2012). Thus, there is a strong stigma against employed women, especially career women. To avoid this stigma, employed women tend to de-emphasize the importance of their jobs. However, Tuti did not; she openly said that her job has equal value and prestige as that of her husband. Moreover, Tuti is not the manager of the housework and childcare; both Budi and Tuti equally feel responsible for these tasks.

Similarly, Budi also challenges common Javanese cultural expectations for ideal masculinity. *Bapak* or father, an important symbol of masculinity, is held to possess characteristics such as self-restraint and calmness; he has mastery in controlling his emotion or feelings, and he rules over his family. It is his *kodrat* to be the leader of his family and these qualities provide him with power and authority over his wife and children (Brenner, 1998). Budi, in contrast, perceives himself as having equal status with his wife. Moreover, his very close emotional relationship with his son and the ease with which he expresses his feelings shows that he rejects hegemonic Javanese notions of masculinity.

"I Saw How my Mom Took Care of the Baby; Sometimes She Even Asked Me to Help Her"

Budi's upbringing seems to have promoted his willingness to share household labor. Budi's parents followed a typical gendered division of labor, "My father tends to think that it is the husband's job and responsibilities to work and earn money for the family, so he was mainly working on the farm and in the office. He did not do household chores and childcare." However, Budi's mother encouraged Budi and his brothers to do family work:

> We, the children, helped our mother to do the chores. I would iron my father's clothes and we washed our own clothes. Since I was a child, my mother sometimes asked me to help her in cooking and going to the market, so I learned from her how to do these ... Relatives, such as my uncle, would leave their babies with my mom when I was a child, so I saw how my mom took care of the baby, and sometimes she even asked me to help her, so I learned it that way. The baby was less than 35 days old at that time.[1]

Budi's mother planted a seed in him to acquire skills in doing housework and childcare and socialized him into the idea that that work is his responsibility as well.

In contrast, Tuti had no experience with household chores when she was growing up. She reports, "Before I got married, my parents, especially my mother, took care of everything for me ... I did not do any household chores at home, not even cleaning or sweeping the floor." Even when she went to college, her parents would visit every week, bring her food, and do her laundry. Although after a few years they stopped, and

[1] The 35th day of a baby's life has a special significance in the Javanese calendar. Called *selapanan*, it is the first celebration after the baby is born.

she had to learn to do her own chores, clearly, she had much less experience of family work than Budi.

Musyawarah and *Gotong-Royong* Reinvented

The ways in which Budi and Tuti defy gendered expectations and experience facilitate their equality in the family. His greater participation in family work growing up, his willingness to limit his career coupled with her commitment to career, their relatively small differences in age and education all reinforce their egalitarian ideas and practices. Their clear principles and goals make them confident and strong, despite Tuti's report of some criticism from others. Budi says, "To be honest, I don't know what others think about us and I don't care about that." Despite rejecting Javanese gendered norms, Budi and Tuti maintain the Javanese values of *musyawarah* and *gotong-royong* (mutual assistance) and, in fact, flexibly interpret them to create a democratic and equal relationship.

They have also upheld the Javanese value of *rukun*, a harmonious relationship (Tickamyer and Kusujiarti, 2012). Tuti sums up how they have created equality with a minimum of negotiation and conflict:

> My husband and I work together well. We both work outside and know that we also need to work together at home to get the chores done and support the children. We just spontaneously do that. We have never intentionally discussed these and explicitly talked about the division of labor. It just flows naturally and somehow we have them balanced. We complement each other.

References

Angloinfo Indonesia (n.d.). *Maternity Leave in Indonesia*. Retrieved from: www .angloinfo.com/how-to/indonesia/healthcare/pregnancy-birth/maternity-leave.

Bowen, J. R. (1986). On the Political Construction of Tradition. *Journal of Asian Studies*, XLV(3), 545–561.

Brenner, S. A. (1998). *The Domestication of Desire: Women, Wealth, and Modernity in Java*. Princeton, NJ: Princeton University Press.

Central Intelligence Agency (2019). Indonesia. *The World Factbook*. Retrieved from: www.cia.gov/library/publications/the-world-factbook/geos/id.html.

Indonesian Census Bureau (2010). *Penduduk Menurut Wilayah dan Agama yang Dianut* [Population Based on the Region and Religious Affiliations]. Retrieved from: http://sp2010.bps.go.id/index.php/site/tabel?tid=321&wid=0.

Indonesian Census Bureau (2012). *Percentage of Population aged 10 years and Over by Province, Gender and Marital Status 2009–2012*. Retrieved from: https://sp2010.bps.go.id/index.php/site/tabel?search-tabel=Penduduk+ Berumur+10+Tahun+Keatas+Menurut+Wilayah+dan+Status+Perkawinan& tid=267&search-wilayah=Indonesia&wid=0000000000&lang=id.

Koentjaraningrat (1967). A Survey of Social Studies on Rural Indonesia. In Koentjaraningrat (ed.) *Villages in Indonesia* (pp. 1–29). Ithaca, NY: Cornell University Press.

Mies, M., Bennholdt-Thomsen, V., & von Werlhof, C. (1988). *Women: The Last Colony*. London: Zed Books.

Mulder, N. (1992). *Individual and Society in Java: A Cultural Analysis*. 2nd ed. Yogyakarta: Gadjah Mada University Press.

One-month paternity leave granted to civil servants. (March 13, 2018). *The Jakarta Post*. Retrieved from: www.humanresourcesonline.net/indonesia-allows-upto-one-month-of-paternity-leave-for-civil-servants/.

Simulja, J., Wulandari, E. H., & Wulansari, S. A. (2014). Gender Inequality and the Division of Household Labor: A Comparative Study of Middle-Class, Working Married Men and Women in Japan and Indonesia. *Makara Hubs-Asia, 18*(2): 109–126.

Soewondo, N. (1977). The Indonesian Marriage Law and its Implementing Regulation. *Archipel, 13*, 283–294. Retrieved from: http://asiapacific.unwomen .org/countries/indonesia.

Suryakusuma, J. I. (1996). The State and Sexuality in New Order Indonesia. In L. J. Sears (ed.) *Fantasizing the Feminine in Indonesia* (pp. 92–119). Durham, NC: Duke University Press.

Tickamyer, A. & Kusujiarti, S. (2012). *Power, Change and Gender Relations in Rural Java: A Tale of Two Villages*. Athens, OH: Ohio University Press.

UNICEF (2018). *Percentage of women aged 20 to 24 years who were first married or in union before ages 15 and 18*. Retrieved from: https://data.unicef.org/ topic/child-protection/child-marriage/.

United Nations Development Programme. (2018). *Human Development Indices and Indicators 2018*. Retrieved from: www.hdr.undp.org/sites/default/files/ 2018_human_development_statistical_update.pdf.

World Population Review 2019. *Indonesian Population 2019*. Retrieved from: http://worldpopulationreview.com/countries/indonesia-population/.

9

Croatia[1]

Lynette Šikić-Mićanović

Nera and Ivo are a cohabiting couple who have lived together for 11 years in the flat Ivo inherited where he had grown up in the center of Zagreb. Both of them have professional full-time jobs and they earn an average joint family income. They met when Nera was still a student of law. She is now 35 and he is 41. Their 5-year-old daughter, Ema, goes to a kindergarten, after having been cared for at home by her father until she was 3. Quite atypically in Croatia, Nera and Ivo are equally involved in housework and childcare. Ivo explains, "It is our intention to be equal, 50/50, not that we divide jobs, but that we both do all the jobs."

A Typical Day

"On a typical day," Ivo says laughing, "you would experience a wake-up call from Ema at least 15 minutes before the alarm goes off . . . She comes into our bed and starts jumping all over us until we tell her to move." Then, while she is watching a cartoon in her room, Ivo takes a shower and Nera prepares breakfast or the other way around. If Ivo has to be at work early, he gets Ema ready in the morning. He notes, "This is not a big job; there's nothing much to do except get her dressed, perhaps choose her clothes or brush her teeth." If one of them is running late, the other takes Ema to kindergarten, but since Ivo's workplace is in the opposite direction, Nera takes her more often. Generally, Ivo's mother picks Ema up and spends a couple of hours with her in the late afternoon. However,

[1] The Croatian Science Foundation supported this chapter under Grant (GENMOD - HRZZ 6010).

when Ivo gets off early from his job, he collects Ema and they go home together. Normally, Nera and Ivo get home at 5:30 p.m. Since they usually have a meal while they are at their jobs, as has Ema while at kindergarten, they do not need to cook dinner then, but instead, they take their daughter to different activities. Nera reports, "I took her to singing lessons and he took her to English lessons. This is the way it worked out most times." Ivo usually bathes Ema in the evening, whereas Nera generally handles the morning routine. Nera explains, "It's easier for me to get up, whereas in the evening I'm tired."

The Republic of Croatia has an estimated population of 4,105,500 inhabitants (Croatian Bureau of Statistics [CBS], 2018b). Most of the population are Croats (90.42%). Serbs are the largest ethnic minority (4.36%), while Bosnians, Italians, Albanians, and Roma, the next most common minorities, each account for less than 1% of the population. Predominately Christian, 86.28% of Croatians are Catholic and 4.44% Orthodox, while 1.47% are Muslim, and 3.81% categorize themselves as non-religious or atheist (CBS, 2013).

Women's rights are protected by the Constitution, which contains a non-discrimination provision and the Gender Equality Act (UNICEF, 2011), but, on average, women's earnings are only 87% of men's (CBS, 2018c). A larger discrepancy exists between women's and men's salaries among higher-paid than among lower-paid employees (Nestić, 2007; Tomić-Koludrović, 2015).

Just over half the population over 15 years of age (52.8%) is married, while 2.69% are in cohabiting relationships. Out of all the families with children in Croatia, 73.4% are married couples, 2.6% are cohabiting couples, while the rest are single-parent families. Approximately, two-thirds of married mothers and 77.4% of married fathers are employed. Over half (54.5%) of married couples with children (under 18) are dual earner, while 37.8% of their cohabiting counterparts are dual earner (CBS, 2018a). For those employed, full-time work (41.1 hours for men and 40.4 hours for women) is the norm in Croatia. The share of employees working part-time in Croatia is small (8.4%), but is still more prevalent among women than men (Dobrotić, Matković, & Zrinščak, 2013).

The Republic of Croatia provides parents with earnings-related parental leave (100%) that begins 28 days before the expected date of birth and lasts until the infant is 6 months old. It is obligatory for the mother to take the first 98 days of this leave, while the father has the right to use the remaining period. After 6 months, either parent has the right to parental leave at a flat rate, for up to 30 months, depending on the number of children and circumstances. However, less than 20% of mothers take parental leave for more than one year (Dobrotić et al., 2013), and only 2% of fathers take any care-related leave (Ombudsperson for Gender Equality, 2018).

Housework is gendered. Women are predominantly responsible for food preparation, cleaning, and washing, whereas men are more responsible for repairs and paying bills (Bijelić, 2011). Employed women do considerably more domestic work and childcare than men, except for playing with children (Tomić-Koludrović, 2015). With preschool-aged children, the only daily childcare fathers perform is playing. Preparing their food, changing diapers, and bathing is only done by fathers occasionally. Twenty-six percent of fathers play with school-aged children, 14% help them with homework, and 12% prepare food for them every day (Bijelić, 2011).

Inflexible work time arrangements as well as inadequate and expensive care facilities are largely responsible for work–life imbalances (Bejaković & Kaliterna Lipovčan, 2007). Between the age of 4 and the age when compulsory education begins, only 75.1% of children attend preschool, compared to 95.3% in the EU-28 (Eurostat, 2018). Coverage for infants is just over 18% (Matković & Dobrotić, 2013). Childcare services are not available in all parts of the country because they are financed by local governments, which vary significantly in financial resources (Šikić-Mićanović, Ivatts, Vojak, & Geiger Zeman 2015).

During the summer months, Ema's grandmother cares for her on weekdays. After work, Nera frequently takes Ema to outdoor events in the city. Ivo recounts, "She usually makes arrangements with another mom to see a play together so while the children are watching the play, they sit and talk about their own things." Meanwhile he is at home preparing what they need for the next day. When they get back at about 9:00 p.m., Ivo takes over so that Nera can have a breather:

> Depending on how much time we have, I give Ema a shower or some food if they want to eat . . . put her pajamas on, teeth brushing . . . then I put her to bed

and either Nera reads her a story before she goes to bed or I do, or perhaps there is no story because she is so tired that she falls asleep at 10:00.

"You Don't Need To Get a Nobel Award for Doing These Jobs"

Ivo asserts that their rejection of traditional role divisions is simply "normal." "We are normal people that think about what we do." It is not "normal" for one person to do all the work. Instead, they do what they are good at and what is more practical. Ivo does the shopping for bread and milk on a daily basis while Nera does the shopping for extra groceries, especially for clothes and houseware because she likes those chores. Cooking is equal but Ivo points out, "We cook less now than we used to before because we don't have the time and we eat at work and Ema eats at kindergarten." During the summer when Nera spends more time outdoors with Ema, Ivo says, "I do what needs to be done at home whether this is laundry, changing the bed linen, whatever ... There is always something to do; you never manage to do everything!" Nonetheless, Ivo says that housework is "nothing special" and "You don't need to get the Nobel award for doing these jobs ... I can get them done quickly and I am left with enough time to sit and read something or to watch a game." On Sundays, while Ema is with his mother, Ivo reports that they have time to clean the apartment more thoroughly. Then, they all meet up for lunch at his mother's.

The division of childcare tasks is accomplished quite flexibly, as Nera explains:

> If I'm making pancakes, then Ivo prepares her backpack for kindergarten the next day. If Ivo is doing a puzzle with her, then I prepare the bathroom for her shower. If I'm out, Ivo will put her to bed and read her a story. If he's out with boys at soccer, then I'll read her a story ... When one of us takes care of Ema this means engagement with the child, not that we are asleep and the child is watching TV. This rarely happens in our home. I think that we spend a lot of that quality time equally either together or separately.

Ema spends more time with her father at home; they play dominoes and do puzzles together, whereas time with Nera is often out at the cinema, theater, or for coffee with her girlfriends and their children.

When asked, "Who do you love more, Mom or Dad?" Ema always says that she loves her parents equally. Nera says proudly, "Children usually sense when one spends more time or that they are closer to one parent; she is equally attached to both of us." Ema asks them both for comfort and help. According to Ivo, "She is not that dramatic. [She runs to] whoever is there at that moment. She doesn't run to a particular person like mom, or grandma, or me when she needs comforting."

One difference between them as parents is in the way they discipline Ema. Nera explains, "He is stricter in some situations ... He can say 'no.' I can't cope with her tears, but he can leave her crying in bed for 10 minutes until she calms herself down." Nera admits, "Perhaps in the long term this is better for her to learn to cope with this, to help her understand that she is not always right," but she spends so little time with Ema that she "can't say no to everything! ... I'd rather not meet one of my needs than not meet hers."

Nera claims responsibility for the mental work of parenting, such as organizing and overseeing details, "I surely do this more because I'm more skilled at these activities ... I don't like leaving things to coincidence." Nonetheless, Ivo explains he is usually the first to know when his daughter is sick and manages her illnesses, "If she sneezes or something like that, I check her temperature." He claims that he is more skilled in this care. Moreover, when Nera is out of town for her job, Ivo is solely responsible for all of Ema's care. Nera does not have to organize what he will do with her. Ideally, however, Nera says, "I would like Ivo to do more things with her independently outside of home ... to take a little more initiative in organizing time with her outside the home, not at home ... so that I can stay at home and look at the ceiling and not do anything at all." Despite this criticism, she has "complete trust in him as a father." She says, "I think that he can do all of these things as well as I can, sometimes even better, sometimes worse, and I think they [he and Ema] work together very well."

"Home Is Somehow a Natural Habitat for Him"

Nera and Ivo lived together as a couple for 7 years before Ema was born and according to Nera, he already knew how to do domestic work when she moved into his apartment. "He did all of this on his own: he washed the dishes, he ironed, these everyday jobs, paid the bills, everything that is involved in maintaining a household." When he first lived on his own, Ivo discovered that learning to cook brought him pleasure, "When you realize that you can do all sorts of things and that this can be very creative, this is something that you can really enjoy and you won't die of hunger!" He also recounts that although he did laundry, he did not use all of the washing machine programs, "I did everything in a 60-degree cycle!"

When Ivo and Nera moved in together, at first he did more of the household tasks because they were living in his apartment. Gradually, she started to take over some of these jobs. He says, "Perhaps she didn't trust me as a man doing these 'women's jobs' so she became involved, but I don't remember any issues about who does what at this time." Nera claims that sharing came "naturally." "It is not normal that one person does all the work and the other sleeps. We always did things in this way."

Ivo was an involved dad even before Ema was born. Nera reports, "When I was pregnant, he went with me to every ultrasound, to the birth ... This is normal for me. It is not normal that men are not interested in this." Ivo went a step further by reading books about childcare.

Ivo describes his role immediately after Ema's birth, "Getting up in the morning, at night time, nappies, feeding. I never had a problem with this ... Washing her clothes was no big deal. They were so tiny. A bigger problem was hanging them all up." Because he couldn't breast-feed, he says, "I did most of these things to help her, to relieve her of some of the work." Nera describes the insecurity she felt as a new mother:

> I never had a small brother or sister. I didn't know any of this. I held her in one of those swaddling blankets for two weeks. I didn't take her out of that except when I bathed her because I was scared that something would break or that something would happen to her.

Nera spent 4 months home on maternity leave. She recalls that period as a "catastrophe" for her, "I am more oriented towards the world outside of home. Those 4 months were very difficult for me ... to be away from other people, in a track suit ... I simply didn't feel good in this role as just a mom." She recalls that Ivo fully supported her wish to go back to paid work and stayed at home with Ema until she was 3 years old. At that time, he was between jobs and was not in a hurry to find a new job, "I didn't have any type of job that I wanted to dedicate myself to, so this was perfect." Ema became his priority and he could do translations and other freelance work in the evening while Ema was asleep. "This was no problem at all for me. On the contrary, this was a pleasure for me, a pleasure to be with her." He had some support from his mother who came every day for 2 hours to play with Ema or to take her to the park.

Initially, Nera worked in a part-time job close to home:

> I was 200 meters away so during my breaks I used to come home and breastfeed ... I was very happy that I could go to work and that I was with other people, with other girlfriends and business partners, that I could get ready, get dressed up, that I could be where my knowledge was appreciated.

Nera reports that during this time, "He did everything for her – bathing, walks ... he surely did more than what I did." Ivo found childcare "easy." He says:

A baby at this age is no burden. She doesn't walk or run; she mostly eats and sleeps ... you see what needs to be done and it was easy to recognize whether she was hungry or whether her nappy needs to be changed. This was very easy for me, a really nice 3-year period.

Nera explains that staying home came easily to him because "home is somehow a natural habitat for him. He has always liked to be at home." He even used to spend his holidays at home reading before they started to live together.

Ivo believes that because he was so much a part of his daughter's life from the very beginning, now it is "absolutely normal" when he takes care of Ema. When Nera needs to go away for job-related purposes, for example, he knows he can manage on his own. Nera first went abroad for 4 days when Ema was 7 months old. Ivo recalls, "There were no problems."

"Men and Women Can Equally Care"

Nera and Ivo's nontraditional egalitarian approach is reflected in their choice of cohabitation over marriage, as well as their decision to give their child, Ema, two surnames. Their egalitarian beliefs underwrite their equal sharing of housework and childcare. Nera asserts:

> We aren't together so that I can be the housekeeper and so that he can be the breadwinner or the other way around ... There's no way he'll be reading the newspaper or watching TV, while I'm doing everything at home and then I'm dead tired at night time and he is full of energy. This certainly never happens.

She thinks that "men and women can equally care" and that even though "men cannot give birth or breastfeed ... these are things that are not important in the upbringing of children ... A man can hug and look after a child and can develop equally good connections with their child just like a mom or a grandmother." Likewise, Ivo firmly believes that "a parent needs to be good at parenting!" He argues, "This has nothing to do with sex. I don't believe in those stories in which a mother possesses natural instincts and that as soon as she gives birth she knows what to do. This is nonsense."

"We Negotiate Everything"

Open communication between Nera and Ivo also facilitates their equal sharing, "We negotiate everything; we come to an agreement about everything." After Ema goes to sleep they often sit with a glass of wine, a plate of cheese and olives, and talk, which is useful for avoiding potential conflicts. Ivo says that these discussions can become quite passionate, "Sometimes we shout at each other, but not in an angry way. We just try to have our say." He adds, "I like to talk about things, more than keeping them a secret, and she's very similar in this way. So we solve matters in this way and they never become conflicts." Nera recalls that parenthood brought new issues. They fought a lot because everything was unfamiliar to them and they did not just assume that as the mother, she was automatically the expert. From their first days as parents, Ivo felt equally entitled to put across his point of view. For example, Nera remembers how Ivo convinced her to take a break from breastfeeding and to go to sleep instead of crying. She was tired but was afraid to have him give a bottle because she had been told in the hospital that she should only breastfeed, "We fought about this for half an hour until he convinced me that I would breastfeed again and that I wouldn't lose my connection with the baby ... He fed Ema and everything was all right."

Communication is an important way they keep things equal without allowing resentments to fester. Nera recalls an example of how they "simply come to some sort of agreement about things":

> When he was at home with Ema for the first 3 years, let's say I come home from work ... there was a sink full of dishes waiting for me and then for 10 days the dishes were still there. On the 10th day I would say, "You don't expect me to wash the dishes when I come home tired from work. You wash the dishes so that we can be together, the three of us in the afternoon" ... and so we agreed to this.

If Nera finds herself burdened by doing more than Ivo, she will say, "I'm dead tired, you wash the dishes." On Ivo's part, rather than being so direct, he playfully teases Nera when he feels that she is not tidy enough and all the tables are full of her papers, "I keep on teasing her and say that if we had more horizontal spaces she would succeed in covering them all up."

"Fatherhood as a Career Rather Than any Job"

Nera is more career oriented and ambitious than Ivo. She sums up her attitude toward paid work, "Success is important to me. My career is important to me. Being with other people is important to me." She adds, "When the children grow up, you have to do something in life!" She is happy at her job in an all-women team in a small private company that deals with EU projects, "I'm very satisfied with my job because it is intellectually challenging and I most often only work 8 hours a day." She appreciates the nice atmosphere at her job, the opportunity to social- ize, and the company's family-friendly policies. "If your child is sick we can work at home ... so whether I do this at work or at home until midnight this is all the same to the owners of the company."

In contrast, Ivo's priorities have changed since fatherhood, which has assumed far more importance than his career. "My job is something now that is in second, third place. In my life, I think fatherhood, in this sense, is by far in first place!" Ivo would willingly stay at home if Nera got a job in the EU in another country because he gives her career priority and imagines that she would have long hours, "I would probably be the homemaker; I would be with Ema."

Ivo does like the organization he works for because it is nonprofit, which gives him "a feeling of satisfaction," which makes him "want to do more, to make more of an effort." Nera adds, "I think that Ivo is also very happy at work as this is an opportunity to show his knowledge and skills ... I think that this is positive." Nonetheless, Ivo complains he does not feel "overly successful at work." He says, "When you complete a task you are not sure that you have done this well. Everything is rushed; there are lots of deadlines that occur at the same time." Although he is basically satisfied with his job/workplace and its family-friendly policies, his priority is fatherhood, "This has never been a basic goal for me – a career. An achievement for me is my family and being a father and fatherhood as a career rather than any job." He notes that other aspects of life outside of his job are also important to him, "We all have social lives, family life, friends – this is the point – there is no point in working as if this is the only facet of your identity. This is a large part but this cannot be the only thing."

Notwithstanding Nera's investment in her career, she is not a work- aholic. They are both adamant about having a balance in life, which means not working more than 8 hours a day. Although Nera earns a bit more money, they feel equally responsible for breadwinning. Ivo de- emphasizes money, however, when he explains: "It's not all about earning money, we have a lot more responsibilities, duties and all of that ... earning money is just one part of this." Neither of them wants a higher salary that would entail more obligations. "It is more important for us to come home at 5:30 and that we can go out with our bicycles and that we can go up to the mountain," Nera adds, "I wouldn't like to work longer hours because we have a lot of activities outside of work with our friends ... This is important to me."

Family Backgrounds

Nera comes from a very patriarchal family. Both of her parents were employed and earned money, but her father was the "money-maker," responsible for family finances. At home, she says, "My mom did everything; my father didn't do anything ... He would eat a meal and then he would leave the plate on the table, he didn't even take it to the sink ... Dad cooked lunch sometimes, once a month, fish or beans." Nera's mother expected her to do more domestic chores than her brother, who was not expected to do housework. Nera remembers that her father used to play with her and her brother while her mother cleaned on Saturdays, "He would take us to the park or for ice-cream or for walks or to the beach when we were at the seaside. He wanted to be involved with us." Her father was also completely responsible for all of their extracurricular activities. Despite the patriarchal nature of her parents' lives, she received egalitarian messages from him throughout her childhood and youth. For example, her father provided his son and daughter with equal educational and extracurricular opportunities. He even encouraged her to have a more equal relationship with her future husband, warning her, "If you're a cleaner and he has a Ph.D., you will be in a subordinate position."

Although during adolescence she questioned her parents' roles, she also saw the logic to them. After some years as a stay-at-home mother, her mother found a job outside the home, but not an ambitious job, and her father was the one who had to worry about money. The logic of her parents' division does not hold up, however, in her relationship with Ivo because the two of them have equal work roles. She consistently invokes a sense of entitlement to an equal life and concludes, "I doubt whether I could live with a partner that is like my father in terms of job and care division. I couldn't do that."

Ivo grew up in an extended household of three generations. His grandmother and grandfather were responsible for domestic chores. "All I can remember is that my father used to go sometimes on Saturdays to the central market to buy special meat like rabbits or wild game as specialities." His geologist father was often away in the field, and died while Ivo was in his teens, and so he grew up with women – his grandmother and mother. According to Nera, even when he lived on his own, he regularly visited his mother. "Every Friday he went home for lunch to see her and to talk with her, to check on her. This was important to him. He was 28, 29, around 30 years old, when he could have been out drinking with the boys." She reflects, "Perhaps his mother took more care of him because his father was away a lot in the field; perhaps he soaked up that family, affectionate way of doing things." His relationship with his mother seems important to the type of father he has become.

"Does He Breastfeed as Well?"

Nera and Ivo live in a highly gendered social world, as Nera observes, "I look at other couples around us and they are just like my dad: the husband who earns a lot of money and the wife who takes care of everything in the household." She explains that most mothers are more involved in childcare. "I think that in only 5% of families the father does the same as the mother." As an unusual couple in their social world, people around them have criticized the way she started paid work early (after Ema was born) rather than being at home. Nera says, "I didn't feel guilty. I felt more bothered when … the doctor said, 'You're going to leave your baby of 4 months to go to work?' But I wasn't leaving her with a stranger on the street or homeless persons; I left her with her father." She thinks that it is still socially undesirable for fathers to fulfill a nurturing paternal role, "People still see this as unacceptable for men here, in the sense, that a child needs a mother and not anyone else." In particular, people in the older generation are puzzled when she explains how they shared childcare when Ema was a baby. Sarcastically, they would say, "What? Does he breastfeed as well?" Nera's mother did not support their unconventional gendered behavior, including her cohabitation, and could not understand that it was important to her "to get out … to have a different world besides the baby."

Nera believes that most men would never stay at home because "this is not appreciated/valued in this society, he's a henpecked person to his friends … there is a negative social context towards men like this." Interestingly, Ivo minimizes their differences with their peers. He did not feel criticized for staying home, and claims that all of his friends are very caring fathers who are involved in their children's lives. He doubts that any one of them would label this as a woman's job. All in all, Nera has suffered from disapproval over their equal sharing, while Ivo has received praise. He remembers, "All of Nera's girlfriends called me 'Mom' [starts laughing] and her, Dad, because I was at home." They thought that this was a great idea and a good example for all of their husbands.

Mothers Who Allow Fathers to Become Involved

Nera pities women who take on too much domestic labor and do not want to share with their partners. "It's women's fault because we are control freaks." Incredulously, she describes a friend who "doesn't let her husband mix the formula for their child, to put milk powder in water and mix and that's it. This is not something sophisticated; this is not a complex activity!"

Nera stresses the importance of helping your partner to be a father so that childcare does not become a burden:

> It's so much easier to say to him that he doesn't know how to do this and that you'll do all of this ... and then you can't change this arrangement ... We are still the generation that was raised by patriarchal families and these young men who want to get out of this patriarchal mode need the help of women to exit this mode. If he heats up the milk incorrectly, you shouldn't say, "What did you do? This is not suitable for a child!" You shouldn't tell him off, but say, "It is a little too hot; cool this down a bit."

Nera asserts:

> This is the battle for equality of the sexes, when you allow your partner to be an equal partner, that you support this in front of other people ... and not make excuses for his choice ... but show that he really wanted to stay home as her father, that no one forced him to be at home.

Nera's approach has given Ivo the opportunity "to be a dad" in the same way that Nera can be a mom. She says, "This is really a pleasure when you let him develop, when he understands that this is his natural role to be a dad."

Nera and Ivo successfully share domestic labor because she is not a gatekeeper and he is motivated to become involved in all aspects of fatherhood and family life. Their straightforward and open communication keeps their equal division of labor on track. The pull of her career and the complementary pull of home for him also supports their equality, as do the lessons they learned growing up. Nera rejected the traditional relationship she saw in her parents, aided by her father's advice about how to avoid becoming second fiddle to her husband. Ivo's nurturing self was fostered by the close relationships he had with his mother and grandmother. Finally, they believe that equality simply makes sense, and that caring comes as naturally to men as to women. Those beliefs foster their equally sharing relationship.

In Croatia, there is a saying that women "hold up three corners of the house" whereby women take over everything in the household and men do what is minimally required. This couple holds up the four corners of the house together. Traditional family life simply makes no sense to them. Ivo says, "If this [the ability to clean] is on the list of partner characteristics when you are looking for a partner, this sounds like they are characters from a really bad novel. I don't see how a normal man can find this enjoyable." Nera insists that their nontraditional life is normal, "He changed Ema's nappies from the first day ... How is this special if we are both a mom and dad, how can he not do these things? That's like 50 years ago when women didn't drive cars ... and were not allowed to drink alcohol ... This is stupidity!"

Nera sums up, "We are partners ... Our relationship is based on the fact that we love each other ..., and Ema is our trophy for this relationship."

References

Bejaković, P. and Kaliterna Lipovčan, L. (2007) *Quality of Life in Croatia: Key Findings from National Research.* Dublin: European Foundation for the Improvement of Living and working Conditions. Retrieved from: www.eurofound.europa.eu/pubdocs/2007/291/en/1/ef0729 1en.pdf.

Bijelić, N. (2011) *Muškarci i rodna ravnopravnost u Hrvatskoj: rezultati istraživanja IMAGES* [Men and Gender Equality in Croatia: Research Results IMAGES] – International men and gender equality survey, Zagreb: Centar za edukaciju, savjetovanje i istraživanje.

Croatian Bureau of Statistics (2013). *Census of Population, Households and Dwellings 2011. Population by Citizenship, Ethnicity, Religion and Mother Tongue.* (Statistical Report 1469), Zagreb: Croatian Bureau of Statistics. Retrieved from: www.dzs.hr/Hrv_Eng/publication/2012/SI-1469.pdf.

Croatian Bureau of Statistics (2018a). *Census 2011.* Zagreb: Croatian Bureau of Statistics. Retrieved from: www.dzs.hr/default_e.htm (additional links for specific data are available from the author).

Croatian Bureau of Statistics (2018b). *Statistical Yearbook, 2018* (Table 5-10, Population estimate of Republic of Croatia by age and sex, 2017). Zagreb: Croatian Bureau of Statistics. Retrieved from: www.dzs.hr/Hrv_Eng/ljetopis/2018/sljh2018.pdf.

Croatian Bureau of Statistics (2018c). *Statistical Yearbook, 2018* (Table 7-7, Average monthly gross and net earnings per person in paid employment, by sex, 2016 average). Zagreb: Croatian Bureau of Statistics. Retrieved from: www.dzs.hr/Hrv_Eng/ljetopis/2018/sljh2018.pdf.

Dobrotić, I., Matković, T., & Zrinščak, S. (2013), Gender Equality Policies and Practices in Croatia – The Interplay of Transition and Late Europeanisation, *Social Policy & Administration, 47*(2): 218–240.

Eurostat (2018). *Early Childhood and Primary Education Statistics.* Retrieved from: https://ec.europa.eu/eurostat/statistics-explained/index.php?title=Early_childhood_and_primary_education_statistics.

Matković, T. & Dobrotić, I. (2013). Promjene u obuhvatu programima predškolskog odgoja i obrazovanja u Hrvatskoj na nacionalnoj i županijskoj razini između 1990. i 2012. godine. [Changes in the Coverage of Preschool Programmes in Croatia at the National and County Levels Between 1990 and 2012.] *Revija za socijalnu politiku*, 20(1), 65–73.

Nestić, D. (2007), *Differing Characteristics or Differing Rewards: What is Behind the Gender Wage Gap in Croatia?* (WP-0704), Zagreb: Ekonomski Institut Zagreb.

Ombudsperson for Gender Equality (2018). *Izvješće o radu za 2017.* [Report on 2017 work]. Zagreb: Pravobraniteljica za ravnopravnost spolova. Retrieved from: www.prs.hr/attachments/article/2404/IZVJE%C5%A0%C4%86E_O_RADU_ZA_2017.pdf.

Šikić-Mićanović, L., Ivatts A., Vojak, D., & Geiger Zeman, M., (2015) *Roma Early Childhood Inclusion+ Croatia report*, Zagreb: Open Society Foundation, UNICEF and Roma Education Foundation.

Tomić-Koludrović, I. (2015) *Pomak prema modernosti: žene u Hrvatskoju razdoblju zrele tranzicije* [Moving towards Modernity: Women in Croatia in the Period of Mature Transition] Zagreb: Naklada Jesenski i Turk, Hrvatsko sociološko društvo.

UNICEF (2011). *Croatia – Analysis of Gender Issues*. Zagreb: Unicef Office of Croatia.

10

Bhutan

Dolma Choden Roder and Tashi Choden

Yangchen and Tshewang live in a rented flat in one of the many colorfully painted, concrete, multi-storied buildings that have sprung up all over Thimphu, the capital city of Bhutan. Their two-bedroom flat is modestly furnished and centered around an open space that serves as the living room and dining room. This is where the family watches TV, entertains guests, and where Tshewang sits with his laptop when he brings work home. Like many other educated Bhutanese urban dwellers, Yangchen and Tshewang are acutely aware that their lives are simultaneously modern and traditional. Their choices about the division of housework and childcare demonstrate this continuous tension. Only about a third of Bhutanese live in urban areas (NSBB, 2017), which means that Yangchen and Tshewang are hardly the typical Bhutanese couple. Yet their marriage and their daily life as a family of four (they have two young sons, Paljor who is 9 and Sonam who is 3) reveal the ways in which questions about gendered labor within the family have become a significant part of the Bhutanese understanding of modernity and progress.

Yangchen provides IT support to a government agency and is able to structure her paid work hours to spend time with their sons. Tshewang's job as a researcher at a well-regarded Bhutanese think tank makes him especially attuned to and interested in the implications of gender norms and hierarchies in his own relationship and family life. To non-Bhutanese observers, Tshewang's better paid, higher prestige work, which he frequently brings home with him at the end of the day, and Yangchen's willingness to take on the majority of caring for their two sons might make for a very "traditional marriage," but the couple makes it clear that Tshewang's willing presence and participation in family life make him an unusually involved husband and father within a Bhutanese context.

Marriage in most of Bhutan, particularly in northern Bhutan, is traditionally a weak institution (Pain & Pema, 2004), with partners moving into and out of relationships with little ceremony or fuss. Even though some contemporary couples choose to hold a ceremony to bless their union, Bhutanese marriages, in general, lack a unified and recognized religious sacrament. Pain and Pema (2004) have argued that this historical attitude toward marriage allowed men to remain unencumbered, free to move beyond their homes and villages to pursue the opportunities provided by a life that could be committed to religion, politics, or trade. Women, on the other hand, were often tied down to land and family obligations. Thus, household concerns and caring for family members (both children and aging relatives) have long been gendered work, with allowances frequently made for Bhutanese men to lead independent lives outside the family sphere. In contrast, Tshewang makes decisions which give him time at home, like leaving the office early and eschewing all-male recreational activities.

Bhutan, a small country in the Himalayas, is a Democratic Constitutional Monarchy. The current population is estimated to be about 692,895 with approximately two-thirds of all households in rural areas (National Statistics Bureau of Bhutan [NSBB], 2017). While Dzongkha is the official language, Bhutan has over 19 different recorded languages (Van Driem, 1994), hinting at the cultural and regional diversity. Most Bhutanese (73.5%) are Buddhist, whereas about 22%, are Hindu (Central Intelligence Agency, 2019). The median age of the population is 28 years. Twenty-eight percent is under the age of 15, while adults over the age of 65 make up only 7% of the population. An estimated 48% of the Bhutanese population is currently married and 58.6% of all Bhutanese households include children. Extended families remain common: roughly one in every five persons in the household is a member of the extended family (NSBB, 2017).

While some scholars have commended Bhutan for its relatively high level of gender equality (e.g., Crins, 2008), many others, including some Bhutanese scholars, have pointed to the often more subtle forms of inequality that might affect women's access to political power (Thinley et al., 2014; Tshomo, Tshomo, Wangmo, & Patel, 2010), education (Choden & Sarkar, 2013; Roder, 2011), and opportunities to practice religion (Zangmo, 2009).

In a survey of time use, Galey (2007) found that while very few tasks were exclusively male or female, men tended to take on "physically demanding work"(p. 24), such as plowing, while women were twice as likely to perform tasks associated with childcare and household maintenance, such as food processing, laundry, and fetching water. Women, on average, spent more time than men each day working (8.9 vs. 7.3 hours), with 3.6 hours devoted to household maintenance.

Large differences exist between the urban and rural populations. For example, the literacy rate in urban Bhutan is 81.7% compared to 58.3% in rural areas (NSBB, 2017). Galey (2007) also found that rural dwellers, especially women, work longer than those living in cities. Urban men work an average of 6.2 hours per day compared to 7.7 hours for rural men, whereas urban women work 7.6 hours per day compared to the 9.4 hours put in by their rural counterparts. Most women in rural Bhutan continue to engage in subsistence agriculture.

There are no reliable measures of maternal employment rates. However, the needs of nursing mothers to get home to their babies at lunch was frequently cited as reason for the failure of Pedestrian Day (which briefly required everyone to walk to and from work once a week), which is one indication of the prevalence of Bhutanese mothers, particularly in urban Bhutan, working outside the home.

Couples rely on extended family, including older siblings, to provide childcare, although today, urban families are less likely to include extended family members who might provide that care. Formal childcare is relatively new to Bhutan, but recent years have seen an expansion in childcare options. As of 2017, of the 307 existing Early Childhood Care and Development (ECCD) programs, 80% are provided through community-based centers. The remaining 20% comprise those run by the private sector, corporations and NGOs. ECCD centers today cater to 21.8% of children aged 3 to 5 (Ministry of Education, 2017).

A "Modern" Husband?

Tshewang also takes on household tasks like cooking, cleaning, or seeing to the children's needs and demands, especially if his wife is busy. He is conscious that his attitudes toward family life and responsibilities are unique. He describes them as "more of modern or western values," values that he learned to see as important through education, reading, and exposure to the world beyond Bhutan. Frequently during the course of the interview he compared himself to other Bhutanese men:

> See, over the last year I've observed some of my educated cousins from my village. Before they used to gamble with dice games; then they moved on to Khuru;[1] then now they're on to archery. Anytime you call, they're out playing this and that. I'm the only one who's not there. So sometimes I call my wife and joke that I'm going off to watch archery games in the grounds. Now if this is the trend among the circle of people I know, surely many others must be doing the same thing. So when they're too active in all these things outside of the house, they don't pay much attention to their kids and family at home.

Yangchen knows of no other husbands like Tshewang, but the "price" of both his extra help and Tshewang's awareness of how different this makes him is his expectation of special acknowledgment from his wife for his contributions. For example, he is upset when his wife criticizes his handling of particular household tasks, such as washing the children's school uniform socks. Tshewang justifies his response by comparing himself to other Bhutanese men:

> I think I react like this because I know that most other men will not be contributing to domestic work, and when what I contribute is criticized, I am touchy. It's basically quite a fragile balance. I know that even though culturally I am not conditioned to be taking such a big part in domestic work, through my own understanding and values cultivated from being an educated person, I've tended to be more considerate ... and yet when suddenly such thankless comments are made, it is very easy to shake that fine balance. At such times I tend to think, "Hey, this is not even my responsibility!"

Clearly, Tshewang still sees domestic tasks and even childcare as mainly his wife's duty. His expectation of special acknowledgment is linked to his assumption that household work and childcare are not his duty, and therefore, any help he provides should be met with gratitude and praise. This perhaps demonstrates the strength of long-standing cultural norms

---

[1] Khuru, like archery, is a traditional Bhutanese sport largely played by men. It is an outdoor game in which teams throw large darts at targets from about 30 meters away.

about the gendered division of labor. In fact, Tshewang complains that observers of their marriage have made fun of him and even described him as "henpecked." He also somewhat dramatically claims that he has been warned that housework might actually diminish his spiritual well-being (*Wangta Lungta* – aura of authority and luck, respectively). Bhutanese believe that individuals are responsible for maintaining their spiritual well-being, for example by performing rituals or seeking blessings from powerful religious personalities. Suggesting that his spiritual well-being is at risk is probably, in part, jest or exaggeration for effect even by those who disapprove of Tshewang and Yangchen's sharing of household tasks and childcare. Tshewang also admits, "For every one person who criticizes, there must be about 40 who appreciate."

Their History

Shortly after Tshewang and Yangchen married, she had an internal cyst that burst and required expensive and painful surgery. She later had to have Caesarean births of both her sons. Tshewang explained how intensely he was affected by her physical suffering and how that helped him to cultivate deep protective feelings toward her. He also noted that having children changed their relationship. Because both of them prioritize the children and their needs, they actually agree more and have fewer disagreements than they had when they first married. He also believes that for his wife, having children made her feel more "secure" about their own relationship.

Tshewang's readiness to do household tasks, however, predates his marriage. Tshewang lived with his older sister after his mother died and it was during this time that he learned to cook as a way to help his sister. Yangchen, on the other hand, grew up in a household with a far more traditional division of labor. For example, she points out that even today, if her father is not actively served meals, he does not eat. These early experiences seem to have shaped both Tshewang's involvement and Yangchen's gratitude. Yangchen points to the way in which this arrangement came about organically and with little discussion, "Ever since we met, I would just get him to do everything together! So I think it just happened naturally, helping each other out."

Yangchen describes the shifts in their division of labor to illustrate their flexibility. For example, in talking about the early days of their marriage, she remembers:

Those days we didn't have a washing machine, and we used to wash our clothes together. I would take out the laundry and separate the big ones for him to wash, while I washed the lighter ones. In cooking as well, we did it together. If he made the curry, I'd make the rice or vice versa. We didn't have kids then, and he wasn't so busy either, so we would do things equally around the house. Now over the years, since we have kids and since he's been busier with office and other work, I do slightly more on the home front. Before, it was really equal sharing.

Though Yangchen now provided most of the active care for Paljor and Sonam, Tshewang provided more childcare when the boys were younger. For example, during his eldest son's first 6 months, he gave Paljor most of his baths because Yangchen was unnerved by how fragile their son seemed. He notes, "Now if we look through his baby photos, we'll not find a single one of her bathing him!"

Tshewang is still more likely than Yangchen to help the boys dress in their ghos, the national dress for Bhutanese men. Before it is put on, a gho resembles a large long coat. To put it on properly, it is fitted to the body, with the "skirt" pulled up around the knees and then secured at the waist with a belt. Being able to make a gho's edges look neat and even takes practice, so children often take time to acquire the expertise to put one on well. Tshewang reports, "If our son or sons happens to be next to me, then I will do it, or she will do it if they're next to her. So it just comes as a natural thing. It's all very organic and happens naturally." Yangchen concurs, "When he's home, he helps and we do things equally ... When the kids ask for something, sometimes he'll take care of it and sometimes I'll take care of it."

Everyday Life

During the workweek, Tshewang is usually up before Yangchen in the morning. He asserts that she should have the "freedom of sleeping in late" in her own household. One of the first activities that Tshewang performs each morning is *chhep phue nyi* or making water offering in the family's shrine room. Most Bhutanese Buddhist households have a shrine room or an altar in their homes which houses statues and images of deities and religious personalities that each particular family venerates. The practice of offering water and other substances is meant to be of a spiritual nature, and not a household chore or task. Making daily offerings of water is one of the many means employed in Vajrayana Buddhism to increase mindfulness, remember motivation, and accumulate merit. Ideally, the person making the water offerings will engage in it as "a meditative, spiritual practice" (Phuntsho, n.d.). However, it is not entirely uncommon in Bhutan for one member of the family to perform this activity regularly as a matter of convention or household responsibility. After making the offering, Tshewang might then start getting breakfast ready: boil hot water, make the rice, and chop up vegetables for his wife to cook later for their packed lunches. However, even at this early hour, Tshewang will then start working on his laptop until breakfast is served.

Yangchen rises an hour or so after Tshewang and finishes making breakfast as well as making lunch for Tshewang and herself to carry with them to their jobs. (The children eat at school.) She then feeds Paljor, her older son, first, since he needs to leave for school. She notes that she has to be there to serve him, "He does try to put it [on the plate] himself, but spills it all over the rice cooker. So thinking that it's going to be extra work in the end, I put [it on the plate] for him." Only after he leaves does the rest of the family sit down to eat. Tshewang then leaves for his job while Yangchen drops Sonam off at his school before she heads off to her own job.

At the time of the interview, Tshewang's half sister was temporarily living with the couple and was able to provide some household and childcare help. For example, she picked up the younger son from school at 1:00 p.m. and watched him until Yangchen got home. She also occasionally cooked dinner for the family or helped with breakfast. Yangchen is usually home with the children before Tshewang arrives and sees to their needs in other ways. For example, on the day of the interview, Paljor had asked her to come with him to an after-school activity informational session to help him decide which program he should join. Tshewang makes a conscious effort to leave his workplace by 5:00 p.m. but as soon as he gets home he is usually back on his laptop. Tshewang describes himself as "addicted" to work, and, as an ambitious and rising academic, he brings work home most days and even on the weekends.

Tshewang does earn substantially more than Yangchen, which means that, while both incomes are important to the family's welfare, Tshewang sees himself as the main breadwinner. Given that Yangchen's salary is relatively smaller, Tshewang has been encouraging Yangchen to quit her job and start a small business, which he thinks might allow her to work fewer hours but earn more. Yangchen, however, likes her job, which she describes as being flexible and understanding of her needs as a parent. She also points out that the work she does is valued by her colleagues:

Even if I take a day off, there are constant phone calls from the office to fix some problem or the other, asking when I'll be in, or to just come even if it means bringing the kids along. Of course it's not a big, important job like others, but still it's an important one.

Once she returns home, Yangchen spends the early evening doing routine housework, like sweeping or dusting, until her favorite Korean TV serial comes on at 6:30 p.m. Interestingly, both Yangchen and Tshewang treat watching television as a legitimate use of time. So while Yangchen is watching her TV shows, Tshewang considers her busy enough to require him to step in and do household tasks or address the children's needs.

Yangchen starts to cook dinner only after her Korean TV serial is over. Most nights the family sits down to dinner at 8:00 p.m. After the meal, while Yangchen cleans up, Tshewang is already back on his computer. Yangchen and the boys are usually in bed before Tshewang finally winds up his work for the day and shuts down his laptop.

On the weekends the family typically shares a late breakfast and then spends most of their time together at home. They sometimes go as a family to visit relatives or on an outing to a park or to the Botanical Gardens just outside of Thimphu city. The whole family also accompanies Yangchen on her weekly shopping trip,[2] although Tshewang and the boys usually wait in the car. Even on the weekend Tshewang spends a lot of time on his laptop, leaving Yangchen the majority of the active childcare.

"I Can Rely On Him"

Tshewang described the usual division of household tasks in this way, "Lighter work she does, and the heavier work I do." In other words, Yangchen does most of the daily cleaning, dusting, and maintenance of the house, whereas Tshewang is responsible for moving and handling heavier, more cumbersome tasks like dealing with the gas cylinder that they cook with or buying and carrying the large 30 to 50 kg (equivalent to about 66 to 110 pounds) bags of rice into the house. He notes that carrying the rice, a daily staple for most modern Bhutanese families, is so decisively considered his job that if he is away from home, "she may buy just 1 kg of rice at a time, and wait until I get back to buy [rice] in

---

[2] In most Bhutanese towns including Thimphu, fresh fruits and vegetables are only available at the weekend market.

bulk." Tshewang calculates that their contribution to household labor is about 50/50 because Yangchen, by doing the daily household tasks, might do housework more often, while he sees the tasks that he does as "heavier and more energy consuming."

Tshewang, however, also stressed his flexible attitude. For example, he reported that the day before the interview he was washing his hands in the kitchen sink and noticed that there were dirty dishes in the sink, so he went ahead and washed them rather than leaving them for Yangchen. Yangchen explained that when Tshewang's job requires him to be away from home, she feels the weight of all the responsibilities that he is usually there to help meet. She notes, "When he's here it is so much easier for me. I feel more relaxed and at ease, and I can get up later in the mornings, because I can rely on him."

Yangchen agrees that Tshewang does a substantial amount of housework but still credits herself with doing a little more (she calculates the division of housework as 60% done by her while 40% is done by him). Like Tshewang, though, she stresses that he will step in when she needs help or asks for help.

She reports that the balance has recently shifted toward equality again as he has started to do more around the house since their household help[3] left. She also notes that she does not always accept her husband's offers to help. For example, she argues that her children prefer her cooking and that she feels she is more attentive than he to their tastes (for instance, she adds less chili[4] to the food for them). So, although her husband and sister-in-law would and could do the cooking, Yangchen chooses to do most of the cooking herself.

One household task that falls on Tshewang most often is entertaining guests. In Bhutan it is fairly common for friends and relatives to visit each other's homes unannounced. During these casual visits, there is an expectation for generous hospitality which includes serving tea and snacks or even a meal to the visitors, as well as spending time with them. Entertaining and engaging with guests is an important household task for most Bhutanese households and one that Tshewang believes has "become more of my responsibility and duty."

---

[3] As in most of South Asia, it is quite normal for even middle-class Bhutanese families to have household help.

[4] Northern Bhutanese cooking is characterized by its abundant use of chili in almost every dish. Chili is frequently treated as a vegetable and not a spice.

Active Parenting versus Independence

Tshewang acknowledges that his wife currently does the lion's share of childcare. While he and his wife are equally present in the home and rarely leave the children "unattended," he admits, "I will be in the other room doing my own work, so physically present but may not be fully engaged with them. Of course they will pop in and out of the room, and I will have to shoo them away!" He has a somewhat ambivalent attitude to his wife's role as a more active caregiver to their growing sons. On one hand he minimizes her childcare efforts by saying, "Actually they're not a lot of work. After helping with their clothes, they're really quite independent and now that they're bigger, it's much lighter responsibility for my wife"; but on the other hand, he praises her as an especially loving and caring mother. He describes her as "naturally nurturing" and notes, "I really appreciate the way she provides childcare, because she does it so passionately and with full responsibility." Similarly, he admits that his wife does the majority of the emotional parenting such as looking after the boys when they are sick.

Yangchen, on the other hand, clearly feels that the boys need more active parental care and supervision. She notes, for example, the need for a parent to help mediate conflicts between the two boys:

> One thing is that since they're both boys, they fight sometimes; there's some sibling rivalry and that creates some extra responsibility, and it can be a bit difficult to control since it involves repeated scolding. If we give something to one, the other one expects the same.

Her previously mentioned desire to cook food that is to their taste and her attendance at extra school events are two additional instances of her taking an active role. Tshewang refers to his wife's more involved parenting as "spoon-feeding." He argues that it is important for the boys to learn how to be more independent and prefers to let them figure things out on their own. For example, Tshewang noted with some pleasure how eager his younger son was to tell his father that he had been able to "stay by himself at school" the other day because he knew that Tshewang would be proud of him.

This difference in opinion on how self-reliant the boys should be is clearly mirrored in their frequent disagreements about how much help and supervision the boys need when studying and doing their homework. Both parents mention that Yangchen often tells Tshewang that he should spend more time helping the boys study. While both parents agree that Tshewang is actually more skillful and effective at helping the boys with their homework (he claims it is because he is stricter, whereas she puts it down to his gender and his higher level of education), he seems reluctant to assume this responsibility. Yangchen explains the conflict:

> Now in the case of my elder son, I tend to pressure him a lot about studying hard, and my husband says I'm pressuring him too much and to let him be. He says that in his own time, he will learn and understand and that it is fine. So when he's around I don't say too much, because even if I do, my son doesn't really listen since his dad doesn't pressure him. But when my husband is out, then I make sure my son studies at home. So even the kids will joke and say, "Oh now Apa [father] is gone, now Mommy's going to fix us up!"

However, education is the only area in which Yangchen comes down harder on the boys than Tshewang. Both parents agree that Tshewang is usually the disciplinarian. He notes:

> When I've scolded the kids and then she treats them very gently and consoles them, I get upset. Then sometimes I tell her, oh you should hit[5] a little harder, you hardly hit him, in the hopes that my son will be alert and learn some value. So basically, I'm more tough on them and she isn't. She'll not discipline them.

Yangchen sees the results of Tshewang's stricter approach in the level of respect the boys have for their father. She claims that even when she does scold them, they don't listen to her. She notes, "When he's around, they'll not watch too many cartoons, and generally behave."

However, despite these differences, she also stresses that "the kids like both parents equally." Tshewang similarly notes, "Even though I'm the one to scold and discipline, my wife tells me that the little one says he doesn't like it if Apa is not around. He explains that the older son, Paljor, usually sleeps with him while Sonam, the younger one, usually sleeps with his mother; however, "They're ready and willing to 'exchange' their places" without making a fuss or complaining. Yangchen reports that Paljor wanted both parents when he was sick, "When my elder son was little, when he got sick, my husband had to be there to take him to the hospital, because then he would not cry so much. But then again, while wanting his father, he also wanted me there."

---

[5] Hitting a child as a disciplinary measure is still very much the cultural norm in Bhutan. Recent attempts to ban corporal punishment at schools have met with mixed results. Debates about the need for it as a way to instill discipline on one hand, the rights of child on the other, continue.

An Unresolved Tension

Tshewang is clearly often proud to be a more involved father and husband but he also has a continued ambivalence about what this active involvement means. For example, he talks about how he occasionally feels compelled, sometimes reluctantly, into this role:

> I tend to talk to others about certain values that should be followed, like the western ones of women's rights, etc … and since I am kind of preaching to others about it, there is a certain self-inflicted pressure on me to follow those values myself! So even if there are certain things that I would rather not do, I have to follow through.

Bhutan's rural past, still so much a part of the country's present, continues to influence the way which marriage, household labor, and equality can be imagined in contemporary Bhutan. Tshewang, for example, is unable to imagine equal marriages for Bhutanese beyond his own urban setting:

> Now in the modern setting, men and women have similar time schedules with work and what not, so sharing responsibilities is logical. But if this is to be replicated in the village, i.e. sharing domestic responsibilities, then it will be waste of time and resources. Because the men being physically stronger have to be working more in the fields, to cultivate rice and what not. If they try to do everything equally at home, it will be a problem.

Yangchen and Tshewang are self-consciously nudging toward equality in a way that is unusual for Bhutan, and yet the household division of labor and their own understanding of what can and cannot be expected suggest that even they are still unable to totally achieve equality. However, their partnership and the priority they give to their children's well-being motivate them to share family work.

Parenthood, Tshewang says, made them more connected:

> Once we had kids, suddenly whatever she said would make sense and she would have a point. The whole context changed, and the way I thought also changed. I no longer thought of her and me as separate entities, but rather as "we," as one entity. Now I don't know what she'll say, but for me whatever I do or think about is for the kids.

References

Central Intelligence Agency. (2019). Bhutan. *The World Factbook*. Retrieved from www.cia.gov/library/publications/the-world-factbook/geos/bt.html.

Choden, P. & Sarkar, D. (2013). Gender Bias in Schooling: The Case for Bhutan. *Journal of the Asia Pacific Economy, 18*(4), 513–528.

Crins, R. (2008). *Meeting the "Other": Living in the Present, Gender and Sustainability in Bhutan*. Delft: Eburon.

Galey, K. (2007). Patterns of Time Use and Happiness in Bhutan: Is There a Relationship Between the Two? *Institute of Developing Economies, Japan External Trade Organization* (VRF Series No. 432). Retrieved from: www.ide.go.jp/library/English/Publish/Download/Vrf/pdf/432.pdf.

Ministry of Education (Bhutan) (2017). *Annual Education Statistics 2017*. Policy and Planning Division, Ministry of Education, Royal Government of Bhutan. Retrieved from: www.education.gov.bt/wp-content/downloads/publications/aes/Annual-education-Statistics-2017.pdf.

National Statistics Bureau of Bhutan (2017). *Bhutan Living Standards Survey Report*. Thimpu: National Statistics Bureau.

Pain, A. & Pema, D. (2004). The Matrilineal Inheritance of Land in Bhutan. *Contemporary South Asia,* 13(4) 421–435.

Phuntsho, K. (n.d.). Yonchap: Water Offerings. Retrieved from: https://texts.shanti.virginia.edu/content/y%C3%B6nchap-water-offering# (Reprinted from article in Kuensel, the national newspaper, 2013).

Roder, D. C. (2011) *Girls Should Come Up: Gender and Schooling in Contemporary Bhutan*. (Unpublished doctoral dissertation). Arizona State University, Tempe, Arizona.

Thinley, D., Aase, B., Dorji, C., Lhamo, D., Lham, N., Dhedup, S., & Robinson, M. (2014). *Improving Women's Participation in Local Governance: An Explorative Study of Women's Leadership Journeys in Eight Districts of Bhutan*. Thimpu: Institute of GNH Studies, Royal University of Bhutan.

Tshomo, T., Tshomo, T., Wangmo, T., & Patel, S. (2010, October). *The Gender Divide in Bhutan: Opinions on the Status of Women Split Along Gender Lines Among College Students*. Paper presented at the 1st International Seminar on Population and Development, Sherubtse College, Kanglung, Bhutan.

van Driem, G. (1994). Language Policy in Bhutan. In M. Aris & M. Hutt (eds.) *Bhutan: Aspects of Culture and Development* (pp. 87–105). Gartmore, Scotland: Kiscadale Publications.

Zangmo, T. (2009). *Women's Contribution to Gross National Happiness: A Critical Analysis of the Role of Nuns and Nunneries in Education and Sustainable Development in Bhutan*. (Unpublished doctoral dissertation) University of Massachusetts, Amherst.

11

Hungary

Judit Takács

Mia and Miki, a well-educated, cohabiting couple, live in Budapest with their daughter, 5-year-old, Anna. Mia is 37 and works as a financial controller at a multinational company. Miki is 49, a self-employed graphic designer, working partly in a computer graphics studio and partly from home. At the moment, they live in a small, one-bedroom apartment in a central, but not well-off neighborhood of Budapest. However, next year they plan to move into a new spacious three-bedroom house in the suburbs, which they are renovating. Miki believes the move will improve their quality of life, "Now, we will have our family house, which is a wider and freer space because it has a garden ... We will be able to spend more time with each other so that it will be even better for the child." Their daughter's kindergarten is close by. Miki spends every Sunday at the new house. According to Mia, "He tries to get out there by dawn and then do all kinds of work on the house, like polishing the ceramic flooring tiles, which will be the floor later, and burning off the paint on the old doors and windows." They both feel great that the work of their own hands contributes to building their new home.

"We Complement Each Other"

Mia depicts their typical daily morning routine:

> Miki gets up first ... 6 o'clock at the latest. He is quickly done with showering himself, and since our child and I are of the types who wake up with more difficulty, it is he who makes the tea for her and my coffee ... Once that is ready he wakes us ... I like it that my little girl comes to me, gets into bed with me; we wake up together, then we talk about how we slept,

how we awoke, then quickly a story ... Everyone's day starts well in that we got out of bed so gently ... After that we go into the shower ... and then we start getting ready, getting dressed ... As Anna is not always prepared to get dressed, however, we try to arrange it that it doesn't end in tears, but that she keeps her good humor. After that ... it is bag-packing. I usually pre-cook something the previous day, so Miki puts our lunch into boxes ... we pack: hat, shawl, coat, shoes, and then we are finally on our way. Together, the three of us, yes, with the car, and ... as my workplace is on the way, I get out first, kiss, kiss, goodbyes, and then they go on to the kindergarten.

So on weekdays Anna arrives at the kindergarten with her father at 8:15 a.m., and he picks her up at 5:00 p.m. After they get home, Miki says, "My partner makes supper, but then I set the table. Then we blow on the soup and the pasta together to cool them so that Anna will eat."

Hungary has an estimated population of 9,655,361 (World Population Review, 2019). According to 2011 census data, less than 5% of the population identifies as ethnically non-Hungarian, with Roma as the largest group, followed by German, Slovak, Croatian, Romanian (Hungarian Central Statistical Office [HCSO], n.d. b). Fifty-four percent of the population identifies with a religious denomination: 68% of them belong to the Roman Catholic Church and 21% are Calvinists. The remaining 11% are divided among multiple religious groups (HCSO, n.d.c). Married or cohabiting couples with children represent 30% of the households in Hungary, 13% are single-parent households, and 20% are couples without children (HCSO, n.d.a).

Discrimination against women in the workplace is forbidden by law, but as of 2016, there was still a 9.4% gender wage gap (OECD, 2019b). Sixty-one percent of women are employed, as compared to 75% of men (OECD, n.d.a).

Hungarian national policy allows for an exceptionally long childcare leave with a maximum of 3 years. Benefits depend on previous employment. The parental care benefit (GYED) is an insured income-related benefit, available until the second birthday of a child, which can be taken by either parent after the 24-week period designated for the mother. There is also a low flat-rate benefit (GYES) for parents who were not in the labor force for at least one year before the birth. Moreover, insured parents can extend their leave an additional year at the flat rate. There is also a 5-day paternity leave (Gábos, 2018). Practically, the generous leave policy discourages the continuous participation of women in the labor market (Plantenga, Remery, & Takács, 2012). In fact, for mothers of children under 2 years old, the maternal employment rate (< 20%) is the lowest of all OECD countries (OECD, 2016a).

As of 2014, in approximately half of families with children aged 0 to 14, both parents work full-time (OECD, n.d.b). Structural features of the Hungarian labor market, such as insecure employment, long work hours, limited opportunities for part-time work, and low wages, which force people to take extra jobs, contribute to an increasingly intense time squeeze for parents, most often mothers because they do the majority of domestic work (Hobson, Fahlén, & Takács, 2014). Hungarian women spend more time on unpaid labor than men, with an average of 4:28 versus 2:07 hours per day (OECD, 2019a).

In theory working parents have an entitlement to early education and care starting at the child's birth, but there are insufficient places available before age 3 (Gábos, 2018). Enrollment of children under 3 in formal care is only 16%. At age 3, the enrollment for preschool education is 79%, rising to 94% for 4-year-olds, and 96% for 5-year-olds (OECD, 2016b).

Mia grumbles a bit about their different styles when they arrive home at the end of the day:

> I quickly get changed and get on with it: I switch on the hot water, start cooking the food, and while I do these he is leisurely getting changed ... While he is comfortably slowly changing, he is talking with the child so it isn't really lost time ... I am more of a let's go, move move move type who runs round the place like a tornado.

After dinner, Miki is usually responsible for bathing, while Mia is tidying up. He says:

> After bath time, it's teeth brushing, pajamas, then "I still want to eat something" ... so this is a kind of evening game, after which she gets put into bed, tucked in snug, "good night," then Mother comes who also says "good night" with a good night kiss. Then they still talk a bit.

Even during his peak work seasons, in the evenings, Miki fits paid work around childcare. Mia acknowledges that he does not let his job demands interfere in their family life:

When there is such a peak period, we come home; we are together; he takes the child out, patiently bathes her without a bad word. We put her to bed, story, good night kiss ... by nine or half past he can finally sit down to work and then works till two or three in the morning and still gets up at six. That is like that for one or two days; that is very, very harsh. Well, then it takes weeks for him to catch up, or there is an evening when he falls asleep because he can keep up no longer.

One day a week students come to Mia for private language tutorials. During these afternoons Miki takes care of the child. Miki reports, "On such occasions ... we have a different program so that we don't get home till after half past six ... because the apartment is tiny, so we can't get out of each other's way."

Mia explains that although they don't always do the same things, overall, their division of labor evens out:

The preparation of food, finding out what to have for supper, making it and warming it up and serving it, that's me, but bathing, and going swimming, morning dressing is very often Father's. So somehow these things are of a different character, but I think, in terms of time and energy that it is divided more or less equally ... we complement each other.

Miki adds:

Her clothes are sometimes put out by me; sometimes by my partner, dressing, undressing, hair washing, combing ... I do the hair washing, my partner the combing. We always try to keep it so that there is no task for anyone that is not desirable, but simply to share ... a significant part of cooking and washing is done by my partner, cleaning we do together, that is really 50/50, and I mainly do the shopping ... We try to share the things so the other one can have time.

Mia describes the flexibility they also give each other: "If he is working late, then I know I won't expect him to do everything ... I take certain things off his shoulders so that they won't burden him extra. If I am snowed under with work, then he helps with those things that make everything go more smoothly."

Miki spends more time with Anna during weekdays, but mother and daughter are together on Sundays when he spends all day working at the new house. Complementing each other extends to the emotional life of the family, as well. Miki says, "The beautiful thing is that when I am impatient my partner is patient ... The thing works by us compensating and complementing each other. So that 'Father, calm now, I'll take over,' or 'Take it easy Mother, and you go over there.'" Although Mia thinks there is something special about the mother–child bond, and that she might have "a better feeling of what the child wants, or what she needs," she acknowledges, "the child loves both of us just as much, is attached to each of us just as much, feels just as secure with Miki as she does with me, embraces, cuddles and kisses both of us just as much." Miki thinks that Mia might have a bit more empathy because they are both girls, but asserts that there is no difference in closeness, "There are days when it is 'Daddy, Daddy, Daddy,' and there are days when it is 'Mommy, Mommy.'"

Except for the kindergarten, Mia and Miki do all of the childcare themselves. Miki generally provides sick care, which he explains, "I am more mobile; I can work from home." Mia adds, "If I were home with her that would either cost me a day's worth of holiday, or it would mean less money, because I would have to be on sick leave on account of the child." They cannot rely on extended family help because Mia has no living parents and Miki's parents are too old and live in the countryside.

Mia is the manager, although Mia does not have to nag him to do things. Miki explains, "She is the one who looks ahead ... the one who does things with a far view, while I give my energy and knowledge towards realizing them. She is more the mover in the family; I am more the one who carries things out." She also brings up issues in parenting, although he is fully engaged.

"I Washed, Cooked and Cleaned for Myself and This Was the Starting Point"

Mia and Miki shared housework equally from the start. Miki points out:

> I washed, cooked and cleaned for myself and this was the starting point ... So it wasn't a strange thing for me that the apartment had to be cleaned, that the wash had to be done ... I used to do these things for myself as well, so I know what it is like to do them and I know how much time they will take.

Mia was sent for a job assignment in the Netherlands when she was in the first month of her pregnancy. After a few months of (mostly Miki) traveling back and forth to see each other, Miki joined her. He arranged to do paid work remotely from abroad, sending his work back to Hungary online. While there he took on most of the housework:

> Most of the cleaning and washing was left to me, because after all, I was at home. So that can be done in between things while working, and with her stomach, how? She couldn't bend down easily by then. So here again the practical point of view is that I do what is needed. And she brought food and cooked, which she can do very well.

Miki wanted to be there while the child was growing in Mia, "This is that feeling that must not be missed, that I put my hand there and felt that she [the daughter] was frolicking and then relaxed from my hand ... I was there and she heard my voice." Mia welcomed that father–daughter bond, "It was an awesome feeling and sight, once my little girl was born and heard her father's voice and immediately turned to him because she recognized his voice."

Even before Anna was born, Miki reports that the two of them would find information about parenting on the internet and send each other links, although Mia took the lead, according to Miki, because she was on leave, "She would say, 'Read this and what is your opinion?' and then we discussed these things."

After returning from the Netherlands, when Anna was born, Mia stayed at home for 2 years on the childcare leave. The parents agreed it would be the best for the mother to stay at home with the baby and breastfeed her, and Mia's higher income also meant the leave was better compensated. Miki's flexible work schedule allowed him to be available without taking official leave.

Mia had originally intended to take a 1-year leave, but then opted for a second year. She explains:

> In Hungary it is quite attractive that mothers can stay at home for a long time ... those 2 years we had were ideal ... I cannot imagine that I would really have had to go back to work after 6 months, because after all, there are countries where the time is so horribly short.

Most days while Mia was home with Anna, Miki came home from his job around 3:00 p.m., and the family went out for an afternoon walk. The parents took the baby to the regular medical check-ups together. Mia points out that although officially she was on childcare leave, Miki was involved too, "It was Miki's task to take the baby to the baby-swimming classes every week, as was the evening bath ... he also shared changing diapers." Mia did the cooking and daily cleaning, but on weekends she and Miki regularly cleaned together. He also usually did the dishwashing and took out the trash.

After Anna's second birthday, Mia went back to full-time employment. They agreed that for a third year, the money would have been too little, and the child would have become "bored" staying at home. Mia felt lucky because her workplace tolerated her absence for 2 years. She has heard about mothers who were threatened with losing their jobs if they did not return to them a few months after childbirth. When Mia returned to her job, Anna went to a crèche where Miki took her by bike every morning, and collected her in the afternoon. At 4 years old, she started going to her present kindergarten.

"She Would Be the Main Breadwinner"

Both Mia and Miki have had atypical career paths. Miki studied engineering but after receiving his degree he got a job in a movement theater. He explains, "I was a complete career-leaver." For 10 years he worked as a dance and movement actor but he couldn't make a living. He recounts:

> So something had to be done to get money. I was doing occasional work ... One of these odd jobs was with this graphic designer, manual work ... At first I glued texts in a shop window, after that I went to the cutting room and I was told what had to be cut, and after that I was sitting at the computer and I did the cutting that had to be done. Now we are at the stage where they say that they want a catalog, and I design it and make it.

He is currently employed at a computer graphics studio and does designing, typesetting, layout execution, all the way to print-ready character work.

Mia also had an unexpected career change, from librarian to a financial controller. She had studied languages, and had been employed at the library of the language department during her university years. However, because of her knowledge of languages, 8 years ago she found a job at a multinational company where she has been working ever since. Despite her liberal arts degree, she now does financial work: "Obviously after one or two diplomas, one is able to learn things, and this is work that can be learned." She adds, "I like my work ... I was in several different positions with various kinds of work, and all of them I liked."

Both of them appear to be very competent at their jobs. Mia notes:

> Whichever field I got into, sooner or later I always managed to build up the knowledge, practice, and insight of a specialist ... all that expertise. So I can quite quickly start working in that role where I have to help others or give advice when there are questions. This has happened in just about all my positions.

Mia acknowledges the link between her work life and Miki's. His flexibility gives her the freedom to work as much as she wants. Mia's career clearly has priority in the family; it carries more prestige and money. However, she admires that Miki's work is creative: "I wouldn't even think that my level would be higher because it is a thing that can be learned, while he creates things."

Mia has more opportunities than Miki for advancement, but both of them assert that they put the family first. More money would be nice, but Miki does not want to take on more work "to the detriment of my family." Mia explains that she gave up some of her ambitions and even some employment opportunities once she became a mother:

> My value system changed completely. Work was no longer the first thing, or career, or anything else, but Anna was and the family ... which doesn't mean that one doesn't perform well at work and doesn't do all that can be done, but it's no longer my aim that I should get into a higher position. My aim is that I can be with my child. ... I used to do a lot more overtime before the child came. At that time a foreign placement was a goal, but not anymore. So just now they offered that I should go abroad to work, in America and Europe, but no ... I wouldn't like to go in for that any more.

However, Miki can imagine that if Mia got a career opportunity, the family would move to another country and he would be a "househusband":

> We spoke about the possibility, that if in Hungary things are not the way we would like ... then it could happen that she would take on foreign work ... She does have a much better chance than me ... I am of the age already that even here [in Hungary] it's getting harder for me to find work, let alone abroad ... We would have to move as a family and then she would be the main bread-winner, while I would do other things and take care of the child.

"We Work as a Family"

Two inter-connected factors facilitate Miki and Mia's equal sharing: the structure of their work lives, and their joint commitment to be responsible for family life. In gendered terms, their careers are structured unconventionally: hers is the more important job. He has fewer opportunities for advancement. He has more flexibility, which allows him to be more available for childcare during the week. Miki explains that Mia's job requires face time, whereas his work just requires productivity, "I have to hand in ready work, while she has to spend a certain minimum time at her workplace."

Mia explains their shared commitment, "For many people commitment is that they marry and say 'I do.' We thought that taking on having a child is an even bigger commitment ... that given 'yes' word is perhaps more easily abandoned these days than that with their own child." Miki adds:

The basic principle is that we have a child to whom we owe responsibility and whom we have to raise. We aren't together because the child binds us tightly together and it is compulsory, but because we feel good together and we have a beautiful child for whom it is worth it to live and work together.

In fact, he says that they didn't have an explicit agreement to share 50/50 but that it grew out of their desire to make their relationship work well.

Mia acknowledges her partner's commitment, but she also expresses a sense of entitlement to share the work, "We are equal partners in the family, and maybe it could literally be stated that I work as much as you do. So I don't necessarily have to do everything at home as a third or fourth shift." She recounts her outrage at witnessing a friend's husband playing on the computer rather than caring for his child, something she would not tolerate, "I didn't have a child and a family so that my partner can play for hours on the computer." Mia reiterates his principle that both parents are equally responsible for the child who is not only her mother's child but her father's as well.

Interestingly, her long parental leave did not create the long-term traditional gender gap in parenting that it often does in other families. Perhaps his sense of responsibility coupled with her sense of entitlement kept him involved and enabled them to share equally once she was back at her job.

Their own family backgrounds may have also facilitated their equal sharing. She says that her parents did try to share, and despite their own gendered roles, her father did teach her some "manly" tasks, like repairing the radio. Both of her parents were employed full-time, and although they divided household labor in stereotypical ways, she implies that her father's household work, around and outside the house, such as picking fruit from their trees, was equivalent to her mother's work inside, but notes that that division wouldn't be fair today, since most of household labor now is "inside" work.

What Miki learned from his family was a work ethic. Both parents worked hard, in somewhat traditional roles, but crossed over when need be. His father certainly did not expect to be waited on, nor did he sit around while his mother was working hard. Miki describes the lessons he learned from his parents:

Most of the housework and cooking were done by my mother, but I know that my father could also cook all kinds of things; I learned a lot from him ... that wasn't the typical male–female division of labor ... both my mother and my father were hardworking ... Mother washed; Father didn't wash. Mother cooked, but the work they did, in a nutshell, around the house was equivalent ... both of them worked until they dropped.

Both Mia and Miki reject stereotypical notions of separate men's and women's work. Miki emphasizes that practicality is what drives them, not gender, "There is no restriction that I am not going to do that because that is the kind of housework men don't do ... I wash up precisely because that will be helpful." When asked if men were as capable as women of taking care of children, Mia responds with a cautionary tale of a woman who didn't think her husband was capable and ruined their relationship. She criticizes mothers who act as gatekeepers, "A lot of people spoil the situation by saying that fathers are unable to do certain things like changing nappies, and instead of letting them learn to try they just let them not do these things ... Women have their role in this, too!"

Mia is adamant, "the only differences are pregnancy and the extra bond of giving birth to the child ... both the father and the mother are capable of doing the same thing." Miki also thinks that men are as capable apart from nursing. Despite the ways in which they undo gender, however, they still hold on to some essentialist ideas about men and women. For example, Miki reports that prior to becoming a mother Mia didn't want children and didn't like them, a decidedly non-stereotypical behavior for a woman, but then he asserts that ultimately all women want children because of biology. Likewise, Mia invokes the biological bond she has with the child because of pregnancy; however, she does add, "What is already basically there with the mother, that has to be established with the father, though that wasn't very hard, because during the pregnancy he always stroked the tummy." She claims, nonetheless, that it is better for the mother to take care of a sick child when the baby is small. Additionally, at one point Mia alluded to a traditional role when friends come over and she acts as "the lady of the house," which is a reference to her serving them.

Another startling aspect of their gendered ideas is the ambivalence with which they approached their different earnings. Both of them agree that Mia earns more, her job is more secure, and is the main source of their family income. Nevertheless, she maintains that in psychological terms, he is the main breadwinner:

> Because my pay is saved entirely, and that is money for our house, we live off Father's income as main breadwinner ... I think that it is possible that psychologically this is a better version, because my pay [is used for] savings for the house, for the child, for the future ... For men, it can be an important point of view that they support the family, are the breadwinners, and since we use his for living, for everything, therefore, psychologically that feeling remains.

Although Mia seems to worry about threats to Miki's masculinity, Miki didn't express any such worries. He concurs that Mia earns more and they live off his income, but he states matter-of-factly, "My partner is the main breadwinner." Despite Mia's concerns, she asserts that if Miki became a househusband that could be "an absolutely workable thing," as long as the work both inside and outside the house were equally valued, "The earnings of the one are in money, those of the other in terms of family and time."

To make sense of these contradictory gendered behaviors and ideas, we should consider the changes affecting women in Hungary, similar to the rapidly changing gender regimes of other post-socialist countries. During the state-socialist era (before 1989–1990), when women's emancipation meant equal rights with men to be gainfully employed, the state provided solutions to the problems of working mothers, partly by free and widely available childcare. After the collapse of state socialism, Hungarian women were no longer forced to participate in paid work nor to maintain the dual-earning nuclear family model. The generous government support for childcare and housing was either abolished or diminished in effectiveness. Renewed nostalgia for traditional gendered roles emerged. Conservative social forces, including political and religious groups, have promoted the view that women can and should resume their "natural" (i.e., traditional), roles as mothers and housewives. Nonetheless, in the 21st century, women in general, and more educated women in particular, are more likely to interpret their job not only as a necessity to earn money but also as an opportunity for personal development. Increasingly women's careers as well as men's are considered in family decisions (Takács, 2013).

In Hungary, similarly to other Central and Eastern European countries, these changes have brought about "the gender yo-yo effect" to describe the contradictory normative expectations about women's roles in post-socialist societies. Women typically feel bad at work because really they should already have children, and if they do, they should have stayed at home with their small children, like their grandmother possibly did before the Second World War; and they also feel bad at home (once they have small children) because really they should have had a full-time paid job, too – like their mother most probably had after the Second World War (Takács, 2013).

In present day Hungary, Miki and Mia are exceptional. Although they do not seem to be getting criticized for the degendered ways they have organized their lives, they do not seem to have a great deal of social support for the unconventional lives they are living either. Miki reported that the traditional model is still dominant. "At the kindergarten I see that ... where the father is the breadwinner, works a lot, and when he's at home then he's resting and tired ... and where it's the mother who takes the child and is responsible for raising the child." The teachers were surprised by his role, "To start with they thought it odd. Why is it always Father who brings the child? And it is the father who gets the child used to the place."

The genuine pleasure they derive from family life promotes their equal sharing. Miki poignantly talks about wanting to watch his daughter at kindergarten, "My problem is that she spends a lot of her time in an institution and I have no idea what she does, I only have indirect information ... I don't see her. Sometimes I would love to sit in and watch what she does." He also talks about the joy of family life that results from the family labor he does: "I am the one who carries things out, bringing me joy, and with that we go forward." They both seem to love spending time together as a family. Mia describes how they use time in the car together to share their emotional lives, "On the way home we talk all the time about what happened to whom on that day. So we arrive home having already talked about the day's events, hurts, joys, learned things."

Conclusion

Mia and Miki do family in exceptional ways. Their coordinated and harmonious efforts to manage family time avoids the time poverty often experienced by Hungarian families, who suffer from a perception that they lack enough hours in the day to fulfill job demands and care responsibilities. Miki and Mia consciously rearrange their priorities to allocate enough quality time for the family. From the very beginning, when Miki moved to the Netherlands to join his pregnant partner, they have been equal sharers. His willingness to adapt his employment to family priorities reflects his commitment.

Responsibility and commitment are conscious, rational motives, but those motives can promote the feeling that keeps equal sharing on track. Miki's involvement in family life leads to a kind of relationship with his partner and child that creates joy, "I look at my child and I am filled with happiness. Beautiful, clever, and my child ... I cannot believe it."

Mia recommends equal sharing as a path to happiness:

It wouldn't be a bad thing if this came up with more families. Then perhaps one wouldn't see quite so many mothers ... who don't look too happy and who are running around in circles. Perhaps a completely new kind of father ... If more people could apply this model, it's possible that more people would be happier.

References

Gábos, A. (2018). Hungary Country Note. In S. Blum, A. Koslowski, A. Macht, & P. Moss (eds.) *International Review of Leave Policies and Research 2018* (pp. 198–204). International Network on Leave Policies and Research. Retrieved from: www.leavenetwork.org/lp_and_r_reports/.

Hobson, B., Fahlén, S., & Takács, J. (2014). A Sense of Entitlement? Agency and Capabilities in Sweden and Hungary. In B. Hobson (ed.) *Worklife Balance: The Agency and Capabilities Gap* (pp. 57–91). Oxford University Press.

Hungarian Central Statistical Office. (n.d.a) Population Census 2011 (Table 1.1.1.1, Population, population density, increase of population; Table 1.2.3.1 Families and persons living in families by family composition and average size of families.) Retrieved from: www.ksh.hu/nepszamlalas/tables_regional_00.

Hungarian Central Statistical Office. (n.d.b) Population Census 2011 (Table 1.1.6.1, Population by mother tongue, nationality and sex) Hungarian Central Statistical Office. Retrieved from: www.ksh.hu/nepszamlalas/tables_regional_00.

Hungarian Central Statistical Office. (n.d.c) Population Census 2011 (Table 2.1.7.1, Population by religion, religious denomination and main demographic characteristics, 2011) Hungarian Central Statistical Office. Retrieved from: www.ksh.hu/nepszamlalas/tables_regional_00.

OECD (2016a). *Family Database* (Chart LMF1.2C. Maternal employment rates by age of youngest child, 2014 or latest available year.) Retrieved from: www.oecd.org/els/family/LMF_1_2_Maternal_Employment.pdf.

OECD (2016b). *Starting Strong IV: Early Childhood Education and Care, Country Note, Hungary.* Retrieved from: www.oecd.org/education/school/ECECDCN-Hungary.pdf.

OECD (2019a). *Employment: Time Spent in Paid and Unpaid Work.* Retrieved from: https://stats.oecd.org/index.aspx?queryid=54741.

OECD (2019b). *Gender Wage Gap (indicator).* Retrieved from: https://data.oecd.org/earnwage/gender-wage-gap.htm.

OECD (n.d.a) *LFS by Age and Sex – Indications: Employment Population Ratios.* Retrieved from: www.oecd.org.

OECD (n.d.b) *OECD Family Database* (Chart LMF2.2.A. Patterns of employment in couples with children, 2014.) Retrieved from: www.oecd.org/social/family/database.

Plantenga, J., Remery, C., & Takács, J. (2012). Public Support to Young Families in the European Union. In T. Knijn (ed.) *Work, Family Policies and Transitions to Adulthood in Europe* (pp. 180–201). Basingstoke and New York: Palgrave Macmillan.

Takács, J. (2013). Unattainable Desires? Childbearing Capabilities in early 21st Century Hungary. In L. Sz. Oláh & E. Fratczak (eds.). *Childbearing, Women's Employment and Work-Life Balance Policies in Contemporary Europe* (pp. 179–206). Basingstoke and New York: Palgrave MacmillanWorld

World Population Review (2019). *Total Population by Country 2019.* Retrieved from: http://worldpopulationreview.com/countries/.

12

USA: Southern California

Alicia Márquez[1]

Xochitl and Felipe, an undocumented Mexican immigrant couple, live in an unassuming part of Indio, Southern California. Cities famous for their luxury hotels, large golf courses, internationally known music festivals, and important sport tournaments surround them. Xochitl and Felipe don't play golf or watch polo matches. When they are not working for pay, they rest and squeeze in time with their daughters. Their two-bedroom, one-bath apartment is on the second floor of a modest complex, comfortable and clean, with functional furniture. Toys can be seen all over the place but not on the floor. The children's room is cozy, with artistic and colorful drawings on the wall made by a proud Felipe.

On weekend days, Xochitl and Felipe's girls, 2-year-old Sonia and 4-year-old Viviana, ride bicycles in the parking lot. Xochitl is slim, with long black hair, and an enigmatic smile that evokes Mona Lisa's. She quietly sits on the fence watching. Felipe, shorter and skinnier than his wife, exudes energy while he chases his daughters' bikes, laughing often. The girls look like a pair of happy, active, defiant little dolls. The pretty picture of a happy family enjoying a Sunday afternoon belies the emotional challenges that the couple confront daily in their struggles for survival. Playing in the parking lot next to their home is a symbol of the reduced physical area of this family's world.

Because they have not been able to obtain legal status in the country, the couple lives under the constant fear of being caught and deported. Going back to Mexico would mean the loss of opportunities for their American-born children. They live close to Xochitl's job, and Felipe tries to avoid traveling far for work. They avoid public gatherings, such as

[1] Francine M. Deutsch wrote the profile of undocumented Latinx immigrants.

dance halls or other meeting places, because they are afraid of raids by Immigration and Customs Enforcement Police (ICE). Their social life has been reduced to family affairs in their neighborhood and excursions to Walmart or Target on Sundays.

Xochitl and Felipe consider their relationship to be completely equal. She cooks and does laundry; he showers their two children and cleans the house. Each one takes care of one of their girls in the evening. How did these two Mexican nationals, who immigrated to the United States while they were adolescents, come to negotiate this egalitarian agreement, contrary to the conservative cultural norms in which they were raised?

As of 2016, there were 5.4 million undocumented Mexican immigrants in the United States (Krogstad, Passel, & Cohn, 2018). In general, Mexican Americans, both immigrants and those born in the USA, tend to be Catholic (61%), while the rest are divided among mainline Protestants, evangelicals, and unaffiliated (Lopez, 2015). The largest Mexican immigrant population lives in Southern California, comprising 13% of the residents there. Sixty-seven percent report limited English proficiency. Undocumented Mexican immigrants typically work at unskilled or semi-skilled jobs that carry no benefits and pay minimum wage or less, such as service jobs or construction. As of 2017, 21% of Mexican immigrants lived below the poverty line (Zong & Batalova, 2018).

Undocumented immigrants live with the constant fear of apprehension. Some describe it like living in jail (Chavez, 2013). They are not eligible for most federal assistance programs, including the food, health care, and income assistance. However, several states, including California, do provide medical coverage to children and prenatal care to undocumented women (National Immigration Forum, 2018; National Immigration Law Center, 2019). If employed in an enterprise of more than 50 employees, undocumented Mexicans are entitled to use the family and medical leave act, which mandates 3 months of unpaid leave for family care or serious illness.

However, they are unlikely to be able to make use of it, given the wide-spread noncompliance with the law, their inability to afford the lost income, and their vulnerable position vis-à-vis their employers (Armenia, Gerstel, & Wing, 2014; Gerstel & McGonagle,1999)

Of the over 5 million children living with at least one undocumented immigrant parent, an estimated 79% are US citizens (Capps, Fix, & Zong, 2016). As US citizens, they are eligible for federal benefits, such as food stamps and childcare subsidies, but often their parents are afraid to take advantage of those benefits because their immigration status might be exposed (Villarreal, 2018). If the family is low-income, the children are eligible for Head Start, a federal preschool education program, regardless of immigration status (National Immigration Forum, 2018). However, only 37% of 3- and 4-year-old children of undocumented parents are enrolled in preschool compared to 48% of American children overall (Capps, Fix, & Zong, 2016).

A study of work–family life in Mexican immigrant, Mexican American, and Anglo parents of 7th graders in southern California and Arizona found that the Mexican immigrant mothers spent fewer hours in paid work per week (25) than their Mexican American (32) and Anglo (30) counterparts. Their husbands' proportion of housework (16.5%) was lower than the other groups of men, who did approximately 25% of the housework, primarily because the immigrant Mexican women spent more hours in housework than the other women (Pinto & Coltrane, 2013).

From Poor Children in Mexico to Poor Parents in Southern California

Both Xochitl and Felipe were born and spent their childhoods in Mexico as the youngest child in their families. They both grew up without their fathers; their mothers used physical punishment to discipline them, and they were both supported financially by older siblings who had previously immigrated to the United States. Xochilt and Felipe were teenagers when they met in California.

Her Story

Xochitl grew up with her parents and two older sisters in Chiapas. Her father used to disappear for long periods of time, coming back at will, always broke. Her mother never worked outside the home. Xochitl fondly remembers a friend, who she considered like a brother, who used to support her family financially. Regrettably, he died the same day she turned 11. Unable to find a job in Mexico, Xochitl's older sister moved to the USA and started sending money to support Xochitl and their mother. Xochitl remembers being poor but always having enough to cover her basic needs, including candy. Her sister continued sending remittances, even after getting married. Xochitl's sister and brother-in-law eventually invited her to live with them in California. For a year Xochitl's mother resisted, but finally, under the popular Mexican idea that life in "el Norte" is better, she agreed. Coming to this new environment without knowing the language or the customs was very challenging for the teenager. Xochitl completed the 7th and 8th grades, but the stress was overwhelming and, at 15, she decided to go back to Mexico. She lived there for one year, happy to be with her mother but struggling to readjust to the seemingly antiquated Mexican culture. When her father returned home, wanting to reconcile once more with her mother but repeating the abusive behavior that Xochitl remembered, she decided to return to California to finish high school. Because she had a valid tourist visa, she was able to travel legally across the border. A few months later, at her sister's house, she met Felipe.

His Story

Felipe was the younger sibling of Xochitl's brother-in-law. Felipe left Hildalgo and had intended stay with his brother in California for just 2 years, enough time to save money to pay for the university in Mexico. He planned to become either an architect or a systems engineer. Growing up with his five siblings had been hard. His father had worked in a retail store, and died after being shot several times by robbers when Felipe was a year old. After that, his two sisters, 4 and 6 years older than he, became his full-time caregivers while their mother worked long hours. His three brothers had to interrupt school and go to work to help support the family. Felipe senses that they still resent having had to sacrifice so much for the family. Their efforts made it possible to pay the bills and always have food on the table, but never as much as Felipe wanted. He remembers his mother coming home every day after dark. Instead of enjoying the children or resting, she dedicated nocturnal hours to sewing, trying to earn a little more money for their survival. Felipe's mother had no time to play. The only interactions he recalls are scolding, nagging, or spanking. As soon as he was old enough, Felipe was taught and ordered to do housework: to cook and clean the house. Unlike his brothers, he was able to graduate from high school, and to dream of becoming a professional.

Their Story

Xochitl and Felipe met at their siblings' home when she was 17 and he was 19 years old. It wasn't the love at first sight made famous in Latin telenovelas. They were cordial to each other but kept a respectful distance. Life for Xochitl and Felipe was relatively quiet. They both had jobs earning minimum wage or less, enough to save a little bit after helping with household expenses. Sometimes, on weekends, with other friends, they risked going to movies or dances. All their acquaintances were Latinxs, most in the same legal situation, trying to maintain a low profile. They didn't travel far, having to take the bus or get rides. Felipe recognized that he was attracted to the enigmatically somber and delicate Xochitl, but at the time they met, Xochitl had a boyfriend she loved very much. However, observing the way Felipe helped around the house, how responsible he appeared to be, and how attentive he was toward her, won Xochitl's heart. She ended the other relationship and soon after the couple moved into one of the rooms. His willingness to help was the main attraction, a quality that Felipe continues demonstrating today. Xochitl explains:

> He is very responsible, attentive. He worries a lot for the house to be ok and for me to be ok. That is what I like about him. He is not like those men, "When she comes, she'll do it; it doesn't matter that she comes from work, she has to do it." He is not like that, and that's what I liked. Even before we had the girls, before we got together. Even today I tell him, "That is why I married you, because you help me a lot."

They married one year later and rented their own apartment. They became parents at age 21 and 23. Both pregnancies were planned and welcomed. In contrast to many other Latinx couples who want larger families, they agree that they don't want any more children. Xochitl and Felipe explain that they want to take good care of their two daughters. Caring for them consumes all their finances, energy, and time.

Felipe has been involved in the care of the children since they were born. Xochitl's mother came from Mexico after both deliveries during the *cuarentena* (the 40 days after childbirth, a time in which the new mother traditionally receives help from family members so that she will have time to rest and recuperate). This was a big help, but although Felipe was employed during the day, he took care of the babies at night. After grandma left, the couple negotiated taking turns for diaper changes and bottles.

Immigrants Have To Work Hard

Xochitl has a full-time job at a dry cleaning store, managing the front desk. Although she studied in the United States, Xochitl doesn't consider herself to be fully bilingual because she only spoke English at school. Nonetheless, she does know enough English to deal with customers. In the summer, when the "snowbirds" leave the area, business is light, and her schedule of 10:00 a.m. to 5:00 p.m., Monday through Friday, and every other Saturday, is manageable, and "even enjoyable." But from September to May, things get really busy, and "even ugly," when the paid work hours become longer, the heat of the machinery seems unbearable, and the bosses urge the workers to hurry up. Obtaining one day, or even a couple of hours off to take the children to the doctor or to the dentist can be a nightmare.

Felipe is a roofer when there is work, and a cook in a restaurant when it becomes necessary to make ends meet. Working in construction in Southern California during the summer is tough. Felipe's crew starts very early, trying to advance as much as possible before the afternoon heat becomes overwhelming. Despite the grueling conditions of the work, Felipe says, "I like to work because it keeps me busy, and I forget everything, and I like what I do. I feel good working. When I don't work I lose energy, and I don't like it."

When the economic crisis caused havoc in the construction business, Felipe's job became unstable. On the days when the company doesn't call him, he tries to help a friend who contracts small jobs. On those jobs, they don't stop until the work is finished, sometimes very late in the evening. At times, he also works in a restaurant in the neighborhood. Recently, his uneven schedule left him with weeks of only 2 or 3 days' employment.

Felipe's hourly income in construction is higher than Xochitl's, and the additional hours at the restaurant meant that he made a bit more money than she over the past year. Yet, his salary isn't always enough to cover the whole rent, and some months she must contribute from her paycheck. When necessary, the couple resorts to food stamps.

When the work slows down and Felipe is unable to be the main provider for the family, it takes a toll on his self-esteem. He explains:

Not that I am *machista* but like I feel uncomfortable that she works; that she helps me and that I stay in the house. I am uncomfortable; I don't like it. Because now, she is my wife, they all are my responsibility. But she is working and she tells me, "I'll help you." We don't fight about it.

However, he is hopeful that soon things will be back to normal. His company is buying some new equipment that he solely has been trained to use, and he expects that money will be coming in steadily once again.

One Diaper for Him, One Diaper for Her

When their children were born, Xochitl and Felipe established their turn-taking diaper-changing rule: one dirty diaper Xochitl, one dirty diaper Felipe. Xochitl is not the stereotypical Mexican mother who is over-protective of her children and limits their interactions with their father. Felipe is certainly not the macho man who feels that bringing money to cover the house expenses, demonstrating authority, or providing protection from outsiders is enough. They both see themselves as equally responsible for the well-being of their family.

On a typical day Felipe leaves the house earlier, so Xochitl takes care of the girls in the morning, giving them breakfast and driving them to the babysitter's place. They are trying to get 4-year-old Viviana into a Head Start program, but for now she is waitlisted. Although extremely suspicious of caregivers who are not relatives, they had no choice but to rely on someone outside the family for childcare, which adds to the couple's stress.

Felipe usually gets home earlier in the afternoon, and cleans up the day's mess before Xochitl arrives an hour later. She makes dinner for the girls. Their efforts at having dinner together, however, have failed. The girls don't sit still and what is supposed to be a positive family interaction used to end up in a daily fight. Now their routine provides some peace. They feed the girls first. Then Xochitl takes them to one of the bedrooms while Felipe eats alone. When he is done, they switch places and Xochitl is able to enjoy her food on her own.

After dinner, each parent takes one of the girls to watch TV or surf the internet in different rooms. For the rest of the evening each adult rests while "his" or "her" girl plays nearby. Because the children are very competitive, the physical separation avoids sibling fights and gives the couple some respite. Xochitl believes that this strategy has been effective in controlling sibling rivalry but has created a gap between her and her husband that they are trying to overcome.

Contrary to the popular belief that mothers have closer relationships with the children than fathers, Felipe appears to be more emotionally involved with their daughters than Xochitl. Felipe says of the older daughter, "[She] is jealous of the other one; I feel she needs more love. I am always with her." His involvement in his children's emotional lives can evolve into gatekeeping and conflicts with Xochitl. She explained:

> He always wants to be the one to solve their problems, with both girls. When I want to do it, he doesn't allow me because he says that I don't know how to talk with them; that instead of soothing them I make them feel worse. And there are times when he makes me mad and I tell him, "No, let me, because you always want to talk with them," but most of the time it is he who talks to them to solve the problems.

Felipe's gatekeeping extends to baths. Xochitl complains, "I used to bathe them every day, but my husband said that I wasn't doing it right." The girls' hyperactivity and their long hair can be challenging for somebody with limited patience. He explains:

> I have told her to bathe them carefully, and not to yell when she is bathing them because they are afraid ... She is improving, but I prefer to tell her, "No, I better bathe them," because they come and ask me, "You bathe us, Daddy." She makes them suffer while bathing them, throwing water on their faces.

Nevertheless, Felipe admits, "I get angrier than her when the kids misbehave. She is more patient than me."

A recent incident challenged their parenting. The pressure of not having enough work, added to the regular stresses of their lives, had been taking a toll on their relationship for months. Xochitl's subtle comments regarding her old boyfriend didn't help. The last straw was Felipe's having an extramarital encounter. They almost separated. Although they have tried to avoid involvement with the local authorities since they immigrated, the couple had a big altercation at home and the neighbors called the police. Felipe says, "We had a fight, without blows but with some pushing and awful yelling, in front of the girls." Nobody was arrested, but because the children witnessed the fight, the County's Child Protection Service required them to take parenting classes. They attended all the sessions and tried to implement most of the suggestions. Xochitl and Felipe were thankful that what they learned made them better parents and also brought them closer together. Felipe explains:

> We have more communication. We had lost it. When I fell in love, it was because we had great communication. I used to come from work ... we lived for a while together, before we got married. We had a lot of trust. And I liked

that very much, because when I grew up I didn't have anybody to talk with ...
I know she still has the thorn of the infidelity bothering her, but like it has made
us to regain some of the trust. I regretted it and after we went to classes ...
I understand ... I have always loved her, I do love her, but I am sorry because
I really don't want to lose my daughters, or my wife. I do love her.

"No, I Don't Want to Pick Up. You Do It"

Felipe and Xochitl don't follow a structured routine for housework. They
bicker about who is doing and should do what. Felipe believes it is he who
wants the house to be clean, and starts by saying "Let's go pick up, do
this." But he admits, "Sometimes she starts cleaning, saying 'Look at this
mess,' like when there are many dirty dishes." They both agree that Felipe
does most of the cleaning, "He vacuums, sweeps, cleans." He proudly
boasts that, "If there are many toys on the floor I pick them up because
I don't like it ... it bothers me that the things are on the floor."

She disputes the claim that he does everything. "He says that I leave
everything for him, but that is not the case," complains Xochitl. He tells
her, "You are taking advantage of me." Felipe insists that because his wife
is home in the mornings, she should be doing more then. She explains that
the daughters occupy all her time, "I am not sitting down watching TV ...
Do you believe they are going to let me watch TV or talk on the phone or
be doing things?" On the one hand, she argues with him and refuses to
cooperate as much as he wants. On the other, she admits, "I am conscious
that I do not cooperate enough." She doesn't hide her strategies. She
avoids chores sometimes by waiting for him to come home or simply
waiting for him to do the work; sometimes she resists the work more
directly. She confesses her response to his entreaties to help, "'No, I don't
want to pick up. You do it.' ... he gets mad and comes, and I go out and
help him or sometimes I don't help." Xochitl defends herself by noting
that she helps by "entertaining the girls while he cleans." When asked,
though, he concedes that it is 50/50, that she does more in the mornings
and he does more in the afternoons. "I feel that there are days when she
does more and other times I do more." Nonetheless, she is worried about
the possibility that one day he will refuse to continue this way. "He
wouldn't help again and I would have to do everything. That would be
terrible for me."

Xochitl does do the laundry. Felipe says, "My wife doesn't like me
doing the laundry because I put all the clothes together. 'Don't touch the
clothes, I'll wash them.'" Because they don't have a washer and drier at

home, laundry involves trips carrying baskets up and down the stairs. When Felipe complains that something he wants to wear is dirty, however, Xochitl replies "Then, wash it yourself," and he does.

Xochitl also does more of the cooking. She makes healthy dishes for the girls, and spicy food for the adults. She enjoys leftovers and her plan is to cook every other day.

> He gets upset because he wants ... me to cook something different each day. But I don't cook every day. Like today I cooked enough for two days, but he doesn't like it. He wants me to do something different each day. And I don't do it. The day that I don't cook ... he does it ... he cooks something only for him.

Their Social World: "She Treats Him like a *Mandilón*"

Felipe and Xochitl have to buck the social norms surrounding them. Their division of housework and childcare is extremely unusual in their social world and draws a lot of criticism. Most of the couple's relatives and friends believe that males are not supposed to help at home. In fact, they expect to be waited on. Felipe explains, "We have also friends ... they come and the women have to warm up the food for the husbands, 'I want my plate' and the men sit down and the women get up at 5 a.m. to make their breakfast." Felipe describes how men talk to their wives when a baby needs a diaper change, "She [the baby] is dirty; you change her." Felipe sums up, "My friends are very *machistas*, my cousins are also very *machistas*. Sometimes they tell my wife, 'Your husband helps you a lot. He helps you to do this, to do that.'" He reports that among themselves, they mock him, "She treats him like a *mandilón*" (i.e., henpecked husband). "But," he asserts, "I don't care because I am comfortable, and I do it because I don't want my daughters to look for a macho when they grow up." He chalks up their attitudes to ignorance.

Xochitl's co-worker is incredulous when she hears that Felipe bathes the children or takes them to the dentist, "My husband would never do that." Her mother and sisters tell her, "If I had a husband like that ... I would even kiss his feet." Xochitl is criticized by men and women alike. Even the husband's ex-lover, in a phone call that revealed the affair, taunted, "You make him sweep and mop; you make him do chores." Relatives warn her that their division of labor is the reason that Felipe had an affair. Xochitl reports that when her mother and sister discuss her sister's divorce with her, they warn, "You should stop being so demanding because the same is going to happen to you."

"I Do Believe Husband and Wife Should Help Each Other"

They both speak of "helping each other." Their sharing is not motivated by a belief in gender equality, at least not explicitly. They simply believe in cooperating with each other. Felipe does not shrink from highly gendered activities like changing diapers, and he rejects the essentialist idea that women have greater parenting ability, "I believe they [men and women] are all alike because they both have to care for the children."

Their non-stereotypical views carry over to their child-rearing. Unlike many other Latinx couples, Felipe and Xochitl allow their daughters to play soccer with the neighbors' boys. Felipe appreciates Sonia's interest in stereotypical male chores, "They see me doing things in the house. I was cutting wood, measuring it, and my older daughter got a pencil and started imitating me. And that doesn't bother me, but I have seen others who [would say] 'Go away, that is for boys.'" As mentioned earlier, Felipe hopes that his modeling will encourage his daughters to find men who will not have *machista* ways.

Breadwinning, however, is the one caveat. Notably, he views breadwinning, not as a source of power but of responsibility. He says, "When I am not working I am only thinking, 'Now the electricity bill is due, the cable bill is coming.' It is not that I feel superior because of the money; I just feel less preoccupied, less stressed." Xochitl, however, shares breadwinning without resentment. She does not believe that he deserves less respect when he can't find employment. "He feels that if he doesn't work he has no value, is worthless. He thinks that, but I don't see it that way."

Yet Xochitl does connect money and masculinity. She asserts that he is in charge of the money because he is "the man." "All Mexican or Latino families, the man is the one who is in charge." However, she goes on to reveal her ambivalence, "Sometimes I don't know if I am kidding or I am serious." In fact, she scoffs at the idea that the man should have more authority because he earns more money, "That is simply *machista* mentality [laughs] ... I think that he doesn't have that mentality and he shouldn't have it because I would complain to him and tell him that shouldn't be." In fact, according to Felipe, Xochitl usually makes purchasing decisions.

If I say "I like this," she says "I don't like that color" and we always end up buying what she wanted ... Sometimes I get mad because I choose something ... regarding the girls. "I like those shoes," and I am happy, but when I go to pay for them. "No, [Xochitl says] I like these other ones." One time I really got mad and I said, "I am going to buy whatever I want." She said "OK." But most of the time ... she chooses everything.

Xochitl seems to be driven by her sense of entitlement. Felipe's willingness to share the work was a key reason that she married him. She
doesn't use feminist language, but she refuses to meet the standards
expected of her, such as making a different meal for her husband every
night. Although she claims that he makes decisions about money, both
of them recount how she reverses his decisions. Clearly, she rejects the
role of woman as less than equal or as servant. She was outraged when
her husband's male cousin pushed her to go help in the kitchen when she
was at his house for dinner, and refused to do so, despite Felipe's
embarrassment. "Why didn't he help his wife? Because if my husband
and I are guests ... Why didn't he help his wife to cook, instead to be
humiliating my husband or me?"

Xochitl invokes the deficits of her own father, who was never around,
to explain why she insists on a husband like Felipe, "I am like this with
my husband because I didn't have my father ... I tell him, 'You have to
help me, you have to do that,' and I make him do things. ... I want my
husband to be like I wanted my father to have been."

Felipe's experience in his own family of origin has also shaped his
views. Felipe grew up with a single mother and his older brothers and
sisters. He hated watching his mother, who struggled to support them,
wake up at 4 a.m. to prepare breakfast for his brothers. He credits his
mother for making sure he was educated, and for teaching him to take on
"feminine" tasks, "There are many men who don't want to change
diapers because they feel like women, but I don't have a problem because
my mother always taught me, since I was a child." However, his mother's
excessively long day at her job left her impatient and as a result, he
reports, "she would scold us, yell at us, hit us, nag very badly." He
wonders whether that accounts for his own impatience with his children.
He does yell, and at times has hit them. Nonetheless, Felipe is determined
to be a different kind of father.

Felipe is deeply committed to involved parenthood, "Everything I do,
I do it for them." And to him, this means, not only supporting them
financially but investing hands-on time with and care for them. He wants
to create a childhood for Sonia and Viviana with better memories than he
has of his own. Felipe recounts a story to illustrate his doing just that:

> [One day] we started cooking. We prepared tuna burgers. I was doing it and
> my daughter came and I started teaching her. That was about 3 months ago.
> And not long ago she asked me, "Daddy, can we make the tuna balls again?"
> because we made the balls and then pressed them down before frying them.
> I told her, "I'll fry them so you don't get burned by the oil." They remember.

She tells me of things that we did together ... The children keep in their heads all their memories, so when they grow up they will get closer to the parents who dedicated more time to them.

Neither Felipe nor Xochitl attended college, and they both have low-status, low-paying jobs. Their equal sharing, therefore, provides strong evidence that equality can be created in the absence of a high level of education, explicit egalitarian ideologies, or a wife's greater earnings. They live within a very traditional social environment, but they resist many of the social pressures of the patriarchal culture that is part of their heritage. Their equality appears to be constructed within a struggle for survival.

In the midst of their mutual complaining, they help and support each other. Felipe sums up his beliefs simply, "I do believe that men and women, wife and husband, should help each other, for their own good and for the good of the children. The children are going to be well, and are going to remember everything." He acknowledges that the rewards of equal sharing make it all worthwhile, "Like my mother says, 'Give love and you will receive love.'"

References

Armenia, A., Gerstel, N., & Wing, C. (2014). Workplace Compliance with the Law: The Case of the Family and Medical Leave Act. *Work and Occupations*, 41(3), 277–304.

Capps, R., Fix, M., & Zong, J. (2016). *A Profile of US Children with Unauthorized Immigrant Parents (Fact sheet)*. Migration Policy Institute. Retrieved from: www.migrationpolicy.org/research/profile-us-children-unauthorized-immigrant-parents.

Chavez, L. R. (2013). *Shadowed Lives: Undocumented Immigrants in American Society*. Australia: Wadsworth, Centage Learning.

Gerstel, N. & McGonagle, K. (1999). Job Leaves and the Limits of the Family and Medical Leave Act: The Effects of Race, Gender, and Family. *Work and Occupations*, 26(4), 510–534.

Krogstad, J. M., Passel, J. S., & Cohn, D. (2018). *5 Facts about Illegal Immigration in the U.S.* Pew Research Center. Retrieved from: www.pew research.org/fact-tank/2018/11/28/5-facts-about-illegal-immigration-in-the-u-s/.

Lopez, G. (2015). *Hispanics of Mexican Origin in the United States, 2013*. Pew Research Center. Retrieved from: www.pewhispanic.org/2015/09/15/hispanics-of-Mexican-origin-in-the-united-states-2013/.

National Immigration Forum (2018) *Fact Sheet: Immigrants and Public Benefits*. Retrieved from: https://immigrationforum.org/article/fact-sheet-immigrants-and-public-benefits/.

National Immigration Law Center (2019). *Medical Assistance Programs for Various States*. Retrieved from: www.nilc.org/issues/health-care/medical-assistance-various-states/.

Pinto, K. M. & Coltrane, S. (2013). Understanding Structure and Culture in the Division of Household Labor for Mexican Immigrant Families. In S. S. Chuang & C. S. Tamis-LeMonda (eds.) *Gender Roles in Immigrant Families* (pp. 43–62). New York: Springer.

Villarreal, A. (2018, December 21). Undocumented Parents Scared To Enroll Citizen Children in Benefits, Say Experts. *The Guardian*. Retrieved from: www.theguardian.com/us-news/2018/dec/21/us-immigrant-undocumented-families-benefit-programs-chip-snap-deportation-fears.

Zong, J. & Batalova, J. (2018). *Mexican Immigrants in the United States*. Migration Policy Institute. Retrieved from: www.migrationpolicy.org/article/mexican-immigrants-united-states.

13

USA: New England

Francine M. Deutsch

Veronica and Sam Callahan and Nick and Patty Ford are two of the rare equally sharing couples in the USA. Both intensely devoted to family life, they differ in two important ways. Veronica and Sam Callahan started with much more gendered arrangements and did not become equal sharers until Veronica went back to full-time employment, whereas Patty and Nick Ford shared the care of their children since they were tiny infants. Although both earn in the top third of the USA income distribution, Veronica and Sam have master's degrees and white-collar professions: Sam is a teacher and Veronica is an accountant; whereas, Patty has a master's degree, but Nick is a firefighter and has not graduated college.

Veronica and Sam: Family First

From the outside, Veronica and Sam's modest house in Northern Connecticut has nothing much to distinguish it from its neighbors. Inside, however, it is a different story. Prints and photos line the walls and shelves. What caught my eye, besides the requisite wedding, happy family, and adorable kid photos, were the items that spoke of their attachment to their historic town. Veronica and Sam's decision to settle in Murrayville was not the artifact of a job search, but the place where they wanted to raise a family. Those 19th-century maps and other town memorabilia on the walls were a testament to what I came to think of as their motto: Family First!

Even before kids, Veronica and Sam were exceptionally devoted to each other. She sheepishly revealed that they had gone into a joint business to be together during work hours:

We had this moment where we both realized that you know, why wouldn't we want to spend every waking moment together? Why? It doesn't make sense that you go to work 8 hours a day and you're apart from the people you most want to be with, right?

Although that ultra-romantic sentiment didn't last, and they eventually gave up the business to move to Murrayville, they express the same kind of devotion when it comes to their kids. When I asked Sam to describe Therese, his 11-year-old daughter, and Kenny, his 9-year-old son, he started by saying, "they are our life." Veronica told me repeatedly, "Family is more important than work to both of us." Unlike many middle-class American families, who seem stressed and whose children run from one organized activity to another, the Callahan's household seems calm. Despite Veronica's full-time job and Sam's contributions to laundry, cooking, and taking care of the children, ironically, the *Leave it to Beaver*[1] videotapes I see in their living room do not seem out of place.

The United States of America has a population of over 325 million people. It is 77% white, 13% Black, 18% Latinx (who can also be white), 6% Asian, and 1.5% indigenous people (U.S. Census Bureau [USCB], n. d.). Predominantly Christian (70.6%), 46.5% of Americans are Protestant (over half of whom are evangelicals) and 20.8% Catholic. Other religions represent 5.6% of Americans (1.7% Jewish and less than 1% each of Buddhists, Muslims, Hindus, and other religions). Twenty-three percent of Americans are unaffiliated (The Pew Research Center, 2015). Thirty percent of American households consist of a married couple with children, of whom 62% are dual earners (USCB, 2018).

---

[1] *Leave it to Beaver* was an iconic American television show that illustrated the ideal 1950s traditional family life.

Among Americans 20 years and over, 56.9% of women are employed compared to 69.3% of men (Bureau of Labor Statistics [BLS], 2019). Workplace discrimination against women is illegal, but, on average, women working full-time earn 82% of what men earn. They are also twice as likely to work part-time (24% versus 12%, respectively) (BLS, 2018b).

The Family and Medical Leave Act, the only national leave legislation, allows eligible men and women (slightly half of the American labor force) only 3 months of unpaid leave for family medical issues, including the birth or adoption of a new baby. Five states and Puerto Rico have some compensated paid family leave (Kaufman & Gabel, 2018).

There is no national childcare system. While mothers work for pay, 38.7% of families have no regular arrangement for childcare. Regular care is provided by fathers (17.8%), grandparents or other relatives (25%), or other non-relative care (e.g., family daycare, in-home nannies) (11.2%). Center-based care (which is usually private and may be for-profit) is used by 23.5% of families, including the 5.6% in Head Start programs (Laughlin, 2013). Head Start is a federal program for low-income children from birth to age 5 that funds early care and preschool education (Office of Head Start, 2019). The preschool enrollment rate is 40.2% for 3-year-olds and 67.9% for 4-year-olds (National Center for Education Statistics, 2018).

According to the most recent time-use data, in couples with children under 18 and two full-time jobs, mothers contribute approximately two-thirds of the parental time spent on housework (including food preparation and cleanup) and about 60% of the childcare time. In families where mothers work part-time, they put in more than three-quarters of parental housework time, and about two-thirds of the childcare time (BLS, 2018a).

Veronica works as a certified public accountant (CPA) at a local community hospital that is affiliated with a medical center. She has a special attachment to it because her children were born there. She had maintained a dream of working there ever since. Sam is a 9th grade English teacher at a middle school a half-hour's drive from their house. Every weekday morning Sam gets up and out to his job quite early, before anyone else is even awake. Veronica wakes up next and is responsible for getting the children off to school. Although they are old enough now to pick out their own clothes, and get dressed on their own, Therese is hard to wake and requires prodding to get through the morning routine. Veronica makes their breakfasts and their lunches and checks to make sure they have what they need to get through the day. Therese takes the bus to her school and Kenny to his, except on some days when Veronica drops him off on her way to her job.

The end of the day is Sam's responsibility. Most days he leaves his job at 2:00 in the afternoon, as soon as classes are over, so he can be home when his children get off the school bus. For a couple of hours each afternoon, he helps his children with their homework, does jobs around the house (e.g., laundry, cleanup), and usually gets dinner ready, although it is a dinner that Veronica has organized for him ahead of time – planning the menu, shopping for ingredients, and defrosting the chicken if need be.

When Veronica gets home around 5, they operate smoothly as a team. She pitches in to finish the dinner. And after dinner they either trade off or work together. Veronica explains:

> It's just whatever needs to be done around the house, as well as helping the kids out if they need help with homework. So we know each – he'll be doing laundry, I'll clean up from dinner. Then it's getting clothes ready for the next day, or getting lunches ready, getting the kids settled for bed ... We both do it. If someone has to do work, or if one of us has to do work on the computer or look something up on the computer, the other one will do getting the kids ready. It just all depends on what each of us has going ... It's never been you know, all me doing the baths, getting their pajamas ready, and reading them stories and tucking them in. We've always both done that.

Sam's comments about housework echo hers:

> I think typically I do more laundry. I do most of the laundry; she does most of the food shopping. Cleaning, I'd say it's kind of a split. Sometimes I'm more gung ho on it, and other times she's more gung ho. But yeah, I think that it's just you know whoever whatever needs to be done you just kinda do it.

Parenting middle-class school-aged children in the USA means a lot of driving. Veronica and Sam seamlessly share that task. For example, after dinner on a day they described as typical, Veronica dropped Therese off at soccer practice and went food shopping with Kenny while Sam cleaned up the kitchen. Then Sam went to pick up Therese while Veronica put away groceries.

Overall, they both see the division of labor as equal. Each admitted to moments of feeling that s/he was doing more, but then immediately took their spouses' perspective to argue that they contributed equally. Sam spends more time with his children, especially because he has school vacations and has the summer off. Veronica is clearly more of the planner. She plans the meals and shops for food, pays attention to permission slips for school, makes dentist appointments, and figures out what to do when the kids have a day off from school. But Sam backs her up by making doctor's appointments when she forgets.

When asked about the psychological aspects of parenting: the comforting, the worrying, the paying attention to children's psychological needs, both claimed that Veronica did more of that. She's the comforter, particularly for the daughter who is closer to her by both of their reports. But Sam expressed the kinds of worries about his children that bespeak an emotionally and psychologically involved parent. He worries whether his daughter should quit the soccer team where she never gets to play but has good friends, and whether his close relationship with his son interferes with his making friends his own age. He lies in bed regretting his impatience with his daughter. But despite his clashes with his daughter, the afternoon I visited their home, Sam very patiently checked her homework and then skillfully engaged her in a conversation about how technology had changed our lives to help prepare her for an upcoming exam.

Winter weekends with the Callahans usually mean a trip to Vermont, where Sam's extended family gathers to ski. Unlike other children their ages, who might spend school vacation in a program or summer vacation at a sleep away camp, Therese and Kenny also often go with their Dad to Vermont for school vacations and spend a lot of time there with him during the summer. Therese reported that she's been skiing with her father since she was 6, and laughingly complained about how on a recent school vacation her father would get her and her brother up early to spend the day skiing, "Yes, it was fun. It was tiring. It was really tiring, but it was fun. Because he [her Dad] likes to get up really really early to go skiing and so he would get us up at like 7:00!" In the summer, Grandma is there and cooks for the family, and until recently, when Veronica and Sam built a cottage on an abutting lot, the whole clan stayed together at Sam's parents' house.

The picture Sam paints is of relaxed family gatherings in Vermont with a lot of "helping hands," a lot of freedom for kids, but where he and Veronica retain ultimate responsibility for watching their kids. Sam told me that he lets them go off on their own, trying to replicate the freedom of the era when he grew up, without helicopter parents, when "nobody paid attention to what you did." Vermont is a place, "where everybody sort of knows everybody so there's a lot of eyes out there." But Sam does pay attention. He notes that his children "don't typically wander too far from venues that they can be seen." And adds, "When I haven't seen them for a while, I'll take a walk."

Surprisingly, given the equality in their current division of labor, Veronica spent 8 years as a stay-at-home mom. Their first days of parenthood, however, foreshadowed their current sharing. When Therese was born, Veronica had 6 months left of a 1-year full-time work requirement to get licensed as a CPA. She took a leave and then negotiated employment at half-time for a year instead of 6 months full-time. Therese was born in the summer, when Sam was home as well. Veronica describes how they muddled through life with a newborn together:

> We asked each other everything. Whenever we had a question or a concern, we would ask the other one. What do you think? Should we do this? I think back to how unsure you are on what to do when you have an infant ... I had her at age 32 you know. I went through college, worked, and yet you have this infant and all these things come up that you have no idea how to handle. So everything that came up we would ask the other one, what do you think about this? ... You know, whether it was what time she went to bed or what time we fed her.

Sam joked in a similar vein, "It's just hard because neither of you knows what to do really. I was looking for the instruction manual and couldn't find it."

Veronica struggled with long hours of breastfeeding, sequestering herself when they were in Vermont with the family, and waking up at night on her own. Except for that, however, Sam was fully involved, as Veronica describes, "We would go for walks with her, you know, just be together a lot with the baby. And he did change the diapers, bath, the whole nine yards. He was right there doing everything with me."

And after a month or two, Veronica started to pump breast milk so her husband could do one of the night-time feedings; however, she couldn't quite surrender control, "When she was up, I had to know how it was going. So I couldn't just roll back to sleep not knowing what was going on in the other room while he was feeding her." After the leave, Veronica worked 2½ days per week, including a half day on Saturday when Sam would take care of his infant daughter. He also picked the baby up the other 2 afternoons when she was cared for either by Veronica's mother or a friend. Veronica reported that other than doctor's appointments and socializing with other mothers, "he still did everything."

Then when Veronica finished the year and got her CPA, she quit her job and, except for some consulting, which she could do at home, she didn't work for pay for the next 8 years. Why? Veronica explains, "I always wanted to do that. That was my intention, I think, even before we had kids. I just didn't want to have them go to daycare. I just wasn't comfortable with that."

Sam concurred, and there was never a question of who would stay home. The division of labor was much more traditional during that period, with Veronica responsible for everything the children needed during the day, as well as the dinners, tidying up, and more of the laundry than she does now. But even then, when Sam came home they "shared responsibilities for the kids: bathtubs, reading at night, getting them to bed." Sam describes his role when he got home, "That's always been my focus – coming home, seeing them, and maybe even giving her a break ... We're just the type that it has always been about the kids. Even taking a break wasn't that desirable, when it probably should've been more so."

When their children were both in school, Veronica found a very flexible part-time job that would allow her to be home when they got home from school and take off if they were sick, but a year and a half ago she started working full-time at her current job. As Veronica picked up more hours of paid work, Sam upped his contributions to the unpaid work of the home. They split being home for the kids, and "he picked up a little more of the housework," Veronica explains, "because I wasn't home as often to keep things tidy – to keep laundry going. Dinners may not have been as planned out ... So I think he started to pick up a little more of that when I went back, even part-time." Veronica goes on to describe the change when she became full-time, "Now he gets the kids after school. He's always the first to get them now usually. Dinners, he's more involved with getting dinners going. And homework, working on homework with them, he's the first there to do that."

Remarkably, they express very little conflict over the division of household labor. He was a bit disgruntled when the house wasn't always tidy when Veronica was home all day; at the same time, he acknowledged, "that's something when you stay with the kids more you understand more." She complained that his recent involvement in their building project in Vermont took him away from routine childcare, but then reflected, "I know that the other piece had to get done, and I wasn't contributing enough in that department at all." Veronica did not have to cajole, nag, or insist to get Sam to share. He simply assumed more responsibilities at home once their paid work lives became equal.

Sam's job facilitates their equal sharing. His schedule also allows him to leave work in the middle of the afternoon. Sam reports working

40 hours, thwarting the trend of 37% of American college-educated fathers who work 50+ hours per week, displaying long hours as a sign of manliness and class status (Williams, 2013). Veronica is thrilled with the benefits of his job:

> Oh I think it's wonderful. I think having him home so much is just great for all of us because we can all share more time together. He has an equally large share in the kids' lives as I do. And I think for a lot of families that we know, the fathers are coming home at 7:00 at night after pretty much the whole day is done and the kids are ready to go to bed or winding down. Also the time that he has in the summer and over school vacations, I think that's definitely a positive for the family.

Sam chose education because of its family-friendly benefits. After college he went back to school to get certified. He confesses, "I think it was partially because I liked English. It was one of my favorite classes in college. But largely I have to admit, it was based on the lifestyle I thought I could live as a teacher." His father had been a teacher, as well, which had enabled the family to spend summers together in Vermont.

He likes his job working with kids and he "feels good about doing something that ... is a good thing – education," but he seems to like even more that it gives him so much time with his family. Although he's "starting to get a little tired of it in some respects," he does not seriously contemplate leaving because he doesn't know if he could "walk away from this world ... I get the summers off. It's great for raising my kids. I have the flexibility."

Veronica is very engaged in her job, and described how she likes learning how all the pieces of the institution are represented in the complicated tax forms that she's responsible for filing. Having this job makes her feel good about herself. Nonetheless, when talking about the relation between her career and her family, she asserted, "I still strongly believe that family comes first and it is more important than work life."

Veronica and Sam have unconventional jobs for their genders. Teaching is a predominantly female profession in the USA and many women choose it for exactly the reasons that Sam articulates: it is good for raising children. Veronica is a CPA, a predominantly male profession, with higher status than a high school teacher. Veronica pursued the career she wanted and never had to make any sacrifices in it to accommodate Sam's career. In fact, at one point, Sam thought he would have followed her to Washington, DC, if a job opportunity she pursued had come through for her there. Nonetheless, when I asked whose job had priority in the family, Veronica answered that it was Sam's. Her answer reflects the gendered nature of their parenting, despite their current equal sharing. Although Sam makes a bit more money because of Veronica's choice to work in a nonprofit rather than a high-paying accounting firm, that's not what gives his job priority in her eyes. Veronica feels both more responsible for being there and more entitled to be there for her children than Sam does, "If for some reason one of us would stop working – say ... [if] one of the kids was really sick or something. I think I would be the one. I don't know if that's just because I would want to be the one."

She also invokes his seniority and the benefits it entails. She interrupted her career, with the accompanying loss of income and seniority, however, not because she is less invested in her career than he is, but because she wanted to be home with her children. Sam reports that when she returned to full-time employment, "she struggled ... feeling a bit guilty that she wasn't necessarily home when the kids came home," even though when she wasn't there, he was.

Both Veronica and Sam grew up in more traditional households. Although their mothers did work for pay, their paid work was clearly secondary to their father's and was fit in around their parenting. Sam's mother was a nurse, but took summers off to take care of her children in Vermont. Veronica's mother started a seasonal business selling beach supplies in the summer where she could bring her children along as helpers. Their fathers, his, a teacher, hers, a firefighter, both took on extra jobs. Notably, although Veronica's father had a schedule that gave him 4 out of 8 days off, he used the time to earn money rather than to change the traditional division of labor: "My mother mostly did everything around the house – cleaning, cooking, washing clothes, laundry, ironing – all of it. She did all the housework. My father did the yard work, the repairs, the traditional father jobs."

Sam witnessed the same gendered division growing up, "My mom did most of the motherly chores and my father did most of the male-oriented chores." His sisters, however, made sure that he wasn't exempt from traditional female tasks. "I think one of the things that has impacted me as a husband is that I had three older sisters ... If they had to do it (e.g. washing the dishes), I had to do it."

Sam's upbringing, albeit traditional in some ways, did underscore the importance of time with family. His wonderful memories of summers in Vermont drove his decision to pursue a career that would afford time away from paid work. Even during the academic year, he prioritizes family over his job. He doesn't stay around after school nor does he put much time into preparing classes:

> There's always new stuff that I could be researching and trying to attack a topic a different way that I don't do as much because of time. Getting home and dealing with the kids, by the time I get them to bed, I'm not one at 8:30, 9:00 p.m. to get on the computer and figure out more ways or more information or create a new lesson plan.

Veronica and Sam did not become equal out of an explicit gender ideology that endorses identical roles for men and women, although they implicitly believe that husbands and wives should contribute equally to the family. When asked how it came to be that he contributes half of the household labor, Sam doesn't take very much credit, "I think my job just enables me to do a lot of that stuff. You know I get home at 3 o'clock. The kids are working on their homework; I'm working. I'll run down and throw a little laundry down. It's not a big deal."

The time Sam's job affords may facilitate their equality, but it doesn't explain it. He chose that job precisely because it would give him time and flexibility. Unlike many American men, Sam's identity is not caught up in either career advancement or money. Both Sam and Veronica have eschewed paths that might have been more lucrative. As Veronica put it, "Work isn't our life. Family is more important than work to both of us."

Veronica explains that Sam's current involvement grows out of his orientation to parenting from the beginning:

> I think that's why he is still so much a part of it now is because from day one he has been doing everything that I do, with the exception of the breastfeeding. I have friends who say, "The girls are only used to me putting them to bed and giving them a bath." It's never been like that in our house. It's always been the both of us.

Modest, like Sam, Veronica doesn't take credit for expecting and welcoming his involvement. Despite Veronica's attachment to the maternal prerogative to be the parent who stayed home, she saw Sam as an equal partner from the beginning of their lives as parents. She didn't expect to be treated as the expert parent or the parent in charge. She did not insist that everything be done her way. She made room for him to parent and they learned together. Sam sums up what they appreciate about each other: "just the caring and the focus on our kids ... that we're doing it together."

Nick and Patty: Equality on a Firefighter's Schedule

"I'm not the type of person that just watches TV all day and then come the weekend have my wife clean the house. I mean, that's ridiculous!" Nick Ford's self-description is quite an understatement. A lieutenant firefighter for a town in Rhode Island, Nick's job schedule entails two 24-hour shifts per week. The rest of the time he works nonstop taking care of his house and his two children: 7-year-old Eric and 5-year-old Annie Sue. Nick, who graduated high school and took only a few college courses, is living proof that a college degree is not a prerequisite to equal sharing.

Patty Ford, Nick's wife, works as an environmental planner for a nearby municipality at a 9 to 5 job, with some evening meetings. So during a typical weekday, Nick is home with the children. If his 2 work-days fall during the week, Patty's mother fills in.

I interviewed him in the summer when the kids were out of school. On Nick's 5 days off, he fed his children breakfast in the morning and lunch at midday, made beds, did laundry, watched them in the pool, took them out to the library, brought them along on errands, did home repairs, and played with them. He's the parent saying, "brush your teeth, brush your hair, all that stuff."

When Nick plays with his children, he regards it as more than recreation. Both he and Patty are proud of how their children excel in sports because of their Dad. He says:

> I used to ride my bike a lot; I run every day. I used to play baseball and stuff, and because of that, my kids at age 4 were riding bikes. They're playing baseball and soccer at upper level ... When we play, I instruct. So every time we play, they learn.

Patty said, "My son catches a baseball like you wouldn't believe, because his dad is out there throwing it with him."

Nick usually does the food shopping and has the dinner going by the time Patty gets home. Both of them are committed to exercising every day, and although he could go for a run by himself when she arrives home, often he incorporates his exercise into his time with children. He runs and they ride along side him on their bikes. So Patty's arrival at 5:30 or 6:00 doesn't necessarily mean a break for him. They finish getting dinner on the table together and are both involved in cleaning up after dinner and getting the children to bed. As Patty explains, "We're kind of tag teaming it. If there's a plate on the table, I grab it and throw it in the thing and then Nick is nagging someone to brush their teeth." She fondly describes bedtime, "We both have our little routines, where we read and ... then we both sing to [each of] them. Then we switch. Except for the nights that he's not there – the two nights – and then it would be just me." Their parenting day isn't over at bedtime, however; Annie Sue wakes up every night and asks for milk and Nick gets up to get it.

Although on weekends they divide the hands-on care of the children equally, Patty acknowledges that during the week, Nick does more of that than she. She explains her role:

> I have a funny way to describe it. I often say ... I'm the project manager of the house, the organizer and the planner, the one who is kind of behind the scenes ... I plan the doctor's appointments, the school activities. There's many sticky notes I have at home like, "Ask dentist about Eric's teeth," or "Nick, if you're going here, please don't forget to check on this."

Nick may take the children to the doctor, but Patty has written out questions for him to ask while he is there. The kids are on her mind all the time, even when she is at her job. Nonetheless, managing at the Fords does not mean that Patty has to nag or that Nick isn't paying attention. Nick sometimes humors Patty and her need to be in control. She admits:

> It's kinda funny ... the kids, they have backpacks and folders in it. And my husband will go through things, but he knows me, so he'd put it all back 'cause he knew that I'd want to see everything. So I'd come home, I'd automatically ... go through everything. I'm like, "Hey did you hear?" and he's like, "Yeah, I saw that."

According to Nick, Patty's greater education shapes the division between them, "My wife, she's educated. So she handles the school portion a lot with the kids, like the homework ... We both do the parent-teacher's conferences, but she's the one that writes questions out ... She takes care of the school stuff."

They agree that she is more attuned to the children's emotional needs. She is closer to their son than he and is quick to pick up on Eric's concerns, like anxiety about starting a new school. Nick admires the way she anticipates and talks to their son about his worries. She's also the disciplinarian. Nick defers to her, explicitly invoking her greater verbal skill:

> When it comes to discipline, if we're both there, she'll take the initiative to do it, and I'll back her up ... She takes initiative to discipline because she's very good at explaining why this was a wrong thing to do or wrong thing to say, while I'm not so good at explaining ... Obviously, if we're apart, then of course I do my best to explain. But if we're together, she jumps on it, which is good.

However, Nick's calm approach to his children's problems can also win out. For example, at times he has convinced Patty not to intervene to solve a problem at school, arguing successfully that working it out would be a learning experience for his children.

Nick has been a hands-on dad since Eric was born, but the origins of their sharing started much earlier. Patty recounted an incident that occurred years ago, an incident that shows her husband's willingness to do housework, his willingness to learn, and her sense of entitlement to share the work and to have it done well:

> I can remember from my college dorm room ... I had 409 [a household cleaner] in there. I said, "Oh, I gotta dust, do you want to help dust or something?" And I came back from the library and he'd used the 409 cleaner on the woodwork. He clearly doesn't do that today. He uses the Pledge.

Before their children were born, Nick worked as a production manager in a pharmaceutical factory. He put in 10 to 12 hours per day, sometimes 7 days a week. Patty did a much larger share of the household labor at that time. He then switched careers and became a firefighter, despite a huge pay cut. Why did he change? "It was the schedule ... because we were anticipating having a family." Unlike the typical American family whose division of household labor becomes more traditional with parenthood, theirs became less so.

Nick took vacation time when Eric was born and the two of them together struggled to learn how to take care of a new infant. Patty might have read all the books, but together they tried to put what she had learned into practice. Nick describes the overwhelming experience of new parenthood:

> The baby is crying, "Why is the baby crying?" "I don't know." "Is he hungry? Did he go poop in his diaper?" We'd take turns doing that: checking diapers, changing diapers ... I think we did a lot of bathing together because the baby was not in a bathtub obviously. We kinda did that together because it was all new to us. Not only that, but I'd be alone with the baby pretty soon – all by myself, you know. I'm trying to learn. What do I need to learn here?

Patty found nursing difficult. She didn't want to quit, but it was painful. And it was scary to discover that you couldn't do what you wanted or planned because "you're latched on." If you thought you were going to organize the closet, the baby might decide, "No, you're not; you're going to come feed me." She recounts how Nick supported and encouraged her by getting up for night feedings:

I remember when in the middle of the night and the nursing was just so bad, [he'd say,] "You can do this. It's great for the baby, you read about it. This is what you want to do." And sitting with me in the middle of the night. He wasn't nursing a child. There was no reason for him to be up, but he would be.

Soon Nick started giving supplemental bottles. Patty laughs, "That's the irony. I don't know how to give bottles to an infant, but my husband does."

Patty went back to full-time employment and they began the schedule that they still follow. Nick recalls those first days when he was totally responsible for an infant:

At first I'm like, "What am I going to do with this baby?" Basically, when she went to work, I had this baby – feed him breakfast, entertain him until he got tired, and then he went to sleep. Whenever he woke up, pick him up, feed him again. Then just kept trying to entertain him because I think that's what babies need, right? ... I don't know what to do next, so I kept on trying new things to see if the baby liked it. I even tried some videos like Baby Einstein, and maybe that's why he reads good now. I don't know, but he seemed to really like that.

The division of labor they established with their infant son has persisted, with adjustments for the ages of the children. Toddlers require a lot of parental attention so Nick couldn't get as much of the housework done during the day at that stage as he can now. School-aged kids mean more dropping off and picking up, but more time for household tasks.

Their journey has seen conflict. Patty mentions earlier disagreements over Nick's getting the housework done while she was at work, but touts their open communication about it, "I just want time with my kids during the weekend. I'm not around that much so I've always communicated, 'Whatever you could get done over the week is more family time for us.' I've always been straight about that." Nick reports that Patty learned to back off on insisting the housework be done perfectly, which was not possible with children in tow. She stopped mentioning that he missed a corner dusting.

Who is to stay home with a sick child, however, was a thorny issue until Patty got her current family-friendly job. Nick sees their jobs as equal and considers Patty, who earns as much as he, a co-breadwinner. Yet calling in sick was very difficult for him:

I've always been told growing up that your job is important. Don't screw with your job. I was never one of those persons to call out sick if I was not sick, and I rarely got sick so I never called out ... I only work 2 days a week. Why does it happen on the days I have to work?

When I first interviewed them, Patty was working as an environmental consultant and had some flexibility, but the flexibility came with costs. Nick was struggling within himself to figure out what was fair. Patty can do some work from home, he argued, whereas "if I call in sick, they get someone to replace me . . . but then again she has responsibilities too, to her job." Nick told me that they had started to alternate, but Patty said that although he had called out sick once or twice when she had a meeting, usually she stayed home or got her mother to come. She admitted getting upset about it, but also acknowledged that her job was more flexible than his. More recently, her new job allows her to stay home for sick children without any penalties. Now she does it without resentment.

Nick loves being a firefighter. He gets a "good feeling" helping others. He also likes the camaraderie, "We call each other brother, brother or sister, because we do have a female. He's got my back; I got his back. We do take care of each other that way. I like that." Nick appreciates the family-friendly environment where people are genuinely concerned if something is wrong in your family. That was missing in the corporate world where "the first thing they ask [is], 'Where's your doctor's note?'"

Patty's recent change has also taken her out of the corporate world and into a municipal job. She's much happier with her current job, especially because it is so family-friendly. Besides having sick time for children's illnesses, if she has an evening meeting she can take compensation time, which has allowed the family to take some additional vacations this year.

Patty's obvious competence shines through in her technical descriptions of zoning requirements, resource management, and environmental issues. She feels much better at this municipal job where she doesn't have to cut corners or "fake it," the way the corporate environment sometimes required. Her current job also better reflects her training in forestry, which makes it feel "like coming home." And although she still feels a pang that her career as an environmental scientist doesn't give expression to the creative part of herself, she feels "blessed" to have this job. Previously, she said she would trade having fewer hours for less money, but now, although fewer hours sounds nice, she wouldn't want to give up the benefits that come with her income. She likes being able to take her kids to Disneyworld and wants to be able to save for college and retirement.

Patty and Nick make about the same amount of money currently. He might get a promotion, which would give him a raise, but both are very clear about their shared income. Nick describes that they are each responsible for paying different bills, but "we consider our money, our money ... We don't have separate accounts. It's our money – totally equal." Both consider themselves co-breadwinners.

A number of factors contribute to the equal relationship that Nick and Patty have developed. Neither of them subscribe to essentialist ideas that men and women are fundamentally different. Although Nick sometimes defers to Patty, he attributes that to her greater education rather than her gender. Neither of them acts like she is the expert simply because she is the mother. Both of them believe that men and women are equally capable of caring for children. Nick says:

> Is there any difference in the ability? No, I don't think so. Just like I think women can do anything they want. If they want to be a firefighter – if you can do it, you can do it, right? No, I don't think so, because there are some women that aren't good mothers, and there're some dads that aren't good dads.

Patty concurs. In response to the question about whether there are differences between men's and women's capability to care for children, she answers, "Well, they can't nurse ... but other than that, no, absolutely not."

Not only does she believe that Nick is capable, she expects him to share the load. Patty's sense of entitlement extends back to college when she handed Nick a dust rag and suggested he help. Along the way, they have worked through the division of labor with "communication." She points out that although Nick does the trash and she trims the hedges, in general, "The daily stuff, we both do it and we both do it well. If we see it needs to get done, we just get it done. It's not, 'that's your job; go do your job.' I think it evolved that way ... [through] the communication, the talking, yeah."

Nick touts his wife's ability to explain things. She demonstrates the relational skills that have been associated with a more equitable division of family labor (Benjamin & Sullivan, 1999). When Patty argued that if Nick got the housework done during the week, they would have more family time on the weekend, her arguments held sway.

Nick's job schedule certainly helps. The schedule was not an accident, however. Nick left a higher-paying job in large part because he wanted that schedule. Both Nick and Patty also note that other firefighters with Nick's schedule do not make the same choices as they do. Nick says, "I know some people in my profession who drop off their kid at a babysitter even though they're home. Why, I don't know, but they do."

Patty credits Nick:

> I do feel blessed because of his schedule, and the person he is. I really should go back to that, because I know that there are other people in that same position who still put children in childcare even given 5 days off ... It has to do with who Nick is as a person.

Nick believes in family care. In fact, he balked when I referred to the preschool they attended as childcare. Unlike the firefighters who take second jobs, Nick would not want to work more even if it meant more pay, "It'd be nice to have more money but I like being with the kids. I don't want to give up that part. I mean, I could do a part-time job. I could start my own landscaping business. A lot of people do. But, I'd rather be with the kids."

Nick's passion for being home with his children is fueled by his determination to be a different kind of father than his father, who abandoned their family when Nick was 11 years old:

> My father wasn't around and I can be around, and ... I'm going to be. I've always said I would never take off from my kids like he did. I said in my head, even before I was having kids, "If I had kids, I'm never gonna take off from them. I'll always be around."

Nick's love for his wife may also underwrite their equality. He speaks of her with great admiration and care. It is worth it to him to do a lot of housework when he's home during the week so they have time to be together on the weekend. Patty confided that when she was struggling with breastfeeding, manly Nick, who prides himself on his physical fitness, rides motorcycles, and fights fires, told her, "If I could nurse, I would do that for you."

It is easy to see how Patty benefits from equal sharing. She can go to her job confident that her children are well cared for, and, unlike many women who work full-time, she doesn't strain under a double shift. Equality enriches Nick's life as well. He may sacrifice leisure and forfeit economic dominance in the family, but he enjoys fun times with his wife and experiences her abiding appreciation. The priceless relationship with his children has changed his life: "They come up and say, 'I love you, daddy,' you know, just that. Just the unconditional love, that's great."

Two American Couples

The stories of these two couples reveal some similarities that may support their equality. Both Veronica and Sam and Patty and Nick earn roughly

equal salaries. The economic equity in these two couples may be necessary for them to create equality (or, at least, may facilitate it), but it is
not sufficient. Perhaps more important, for American men, both Sam
and Nick have unusual work lives. Men's investment in career and/or
breadwinning, which often requires long hours away from the family, is
usually a barrier to equal sharing, even in families that believe in
equality. In contrast, both Sam and Nick have jobs with schedules that
enable them to spend a lot of time with their children. Sam puts in fewer
paid work hours than the average man in the USA and seems less
invested in his career; Nick's schedule gives him time off during the
week. Both had previously worked in the corporate world, but specifically chose these careers instead because of their compatibility with
hands-on fatherhood. Both eschewed maximizing their incomes. Nick
took a big pay cut to become a firefighter.

Both Patty and Veronica opened the gates to parenting and welcomed
their husbands in. Although Veronica maintains an unchallenged prerogative to be the stay-at-home parent if one is needed, in all other ways
she is as open and encouraging to Sam's involvement as Patty is to Nick's.
The couples' remarkably similar accounts of the early days of parenting
emphasize that they learned how to parent together. Neither assumed the
mother was the expert or was in charge. They spoke with humor about
the challenges of trying together to figure out how to manage an infant's
needs. Patty and Veronica reinvented motherhood by letting their husbands in, and their husbands reinvented fatherhood by going "the whole
nine yards" as Veronica put it. Veronica and Patty also expected and felt
entitled to their husband's equal involvement. Patty persuaded her husband to do more of the housework so they could have more leisure time
together. Veronica, although traditional enough to want to be home with
her children for 8 years, was not traditional enough to believe that in a
dual-earner family more childcare or housework was the mother's
responsibility. These couples were free to reinvent motherhood and
fatherhood because they all rejected essentialist beliefs that mothers had
more natural ability to parent than fathers (Gaunt, 2006).

Moreover, these two couples were similar in that they approached all
aspects of life together. Both evinced an unusual level of togetherness.
Notably, Veronica and Sam had shared a business together before they
became parents. Nick expressed an unusual level of empathy when Patty
struggled with nursing, and was convinced to do more housework by the
argument that it would give them more time together over the weekend.
Both couples also put a strong emphasis on family time and family care.

Neither couple had used paid childcare, which created more room and more need for paternal participation.

The families they grew up in influenced them in different ways. All four of them had mothers who had been employed, yet none had experienced a nontraditional division of labor by their own parents. Nonetheless, although Sam's parents had traditional roles in the division of family labor, his sisters made sure that he did his share of the female chores. Thanks to them, he is no stranger to washing dishes or doing laundry. Likewise, the happy memories he has of spending summers in Vermont underlies his desire to have a more relaxed lifestyle that doesn't revolve around career and, consequently, leaves him available for childcare. For Nick, in contrast, unhappy memories propel him to be a different kind of father than his was. Because his father abandoned the family when he was 11, he is determined to be a very different kind of father, one who is there for his kids.

In both of these families, equality was created with a minimum of conflict. When resentments do arise between Veronica and Sam, they are quicker to convince themselves that they are in the wrong than to instigate an argument. In Patty and Nick's family, however, good-natured negotiation is the norm. Patty persuaded Nick to do more of the housework. Nick got Patty to let up on her standards. They discuss and persuade each other when problems come up with their kids. Although the styles of the two couples differ, the overwhelming sense they both give is of well-functioning cooperative couples, working together. They don't invoke gender equality to explain why they share. Their equality appears to be a byproduct of how they cooperate with each other to make their dual-earner families work, rather than the result of the ideological goal of gender equality.

References

Benjamin, O. & Sullivan, O. (1999). Relational Resources, Gender Consciousness and Possibilities of Change in Marital Relationships. *The Sociological Review*, 47(4), 494–820.

Bureau of Labor Statistics (2018a). *American Time Use Survey*. (Table A-7C: Time spent in primary activities by married mothers and fathers by employment status of self and spouse, average for the combined years 2013–2017.) Retrieved from: www.bls.gov/tus/tables/a7-1317.htm.

Bureau of Labor Statistics (2018b). *Highlights of Women's Earnings in 2017*. Retrieved from: www.bls.gov/opub/reports/womens-earnings/2017/home .htm.

Bureau of Labor Statistics (2019). *Economic News Release.* (Table A-1: Employment status of the civilian population by sex and age.) Retrieved from: www.bls.gov/news.release/empsit.t01.htm.

Gaunt, R. (2006). Biological Essentialism, Gender Ideologies, and Role Attitudes: What Determines Parents' Involvement in Child Care. *Sex Roles, 55*(7), 523–533.

Kaufman, G. & Gabel, S. G. (2018). United States Country Note. In S. Blum, A. Koslowski, A. Macht, & P. Moss (eds.) *International Review of Leave Policies and Research 2018* (pp. 443–449). Retrieved from: www.leavenetwork.org/lp_and_r_reports/.

Laughlin, L. (2013). *Who's Minding the Children? Child Care Arrangements: Spring 2011.* (Table 1: Preschoolers in types of child care arrangements: Spring 2011). Retrieved from: www.census.gov/prod/2013pubs/p70-135.pdf.

National Center for Education Statistics (2018). *Digest of Education Statistics.* (Table 202.20: Percentage of 3-, 4-, and 5-year-old children enrolled in preprimary programs by level of program, attendance statistics, and selected child and family characteristics 2017.) Retrieved from: https://nces.ed.gov/programs/digest/d18/tables/dt18_202.20.asp.

Office of Head Start (2019). *Head Start Programs.* Retrieved from: www.acf.hhs.gov/ohs/about/head-start.

The Pew Research Center (2015). *America's Changing Religious Landscape.* Retrieved from: www.pewforum.org/2015/05/12/americas-changing-religious-landscape/.

U.S. Census Bureau (2018). *America's Families and Living Arrangements: 2018.* (Table H2: Households by type, age of members, region of residence, and age of householder: 2018 and Table FG1: Married couples family groups, by labor force status of both spouses: 2018). Retrieved from: www.census.gov/data/tables/2018/demo/families/cps-2018.html.

U.S. Census Bureau (n.d). *Quick Facts: United States.* Retrieved from: www.census.gov/quickfacts/fact/table/US#.

Williams, J. C. (2013, May 29) Why Men Work So Many Hours. *Harvard Business Review.* Retrieved from: https://hbr.org/2013/05/why-men-work-so-many-hours.

14

Brazil

Maria Auxiliadora Dessen and Cláudio V. Torres

João and Cecília Silva have been married for 7 years. They live in Brasília with their 7-year-old son, Davi. Both have received bachelor's degrees, which is unusual in Brazil (IBGE, 2019). Cecília works 40 hours per week as a public employee involved in the supervision and control of Brazilian flora and fauna. João is a commercial airline pilot, working at a very well-known Brazilian company.

"When I'm Here I Take More Care of Him than She Does"

The family's current division of domestic labor has been structured around João's job. His work schedule demands that he be absent from home for approximately 3 days per week. He explains, "I have lunch at home. I leave after lunch. I stay 2 days completely away, and on the 4th day I am home for lunch too. Thus, in reality, it is only 3 days away from home."

In João's absence, Cecília is totally in charge of the family's routine. She takes Davi to school in the morning, she picks him up at the end of the morning to have lunch together at home, and then takes him back to school by 2:00 p.m. to attend an extracurricular program. At the end of the afternoon, she picks him up again and they return home. On these days, Cecília, who works for pay from 8:00 a.m. until 6:00 p.m., with a 2-hour lunch break, is always in a rush because they live far from the city center where the school and her job are located.

On the days when João is at home during the week, he takes the bulk of childcare responsibility. He reports:

> I would say that when I'm here I take more care of him than she does. I spend the whole morning here with him. So I give him breakfast, bathe him, and put

181

on his clothes, and take him to [school]. She basically only brings him from [school] in the car to home, and when he gets home I bathe him, give him dinner, put on his pajamas, brush his teeth, and put him to sleep ... because I miss the child. I love smell of his hair; I love the smell of it.

Brazil is the largest country in South America with the biggest population in the region: approximately 210 million inhabitants (Worldometers, 2018). Brasília, where the interview was conducted, is the capital of the country. It has approximately 2.8 million inhabitants and the lowest rate of illiteracy (2.08%) in the country (Companhia de Planejamento do Distrito Federal, 2018).

A lot of cultural and ethnic variation is present in Brazil (Torres & Dessen, 2008). Beginning with colonization in the 16th century, up to the middle of the 20th century, immigrants arrived from Portugal, Italy, Germany, Holland, and Japan, settling in different areas, to work mainly in agriculture and cattle ranching. However, the majority of the population are descended from African slaves, who were not freed until 1888. Official data for the first time in 2016 confirmed that the majority of the Brazilian population identified as Black (8.2%) and *Mestiços* or *Pardos* (46.2%) (mixed Black and either indigenous or White) (Instituto Brasileiro de Geografia e Estatística [IBGE], 2017).

The population is predominantly Christian (89%), with the majority being Catholic (64.6%), 22.2% Protestant, and 2% Spiritual (IBGE, 2011), making Brazil the largest Catholic country in the world. Other religions were identified by 3.1% of Brazilians, and are mainly represented by the Afro-Brazilian religions such as *Candomblé*, *Umbanda*, or Native traditions. Yet, in Brazil, Christianity is also often mixed with African religions (Torres & Dessen, 2006). Eight percent of the population are unaffiliated, and a small minority of people are Jewish, Buddhist, or Muslim.

Brazil has huge economic and social inequalities. The richest 10% of Brazilians earn, on average, 45 times more than 40% of the poorest Brazilians, as well as having better access to education and jobs. Moreover, 22% of the population lives below the poverty line (IBGE, 2017). Over half of the population 15 years old or older is illiterate or did not finish elementary school, and 1.4% of the children between 6 and 14 years old have never attended school (UNICEF, 2017). Only 12% of the adult population have college degrees (OECD, n.d.). The most common household type is couples with children (40%), followed by extended families (21%), couples without children (14%), single person households (12%), and single parents with children (10%) (United Nations, 2018). In households with couples, 62.7% are dual earner (IBGE, 2011).

The position of women in the Brazilian economy is still unequal. Women earn 23% less than men, and the gap is relatively greater at higher levels of education (Canineu & Carvalho, 2018). Inequality continues at home as well. A national survey found that women who had paid jobs outside their homes spent, on average, 20 hours and 11 minutes per week taking care of the house, while men spent in average 10 hours and 7 minutes a week on the same tasks (Pesquisa Nacional por Amostras de Domicílio, 2011).

The law allows women 4 months of paid leave on the birth or adoption of a child, with an optional extension to 6 months, while men have 5 days of leave with an optional extension to 20 days (Governo do Brasil, 2018). There is no national childcare system, although preschool children may attend public kindergarten and preschools. However, the majority of poor children do not have access to them. Although the Brazilian government supports poor families with social welfare programs, such as "*bolsa família*" (a monthly minimum salary), it is not enough for the needs of those families (Campello & Neri, 2013).

João enjoys taking care of his son and sharing activities with him, "I like to take the kid to school or to buy popcorn at the end of school, to share, to play. When I arrive at school earlier we play ping-pong. Then I think it's a nice contribution. I enjoy it; I enjoy being with him too."

João explains that on the days when he is present, he tries to compensate for his absence by spending more time with his son and by giving Cecília a break. She elaborates, "In these moments, I use the time to sometimes have some leisure, read a book, do some yoga, something that I like to do, such as go for a walk in the garden." But she also appreciates the time they spend together with Davi. Cecília believes that the family moments when they play cards all together, watch a movie together, or go for a walk are possible because "everything is very equally divided" between her and João. She can relax while he retains responsibility for caregiving. João reports:

> Rarely does she go out alone, and I stay alone with him ... I go out with him for a walk in the neighborhood, to play ball ... She wants to come along, but without the responsibility of being with him at this time to take care of him. She knows that I am the one who is responsible for him, so she comes along just to enjoy that family moment.

Cecília is in charge of managing the family's agenda. She organizes their social life, makes doctor's and dentist's appointments, and arranges school affairs. Like other middle-class Brazilians, they buy clothes abroad and, because of João's profession, they agreed that he would be responsible for that. He also takes Davi to the doctor's because of his free days.

The two parents pursue different activities with Davi. With João, Davi shows more interest in "masculine" activities, such as playing ball, watching Formula 1 races, or watching soccer. With Cecília, he goes to the pool, goes for a walk in the park, does a puzzle, or paints.

The parents differ in discipline, as João explains:

> I am even stricter than she, because I am a man. And I think she is way more flexible, she is more relaxed ... With me, I treat him like a prince, I carry him around, but when we need to, I say, "Dear friend, I am the one who rules here, and you are the son."

However, Cecília is the stricter parent when it comes to feeding. For her, it is very important to have meals at the right time, whereas for João, it is better to be more flexible, for example, to delay lunch to have another hour at the swimming pool.

Davi seems to be closer to the parent who is most available, to his dad on his days home and to his mom when she is the sole caregiver. Cecília notes, "When [João] is with Davi ... he is really with him, with body and soul. He is there 100%, he is donating himself, he is giving all attention he can." She admits that when she is with Davi, she is often worried about managing everything, "I am, at the same time, thinking about the dishes, or an appointment that I have to schedule ... the market that I have to go to."

But João acknowledges her greater patience with the child, "I think it is natural, in the sense of the animal instinct. The mother usually has more maternal instinct, of being together, caring, and being patient."

Housework

Because they have a housekeeper, which is typical for rich and middle-class Brazilian families, João and Cecília are free during the week from domestic tasks, like laundry, cleaning, ironing, and cooking. Even during the weekend, the housekeeper leaves them prepared food. Cecília describes how they share some of the remaining household tasks:

> That would be to set the table, be it for breakfast, dinner ... to warm up the food, because food is basically ready, and on the weekends, cook some

pasta ... We divide things a lot, and sometimes he ends up doing a little more, to compensate for the days that he is not at home ... Regarding feeding, cooking, and setting the table, it would be equally divided, really, considering the days he is at home and the days that he is not, right?

João adds:

We're always sweeping and washing dishes, like this morning for breakfast. We cooked lunch together and while one was making a juice, the other was cooking, one was washing, and the other was bringing Davi to eat. So yeah, I guess I'm pretty active these days I'm home again, and when I'm not, of course, she assumes all functions.

João is also involved with other kinds of tasks, such as the organization of the cabinets, the towels, bed linen, or separating dark from white clothes. He asserts that he and Cecília equally share of all the additional little day-to-day tasks not done by the maid, such as making a specific meal or a different dish, or organizing the guestroom when someone is visiting them.

João always does the typical Brazilian big monthly shopping for the family. Cecília buys some food, bread, and vegetables in the middle of the week. João also assumes the home repairs, mixing these tasks a little bit with his leisure activities when he is home:

I can see a program on television, something, then I stop and from there I'll do something and fix something in the house. But I wash enough dishes, I cook, and there is a task, well, very, very important, I think, which is also being the liaison with our maid here at home.

Although the couple has routines for domestic labor, from time to time they exchange tasks. Cecília comments:

Let's suppose that he takes more care of maintenance, and I take care of the market, but from time to time, he also buys things at the market, and I take care of maintenance. Thus, this way everything is very natural, with small adjustments throughout the relationship. Little things, right? And everything in a very intuitive way, with a lot of sensitivity, and a lot of attention given one to the other.

The couple is very attuned to each other's needs. For example, if João arrives at home very tired, Cecília continues taking care of Davi so that he can rest. She elaborates:

[We] are very careful in knowing when the other is tired, and when is the time to step in ... I think that João is a very involved person, he is always paying attention to my needs, so when I am sick, when I am having my period ... [if]

he is at home, he responds, you know? We have this exchange, I give him the ball and vice versa.

Having a housekeeper allows the couple to be together without worries about cooking and cleaning during the week. Unlike other middle-class families, however, João and Cecília take complete responsibility for taking care of their son; their maid does not do childcare.

"It Was Something Very Natural; There Was No Negotiation"

Cecília and João got married when she was pregnant and they were living in Rio de Janeiro. Although Cecília did not have a job then, the Silva family has shared housework since the beginning of their marriage. At that time, she was attending courses and studying to apply for her dream job in a government environmental institution. She reports that they established a division of labor without serious conflicts or even explicit negotiation:

> This was very natural, due to the sensitivity of each of us, one paying attention to the other, knowing that this is the time for you to step down, or to step in, to be in charge of some responsibilities, an obligation in that moment. So it was something very natural; there was no negotiation.

When Davi was born, they also started sharing childcare without explicit negotiation. Although Cecília breastfed, at 4 in the morning João gave the child a bottle so that she could "sleep a little more during the night." When Davi was 5 years old, Cecília got a full-time job in Brasília, so the family moved there from Rio de Janeiro. They adapted to their new schedule in a natural way. Although João supports her career, he also misses the time when her energies were completely devoted to the family:

> She was fully available to meet our desires and wishes before … it's not a complaint, but an observation … Her work has decreased her available time to do things for us.

Paid Work and Family Balance

Cecília's challenging government job entails writing technical reports and analyzing lawsuits about the environment. She says of the agency where she is employed, "I feel I am very fulfilled because it is a place that I always wanted to work at, something that I used to say since I left college." João points out that she was hired after her success on a very competitive exam in which 8,400 applicants vied for 30 positions. Cecília is satisfied with her salary, her co-workers, and her boss. She also values the financial independence her earnings provide, as João explains:

> It is not about the money itself, but it is about the possibilities that money gives you to have an opinion and make it happen, to create a chance for the child or for herself. "No, I'm going to do X, a gym, even if it is more expensive, but I'll give myself this right."

Nonetheless, Cecília is stressed by her long hours. She leaves home at 7:30 a.m. and is not back home until 7:30 p.m. When João is absent, her morning routine with Davi often makes her late for her job. She feels relaxed there only when João is at home. According to her, his job strongly affects their family life and, consequently, her productivity at her job:

> I think it affects my work because everything is very tight, our schedules are tight, and I do not have him here to help me to put the uniform ... Sometimes I arrive late for work and then I have to work overtime, and sometimes when he is not home I do not have time to work overtime and that makes me feel very stressed.

It is easier for João to concentrate fully on his job. Unless the child is sick or his wife is facing problems, he is able to work without worries:

> I think when I'm in aviation I can completely forget my role as a father or as a husband, and I can really focus on my professional side ... My family life, in general, is good and I feel balanced, healthy and happy. Then I go to work without major problems, without taking any problems from home to work.

João says of his career, "I have the satisfaction of being able to do what I do well. I know that technically I am a very good pilot." He is also very satisfied with his salary, which is almost 10 times as much as the average Brazilian earns (Empresa Brasil de Comunicação, 2015).

Although both of them have prestigious jobs and treat the two careers as equal, Cecília believes that her husband's career commands more respect:

> His profession is rarer ... no one ever saw an airplane pilot. Nobody ever talked to an airline pilot. So people tend to give a little more importance and value to his career ... Environmental issues as a career is still undervalued ... I think people still do not know exactly what our job is, what we do, and what the effects our work has on ... the preservation and conservation of the environment.

In the last 2 years, João turned down two career opportunities, including one to become a commander, which would have entailed a promotion and a significant raise. He gave up these chances to enhance his career, he explains, because he didn't want to compromise the quality of his life with his wife and son. As commander, for example, he would have had to spend 5 or 6 days away from home. In fact, for the sake of the family, João is planning to limit his work to Brasília, working and earning less than he does now:

> I'm trying to make a change. I'll give up this "glamor" of visiting the world to others, to stay only here, in Brasília: to fly here in Brasília, to sleep almost every day at home … to take my son to school, to see my wife, to have a greater family contact.

Cecília would like him to be at home every day so she could have lunchtime free. She also plans to reduce her daily paid work hours from 8 to 6, despite a significant financial loss. She wants to have more time, not just for the family, but also for herself, "to go to a gym, to read a book, to play the guitar or to study a language."

What Explains the Equality of this Brazilian Couple?

Typically in Brazil, fathers are far from playing an equal role (Vieira et al., 2014). Married fathers are not used to cooperating with their wives on domestic tasks, although recent studies have indicated a small increase in parental sharing (Carvalho, Franco, Costa, & Oiwa, 2012; Jablonski, 2010). Fathers participate more in activities like playing, bathing, and taking a child to the doctor. But these subtle trends, observed especially in the middle to upper class, do not extend to household chores, which are done by Brazilian mothers even when fathers are available. Those tasks are seen as feminine (Vieira et al., 2014).

The resistance to change reflects widespread social pressure on women to place motherhood at the center of their identities, and on men to maintain masculine identities by eschewing female tasks (Bossardi, Gomes, Bolze, Crepaldi, & Vieira, 2016). The macho man Latin culture is very strong in almost all Brazilian sub-cultures, particularly in the Northeast and South (Torres & Dessen, 2008; Torres, Porto, Vargas, & Fischer, 2015). According to Cecília, men tend to be more selfish and individualistic than women.

João is different. For example, he takes their son to places rarely frequented by fathers. He recounts:

> Once I took him to a birthday party and I was the only father there. There were eight mothers with children and I was the only father. And I take him to the

pediatrician or dentist. So compared with other fathers, I believe I do it more on the days that I'm here.

What then, can explain why their marriage, differs from the norm in Brazilian society? The equality in the Silva's family is supported by four key factors: 1) the structure of their jobs; 2) their experience in their families of origin; 3) their views of fatherhood and motherhood; and 4) their marital relationship.

The Structure of Paid Work

During the interview, João emphasized that he is always trying to compensate for his absence from home. On the days he is home, he points out, he can be totally dedicated to the family; he does not need to rush like other dads. He has the time to take his son to the doctor or to go to the city park. Cecília notes that it is only his job-related absence that prevents him from contributing even more, "Compared to other men, when he's at home, he assumes so much. And he is a good husband, a super dad. It is more on account of his profession that he is out so much."

Although his days at home allow for João to take as much responsibility as he does, they do not ensure it. Presumably, many other pilots play a much more typical masculine role even if they could be available to take a bigger share of domestic labor. João reports that his motivation to be the kind of father he is grows out of his own experience growing up.

Families of Origin

Although João's father was the breadwinner, the emotional tone and the division of labor in his family of origin were nontraditional. João's parents' loving relationships with their children, grandchildren, nieces, and nephews inspired him to forge that kind of relationship with his own son, "I want be for my son what my parents were for me."

João describes how his father's behavior defied conventional masculinity, "He was not a macho man. He was a man who helped with the housework, helped to educate his children." His parents strongly conveyed that care of a child was not the exclusive domain of mothers:

> Our parents who have helped us to see ... the mother by the side of the father, or the man on the woman's side. They helped us to see that the function of the couple is to take care of the child ... things that have helped me as a father too, as being close to my child and not letting it be only with the mother.

Cecília added, "He [João's father] was always a person who cooked, washed the dishes, cleaned things at home. So I think that culturally, he ended up getting these characteristics from his own father."

Cecília's father also defied masculine stereotypes because he was the more emotional parent, more easily prone to crying. However, he did not share housework and childcare. Having noted her mother's dissatisfaction with this traditional division of labor during her childhood, Cecília is critical of her father's failure to take children to school, help with their homework, fix their backpacks, or help get them into their uniforms. "It was always my mother who took those responsibilities." Her mother, however, eventually succeeded in getting her father to change. "About 10 years ago he began to take a bit more of these functions at home. And now he even cooks and irons when he needs clothes [laughter]. It took a long time but it happened."

Views of Fatherhood and Motherhood

Despite their egalitarianism, João and Cecília believe that some aspects of parenting differ by sex. João says, "It is human that the woman is one way, and the man another ... Perhaps this experience for the child, to see that there are two different sides, will give him a more complete upbringing." But both of them think that whatever is instinctual in men and women is also shaped by what they have learned in childhood. João believes that the woman has been taught to dream about being a mother since childhood and the man to pursue a prestigious career.

Cecília says about motherhood:

> I think it's also a very instinctive thing. I usually say that, from the moment the baby is born, the feeling you have is that someone installs something inside your head, a program to be a mother, and that probably comes from what we learned from our mother and our grandmother that is in our memory.

She believes that becoming a mother made her a much better person, and sees the same change in her husband, even though he is a man and she, a woman, "I find that what fits me also fits him as a human being." Cecília's valorization of João's parenting contributes to their ability to share. She never gatekeeps; she is happy when she sees João playing with their son, giving him attention, putting him on his lap and to sleep, or bathing him. She appreciates having more time to herself after her hectic days when he is absent.

João feels rewarded for his type of fatherhood. He says:

> I know I'm not perfect, I have my flaws, my moments of fatigue, my moments
> of my lack of patience. But on the other hand, I lay him on my lap; I love;
> I bathe; I put on clothes ... And I'm learning along the way ... I'm developing
> myself to be a better father. I believe this also ends up having an evolution for
> me as a person, a complete human being ... I am proud when I hear my son
> talk to the teacher or someone else, "I like my dad; my dad is cool."

Their Relationship

The strength of the couple's relationship is key to their equal sharing of
family work. João points to the similarity in their education as part of the
foundation for their equality, "We both had the opportunity to finish
college too, so we have a very high level ... So I guess that this puts us in a
very close position, distinct areas of mutual respect." He also expresses a
strong sense of fairness in explaining his involvement, "I do it in order not
to leave my wife with all the responsibilities ... because I think this is not
fair or correct. If she works, if she tries ... I also have to make an effort to
be with my son, at home."

But many couples share a similar educational background and profess
a belief in fairness without achieving equality. The emotional tone of their
relationship may be what sets them apart. João explains:

> Before we had the child, we always had a very open relationship, very out-
> spoken conversations, and we would talk about our internal feelings, our fears,
> because in ... conflicts, usually an attack is a response to fear ... because
> you're defending yourself, so we have a capacity to be open to the other while
> we still have fear.

João also jokes that he is one of the last romantics alive. He showers
Cecília with attention from the little gifts he brings home to opening her
car door. More importantly, they are very sensitive to the needs of each
other with respect to the division of labor, showing flexibility and mutual
understanding. Both of them believe that they are a "good team." João
comments:

> From the moment that for some reason a task is getting a little heavy for one of
> us, or one of us feels a need, needs a relief, needs to do something, then this is
> stated. But not as a criticism, but is expressed in a companionship manner. We
> are a team here, which we like very much. As a tennis game, there is not a
> winner, the two of us have to be constantly lifting the ball in the game, so that
> the ball does not fall, the two have to be throwing the ball.

João does not feel criticized when his wife gives him feedback about his parenting, "The way she points out some observations, it is not criticism or judgment. It is to reinforce something that for some reason I am not seeing or at some point I'm exaggerating, and she warns me. Then she helps me in our everyday lives." Their communication, which strongly supports equality, reflects the Brazilian cultural notion of *jeitinho*, that it is possible to find a solution to a problem even if it seems there is no way to reach it (Torres & Dessen, 2008).

João sums up:

> I believe that Cecília is my soulmate and she feels that I'm her soulmate. So there is this feeling of complementarity, empathy, strong friendship. We know that neither of us is walking alone, that we are really a team and that our son is part of this team along with us too. So this effort we do, that energy that we bring with us is love. And this love is also the one I see in my father and my mother and that I see in her father and her mother, which is the energy and strength that give us the opportunity to become better, not only as a couple but as parents. So that's it: love and soulmate.

References

Bossardi, C. N., Gomes, L. B., Bolze, S. D. A., Crepaldi, M. A., & Vieira, M. L. (2016). Desafios de ser pai em uma sociedade em transformação [Challenges of Fathering in a Changing Society]. In L. V. C. Campos, E. P. Rabinovich, & P. S. V. Zucolloto (eds.), *Paternidade na sociedade contemporânea: O envolvimento paterno e as mudanças na família* (pp. 81–100). Curitiba: Juruá.

Campello, T. & Neri, M. C. (eds.). (2013). *Programa Bolsa Família: uma década de inclusão e cidadania* [Family Grant Programe: A Decade of Inclusion and Citizenship]. Brasília: IPEA.

Canineu, M. L. & Carvalho, A. (2018). *Working for Less in Brazil*. Human Rights Watch. Retrieved from: www.hrw.org/news/2018/03/08/working-less-brazil.

Carvalho, A. M. A., Franco, A. L. S., Costa, L. A. F., & Oiwa, N. N. (2012). Rede de cuidadores envolvidos no cuidado cotidiano de crianças pequenas [Caregivers Network Involved in Daily Care of Preschool Children]. In M. G. Catro, A. M. A. Carvalho, & L. V. C. Moreira (eds.), *Dinâmica familiar do cuidado* (pp. 63–109). Salvador: EDUFBA.

Companhia de Planejamento do Distrito Federal (2018). *Pesquisa distrital por amostra de domicílios: 2015* [District Sample Household Survey: 2015]. Retrieved from: www.codeplan.df.gov.br/wp-content/uploads/2018/02/Resumo-PDAD-Distrito-Federal.pdf.

Empresa Brasil de Comunicação (2015). *Renda média domiciliar per capita do brasileiro é R$1052, diz IBGE* [Average Home Income Per Capita of the Brazilian is R$1052, says IBGE]. Retrieved from http://agenciabrasil.ebc.c om.br/economia/noticia/2015-02/rendimento-domiciliar-capita-do-brasileiro-e-de-r-1052-mil-diz-ibge.

Governo do Brasil (2018). *Lei trabalhista garante Licença-paternidade e outros direitos aos pais* [Labor Law Guarantees Paternity Leave and Other Parental Rights]. Retrieved from: www.brasil.gov.br/noticias/emprego-e-previdencia/ 2018/08/lei-trabalhista-garante-licenca-parternidade-e-outros-direitos-aos-pais.

Instituto Brasileiro de Geografia e Estatística (2011). *Censo Demográfico 2010* [Demographic Census 2010]. Retrieved from: www.ibge.gov.br/home/estatis tica/populacao/censo2010/educacao_e_deslocamento/default.shtm.

Instituto Brasileiro de Geografia e Estatística (2017). *Síntese de indicadores sociais: uma análise das condições de vida da população brasileira – 2017* [Synthesis of social indicators: an analysis of the living conditions of the Brazilian population – 2017]. Retrieved from: https://biblioteca.ibge.gov.br/ visualizacao/livros/liv101459.pdf.

Instituto Brasileiro de Geografia e Estatística (2019). *Brasil em síntese. Educação: anos de setudo e sexo* [Brazil in Summary. Education: years of schooling and sex]. Retrieved from: https://brasilemsintese.ibge.gov.br/educacao/anos-de-estudo-e-sexo.html.

Jablonski, B. (2010). A divisão de tarefas domésticas entre homens e mulheres no cotidiano do casamento [The Division of Household Labor Between Men and Women in Everyday Married Life]. *Psicologia: Ciência e Profissão*, 30(2), 262–275.

OECD (n.d.). *Education at a Glance, Brazil*. Retrieved from: www.oecd.org/ education/Brazil_EAG2013%20Country%20Note.pdf.

Pesquisa Nacional por Amostras de Domicílio (2011). *Definições fundamentais e aspectos do questionário com destaque para trabalho e rendimentos* [Fundamental definitions and aspects of the questionnaire with details regarding the work and earnings]. Retrieved from: www.ibge.gov.br/home/estatistica/indi cadores/sipd/segundo_forum/segundo_pnad_continua.shtm.

Torres, C. V. & Dessen, M. A. (2006). The Brazilian *Jeitinho*: Brazil's Sub-Cultures, its Diversity of Social Contexts, and its Family Structures. In J. Georgas, J. W. Berry, F. J. R. van de Vijver, C. Kagitçibasi, & Y. H. Poortinga (eds.), *Families Across Cultures: A 30-Nation Psychological Study* (pp. 259–267). Cambridge University Press.

Torres, C. V. & Dessen, M. A. (2008). Brazilian Culture, Family, and its Ethnic-Cultural Variety. *Arizona Journal of Hispanic Cultural Studies*, 12(1), 189–202.

Torres, C. V., Porto, J. B., Vargas, L. M., & Fischer, R. (2015). Uma meta-análise de valores humanos básicos no Brasil: diferenças observadas dentro do país [A Meta-Analysis of Basic Human Values in Brazil: Observed Differences within the Country]. *Revista Psicologia: Organizações e Trabalho*, 15(1), 89–102.

UNICEF – United Nations Children's Fund (2017). *Cenário da exclusão social no Brasil* [Scenario of Social Exclusion in Brazil]. Retrieved from: https:// buscaativaescolar.org.br/downloads/guias-e-manuais/busca-ativa-escolar-v10-web.pdf.

United Nations Department of Economic and Social Affairs, Population Division (2018). *Household Size and Composition.* Retrieved from: https://popula tion.un.org/Household/index.html#/countries/76.

Vieira, M. L., Bossardi, C. N., Gomes, L. B., Bolze, S. D. A., Crepaldi, M. A., & Piccinini, C. A. (2014). Paternidade no Brasil: revisão sistemática de artigos empíricos [Paternity in Brazil: A Systematic Review of Empirical Articles]. *Arquivos Brasileiros de Psicologia, 66*(2), 36–52.

Worldometers (2018). *Brazil Population.* Retrieved from: www.worldometers .info/world-population/brazil-population/.

15

Australia

Judy Rose and Janeen Baxter

Mike and Joanne Lally appear to be an average married Australian couple. They live in a neighborhood of Adelaide just outside the city center with their three children Lily aged 10, James aged 13, and Hayley aged 17. However, the Lallys are far from average. Not only do they share equally in housework and childcare, but they also both hold strongly egalitarian views about family life. Mike's egalitarian attitude is most evident in his adoption of Joanne's last name, "Lally," the surname they have also given to their children. Men who change their surname after marriage are extremely rare in Australia. Most women still take their husband's surname following marriage and typically, even if women retain their maiden name, children are given the husband's surname. Mike and Joanne are highly unusual in this respect.

The Lallys live in a red brick and wrought iron terrace house which, like most terrace homes in the area, is long and narrow, with three bedrooms, one bathroom, and a small paved courtyard out the back with a lone leafy tree. Their neighborhood was originally working class, but it has become increasingly gentrified and is now predominantly inhabited by middle-class professionals, who typically hold liberal (non-conservative) political views and support alternative lifestyles. Its residents are deeply involved in their community, which comprises a large number of cyclists and pedestrian commuters. Mike reflects on how he and Joanne (who is originally from the UK) have established deep roots in their community:

> Well, we've lived here 22 years, and before that I rented a house over the other side of the neighborhood. So [it's been] a very long time. We know most of the

shopkeepers by name, and we walk everywhere. And you go to the dog park, so you know people who have dogs and you know people who have kids ... we spent 13 continuous years at the local primary school.

Australia is a constitutional monarchy and a parliamentary democracy. According to the 2016 census, Australia's population is approximately 23.4 million people. Although Australia is the sixth largest country in land mass, almost 80% of the people live in the eastern states and over two-thirds live in capital cities. Australia is a culturally diverse nation with more than a quarter (26%) of the population born overseas. The top four countries that overseas-born Australians come from are the United Kingdom, New Zealand, China, and India. Approximately 3% of Australians identify as either Aboriginal or Torres Strait Islanders. The majority of Australians are Christian (52%), with 8.2% of the population affiliated with non-Christian religions, the most common of which are Buddhism, Islam, and Hinduism. Thirty percent report "no religion" (Australian Bureau of Statistics [ABS], 2017).

Although the Sex Discrimination Act of 1984 (Australian Government, 1984) and the Equal Opportunity for Women in the Workplace Act of 1999 (Australian Government, 1999) were established to protect the rights of working women, pay equity issues persist. The gender pay gap between full-time working women and men is 14% (Workplace Gender Equality Agency, 2019). While women are on average paid less than men in Australia, more women than men attain bachelor's degrees (ABS, 2018a).

The 2016 census figures show that of families in Australia, 44.7% were couples with children, 15.8% were single-parent families, 37.8% were couples without children, and 1.7% were other types of families. In 2016, 65% of men and 56% of women were employed, with men employed an average of 39 hours per week and women employed an average of 30 hours per week (ABS, 2017).

Most Australian couples with children adopt traditional or neotraditional arrangements in which fathers work full-time and often long hours, while mothers either withdraw from the workforce or transition to part-time employment while their children are young. The proportion of couples with children in Australia who were dual earners was 66.1% in 2011. However, among these dual-earning couples, over half adopt the full-time/part-time model, whereas fewer than a third comprise two full-time working parents (Australian Institute of Family Studies, 2013). This pattern of family life has been shaped by the pervasive male-breadwinner ideology, but is also related to the structure of the labor market, which provides greater opportunity for part-time employment among service sector jobs dominated by women.

Regardless of employment hours, women spend far longer on domestic tasks than men. Women spend, on average, 24 hours per week on domestic tasks compared to approximately 9 hours per week for men (Baxter, Hewitt, & Haynes, 2008). Australian longitudinal data shows that men's domestic work time remains very stable over the life course, regardless of key events such as entry to marriage and the birth of children. Women's domestic work hours, on the other hand, vary much more widely across the life course, especially increasing after the birth of a first child (Rose, Brady, Yerkes & Coles, 2015).

The national Paid Parental Leave scheme includes Parental Leave Pay for eligible working parents, which is paid at the national minimum wage for 18 weeks, and The Dad and Partner Pay for eligible working fathers, which provides 2 weeks leave, also paid at the national minimum wage (Australian Government, 2018).

In 2017, 49.3% of children aged 0 to 12 years attended childcare. The Australian Government provides some support to families to meet the costs of childcare through the Child Care Benefit and Child Care Rebate (ABS, 2018b). In addition, the Fair Work Act 2009 introduced a right to request flexible working hours for eligible employed parents with children under school age (Australian Government, 2009). To date, mothers, rather than fathers, have predominantly used flexibility arrangements to care for children (Rose et al., 2015).

The Lally's home is warm and unpretentious, much like Mike and Joanne themselves. The soft furnishings are colorful, if a little worn, and many of the hard surfaces hold accumulated artifacts of family life, including CDs, magazines, and family photographs. Mike and Joanne's functional use of space is visible in the courtyard where they simultaneously dry clothes, store buckets and mops, and have cups of tea and meals on a no-fuss picnic table.

Mike and Joanne have a division of household labor that is organized around their work schedules and the family's needs. They are both employed in hospitals, Joanne as a clinical nurse manager and Mike as an operating theater technician. They have both negotiated complementary shift work schedules that allow them to work alternate times and fit their jobs around their care responsibilities. Their job schedules entail each of them working in different hospitals, at different times of the day and on different days of the week, except for Monday when they both work. Mike explains how their intricately scheduled arrangement works to facilitate childcare and helps them keep up with housework tasks:

> I leave before the family gets up. Joanne does breakfast and lunches, house-work, cooks or sorts out tea. Hayley picks up Lily; I come home, do dinner and housework, and bring in washing and put it away. The children all help with cleaning up after tea.

There is a high level of cooperation in the Lally's daily routines and their children are encouraged to help out as well:

> If I'm working, and Joanne's on a late, she will get the dinner organized. She'll buy the ingredients, or if she gets time she'll cook, and I'll come home and finish it off, or now that the kids are older, Hayley will come home and put it in the oven, or warm it up for when I get home.

Only Joanne works for pay on the weekend. Mike explains his routine:

> Because Joanne often works weekends, Sunday is often spent preparing for the week ahead. While Joanne is at work, I'll organize tea [dinner] for Sunday and Monday, and make sure that there's food for the lunches, morning teas, etc. The kids and I will often go for a bike ride or, as its footy season, take James to his footy game where I'm also the trainer.

Mike and Joanne take a fairly rational approach to the division of household labor, based on who has the most time available. Joanne explains:

> If I'm working more, then Mike will do more housework, or vice versa, and it's never really been that much of an issue, because, you know, if you're not at home, then you're working, so you're still working either way [laugh] ... it's never been something that we've discussed, but I don't really think it would be an issue anyway.

Both Mike and Joanne perceive doing a 50/50 split in family work. On childcare Joanne reports:

> It would be 50/50, I think. It would work itself out, because Mike goes to work before seven in the morning. I'm always the one that gets up and gets the breakfasts and does the lunches and all of those types of things. But then five of my shifts in the fortnight are usually evenings, so he does the stuff at the other end of the day.

On housework, Joanne also perceives a 50/50 split, although she does more of some tasks like food shopping (mainly because she has the car), while Mike does more cooking and cleaning:

> Oh, that's all 50/50. Shopping, I would do the majority of the shopping. But again, that's because I'll do the morning run. I'll be walking the kids to school, and I usually go and do the shopping on my way back, because we've only got a little house. We've only got a little kitchen, so I do tend to shop probably every day, or every couple of days. So I probably do more shopping. Mike probably does more cooking. Mike probably cleans more than I do, actually. He'll sort of vacuum and clean through, although I do things like dusting and give the bedrooms a good go. Laundry's 50/50. He's done two loads of washing this morning.

Mike echoes Joanne's report that they share housework evenly:

> I don't know – 50 per cent, I suppose. Yeah, there's no tasks that I don't do and Joanne doesn't do. Yeah, I don't really like doing the bathroom [laugh], but if I have to do the bathroom – if the bathroom needs doing, I'll do the bathroom. Yeah, if there's a load of washing to do, I'll do it. You know, there's that sort of running joke about "domestic blindness." I see James's pants behind you that have got a big stain on the leg. I washed 'em this morning, brand new pants, and he spilled something on them. [laugh] Well, yeah, so we both do the same – there's no division really. I don't think so.

These accounts suggest that the Lallys adhere to the principle of substituting for each other in most household tasks. However, Joanne acknowledges, "There are some tasks that I don't like to do: cleaning floors, folding the washing, and some Mike doesn't like to do: paying the bills, cleaning the bathroom. It's an unwritten division of tasks without resentment from either party."

While the Lallys demonstrate a high level of responsiveness to their children's needs, Joanne explains there are certain childcare tasks each can do better than the other:

> Lily didn't let Mike do her hair this morning. "No offense, Dad," she said [laugh]. But I don't think they really go to anyone in particular. James has got certain issues, then he might come to me 'cause he thinks I'll be more sympathetic than his dad, but, really, they don't usually save things out until one or the other of us is there.

Mike concurs that they have different strengths in parenting. He recounts how he is able to respond more ably than Joanne when his children are upset or anxious:

> I think Hayley and Joanne, they tend to clash more and then I will come in and negotiate a truce. James tends to, for some reason, James tends to implode in

the mornings and so Joanne tends – because I work, I start work at 7 for 3 days, I'm not here in the mornings, so I'll ring Joanne up halfway through my morning, and James will have, you know, gone and been upset or whatever. He tends to do that on those mornings I'm not here. Yeah, he does get a bit anxious, and he doesn't get a headache; he gets a brain tumor. [laugh]

Joanne believed that their overall emotional bond with their children was equivalent, although their roles were different:

Emotionally, I think it's probably pretty even. There's certain times when, you know, different things may rub. Say, for example, with Hayley, we might clash, so therefore dad comes and is the mediator, but then there's other times when, when people need their mum. So I think that's pretty even.

Despite Mike and Joanne's awareness of their different parenting styles, they were also conscious of supporting each other in parenting decisions. Joanne explains, "We try to be consistent, because we've never wanted them to try and sort of play one off against the other."

Reflecting back on Mike and Joanne's backgrounds and relationship histories, we can track the evolution of their equally shared arrangements. The seeds of an egalitarian domestic lifestyle were sown early for Mike. Mike's personal history, being the oldest child in a single-parent household, contributed to his experience with household duties at a young age. His father's absence meant that he didn't witness a traditional division of labor. Mike recounts, "I don't know whether it sort of stems from my parents were divorced when I was quite young, so I didn't have really a male role model." Joanne suggests that her husband's nontraditional start to life meant that he was also exposed to running a household from an early age, "Mike's dad wasn't around from about the age of 8, so Mike probably assumed a more dominant role in that household." Mike remembers that even before he met Joanne, when he lived in shared houses, he did more housework than his male housemates. He reflects, "When I did move out into shared houses, I always liked things tidy. I guess I did that."

Despite this early exposure to domestic life, after meeting Joanne and living together for a time before they married, Mike remembers that Joanne used to cook more than he, "We both worked full-time. Joanne cooked at the beginning more than I did. Joanne, in England, lived with an Indian girl, so she cooks curries and things like that which we didn't have at home. So she was certainly a better cook."

Neither of them remember any disputes over housework during their early married life before children. Joanne recalls that they both contributed to housework together, and if one was sick or unavailable, the other would take over:

> As far as cleaning and things, when you're both working full-time, when you're pre-children, it just happens ... I had a sore back a few years ago, so Mike always used to do the vacuuming. He's got a sore back now, so I seem to do it, but [laugh] yeah, we just used to share it. When it came to decorating and things like that, we used to do that together.

When they became parents, Joanne's difficulties with breastfeeding meant that Mike was a hands-on dad right from the start. As Joanne says, "I couldn't breastfeed so we shared that after a month, I think. That was a shared thing."

The pattern of one of the couple substituting for the other has continued as their children have grown, and as the family's needs and schedules have changed. Joanne's job as a nurse manager has always been at a higher pay level than Mike's theater tech position. Mike matter-of-factly notes, "Joanne's job gets priority because she gets paid more." Joanne's greater breadwinning capacity led her to go back to full-time employment, while Mike was able to withdraw from the workforce for short periods and take the main responsibility for their children's care, "I suppose it started when Joanne, with Hayley, when Hayley was born, Joanne went back to work, and I didn't work, so I was the 'househusband,' as they say, and I guess it started from there."

Joanne reflects on how their nontraditional arrangements seem natural to their children:

> I worked full-time a couple of times since I've had kids, but Mike's always worked part-time ... They've only ever been in a maximum of 2 days child care ... I earned more than he did, so it was a natural thing that I would work more than him. So he was able to be at home. And the kids have never thought of it as being particularly special.

Joanne has been employed full-time when they have needed the money, but when a third child was on the way, Mike recalls that Joanne admitted she could not do it all, "Joanne went back to work full-time for about 6 months while pregnant with Lily. At this time Joanne realized that it was too hard to juggle a demanding job, our relationship, and time with the kids, which she felt all suffered."

These changes in jobs and hours over time ultimately led to their current arrangement, with each employed 30 hours per week. This part-time job schedule has facilitated an equal division of household labor, and reflects their strong priority on family well-being. Mike explains that planning their employment schedules to avoid as much formal childcare as possible has been an important family goal:

> We both work on Monday, but basically what we've tried to do is keep the kids out of childcare. The school where they've all gone offers morning care and afternoon care. They've never gone to morning care. Lily goes to afternoon care occasionally, not very often, like on a Monday. But now, as the other two have got older, they pick her up from after care, so she's not there for that long.

Joanne has also demonstrated determination by negotiating her part-time senior role at the hospital. Joanne initially had to convince hospital management that a part-time, job-share arrangement would be viable:

> When I first started ... when Hayley was a baby, I worked full-time. But basically, when I got pregnant with James, I went back as a job share in my unit manager role. We had to sell it to them, because they'd not had a job-share management role before, so, you know, we said, "Look, this is the way it will be."

Mike was able to negotiate three 10-hour days per week, with the option of being available to work different shifts if needed. Both Mike and Joanne's agency at their jobs enabled them to attain their ideal hours. While Joanne's management role gives her more power to say, "This is the way it will be," Mike has relied more on his reputation as a good worker. Mike explains:

> I guess as you've worked in hospitals a long time, you get yourself into a position ... They're sort of big places, but they're small enough that you know the people that are in charge of you, and they know you're a good worker, and you can say to them, "I want this shift, this shift, and this shift." They appreciate your work.

Mike's aptitude for keeping a tidy environment at his job also transfers into a well-organized household:

> I think it's got something to do with working in an operating theater. It's a work environment, that everything's labeled, and shelves are neat, and if you want a piece of equipment or you want something, you go to a shelf and it's there. It's a tidy environment, so now I've worked in operating theaters forever. So I think maybe that's – there might be something to do with it.

Mike clearly values time with his family. When asked whether he ever craved some time alone, he scoffed at the advice in a book about the men's movement in Australia written by a well-known author:

> He said about how men should go off for a weekend by themselves, you know, choose like your birthday weekend or something like that, but I couldn't think of anything worse! And maybe 'cause I've got daughters as

well, I couldn't relate to much of it. But, yeah, so maybe that's why I sort of can't relate to that sort of male thing, and maybe that's got something to do with not having a role model. But no, no, I'd rather spend time with my family than by myself.

Joanne and Mike reflect anti-materialist values when they discuss paid work and family time. They are critical of parents who prioritize their jobs and money ahead of time with children. Joanne complains:

> It does annoy me when you see people that are working, they're both working full-time, and they seem to outsource their parenting. I think, "Why have you had them?" Okay, they might live in a really nice house; they might have two nice cars, but your children are being outsourced. I must admit, actually, I thought that recently, because I've been doing the netball run . . . for the kids' netball training, and I'm taking this particular kid whose parents both work full-time, and I'm not even getting a "thank you," and I think, "What's that about?"

By deliberately deciding to work part-time, the Lallys have made a conscious decision to trade off earning more money to spend more time with the family. However, their decision to earn less means that some luxuries, including overseas holidays, are not currently possible. Mike explains:

> I guess that's one of the things with working part-time. Saving up for things like holidays, ten plus thousand dollars for airfares, is really difficult. You know, we've just given up on that sort of thing. We still have great holidays. We share a house with some friends every year over in January. So yeah, I think those sort of things have fallen by the wayside, but it'll come again.

Joanne reports that having become less materialistic and more modest in their leisure pursuits over time has affected the types of people with whom they associate:

> Before we had kids, we had a group of friends that we used to go out with, and go on holiday, or go away for weekends and things, but we've drifted away from them . . . They seemed to be more materialistic, still wanting the fast cars and the flash holidays. And so I suppose we have gravitated towards different people.

Joanne touts the bit of couple time she and Mike spend together in activities that do not cost a lot of money:

> We're fortunate because we might not go out so much in the evening, but we've just had a really nice morning. We just walked the dog out to Marphet Street, and had a wander around, and gone for a coffee, so we spend different time together, but it's just as nice.

The Lally's egalitarian division of labor has developed out of their different earning capacities, Mike's background, their ability to negotiate part-time employment, and their goals for family life. Mike talks about Joanne's breadwinning role as the most natural thing in the world, and, in doing so, has undone the male prerogative to be the family's breadwinner. Likewise, Joanne's willingness to let Mike assume the role of primary carer when their first child was born debunks the idea that only mothers can be primary caregivers. Joanne's stance against gatekeeping is also an important piece of the puzzle of how they create equality:

> But there are also women – someone said, "Oh, no, no, no, no … I don't let him do that, because he doesn't do it right." I mean, yeah, okay, I prefer to use two pegs to hang up something on the line than one, but if it gets done, it's really not the end of the world, is it? If you want things to change, then you have to give a little as well, whether it's your job or whether it's your house-keeping duties, you need to be respected.

In many ways Joanne and Mike's collaboration in sharing household tasks contributes to a lack of angst over whether each is doing his or her fair share. Their married life is largely devoid of the conflicts and resentments over housework that might be typical in more traditional marriages.

Given the deeply entrenched gender norms that still pervade home and family life in Australia, the Lally's story is remarkable, and clearly demonstrates how equally shared arrangements can provide positive outcomes for men, women, and children. However, while Joanne and Mike contribute equally to housework and childcare, in a manner unique in Australian culture, they are outwardly dismissive of this fact. When asked why they choose to share domestic work equally, Joanne reflects, "I don't know; it's never really been an issue." Mike seems surprised at the question, "I can't believe this is interesting. Don't other families live like this?" The short answer to Mike's question is "no." Equally sharing households are rare and difficult to find in Australia.

References

Australian Bureau of Statistics (2017). 2071.0 – *Census of Population and Housing: Reflecting Australia – Stories from the Census, 2016*. Retrieved from: www.abs.gov.au/ausstats/abs@.nsf/Lookup/by%20Subject/2071.0~2016~Main%20Features~Snapshot%20of%20Australia,%202016~2.

Australian Bureau of Statistics (2018a). 4125.0 – *Gender Indicators, Australia, Sep 2018*. Retrieved from: http://abs.gov.au/ausstats/abs@.nsf/Lookup/by%20Subject/4125.0~Sep%202018~Main%20Features~Education~5.

Australian Bureau of Statistics (2018b). 4402.0 – *Childhood Education and Care, Australia, June 2017*. Retrieved from: http://abs.gov.au/ausstats/abs@.nsf/o/F924A95E815CD063CA257657001619DE?Opendocument.

Australian Government (1984). *Federal Register of Legislation: Sex Discrimination Act 1984*. Retrieved from: www.legislation.gov.au/Details/C2004A02868.

Australian Government (1999). *Federal Register of Legislation: Equal Opportunity for Women in the Workplace Act 1999*. Retrieved from: www.legislation.gov.au/Details/C2009C00329.

Australian Government (2009). *Fair Work Legislation, Fair Work Ombudsman*. Retrieved from: www.fairwork.gov.au/about-us/legislation.

Australian Government (2018). Department of Social Services. *Families and Children. Paid Parental Leave Scheme*. Retrieved from: www.dss.gov.au/our-responsibilities/families-and-children/programmes-services/paid-parental-leave-scheme.

Australian Institute of Family Studies (2013). *Parents Working Out Work*. Retrieved from: https://aifs.gov.au/publications/parents-working-out-work.

Baxter, J., Hewitt, B., & Haynes, M. (2008). Life Course Transitions and Housework: Marriage, Parenthood and Time on Housework. *Journal of Marriage and Family, 70*(2), 259–272.

Rose, J., Brady, M., Yerkes, M. A., & Coles, L. (2015). 'Sometimes They Just Want To Cry for their Mum': Couples' Negotiations and Rationalisations of Gendered Divisions in Infant Care. *Journal of Family Studies, 21*(1), 38–56.

Workplace Gender Equality Agency (2019). *National Gender Pay Gap Remains Stable*. Australian Government. Retrieved from: www.wgea.gov.au/newsroom/media-releases/national-gender-pay-gap-remains-stable.

16

Singapore

Karen Mui-Teng Quek and Carmen Knudson-Martin

Siti and Osman Hamzah are among a growing group of young, well-educated dual-career couples in Singapore. A Muslim Malay couple, they have been married for 11 years and are both 37 years old. Siti is a senior teacher in the neighborhood primary school that their 9-year-old son, Adrian, attends. Osman is an educational administrator in a secondary school.

In Singapore, changing economic roles for women have challenged deeply ingrained gender traditions (Quah, 2004), promoting a shift toward more equality among couples (Quek & Knudson-Martin, 2006; 2008). Siti and Osman demonstrate a particularly strong commitment to a shared partnership. Ever since their first interview as newlyweds over 10 years ago,[1] they have maintained an equal division of labor; both partners take responsibility for paid work and care, and both make family a priority.

Achieving the Singapore dream of the five Cs (cash, credit cards, condo, car, and country club) is a family goal. Like many Singaporeans, Siti and Osman began married life in a government flat that was set up to provide affordable homes in integrated towns. Five years later, Osman said, "We have a car now ... we get to dream about moving to a nicer place." Finally, they moved to a privately developed luxury condo, complete with swimming pool, landscaped gardens, clubhouse, and air-conditioned gym.

---

[1] This couple was originally interviewed during their first year of marriage as part of the first author's dissertation research. She subsequently interviewed them during their 5th year and 10th years of marriage. Couples were interviewed together on all three occasions. To read more about the larger longitudinal study, readers are referred to Quek and Knudson-Martin (2006; 2008).

 Singapore is a cosmopolitan city-state of an estimated 5.6 million, with 4 million Singapore citizens and permanent residents and 1.6 million non-resident foreigners, as of 2018 (Department of Statistics Singapore [DOSS], 2019b). Chinese represent 75% of the resident population, followed by Malays (13%), and Indians (9.2%). Religiously diverse, Buddhists and Taoists account for 44% of the resident population; 18% identify as Christians, 15% as Muslims, and 5.1% as Hindus. The remaining 17% have no religious affiliation (DOSS, n.d.).

The labor force participation rate for men is 75.6%, for women 60.2% (DOSS, 2019a). Although there are more employed female university graduates (38%) than male graduates (35.6%) (Ministry of Manpower, 2019), men's income exceeds women's by 12% (Hofmann, 2019).

Married couples with children account for 51.5% of households, couples without children are 17%, 13% are people living alone, and 7% are lone parents (DOSS, 2018). Over half (53.8%) of couples are dual earners; male-breadwinner couples account for only 27.7% (DOSS, 2015).

From its humble beginnings as a fishing village to a thriving city-state, Singapore is widely regarded as an economic success story. To promote economic development, government family policies are designed to encourage women's employment and to increase the birthrate (Yenn, 2007; Quek, 2014).

Working mothers are entitled to a 16-week paid maternity leave; working fathers are given 1 week paid leave, and can share 4 weeks of the maternity/parental leave. In addition, fathers and mothers can each take 6 days of paid childcare leave per year until children are 7 years old (MSFD, 2018b).

Government childcare and early education services are available and being increased (Early Childhood Development Agency, 2019). To encourage more births, the government also provides cash gifts for each child ("baby bonuses") (MSFD, 2018a).

The combination of pro-natalist and pro-employment policies can burden women (Yenn, 2007) because fathers' roles in domestic labor have not kept pace (Quek, Knudson-Martin, Orpen, & Victor, 2011).

Siti made the final choice of the condo with a balcony facing the pool, despite Osman's reservations. Osman says, "After having moved here, I saw the wisdom of her choice." Both of them beamed when they said in unison, "Everyone in the family is happy." Siti likes to sit at the balcony and watch Osman swim laps and Adrian play in the pool.

Family is Osman's priority:

> I have a happy family. That's my goal. I believe that I'm working to support my family. I'm not working to make myself a great man or to earn 50 million bucks or whatever. I mean as long as we are living in a great place ... we're happy ... we're very, very comfortable ... [I] want to be a good father, a good husband, and to be happy among the three of us ... I'm content.

Siti invokes her partnership with Osman to explain her happiness in their family:

> I am happy, we are happy ... he's a partner ... he's a companion. He doesn't order me around ... he talks to me and [does] not shout ... ... [does] not belittle me. And he doesn't expect me to come back and cook, fetch Adrian, and do all those menial tasks.

When asked the difference between them and a traditional Muslim Malay couple, they provide a stark contrast. Siti explains:

> In our culture, the male would be more dominant and the female the submissive one. When eating out at the food court ... many times the husband will be sitting down and the wife would be going over to the food stalls to buy the food ... In a Malay couple, more often than not the wife would be serving the husband ... whether at home or outside. But that's not what happens with us ... He serves himself. He will take his own rice.

Osman concurs, "I don't like her to serve me. I go over to [the kitchen] and take my own stuff. In a typical Malay household that would be the wife's duty: cleaning the house and taking care of the children and husband, but we are very different."

"We Do Everything Together"

Siti and Osman are a team of equals with similar educational backgrounds, careers, and family goals. Since the beginning of their marriage they have shared everyday duties. Siti says of housework. "Whoever cannot stand the mess" will be the first to wash and clean. Osman remarks, "whoever's available, just do it." The couple does not have fixed rules to guide them. They explain that they divide domestic work according to availability, interests, level of tolerance, and ability. Although those explanations are often used to justify wives' greater share of housework or childcare (e.g., "she's better at it;" "she cares more about tidiness") (Knudson-Martin & Mahoney, 2005), for Osman and Siti the outcome is a non-gendered division of labor.

They intend to share household tasks 50/50. When asked to elaborate, they responded in unison "we will just do it together." For example, whenever Osman vacuums the floor, Siti does the mopping. With laundry, he washes and hangs the clothes; Siti takes them down and folds them. Knowing that she does not like to iron, Osman does most of the ironing for himself and their son. Siti usually makes the bed but says, "if I'm tired or I'm really late … " Osman interrupts, "if she doesn't make it, I'll do it."

Siti and Osman do specialize in some responsibilities. Osman remarks, "like … buying food, buying groceries … the weekly stuff everything I buy." Osman makes sure that the pantry is stocked with cereals, cheese, and milk. And Siti quickly adds, "If there is any cooking, I will be the one to do cooking." But she doesn't like to cook. Most weeknights they eat at food courts.[2] They agree that dinners cooked at home are too much of a hassle. Osman says, "Cooking is just one of those things that take up time unnecessarily. Outside food is ok." He is relieved to avoid cleaning up the after the dinner "mess." Thus, during the week, little cooking is done. On weekends they usually have meals at her parents' or his parents' homes.

The Hamzah family gets up at 5:00 a.m. during the workweek. Adrian dresses himself in his school uniform. Each parent takes care of his/her own breakfast and one of them gets Adrian's. They leave home together by 6:15 a.m. Osman drops Siti and Adrian at their school and then drives to his workplace. Adrian takes a school bus home by himself after school and their in-home nanny is there to greet him and give him lunch. Between 4:30 p.m. and 5:00 p.m., Osman and Siti return home together, the nanny leaves, and they take care of Adrian. According to Siti, "He

---

[2] Famous as a cultural attraction of Singapore, food courts, typically situated in the basement or top floor of nearly every shopping mall and other commercial venues, are the air-conditioned, indoor version of hawker centers. They usually house many small food stalls next to each other with properly maintained tables and chairs for convenient dining under one roof. Most Singaporeans choose to eat at food courts rather than at actual restaurants because of their abundance and cheaper price. They serve a wide variety of favorite local food, including Hainanese chicken rice, prawn noodles, Indian prata, Malay curries, satay, pork rib soup, fish rice porridge, and barbecued seafood. Some even offer Thai, Vietnamese, Korean, and Japanese cuisine, and Western dishes.

[Adrian] is quite independent," and Osman added (pointing to their son), "A lot of the time he is just playing with his toys hanging around us ... content that we are around, and we are content that he is around." Before bed, Adrian chooses a parent who reads to him and lays down with him until he falls asleep.

When overnight trips for their jobs are required, they arrange childcare between themselves rather than rely on the nanny. Osman describes their coordinated efforts:

> I went off for a field trip to New Zealand for 10 days with the school kids ... Then on the day I came back ... my flight landed in Singapore at 6 p.m. Siti was flying off to Japan for a 6-day conference at 9 p.m. on the same day. She handed Adrian over to me when we met [at the airport].

Both Siti and Osman see themselves as primary parents. Although they sometimes do different child-related tasks, they agree it is 50/50. Because Adrian goes to Siti's school, she sees to his academic needs. Osman takes responsibility for Adrian's outings, "If he wants to go to a farm or any special outing or swimming, I will be the one." Osman worries though, "It is unfair that mine's more fun stuff and hers is more work related." But Siti protests, "I have no interest [in those activities]." She says she was not brought up to enjoy them.

Equal from the Beginning

"It all started in the science library." Siti and Osman tell their story with energy and enthusiasm. They began their relationship at the National University of Singapore on an equal footing. On their first date, a trip to the movies, Siti recalls, "We met halfway." She describes the freedom she felt with Osman early on: "I didn't feel pressurized, I didn't feel stifled, I didn't feel suffocated. I felt free; I had a boyfriend, yet I had my own life, with my own friends. It wasn't just with him 100%. It was a very fair balance."

Despite their preference for an egalitarian marriage, like other Singaporean couples, they had internalized gendered cultural obligations (Quek & Knudson-Martin, 2008). As newlyweds, Siti said, "We are very binded by our religion, so we have religious expectations we have to follow." Osman concurred, "Husband provides for the wife: food, clothing, money, and shelter. So no matter what, I have to be financially able to support her. That's an obligation that is non-negotiable." Siti added, "I cook and I would lay the table ready for him when he comes home from work." In truth, the reality was quite different. She rarely cooked. From the start, they shared breadwinning and housework. Osman described the non-gendered pattern they continue today, "I do my own laundry most of the time; iron my clothes all the time; she works and I don't expect her to cook."

Nonetheless, maintaining cultural values has been important to them. Siti did not speak of motherhood in terms of personal fulfillment, as is common in American couples (McQuillan, Greil, Shreffler, & Tichenor, 2008). Instead, she associates motherhood with upholding family loyalties and ethnic traditions (Kagitçibasi, 2007). For example, when she became a mother, Siti began to wear the *tudung*, a Muslim headscarf, as a reflection of Islamic piety. Siti wears the *tudung* to impart the core values (Islamic teachings) to her child, "I put on the tudung … to be a good role model for my son. Although I still complain because it's hot and I'm not used to it. But if I see it in another light … like now I'm a mother, it's something good."

When Adrian was born, Siti and Osman assumed that parenting responsibilities would be shared. They discussed and made all childcare and housework decisions together, such as the decision to hire a housecleaner for 5 hours a week to give them more time to cope with a newborn. When asked who did the diaper-changing and baby-related tasks, both responded "50/50." Although they did most tasks together, Osman noted, "But waking up at night [to feed the baby] I did mostly. Siti was a light sleeper and had a hard time going back to sleep when she was already up. Since I didn't have any problem with that [sleep], I did the night feedings for him." Siti chimed in to emphasize their overall shared responsibility, "and for bathing him … also 50/50. It also depended on who is free."

After Siti's 4-month maternity leave, they had to make babysitting arrangements. Although many parents in Singapore hire live-in help to care for their children (Quek, Knudson-Martin, Orpen & Victor 2011), Osman had concerns about doing that, "There would be nobody to supervise the maid at home, and I have trouble trusting an 18-, 19-, 20-year-old with my baby."

Thus, for the next 7 months, while Siti took public transportation to her job, Osman dropped off and picked up their baby at his parents' home on his way to and from his job, which added 25 miles to his daily commute. Siti described those first months, "The initial [7] months were quite trying. It was too far of a journey in the morning. It was kind of tiring." Siti explained that when Adrian was 11 months old, "He

[Osman] requested and was granted a transfer nearer to home ... we decided to get a nanny instead, a local [older] nanny."

Although Osman still worried, they managed. While they worked out this stressful transition, Siti and Osman organized their life to do nearly everything together: taking Adrian to the nanny, picking him up at the end of the day, and spending evenings together. They explained that the only exception was sick care:

SITI: Yeah, most of the things we do together ... The only problem is when it comes to the childcare leave; that is beyond our control.
OSMAN: If he has a fever and he needs to stay at home,
SITI: we cannot leave together 'cause there is only one medical certificate,
OSMAN: so we take turns.

Although Osman has the right to take the leave, his boss doesn't make it easy, as he explains:

Yeah. As a man, I am entitled ... my boss doesn't like it ... he makes it hard for us. When you want to fill out a form, he makes it tough. I got called in by my boss. He said, "Yesterday you took childcare leave." I said, "Yes." The boss asked, "Why didn't your wife take [it]?" But if I insist, there is absolutely nothing he can do about it.

Osman was willing to forego advancement in his career to share parenting, "We decided that if by doing this, I don't get promoted to principal or vice principal, then so be it."

Osman and Siti have worked together cooperatively to figure out how to put the principle of equal sharing into practice. However, all was not idyllic in the early days of their relationship. Siti and Osman recalled, "We fought so much, almost every ... other day." They argued about decorating their home, about where to live; and about discipline for Adrian when Siti thought Osman was too harsh. Osman would usually give in or they would come to some compromise. Now Osman is proud of his nontraditional parenting, pointing out, "See he [pointing to Adrian] is making noise and I did not "*han-thumb*" [colloquial for punish] him ... I am milder in discipline [than my father was]."

Balance of Paid Work and Family

Although Siti and Osman do not make career success their first priority, they are financially successful. Each earns about S$90,000 (US$70,000) annually. They need both incomes to afford the expenses that come with what they consider "a good life." Both view Siti as a co-provider, but Siti struggles a bit with her internalized cultural ideal that childcare is a woman's responsibility, "In fact, it would be better if I would devote my time to looking after him." Nonetheless, those traditional ideals conflict with the material advantages of a dual-earner family to which they both aspire. Siti explains, "Because we want this lifestyle, we want the car. We want all these, so we know that we have to work, both of us have to work in order to achieve what we want."

Osman recognizes that the dual-career family is becoming standard in Singapore and that he cannot maintain the family finances alone. Even before their son was born, he said, "If she doesn't want to work, I will try to persuade her, 'Look, it's going to be really hard for me.'" He treats her job as equally important as his, and does not expect her to alter her work to accommodate his plans, "On some weekends we didn't go [to visit his parents], because she had too much work to do. I got it and it doesn't matter [not visiting my parents]." Moreover, viewing his wife as a co-provider gives him the impetus to redefine household roles. Osman remarks, "I know she works so I don't expect her to cook ... I mean, if she does not have the time, just say so. It's not a big matter."

Siti is already on her way to becoming a senior teacher, but she turned down a promotion to be head of the department because it would have required more time away from home. Osman respects her right to make that decision, "I didn't mind the fact that she wanted to spend more time [with the family]. It was a nice decision for her to make, but I wouldn't have had a problem if she wanted to take it [the promotion]."

Siti and Osman maintain similar attitudes toward their careers. He says, "We work to live," and she adds, "and not live to work." Neither shows interest in a "fast track" career track. Like Siti, Osman doesn't want a promotion that would mean long hours away from the family. Both put in regular hours, and focus their time at home on their son, agreeing not to bring work home. Osman says, "I still work ... maybe 50 hours a week. These are my 50 work hours and I do not bring my work home."

Doing Marriage Differently

Traditional marriage in Singapore is patriarchal. Traditional collectivist cultural standards require individuals to adhere closely to what is demanded, what is permitted, and what is taboo for their genders. Siti and Osman maintain some internal loyalty to these cultural values. Yet by focusing on togetherness and shared partnership, they are doing marriage very differently. A number of factors contribute to their transformation of the traditional marriage model including conflicting economic and cultural pressures, the ways in which they have adopted nontraditional ideologies and transformed traditional ones, the models and anti-models of their families of origin, collectivist norms, and the creation of harmonious relationships.

Siti and Osman's generation has been greatly affected by the rapid socioeconomic changes in Singapore. The government has instituted policies to spur economic development by promoting equal educational and employment opportunities for women (Lazar, 2001). When Siti and Osman were newly married, only 35% of women earned as much as their husbands (Leow, 2006). Singaporean women are now as well educated as men. That Siti and Osman would meet at school and have jobs with similar prestige and income reflects these policies.

Siti expresses strong commitment to job demands, illustrating the success of government efforts to engage women in the workplace. Her career is also strongly supported by Osman. Equality emerges pragmatically as they develop workable arrangements that honor her job as much as his. Osman, for example, automatically takes on household responsibilities when Siti is busy with job demands. When Siti had additional classes to teach, Osman did a lot more laundry. Nonetheless, with few cultural models to guide them, dual-career couples like Osman and Siti face tensions and ambivalence between tradition and modern society.

Reconciling Traditional and Nontraditional Ideologies

As newlyweds, Osman and Siti identified with their culture's gender traditions. Osman saw himself as financially responsible for the family, Siti for family cooking. However, he shared the breadwinning and she didn't really cook much! Their conception of what they should do clashed with the less gendered reality of what they actually did. Whereas their American middle-class counterparts often create a myth of equality and describe unequal relationships as equal (Knudson-Martin & Mahoney, 1996), Siti and Osman seemed to be constructing a myth of traditionalism, saying that their relationship is structured traditionally, while in practice living a more equal relationship.[3] As the Hamzahs grappled with

---

[3] In the US, working-class couples who hold traditional gender ideologies sometimes work alternate shifts and share the care for their children to avoid paid childcare. They also often create a similar myth of traditionalism (Deutsch, 1999).

contradictions between their gender training and cultural ideology and the day-to-day realities of prioritizing two careers, new possibilities for equality were constructed. Ten years later, they both articulate more clearly their expectations for an equal relationship and state unambivalently that equality is what they want.

Yet, even before marriage, Osman and Siti did not conform to gendered norms. Although Siti has decided to "cover up" now that she is a mother, she previously felt free to rebel and even went to bars, a prohibited place for Muslim girls. And they gave each other the freedom to go out with friends. They described their equality as a natural outcome of their orientation to each other. They have avoided the model of Siti's traditional family and learned from the nontraditional model of Osman's.

Families of Origin

Siti grew up in a typical Malay household where her father gave her mother a sum of money for household expenses, and her mother took care of all household tasks. Siti witnessed the oppressive effects of this gendered division of labor on her mother, and disliked the sense of dependence on men inherent in it. She insisted on a different kind of marriage, and chose Osman with that in mind, "I want a partner … a companion. I don't want to be a maid … to be controlled. I like him [Osman] because I can be me." Siti vowed that she would rather be single than be in a marriage like her mother's. She "almost always obeys him [her father] without question". He does not lift a finger on household tasks. In all three interviews, Siti used similar words, "I want to be in a partnership for companionship and not to be a maid."

In contrast, Osman grew up in a dual-career home where his dad modeled an unconventional family role. Both his parents were police officers and each achieved career success. It never occurred to him to seek a traditional wife nor to expect traditional wifely services. Although he is aware of cultural expectations that he support the family, Osman assumes his wife will be his equal and will work.

Osman's parents also divided domestic labor nontraditionally. He says, "In my opinion my dad does more in the household than my mom." Osman was expected to do housework and childcare as well:

> When I was old enough … my dad made me do chores … vacuum the house, wash toilets. Basically, my dad set the example for me, so I'm not averse to

doing housework. It's always been like this, so it's nothing new. When I was 17, my younger sister was born. So I helped look after her. I was already doing things with a baby so I was used to taking care of a baby.

Collectivism and Equality

In the past, a collectivist family ideal reinforced the patriarchal family. Today, while rejecting patriarchy, several aspects of collectivist world views actually enhance Siti and Osman's practice of equality (Quek & Knudson-Martin, 2006). Collectivist family ideology, for example, encourages women and men to marry someone of similar or equal status, a good match that maintains the reputation of each family. Siti and Osman have equal educational qualifications and equal-status jobs. Thus, they are peers who can negotiate as equals.

Harmonious family relationships are prized in a collectivist ideal in which personal interests are subsumed to the group (Tan, 2008). In the past, that meant that women, in particular, suppressed self-interest to serve the family. In Siti and Osman's family, however, both of them subsume their career self-interest to the good of the family. Both Siti and Osman deeply value family relationships.

Moreover, in collectivist culture the importance of maintaining harmonious relationships also means that people may not directly express their feelings. Instead, partners must "read" each other's non-verbal cues. Osman takes the initiative to engage with Siti when he observes that she is angry:

SITI: If I'm upset, . . . he will ask and then he will comfort me. If I'm sad, then I will tell. But if I'm angry or bothered, I'll keep quiet.
OSMAN: I will try to talk to her. If she's still angry . . . she doesn't respond. She will respond, but curt, short words . . . Then after a few hours later I will try again.
SITI: He always breaks the silence.

Traditionally, the dominance of men freed them from noticing the needs of others. In contrast, Osman has learned to attend to Siti, to "read her face." "It's very easy to read her. If she's unhappy, she will show it. She doesn't have to say it all most of the time." Focusing on the well-being of wives represents a shift in the hierarchical gender structure. Osman proactively anticipates Siti's needs, helps her relax, and makes her feel good.

Despite the focus on harmony in collectivist cultures, Siti and Osman are not afraid to engage in conflict. However, the desire for harmony shapes the ways that they communicate. Siti describes how she gets Osman to paint the wall, "I will try, I will just try . . . If he does it, good. If he doesn't, I'll just try again." She is persistent, "I will sense that he doesn't want to do it, but . . . I'll just ask nicely again." According to Osman, her persistence without aggression is effective, "She doesn't get angry, she just does it her own way . . . I'll warm up to her idea. I will just do it."

Conclusion

When the Singaporean government made national polices to prepare the workforce for knowledge-based, high-tech industries in global competition, and to engage women as part of this workforce, these moves directly affected how gender is experienced and practiced in daily life. Siti and Osman exemplify how women's changing positions in the public sphere can translate into changes within marriage (Quek & Knudson-Martin, 2008). Osman recognizes Siti's contributions to the family, notices and attends to her emotional needs, and views parenting and household chores as his responsibility. Siti feels entitled to make demands and communicate her views. She is drawn to Osman because with him she feels free to transcend societal gender patterns.

Both Siti and Osman initiate and maintain career and family equality. Osman has responded cooperatively to their dual careers due to his own egalitarian socialization and Siti's clear expectations for personal autonomy and equal status. He shows no animosity or resistance to dismantling the traditional division of labor because since childhood he has been involved in household tasks. Although Siti occasionally feels guilty for not being a stay-at-home mother, she was clear from day one of their relationship that she would not accept a subservient status or the role of servant.

They genuinely desire a mutual partnership. For them, it is not simply who does the laundry or feeds the baby. By doing these tasks, they express mutual support for each other and their commitment to sharing the load. Each was willing to sacrifice income and ambition to make family a priority. In many ways, their commitment is less a repudiation of collectivist cultural values and more a transformation of them in a new social context in which separation of roles for women and men no longer serves the collective good.

Their equal sharing is underwritten by their mutual prioritizing of family over career. They repeatedly reiterate that accumulating wealth is not as important as maintaining their family and their relationship. Siti says, "There is no point in working if in the end your relationships suffer and your life gets turned upside down." Osman echoes her:

I try never to lose sight of what this life is all about. You can get caught up and so excited about your own success that it is easy to get a warped view of what's important. But you need to step away from it and you realize that the only thing enduring is the people you love.

References

Department of Statistics Singapore (2015). *General Household Survey*. Retrieved from: www.singstat.gov.sg/-/media/files/publications/ghs/ghs2015/ghs2015.pdf.

Department of Statistics Singapore (2018). *Population Trends 2018*. Retrieved from: www.singstat.gov.sg/-/media/files/publications/population/population 2018.pdf.

Department of Statistics Singapore (2019a). *Labour, Employment, Wages and Productivity*. Retrieved from: www.singstat.gov.sg/find-data/search-by-theme/economy/labour-employment-wages-and-productivity/latest-data.

Department of Statistics Singapore (2019b). *Population and Population Structure*. Retrieved from: www.singstat.gov.sg/find-data/search-by-theme/population/ population-and-population-structure/latest-data.

Department of Statistics Singapore (n.d.). *Singapore Census of Population 2010, Statistical Release 1: Demographic Characteristics, Education, Language and Religion*. Retrieved from: www.singstat.gov.sg/-/media/files/publications/ cop2010/census_2010_release1/cop2010sr1.pdf.

Deutsch, F. M. (1999). *Halving It All: How Equally Shared Parenting Works*. Cambridge, MA: Harvard University Press.

Early Childhood Development Agency (2019). *A Good Start for Every Child*. Retrieved from: www.ecda.gov.sg/PressReleases/Pages/Making-quality-pre schools-more-affordable-and-accessible.aspx.

Hofmann, W. (2019). *Singapore's Gender Wage Gap Widened in 2018*. Singapore: Value Champion.

Kagitçibasi, C. (2007). *Family, Self, and Human Development Across Cultures*. New Jersey: Lawrence Erlbaum Associates.

Knudson-Martin, C. & Mahoney, A. R. (1996). Gender Dilemmas and Myth in the Construction of Marital Bargains. *Family Process, 35*(2), 137–153.

Knudson-Martin, C. & Mahoney, A. R.(2005). Moving Beyond Gender: Processes that Create Relationship Equality. *Journal of Marital and Family Therapy, 31*(2), 235–246.

Lazar, M. (2001). For the Good of the Nation: 'Strategic Egalitarianism' in the Singapore Context. *Nations and Nationalism, 7*(1), 59–74.

Leow, B. G. (2006). *General Household Survey 2005: Socio-Demographics and Economic Characteristics*. Singapore: Integrated Press.

McQuillan, J., Greil, A. L., Shreffler, K. M., & Tichenor, V. (2008). The Importance of Motherhood in the Contemporary United States. *Gender & Society, 22*(4), 477–496.

Ministry of Manpower (2019). *Employment 2018*. (Table 68, Employed residents aged 15 years and over by highest qualification attained and sex.) Retrieved from: https://stats.mom.gov.sg/Pages/Employment-Tables2018.aspx.

Ministry of Social and Family Development (2018a). *Child Development Co-Sav ings (Baby Bonus) Scheme.* Retrieved from: www.babybonus.msf.gov.sg/ parent/web/about?_afrLoop=1006270792567954&_afrWindowMode=0&_ afrWindowId=tfky86ti9_1#%40%3F_afrWindowId%3Dtfky86ti9_1%26_ afrLoop%3D1006270792567954%26_afrWindowMode%3D0%26_adf.ctrl-state%3Dtfky86ti9_17.

Ministry of Social and Family Development (2018b). *Government Paid Leave.* Retrieved from: www.profamilyleave.gov.sg/Pages/About.aspx.

Quah, S. (2004). *Home and Kin: Families in Asia.* Singapore: Eastern Universities Press.

Quek, K. (2014). The Evolving Challenges of Modern-Day Parenthood in Singapore. In Selin, Helaine (ed.), *Parenting Across Cultures: Childrearing, Motherhood and Fatherhood in Non-Western Cultures* (pp. 145–162). New York: Springer Publishers.

Quek, K. & Knudson-Martin, C. (2006). A Push Towards Equality: Processes Among Dual-Career Newlywed Couples in a Collectivist Culture. *Journal of Marriage and Family,* 68(1), 56–69.

Quek, K. & Knudson-Martin, C. (2008). Reshaping Marital Power: How Dual-Career Newlywed Couples Create Equality in Singapore. *Journal of Social and Personal Relationships,* 25(3), 513–534.

Quek, K., Knudson-Martin, C., Orpen, S., & Victor, J. (2011). Gender Equality During Transition to Parenthood: Longitudinal Study of Dual-Career Singaporean Couples. *Journal of Social and Personal Relationships,* 28(7), 943–962.

Tan, E. (2008). A Union of Gender Equality and Pragmatic Patriarchy: International Marriages and Citizenship Laws in Singapore. *Citizenship Studies,* 12(1), 73–89

Yenn, T. Y. (2007). Inequality for the Greater Good: Gendered State Rule in Singapore. *Critical Asian Studies,* 39(3), 423–445.

17

Austria

Sabine Buchebner-Ferstl and Mariam Irene Tazi-Preve

Richard and Christine live in Vienna, the capital of Austria, with their two daughters, 7-year-old Hannah and 4-year-old Lucy.[1] Richard is self-employed in computing and environmental consulting. He estimates his workweek at 40 hours, which, for the most part, he can schedule as he likes. Christine, who was born in Germany, works approximately 44 hours Monday through Friday as an executive assistant in a large enterprise in Vienna.

A Day in the Life: "Papa, it's Fun to Puke with You; with Mama, I Can't"

On a normal workday, Christine wakes the kids and gets them dressed. After breakfast, which Richard prepares, both parents "help the kids get ready for school or kindergarten: get their teeth brushed, shoes and coats on, schoolbags, pack what they need for the day, and then out the door." While Christine leaves the house with the older daughter (the school is on the way to Christine's office), Richard takes the younger girl to kindergarten. When the family is gone, Richard does some of his freelance work at home, but also fits in some housework, such as laundry. His day

---

[1] The couple used for the Austrian case study originally participated in a qualitative study conducted in Austria, the Netherlands, and Belgium that examined the division of employment, housework, and childcare, and addressed the changes that transpired after the child's birth (Audenaert et al., 2004). In that study, Richard and Christine were interviewed using "pair interaction" interviews in which both partners were separately interviewed first. In a second interview, conflicts in their assertions were addressed. At the time of those interviews their first child was 15 months old. Because of their equally sharing relationship, they were selected for the current research and interviewed a third time (Cuyvers, 2000).

is flexible and depends on the kids as well as on his current workload, which varies according to the assignments he has taken on. Richard usually picks up the youngest daughter around 2:45 p.m. and the older one gets home from school at 3:30. Richard then often goes out with the kids in the afternoon, especially for sports (both girls play hockey). He explains, "We're not at home very often and when we are we usually have company. That is how the girls like it; they always want excitement." When Richard is out with the girls he organizes the activities himself, packing the backpacks for the girls and making sure that they have all their sports equipment and snacks.

By the time Richard comes home with the kids, Christine is often already at home and has dinner on the table. In the evenings (brushing teeth with the kids, reading aloud, putting the kids to bed, etc.) both are responsible, according to Richard, but Christine says, "Usually I put them to bed, so that I get a chance to see them after I get home so late." Then Richard usually works on his computer, while Christine often straightens up and either reads or watches television.

Thus, on a typical workday for Christine, when she leaves the house around 7:45 a.m. and comes back between 6:00 and 6:30 p.m., Richard spends more time with the kids than she. On weekends the two of them frequently go out and do things together with the kids, but sometimes Richard pursues his favorite activities (mostly sports) without the family and Christine takes care of the kids on her own. Richard admits that he has a bit more leisure time than Christine. The only time she goes out is on Tuesday nights for Pilates.

Austria has a population of about 8,773,000 inhabitants. About 15% of the population is foreign-born, the majority of whom come from Germany and the states of the former Yugoslavia. Vienna, the capital, has the highest proportion of foreign-born residents (28.6%) (Statistik Austria [STATA], 2018). According to 2001 data (since then religious orientation is no longer requested in the population census), the Christian faith dominates (81.4%), and most Christians are Roman Catholic (73.6% of the population). Four percent are Muslims and approximately 3% identify with other religions. Twelve percent of Austrians are unaffiliated (Statistica, 2019). Although no recent data are available, it is generally believed that the number of Muslims and people without any religious affiliation has risen since 2001.

Despite ongoing political efforts to ensure gender equity, the gender pay gap of 20% in Austria is one of the highest in Europe (Eurostat, 2018).

Austria practices a rather generous, but also complicated parental leave policy. Obligatory maternity leave comprises 8 weeks before and 8 weeks after the birth of the child, and is remunerated at 100% of the mother's average income for her last 3 months of employment. After these 16 weeks, regardless of former employment, all parents are entitled to the Austrian childcare subsidy, *Kinderbetreuungsgeld*. Mothers and fathers are eligible for parental leave until a child reaches 2 years old with a monetary bonus if they share. The so-called "family time" bonus for fathers who exclusively provide childcare for a month during the first 3 months after birth does not provide job protection (Rille-Pfeiffer, Dearing, & Schmidt, 2018).

In 2016, single-person households were the most common type in Austria, followed by couples living with their children (younger than 27) (26%), couples without children (23%), single-parent households (6.8%), and other types (6.2%). Approximately two-thirds of the mothers of childen under 18 currently work for pay, 77% of them part-time. An additional 9.3% are on parental leave (Kaindl & Schipfer, 2017). Based on the most recent data available, in dual-earner couples with children under 16, women spend 3:44 hours per day on household tasks and 3:47 on employment. Men do less housework (1:37 hours per day) but are employed for more hours (6:52). Regardless of employment status, on average, men spend about 1:30 hours and women 2:21 hours per day on childcare (STATA, 2009).

The most important childcare service in Austria is the kindergarten, which is open for children aged 3 to 6 (in some federal provinces from 2½). In 1872, Austria was one of the first countries in the world to establish a legal framework for the kindergarten system. Each federal province has its own kindergarten law, although the kindergarten is compulsory for pre-school children (one year before school) in all federal provinces. In Austria 93.4% of children aged 3 to 6 years old attend some kind of institutional care, most of whom attend the kindergarten. For children younger than 3, there are crèches, parent-toddler groups run by parent associations, and family daycare. However, children from birth to 2 years old are mainly cared for within the family; only about 28% had been placed in childcare outside the home in 2016/17 (Kaindl & Schipfer, 2017).

While Christine's paid work hours are fixed, Richard's fluctuate. Sometimes he has to work extremely hard in order to finish a project. Other times, when he has nothing to do, he picks up the kids earlier and takes them swimming or to do something else. An annual business trip takes him out of town for a week to 10 days and he bears responsibility for arranging childcare during his absence. He asks other parents for help or he arranges for them to stay in school or kindergarten longer. But Christine also uses vacation days to take care of her kids if other arrangements can't be made.

Richard clearly takes pleasure in handling some of the everyday details in their daughters' lives. One morning before school when the older daughter told her parents that she needed to bring "something with butterflies" to school that day, Richard went looking for the appropriate objects. He proudly reported:

> I saw that I have two stamp collections that I made when I was 14, I think ...
> I looked inside and found stamps with butterflies from all over the world. So
> I gave her 10 stamps with butterflies ... Surely no one else had something like
> that, because they were from Indonesia, Bulgaria, and other places. That is
> something that surely no one else brought – you have a real butterfly and
> stamps. That was perfect and made her really happy!

Even when it comes to unpleasant things in relation to his children, Richard doesn't succumb to the temptation to delegate the responsibility to his wife. That is how he came to receive the memorable compliment from Lucy, his younger daughter, when she had a stomach virus, "Papa, it's fun to puke with you; with Mama, I can't."

Both parents emphasize that the two of them have equally close emotional bonds with the kids. Christine says:

> I think it's the same. Yeah, it is really the same. Naturally the girls have a
> stronger bond with their father than a lot of other kids, just because he's there,
> yeah. That is a huge advantage for the kids, because I believe that kids, in
> principle, start out with a stronger bond with their mother and the bond with
> their father is less strong.

Both parents report that the relationships between Richard and his daughters are nearly free of conflicts, but Richard mentions that there is some tension between Christine and Hannah, the older daughter, "because they are so similar." Nonetheless, the children come with the same frequency to both parents with questions and problems or when one of them is sick or hurt. Richard reports:

> Well, if I am the only one home, then sure, there's only me, but if we're both
> home and something happens, then yeah, depending on how they feel, well

there isn't one who is closer to the kids or one who is distant or one who has better relationships or anything like that.

Christine says:

> When they fall down and get hurt they cry for whoever is closest, yeah. Well [short pause], yeah, the only thing is when they get more seriously hurt, then I'm responsible, because he won't touch medicines and Band-Aids aren't his thing. That's my responsibility. But that is the only case when the girls make a distinction [and] specifically ask for me.

Dividing Household Tasks

Housework is not a big priority for them. Christine reports 8 hours of housework a week, whereas Richard reports 4, far below the Austrian norm of 25 hours a week for women and 14 hours for men (STATA, 2009). Notably, the family doesn't live in a small apartment, but in a house of 180 sq. meters with a garden. Richard does "his" portion of the housework during the week, while Christine does "hers" mostly on the weekend.

For Christine, making such a minimal effort meant lowering her standards, which sometimes irritates her. She complains, "It always looks chaotic here," whereas Richard jokes, "This is what it looks like straightened up." Although the furnishings and houseplants create a light and friendly atmosphere in their home, the stacks of papers and toys strewn about confirm the disorder.

Richard's negligence sometimes leads to conflicts. "One example is that I've been asking him for a year to clean up this pile of papers on the window sill," Christine says. She argues that her husband should clean more, while trying to avoid falling into the trap of doing much more than he to maintain her standards. Doing it for him is not an option for her, so she has no alternative but to live with it, "Well, I don't have a choice; I work 40 hours a week. I can't clean up all the time so I have to get used to him not straightening up." One part of their solution to the cleaning conflict is to rely on a housekeeper who comes for 4 hours every 2 to 3 weeks.

They don't completely agree about who does the laundry. Christine claims that it is mostly she, although Richard will do some if she sorts it first. Although he agrees that she does a bit more than he does, he claims to be doing a relatively bigger share now that he is home. "I've started washing a lot of clothes. That means I do the laundry and hang it up and take it off the line." Richard also does his father's laundry, which Christine makes clear is not her job, "I don't touch it. That's all his." Ironing is not done much in their household.

All tasks are shared with the exception of cooking. "When something comes up, it's taken care of by the person who has time," explains Richard. But Richard admits that he doesn't like to cook, and Christine prefers her own cooking, so, generally, the hot meals that the family eats on the weekends are cooked by Christine. During the week, she sometimes cooks, sometimes prepares a cold meal, and sometimes they go out. Still, Richard prepares breakfast during the week and packs lunches when the kids are going out. He often makes sandwiches for dinner, and occasionally Christine reports that if she is getting home late, "Sometimes I can convince him to make noodles; then the girls help him because Papa could even somehow manage to burn water." These acts are not seen as actual "cooking."

Jobs

Christine and Richard have very different careers. She has switched fields and held multiple jobs, but has the more secure and lucrative job in the family. Richard has always been self-employed, which he considers a privilege because it brings freedom and flexibility with it. "I want to be independent; I need to feel free," Richard emphasized. He sees the coercion of being an employee as the price of the higher security of a conventional job.

Although he takes great pleasure in his work, he does not try to increase his customer base and earn more money:

> I could … put a lot of effort into growing my business, take on big projects, hire people and things like that. I have had several opportunities to do that. I never wanted to. Yeah, I wanted to work on my own and stay independent, which is great for the kids now.

Christine seems more invested in her career. She can't imagine a life without employment. "Even if I had married a super millionaire," she says, "I still probably wouldn't stay at home the whole day and do housework."

She likes the international company she works for. She senses a lot of respect for different cultural ways of doing things, and feels appreciated at her job. Moreover, she emphasizes that her job is compatible with motherhood. For example, her workplace grants some flexibility when she has to leave to pick up her daughter. At the same time, she argues that motherhood enhances her performance in what can be a very demanding job:

> Well, sometimes it's crazy. But in certain situations, I don't let it get to me, because I have kids [chuckle]. I personally say that putting mothers in those kinds of positions is the best thing that can happen ... They do better because they are more relaxed about a lot of things and always have at least a Plan B or a Plan C up their sleeve.

Husband and wife share financial responsibility, but Christine earns more than her husband and her job provides more financial security. She is proud of her superior earnings. She can imagine limiting her job to only 30 hours and even thinks her company "could also manage it," but she says, "to be honest, I haven't brought it up, because then, naturally, I would earn less."

Christine doesn't feel at all torn between the demands of motherhood and her job because she is confident that her kids are comfortable with her career. In fact, she thinks that working makes her a better mother:

> For the girls it's normal that I go to work. They don't see it as a big problem or whine about me going to the office every morning ... because they see that I feel good about going to work. So it's good for them, too, because I'm not stressed or angry and so we have good relationships.

Christine tells an anecdote that reveals the two girls' natural acceptance of their parents' alternative gender roles. They don't present a problem at all and, in fact, appear to them as the only possible way to arrange family life:

> When I went on maternity leave with Lucy, Hannah was about 3¼. After I had been home for a week, I got up one afternoon and did some ironing. Hannah was sitting on the floor. After about 5 to 10 minutes of staring at me, she said, "Mama, why are you at home?" I said, "Well, we had a baby and I'm at home so that I can take care of you and the baby, and now Papa can go back to work." She looked at me again and said, "But Mamas go to work, Papas stay at home."

History

The story of their equality begins even before the children were born. Christine had studied social science, but could not find employment in her field. Rather than resign herself to underemployment, she retrained in economics and finance and then found full-time employment in banking. Richard was already a successful self-employed computer software engineer. Both of them did their own housework. Richard explained, "For 5 years we each had our own places and each of us took care of our own household, more or less. And when we moved in together here it was clear that the work should be divided up, because each of us already was used to doing housework."

The most traditional time in their relationship was after the children were born. Christine took maternity/parental leave for a year after the birth of each child. During the brief time when Christine was on leave, she even cooked lunch for everybody every day. Nonetheless, from the beginning Richard really wanted to be an involved father. Christine did not have to fight for his participation, Richard reported, "We fought more about which of us was allowed to do something with the kid." Childcare was regarded as a privilege in their family.

Richard emphasizes that he has "always been the type to spend a lot of time with kids," and always wanted children of his own. Although he has some regrets that he didn't decide to have children earlier, he sees a certain advantage to being an "old father":

> I enjoyed life for a long time without kids. That means that I enjoy life with kids that much more, because I'm not missing out on anything. I can imagine that if I had kids at 20 or 22, I would have thought more about whether I wanted kids at that age. Then, naturally other things had priority: things like going out, vacation, fun, studying, an easy life, not being tied down.

When their first child, Hannah, was born, Richard cut back his hours while Christine went on maternity/parental leave. She went back part-time when their daughter was 7 months old and resumed full-time employment a year after the birth. According to Richard, due to his flexible employment situation, it "was always clear" that Christine would return to work soon after her maternity leave and that he would then take paternity leave, but that they would leave open how they would respond subsequently. He explained:

> We really thought a lot about what we would do ... We said she would stay on maternity leave until [the daughter] was about a year old, and then I would go [on leave]. Then we would see what happens, which would depend on her job. It [also] would depend on how much work I have – if I get three new major projects, or I don't do any active acquisition. We could rethink things or switch them around.

Nonetheless, when Christine lost her job after her parental leave ended, they did not implement the option of extending her maternity leave and having Richard take on more work. Christine soon found a new job and

Richard remained on paternity leave for 2 years, until the birth of their second child. With the second child, this pattern was repeated – Christine was again on maternity leave for about a year. Again she was fired (after the legal retention period required) and forced to change jobs, but found another job. Richard took over the primary childcare responsibility with a subsidy for his reduced employment hours.

They invoke the financial incentives, in part, to explain their ongoing decisions about how they would divide parental leave and childcare. Christine says, "From the very beginning we divided things up that way ... because I actually always [laughs] had a higher income, so it made sense to do it that way. It wouldn't make any sense now for me to work less, because that wouldn't result in him earning more." Richard explains that they needed the money and that he had more flexibility to adjust his hours to retain the childcare subsidy.

However, Christine's return to full-time employment after her children were born was not simply motivated by financial concerns. Christine was not happy with the part-time option she took when Hannah was 7 months old. Richard says, "She didn't feel satisfied during the brief period of time when she only worked 16 hours a week, particularly because she had simpler work to do than before her maternity leave." Moreover, being home full-time didn't suit her, "When I was at home with the baby, the second time, it didn't work so well ... He was working at home – it doesn't work. We argued too much during the day ... we got on each other's nerves a little."

What Helps?

Employment

The couple's employment situation promotes their nontraditionally gendered life. Being self-employed allows Richard to work flexible hours, which is compatible with childcare, whereas the standard hours of Christine's job are a constraint on childcare. Richard can pick up the kids from school at 3:00 p.m., while Christine doesn't get home until 6:00 p.m. As mentioned earlier, his self-employment was also an important factor in the decision to share the infant care leave as well as the childcare subsidy.

The Austrian childcare subsidy reimburses mothers and/or fathers for at least part of the effort of caring for small children. Using the subsidy generally means a significant reduction in income. The larger the previous income, the bigger the financial loss would be. In Richard and Christine's case, Christine's larger income and Richard's self-employment, which gave him the ability to regulate his additional earnings, both monthly and yearly, promoted their nontraditional division of labor because it made economic sense for him to take greater advantage of parental leave.

However, it would be a mistake to assume that the external conditions were solely responsible for the less traditional division of responsibility within the family. The external conditions were created by choices the two of them made. As Richard says:

> Well, this constellation didn't come about by chance. We decided to do it this way, that one of us has the security of a regular income with benefits and insurance and the other brings in extra income, icing on the cake, but has the freedom to take care of the household, the kids and everything. I mean it's no accident that it came about; we actively decided. Well that's the way we wanted it.

Attitudes Toward Career and Family

Richard's unconventional attitude toward career and his desire to spend time with his children, coupled with Christine's commitment to her career and her willingness to share childcare and to credit men with the ability to care, go a long way toward explaining their nontraditional choices. For Richard, enjoying work, avoiding monotony, independence, and flexible hours are central issues for him, whereas money and prestige are less important, "In my life I only do things that I love doing ... In the short run, there are things you have to do ... but in the long run I only do what I love doing." Unlike his wife, he does not have a university degree and chose not to pursue the prestige of an academic title, although he has fulfilled nearly all the requirements for graduation, "Well I could have finished my studies and gotten a degree – but status, what other people think, isn't important to me ... I couldn't care less." He isn't the least bit threatened by Christine's outearning him.

Moreover, Richard admits that the choice to limit his paid work is not simply attributable to parenting:

> If I had more time, because ... I didn't have any kids ... I could actively try to get more jobs – acquire more contracts. I don't know if I would do it or not. Well, I'm more of a lazy dog than a workhorse [laughs]. Just to have a little more money, I don't know, probably not.

Christine seems more committed to her career. At several turning points, Christine faced obstacles that could have derailed her, but in each case she redoubled her efforts to secure full-time challenging work. She retrained when her university degree did not provide a ticket to employment. Twice she was undaunted when she was fired immediately after the (legally defined) retention period following the birth of each daughter. Rather than give up and take a more traditional role in the family by working part-time or staying home, as many mothers might have done, she found new full-time jobs. Part-time employment was not a satisfying option for her.

Their nontraditional career balance also gives Richard the opportunity to spend a lot of time with his children, which he relishes, "I am crazy about the kids and love the time I spend with them ... I enjoy it, yeah, I love it ... You get so much back from the kids. It's unbelievable how many positive experiences you have."

Both Christine and Richard reject essentialist beliefs that mothers have a stronger attachment to children or are naturally more well-suited to care for them. Full of conviction, Richard asserts, "There is no difference. It's just how much time do you invest and how much you are involved. Men and women can both do it equally well if they want to." The only hint of some reluctance on Christine's part was Richard's statement that they initially fought about who was "allowed" to care for their first baby. However, now Christine does not seem the least bit threatened by sharing the caregiving with Richard.

The couple admits that just after a birth there was definitely a danger of slipping, of being drawn into traditional roles. That they didn't was due to their active efforts to prevent it: Richard's willingness to restrict his professional commitments to support her return to her career, and Christine's choice to find a new job and trust Richard with infant care. Richard's choice not to pursue advancement in his own career isn't seen as a sacrifice. He sees Christine's carrying the greater burden of financial responsibility as a valuable gift, which allows him to spend more time with their children than most fathers can manage. He doesn't feel that his masculinity is threatened in any way by the higher salary his wife earns. Likewise, she doesn't appear to be threatened by his close relationship with their children.

The two agree that sharing the responsibilities, which includes full-time employment for both parents, would be extremely difficult without the support of all-day school or kindergarten. Their children receive a hot lunch, and although they usually leave by mid-afternoon, they have the option of staying later, which the parents rely on when there are extra demands from Richard's work. What's decisive here is the couple's access to and approval of this kind of external care. All-day school in Austria exists mainly in the large cities and, in general, there is little social acceptance of it.

Family Background

Richard and Christine's childhoods reveal some parallels. Both of their fathers were self-employed, and both mothers worked in the family business. However, employment for mothers did not imply active fathers. In both Christine's and Richard's families, child raising was women's work, and was delegated to an external care provider. One striking difference between their parents and them is that both fathers, although self-employed like Richard, bore the primary financial responsibility. Instead of taking advantage of the opportunity for flexible hours, they invested long hours in their businesses.

Richard's father was a negative model for him. His father was never able to deal with children and often expresses his bewilderment in the face of Richard's efforts. Richard identifies his mother as his role model:

> It was mostly my mother; she showed me the most. My father ... and kids – I couldn't learn anything from him except how not to do it. My mother was the super nanny for kids, yeah, right. She was always the one. She filled kids with love, me too, and her grandchildren. Yeah and I saw how she did it; I remember a lot of it.

Although Christine's and Richard's fathers were similar in their traditional roles, their mothers differed in one essential point. Whereas Richard describes his mother as a warmhearted, loving woman, who served as his role model for his interactions with children, Christine describes her mother as "actually a very cold person in many respects," who has not connected with her own children or her grandchildren. Christine doesn't have a role model for maternal behavior.

The Social Network: "They Think I'm the Pied Piper of Hamelin"

Richard has gotten to know many parents, mostly mothers, and has been instrumental in developing a large network of them. In the absence of any help from grandparents, this network provides important support when Richard can't take care of his children in the afternoon due to appointments with clients or when he has to make his annual business trip.

> Kindergarten has helped us to make lots of friends. Mostly through me, I have to give myself some credit here ... mostly the mothers. I brought the mothers together and today they are people who take vacations together and have become best friends ... ten families ... Naturally they all live here; they all have kids the same age ... That's why I tried to get them together from the start. Because it makes sense ... I can always ask them, "Can you take my kid?" ... You can just come up to someone – you don't even need to call ahead ... But it goes the other way, too; I take kids a lot. Sometimes I come home with five kids. They think I'm the Pied Piper of Hamelin, because it happens so often. The kids love it, of course, whenever someone comes over or they can go somewhere else. They have a lot of fun and for us it gives us flexibility. We've partially replaced the grandparents with these friends, yeah. Naturally you can't abuse it. It has to be give and take.

This social network comes in especially handy when Richard takes his one-week annual business trip to Belgium. He does his best to organize substitutes to take the burden off Christine:

> When I'm in Belgium ... I call everyone and say, "Okay boys and girls, how do things look this week, is there any time you can take my kids?" So when someone takes them on one day, someone else another, then a third, we have three days covered, and there are only two days where Christine has to be home, or we'll do something else, find some other solution.

In addition to the help he gets from the other parents, their acceptance of him validates and supports his nontraditional role as an involved father. He brags about taking care of their kids as well as his own and he is proud of his unusual role among the mothers:

> Naturally I love being with all the wonderful mothers ... whether we are drinking coffee in the park or if we've decided to go out somewhere together. I've already gone to mother-child gymnastics with our older daughter; now I'm going with the younger one. It's called mother-child gymnastics and I always go. We've already discussed whether it should be called mother-child gymnastics, but ... I am almost always the only father.

While other fathers might not feel comfortable around all the mothers, or even feel excluded, Richard's special status is a reward for him, beyond the enjoyment he feels from spending time with his children:

> Standing out, yeah, being someone special in society, I like that just as much ... Even at the park or someplace in the afternoon, the kids are playing, you're drinking coffee, the moms and I or sometimes eight moms and two dads ...

And I like that, the fact that it's unusual, that I'm doing something unusual and am really actively living it.

Undoing Gender

Richard and Christine are undoing gender in the ways that they organize and share family life. Each of them is proud of how they have invested and succeeded in realms that have traditionally been associated with the other gender. Richard's masculinity is not threatened by his childcare, his time among mothers, or his prioritizing his wife's career over his. Likewise, Christine is not threatened by Richard's time with their children or by her involvement in her career.

Christine pursues her career with more vigor than the majority of women in Austria; Richard cares for his children more than most Austrian men. At times, their equal sharing can seem like a reversal of traditional roles. However, unlike traditional wives, Richard has a full-time successful career and unlike traditional husbands, Christine assumes as much or more responsibility for the children as her husband when she is at home. Christine also still does a bit more of the housework than Richard.

For both of them and their children, their arrangements work well. Christine shudders when she contemplates a dual-career life without sharing:

> It's simple. If I had to do it alone in addition to my 44-hour-a-week job, I would explode. It's impossible for one partner to be responsible for all the housework, kids and everything that goes along with it, so that the other partner can come home [and] throw his coat on the floor. I mean that's impossible!

Richard repeatedly extols how much he gets back from the time he spends with his children; he can't imagine a better life, "It is a perfect fit . . . I love it and wouldn't have it any other way."

References

Audenaert, V., Buchebner-Ferstl, S., Cizek, B., Cuyvers, P., Deven, F., Hoogiemstra, E., Lucassen, N., Pfeiffer, C., & Pool, M. (eds.) (2004). *The Glass Partitioning Wall: The Difference Between Equity and Equality in Partner Interaction on Work, Household and Care*. The Hague: Nederlandse Gezinsraad.

Cuyvers, P. (2000). *Partner Interaction: Partner Demography and Equal Opportunities as Future Labour Supply Factors*. European Commission SOC 98 101387-05E01. The Hague: Netherlands Family Council.

Eurostat (2018). *Women in the EU Earned an Average of 16% Less than Men in 2016*. Retrieved from: https://ec.europa.eu/eurostat/documents/2995521/ 8718272/3-07032018-BP-EN.pdf/fb402341-e7fd-42b8-a7cc-4e33587d79aa.

Kaindl, M. & Schipfer, R. (2017). *Familie in Zahlen 2017. Statistische Informationen zu Familien in Österreich* [Family in numbers 2017. Statistical information on families in Austria]. Vienna: Österreichisches Institut für Familienforschung (ÖIF). Retrieved from: https://backend.univie.ac.at/file admin/user_upload/p_oif/FiZ/fiz_2017.pdf.

Rille-Pfeiffer, C., Dearing, H., & Schmidt, A. E. (2018). Austria Country Note. In S. Blum, A. Koslowski, A. Macht, & P. Moss (eds.) *International Review of Leave Policies and Research 2018* (pp. 57–65). Retrieved from: www .leavenetwork.org/lp_and_r_reports/.

Statistica (2019). *Anzahl der Gläubigen von Religionen in Österreich im Zeitraum 2012 bis 2018* [Number of believers of religions in Austria from 2012 to 2018]. Retrieved from: https://de.statista.com/statistik/daten/studie/304874/ umfrage/mitglieder-in-religionsgemeinschaften-in-oesterreich/.

Statistik Austria (2009). *Zeitverwendung (2008/2009). Ein Überblick über geschlechtsspezifische Unterschiede. Endbericht der Bundesanstalt Statistik Österreich an die Bundesministerin für Frauen und Öffentlichen Dienst* [Time use (2008/2009). Overview over gender-specific differences. Final report of the federal agency Statistic Austria to the Federal Ministry for Women and Public Service]. (GZ: BKA-F140.300/0003-II/1/2008). Retrieved from: www.statistik.at/web_de/static/zeitverwendung_200809_ ein_ueberblick_ueber_geschlechtsspezifische_untersc_052108.pdf.

Statistik Austria (Hrsg.) (2018). *Statistisches Jahrbuch Österreichs 2011* [Statistical Yearbook 2011]. Vienna: Verlag Österreich.

18

Turkey

Cagla Diner

Hande and Burak Yilmaz are a married couple who live with their 7-year-old son, Deniz, close to the center of Istanbul. Their gentrified neighborhood, Cihangir, is favored by artists, writers, and young professionals, and the rents are quite high, but the couple lives in an old, small, and modest apartment and, as long-time tenants, they pay a relatively inexpensive rent. Hande got a degree in engineering and Burak in philosophy at one of the best universities in Turkey, but both of them have been working in publishing since then.

Hande and Burak met and started dating while at the university. After living together for over a year, they married. Burak was employed full-time and Hande part-time as editors in prestigious publishing companies. Hande also did freelance translation in the evenings. They shared the housework equally.

When Deniz was born, a year after they married, they continued to share housework. Burak's parents moved nearby to help with childcare and they hired household help once a week to clean, do laundry, and iron. They reminisce about these years as the "good old days" because they had enough money and leisure time.

Hande breastfed for almost 2 years. She was Deniz's primary caregiver with the help of the grandmother until he was 2½ years old. She picked him up from the grandparents when she was done with her job and later picked him up from the nursery after the grandparents moved away. Burak prepared meals, occasionally bottle-fed Deniz, and occasionally changed his diapers. But when Hande traveled abroad for her job, Burak stayed home and took care of Deniz alone. Hande says, however, that Burak's main way to help during those years was to entertain and play with the baby.

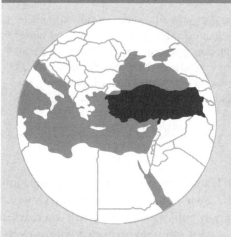 Turkey's population is approximately 81 million. It is predominantly Muslim with only 0.2% Christians and Jews (Central Intelligence Agency [CIA], 2019). Most Muslims are Sunnis, but a minority are Alevis who embrace a form of Shia unique to the Anatolian region, more liberal in religious belief (Dombey, 2014). Approximately 70 to 75% of the population is Turkish, 19% is Kurdish, and the remaining 7 to 12% belong to different ethnicities (CIA, 2019). Couples with children comprise the most common type of household (43%), followed by extended families (16%), single persons (15.4%), couples without children (14.2%), lone parents (8.5%), and unrelated groups (2.5%) (Turkish Statistical Institute [TSI], 2019c).

Women's labor force participation rate is 36.1% versus 77.4% for men. Women earn less than half (43%) of what men earn. A quarter of employed women work part-time (World Economic Forum, 2018).

In the private sector, women have the right to a 16-week paid maternity leave and an additional 6 months of unpaid leave, whereas men have no right to parental leave. In the public sector, which comprises only 3% of the workforce, women receive 16 weeks of paid leave, men only 10 paid days; both can take up to 24 months in unpaid leave (İlkkaracan, 2014). However, more than half of employed women work in the informal labor market and are not covered by these policies (Baslevent & Acar, 2015).

There is low public investment in early childhood education, and the preschool enrollment rate is only 37% for children between 3 and 5 years old. In fact, less than 10% of 3-year-olds are enrolled (OECD, 2018). İlkkaracan (2014) has argued that Turkey has a conservative family-based care regime. The lack of available institutionalized childcare is one of the contributing factors underlying the masculinized labor market in Turkey. Government policies perpetuate mothers' roles as the primary caregivers. In 86% of families, care of children aged 0 to 5 is done by the mother, with the rest going to (presumably female) grandmothers, relatives, nannies, and kindergarten (TSI, 2019b).

> Based on 2014–2015 time-use data, overall, women spend substantially more time (4:35 hours per day) than men (0:53) on household and family care. Employed women's contribution drops to 3:31, versus men's (0:46) (TSI, 2019a). Household tasks are gendered. For example, in 91.2% of families, women do the cooking and in 89.7% they do the ironing, whereas in 77.7% of families men are responsible for bill paying and in 89% men do the small repairs (TSI, 2019d).

When Deniz was 2 years old, Hande was fired from her part-time job. She and Burak established their own publishing company, "Omega." Burak kept his full-time editing job until a year and a half later, when he also got fired. After Burak lost his job, they struggled with poverty. Burak depicts the difficulties of life without enough money, "You would walk the whole Istiklal Street with a 3-year-old in your arms because you didn't have a lira in your pocket. You don't have money to get on the tram . . . There are times you can't have lunch." The grandparents had left Istanbul by then, and because there was no public daycare slot available, Deniz went to a private full-time nursery, which increased the financial strain on the family. Even when Deniz started attending a free public preschool at 5½ years old, they had difficulty making ends meet and were always in debt. They had no regular income and their publishing company, Omega, had huge expenses. The family had to give up paid household help, which, Burak reports, was hard on Hande. She got mad about spending the weekends cleaning. He quotes her complaints, "Why can't we go to Bebek Park on Saturdays and Sundays?"

Things started to improve financially when Hande started her current full-time job as publishing coordinator at a major university press. Thanks to her salary, after a year they were able to alleviate the debt they had accumulated since establishing Omega. Burak's childcare and housework responsibilities increased, especially after he started working from home. Deniz had turned 7 by then.

A Typical Week

On a typical weekday Hande wakes up before everyone else. She prepares breakfast and the breakfast table for Burak and Deniz; she leaves home at 7:20 a.m. Burak wakes up about 10 minutes after Hande leaves, makes Deniz's hot chocolate, and by 8:00 a.m. wakes up Deniz. They have breakfast together while watching the cartoons that Deniz likes. If Deniz had not completed his homework the night before, Burak makes sure that he does it in the morning. Deniz can get dressed and get ready for school on his own, but Burak picks out what he will wear to speed things up. He makes sure that Deniz brushes his teeth, and oversees his packing of the school bag. Then Burak walks him to school, which is close by.

Burak runs his publishing business from home. During the day, he cleans and vacuums when he takes a break. At 5:30 p.m., he picks Deniz up from school. On the way home, they shop for whatever is needed for that day's dinner. Shopping for food, planning what to cook, and cooking are all Burak's jobs. Usually Hande does not even know what they have in the fridge. If Burak forgets to buy something, he calls her and she buys it on her way home. When Burak and Deniz arrive home, Burak prepares dinner, which takes about an hour, while Deniz plays by himself, does homework, or watches cartoons. Hande comes home between 6:30 and 7:00 p.m. Burak reports that she then rests for about half an hour, or sometimes for an hour. But Hande says that when she lies on the couch, she is also spending time with Deniz and checking to see if he has done his homework.

The three of them sit down to eat at around 7:30 or 8:00 p.m. and typically spend more than about an hour at the table. Deniz sits with them and the conversation focuses on his interests. For example, Deniz had been very interested in the lives of the Ottoman Sultans. Intrigued because he read that brothers assassinated each other to become the Sultan, he peppered his parents with questions. Burak, who wants Deniz to develop the habit of pursuing his interests, sometimes did research himself to answer Deniz's questions. Burak also takes him on excursions following his interests. For example, Hande recounts, "When he was into streetcars, Burak took him all the way to the airport just so they can see the route of the streetcar. He cares that much; he goes out on a Sunday and takes him all the way to the airport."

Hande says that she takes over both housework and childcare in the evenings because Burak has done so much during the day. At dinner, Burak starts to drink *raki*, an alcoholic Turkish drink, which reduces his evening responsibilities.

Hande tidies up the apartment a little bit during the evening and makes the beds, despite that they will be going to bed within a few hours. She usually cleans up from dinner and loads the dishwasher, but Burak does it sometimes, and sometimes they just leave everything for the next day. Hande's main task in the evenings is to put Deniz to sleep. In fact, Hande reports that one night during the past week she went out and came back at 11:30 p.m. and Deniz was still awake waiting for her; his father had already fallen asleep. After Deniz goes to bed, Hande sometimes does some freelance translation. Typically, Hande and Deniz go to bed together. They study English for about half an hour while lying down, then each reads his/her own book, and finally, they turn off the lights and go to sleep hugging each other.

Because Burak is mainly responsible for Deniz on weekdays, Hande takes over on weekends. She takes him regularly to French class on Saturdays and to basketball class on Saturdays and Sundays. Occasionally, Burak takes him to these classes if Hande is very tired or if she goes out to meet a friend. They continually search for a balance in parental chores. For example, Burak goes to the PTA meetings because they are usually during the weekdays, but if they occur on a weekend, then Hande attends.

They share cooking during the weekend. Hande usually cleans the bathroom, washes the clothes, folds them, and puts them away on the weekends as well. But she makes a point of saying she does not iron, "Ironing is never on me, I wouldn't even touch it." Burak cleans the windows once every 2 to 3 months. He takes care of repairs in the house. He also takes care of the car and takes it to the mechanic when needed. Hande pays most of the bills and manages the household budget, but Burak pays the rent. They both believe that Burak does more housework than Hande.

Hande focuses on Deniz's emotional needs and psychological development. Every night she asks him about what happened in school. If he hints that something is bothering him, she probes deeper. She worries that he may be too passive. Burak neither asks about Deniz's emotional life nor understands Hande's approach. Nonetheless, Burak is more concerned than she about illness. Hande reports that as soon as Deniz coughs, Burak takes him to the doctor, whereas she typically thinks it is nothing. However, when Deniz is sick or upset, both Hande and Burak try to comfort him by distracting him with new games or books. Burak is also more protective than Hande; for example, he took pains to childproof the house when Deniz was young, and he is more watchful of Deniz when they are out in public. Despite Burak's involvement, Burak reports, "He is closer to her, of course. He says it clearly, 'I love my mom more.'" He is also more likely to give in to her; he is more demanding and stubborn with his father. Hande adds, if they all play a game together, Deniz always sides with her against his father.

Both Hande and Burak are invested and involved in Deniz's intellectual life, but their views differ. Hande believes success at school is critical. She wants him to get high scores on competitive national examinations so he can go to a good high school and a good university. She worries that in the public primary school he attends, he is using only 10% of his potential. Having already known how to read and write when he started first grade, Hande believes that Deniz is more advanced than his classmates and that he would learn more at a better school. Burak, on the other hand, is confident that the upbringing they provide will serve him well enough, no matter which school Deniz attends.

Both Burak and Hande want Deniz to be a person who knows how to think, and who has values and principles. Burak asserts, "A man has to have the capacity to go after his own passions rather than imitating others." Both of them are critical of Turkey's educational system, but Burak is more relaxed about whether or not Deniz gets into a good university. He can afford to be relaxed because he knows that Hande is quite concerned about this issue. He admits, "I have peace of mind about that because his mother makes the choice of his school, because she takes care of all that."

In general, Hande claims to take responsibility for more of the management of parenting. She thinks and worries about the details of his everyday life, such as haircuts, clothes, and school supplies. If he is going to a friend's birthday party, she buys the present and arranges how Deniz will get to and from the party.

In sum, although Hande and Burak perceive the division of childcare as equal, Hande spends more time with Deniz overall, has a closer relationship with him, and is the manager of parenting responsibilities. Equality is achieved through the balance with Burak's greater contribution to housework. Burak does not complain about doing more housework because he is happy that his wife has a prestigious well-paying job, which relieves them of financial stress. They still live in the same rather small apartment, and they still have debts to pay, but they are now able to buy their necessities without getting into further debt. Sometimes they even eat out.

The financial hardship they suffered intensely for about 3 years seems to have made them closer as a couple. They are happy with their current division of labor, although both feel overburdened with work and wish they had more leisure time. Clearly, they care about each other's well-being and would like to make life easier for each other. For example, Burak says that he makes the ingredients of the salad ready for Hande to be chopped and seasoned to protect her hands from water as she has eczema. Hande worries that Burak feels like a "housewife," and wants to have more money to hire household help and to afford office space for Burak. He would not feel like a "housewife" if he did not work at home.

"Omega ... Is Like Another Child for Us"

Burak runs Omega, the publishing house, by himself. He does all the intellectual and administrative work, as well as the physical work: deciding what will be published, designing the layout, and loading the books into the car for delivery. He cares deeply about this part of his life. He says that he "does it with love," and he believes that he is successful because, despite the lack of money, Omega is well respected.

Hande is also very proud of her work as the publishing coordinator at the university. She chooses the books to be published by the university press and works with the relevant people to publish them. She reports, "People around me say that I do it very well. They always compliment me, 'You came here, and you saved it, this place became something.' I hear these things once or twice a week." She wants to remain at her current job for 10 more years to continue to draw a good salary, and to build her reputation, "That place should become something and reach 50 or 100 books; they should say in the future 'one woman came by and made something out of here.'" Nonetheless, when considering whose career is more important she muses:

> Which is more important? That's really hard for me to say ... somewhere deep in my heart Omega is more important than University Publishing ... Omega, other than being Burak's career, is like another child for us ... When I become 50 or 60, Omega will be very big and important. They will either fire me or I will retire [from University Publishing]. Because Omega will be the place I will end up at.

She points out the sacrifices they make for Omega, "We could send Deniz to a very expensive school. We could close down Omega and pay all the debt off ... But we don't do that ... Deniz goes to public school. We continue to invest everything in Omega ... We think that's the right thing to do."

Why Burak and Hande Became an Egalitarian Couple

Hande asserts that how much they work outside the home determines how they share housework and childcare. The care Burak gives Deniz, as well as his greater share of housework, is shaped by the structure of their work lives, with Burak working at home, while Hande puts in long hours at her workplace. They have been able to create this structure because Burak does not resent doing more housework than she, and she does not resent being the breadwinner. Hande says, "There are women who think,

'This man is going to take care of me and I am going to lie down. The man has to earn money and take care of me and my child.' ... I am not like that. I work and I don't see that as a burden."

Hande's determination that she will not do more housework than Burak, however, is another key factor. Even when she was employed part-time, she did not take a larger share of the household labor. Hande waited until Burak came home to start the housework so they could do it together. She explains:

> When Burak was working in a full-time job, I was working in a part-time job. Deniz wasn't around then. Even then, when he came home, we usually did everything together ... When I am sitting at home, I will get up and vacuum the place? Never! I never do that. I never iron, never. I mean when I was at home and he was working full-time, I never do more work, under no condition ... I never do more than Burak does.

Hande is adamant that she would never take the role of a "proper" wife who serves her husband:

> I can never be the type of woman that [society] would like. If I am home in the afternoon, I am doing editing. I am definitely working: I am translating, I have something in my hands. When I am doing editing, it's not like I am going to get up and cook or say, "I should put those dishes away." ... Also, if I had done all that and Burak had done less, I would have been really bothered. I can never establish that kind of marriage or relationship. I am always serving a man, everywhere is clean, magnificent house, food is being prepared, dishes ... that can't happen.

She made sure it didn't happen:

> When he comes home at night, I would have done nothing so far. Everyone helps. Or if he is not putting away the dishes, I don't either. And because I am not the kind of person that is clean and neat and "everything should be put away neatly," those dishes there never bother me. If he is not putting them away, then I am not either.

Despite their perception that Burak currently does more housework than Hande overall, Burak does not think it is unfair. Reflecting on the experience of poverty, Burak explains, "When you get through all these really bad times, this doesn't seem that important anymore. An external thing, like unemployment, would be very hard on me. I don't care if I work 2 hours more in the kitchen." He even talks about the pleasure of cooking for others, "As long as there is a meal being eaten here with nice people, I can work for 4 hours in the kitchen ... I think people ... think of it as a burden they don't want to do. I think of it as something that brings happiness."

Hande gives Burak some credit for their egalitarian arrangements, and herself some credit for choosing someone like him, "I don't think that I transformed him or I educated him on this. It's because he is that kind of person and I found him and I felt that." In addition to his lack of resentment toward her for his greater share of housework, neither of them are bothered that she is the higher earner in the family.

Nonetheless, their equal sharing could potentially be undermined because both feel uncomfortable about the degree of Burak's involvement with housework. Both of them see it as a threat to his masculinity and worry that he is becoming "a housewife." Hande relates an incident that illustrates her unease:

> The other day we came back from a picnic; we spent the whole day outside. When I was cooking the okra, he went and vacuumed because it was too dusty. He thinks that he is becoming more of a housewife and I think it is so. Think about it. He says, "I should go vacuum over there really quickly." ... It seems so odd to me, a man saying out of the blue, "I should vacuum." I have also never been that way ... There is dust ... I never see it. After weeks I would say, "I should clean a bit." After 5 hours [outside] ... would you come home and think about vacuuming? Would you even think that way as a woman?

Burak reveals the same worry. For example, in the past he would never think in advance about what to cook for dinner. He would simply go to the grocery store and decide what to buy there. He confesses, "After we moved the Omega office here at home is when I said I turned into a housewife. I got scared one day when I thought about it when I was in bed."

He says that his transformation came about partly as a result of pressure from family and friends to have a cleaner house. His sister would say, "Your shower curtain is really dirty, let's clean that up; I'll get a new one for you." Or a friend would ask, "How do you even touch your hand on the kitchen light?" The last straw, though, was when an insect colony formed in the house and they had to call an exterminator. After that, Burak says, he started to clean some of the very dirty spots around the house. One day he wiped the kitchen cabinets, another day he cleaned the fan in the kitchen, which was covered in oil dust. And so it continued until one day he found himself lying in bed and making plans about where to clean the next time. Hande worries about Burak, but notes the double standard:

> As a man he is going to feel "that's enough." I think he might feel like, "All this woman's work is being put on the man." ... It's like his manhood is becoming a woman, like we switched roles. I earn good money; I go to work. I come home at night very tired. There are thousands of examples like the man comes home all tired at night, lies on the couch, never thinks "I should go and load the

dishwasher, the woman has been dusting all day." That man thinks, "I am a man, I came from outside, I read my newspaper, I eat my dinner when the table is set, then I go to bed, I watch TV and I sleep."

Although Hande is well aware of the injustice of this double standard, she can't help feeling guilty. So sometimes she forces herself to do housework at night:

> Burak has this feeling, "I am like a maid; I have become a housewife." ... I worry about that. I say, "It shouldn't be like that." Even if I am really tired when I come home at night, just so he doesn't think that way, even though I really don't want to, I go into the kitchen and I prepare something. Or some days, I get so tired that I throw myself on the couch and I don't want to move a finger ... but I say, "The man has been doing all these things since the morning; I should get up and help." I go and load the dishwasher with those feelings ... If it was up to me, those dishes could stay there in filth, they could smell, bugs can go in them; that might happen ... If he gets up to do it, I think, "He shouldn't do it, I should." It's 10 at night, Deniz is asleep, and the table is dirty. He really would have been working since 7:30 in the morning, always either for Omega or for housework.

She is ambivalent about what to do. As much as she thinks she should not let him do more housework, she says, "I don't want to kill myself just so he doesn't feel bad either. I can't do that." Her fantasized solution to their dilemma is to get paid help for the housework. Her biggest dream is to hire a woman who could do all the work: the food, the dishes, the laundry, and the cleaning. "When I come home at night, the food would be ready, and I could just sit down. ... I wouldn't have to make the beds when I come home. The house is all clean; I come home to a magnificent house ... how nice. I could spare more time for Burak, for Deniz, a happy family."

Hande has also been working since 7:30 in the morning, and seems to take greater responsibility for childcare. The reactions from their families may account for her guilt and worry. Burak says, "My parents think I do a lot of work, like I am here washing the dishes and Hande is there sitting. They think, 'Why doesn't Hande do it?'" Hande reports that both of Burak's sisters, his dad, and his mom all think that Burak takes on a lot more responsibility. "They think it's very asymmetrical ... My own mom says, 'You are using this man; you are leaving it all on him.'"

Both of them grew up in traditional households. Burak's father worked for the government; his mother was a housewife. Burak describes his father's role sarcastically, "Mom did everything. Dad went back and forth to work ... He didn't do anything ... but it looked like he did everything. He did the *holy* breadwinning work." Hande says of her parents, "Both of my parents worked, they both came home at the same time at night. My dad would lie on the couch and read his newspaper, drink his alcohol; my mom would cook – totally asymmetrical." Although they have rejected the lifestyles of their parents, those traditional gendered roles may still insidiously influence them.

Burak and Hande have achieved equality by undoing gender. Hande is the main breadwinner, and Burak does a larger share of housework and, moreover, manages the housework by thinking about, noticing, and planning what needs to be done. Although they have undone gender in their actions, they still think in gendered ways. Burak's contribution seems to be exaggerated and Hande's minimized. Burak's involvement in housework threatens to emasculate him, and Hande suffers from worry and guilt because of that. Although she doesn't want a "housewife" role, she doesn't want him to have it either. They pay a price for equality.

References

Baslevent, C. & Acar, A. (2015). Recent Trends in Informal Employment in Turkey, *Yildiz Social Science Review*, 1(1), 77–88.

Central Intelligence Agency (2019). Turkey. *The World Factbook*. Retrieved from: www.cia.gov/library/publications/the-world-factbook/geos/tu.html.

Dombey, D. (2014, July 28). Alevis Fear for Future Under an Erdogan Presidency. *The Financial Times*, p. 4.

İlkkaracan, İ. (2014). Political Economy of Caring Labor, Gender and Deepening Conservatism in a Developing Economy Context: The Case of Turkey. *Working Paper Series: Work-Family Balance And Gender Equality – A North-South Policy Perspective*. Retrieved from: www.kaum.itu.edu.tr/dosyalar/3013WorkingPaper.WorkFamilyBalance.Turkey.pdf.

OECD (2018). *Education at a Glance 2018. (Turkey)*. Retrieved from: https://read.oecd-ilibrary.org/education/education-at-a-glance-2018/turkey_eag-2018-69-en#page1.

Turkish Statistical Institute (2019a). *Average Activity Time per Person by Type of Activity, Sex and Employment Status, 2014–2015*. Retrieved from: www.turkstat.gov.tr/PreTablo.do?alt_id=1009.

Turkish Statistical Institute (2019b). *Daycare of Kids by SR level 1 and Three Major Provinces*. Retrieved from: www.turkstat.gov.tr/PreTablo.do?alt_id=1068.

Turkish Statistical Institute (2019c). *Number of Households by Size and Type, 2014–2017*. Retrieved from: www.turkstat.gov.tr/PreTablo.do?alt_id=1068.

Turkish Statistical Institute (2019d). *Persons Responsible by Household Chores by SR level 1, Three Major Provinces and Sex*. Retrieved from: www.turkstat.gov.tr/PreTablo.do?alt_id=1068.

World Economic Forum (2018). *The Global Gender Gap Report 2018*. Retrieved from: www3.weforum.org/docs/WEF_GGGR_2018.pdf.

19

Czech Republic[1]

Hana Maříková

Magda and Martin Svoboda have four children and represent the "older generation" of parents, not in terms of their age, but because they lived during the socialist period. Denisa and David Urban are a young married couple, aged 32 and 35, respectively, who represent the new generation who became parents after 1989 (Chaloupková, 2009). Both couples, residing in Prague, represent a small group of equally sharing couples in Czech society. Magda and Martin have progressively moved toward a more equal arrangement of paid work and care responsibilities over the past 21 years. Unlike them, Denisa and David, started their life together with a more equal arrangement, and continued to share once they had a child. Their stories show that despite the difficulties of equally sharing care for children and housework, it is possible, even in a society as gender-conservative as the Czech Republic (Crompton, Brockmann & Lyonette, 2005).

Magda and Martin: A Long Path to Equality

Magda and Martin Svoboda, both secondary school graduates, are parents of a 21-year-old daughter, Nora, a 7-year-old son, Norbert, and 4-year-old twins, Petr and Pavel. Martin has been at home on parental leave with the twins for almost 2 years. He still engages in his business activities, but because he does so from home, he can care for the two youngest children until they start preschool. Magda is employed part-time. Their family

[1] The research for this chapter was supported by CSF (grant no. 17-04465S and grant no. 18-07456S) and by RVO (No. 68378025).

arrangement defies the conventional gendered structure of the family; Martin devotes more time to caring for the children, Magda to paid employment. Both parents view their respective contribution to housework and caring for the children as equal, if not entirely "identical." However, the Svobodas followed a long path before they reached this more balanced arrangement of the shared paid and unpaid work.

The Czech Republic was established as an independent state on January 1, 1993 after the split of the former Czechoslovakia. Over 10.5 million inhabitants live in the Czech Republic, of which more than 64% declare Czech nationality, 25% do not specify a nationality, and the remaining 11% of the population declare Moravian, Silesian, Slovak, Ukrainian, Polish, Vietnamese, German, or Roma nationalities, although the Roma, a disadvantaged minority, may be vastly under-counted (Czech Statistical Office, 2019a; Sekce pro lidská práva, 2017). In the last census, only 20% of Czech inhabitants declared a religion: 34% declared no religion and 45% respondents did not answer the question on religion. The biggest religious group is Roman Catholic, comprising 10% of the population (Czech Statistical Office, 2019a).

The equality of women and men is legally guaranteed in the Czech Republic. The Antidiscrimination Act mandates equal treatment for men and women in employment and in a wide range of societal benefits. Nonetheless, women earned on average 78% of what men earn. In the European Union, only Estonia had a larger pay gap (Czech Statistical Office, 2018). At the end of 2018, the labor force participation rate of women was 68.7% and men 82% (Czech Statistical Office 2019b). However, women's rate is significantly lower when they have children under 6 years old; less than half of them are in the labor force (Czech Statistical Office, 2018).

Paid maternity leave is typically offered for 28 weeks. The parental leave is one of the longest in the European Union; parents can take paid leave up until the child's 2nd, 3rd, or 4th birthday. Payments are based on previous salary and the length of the leave. The right to return to one's job after parental leave is guaranteed until the child is 3 years old. Women, on average, take off 3 years, which employers use to justify gender discrimination. More than 50% of mothers become unemployed after taking parental leave. The employment impact of parenthood on women is the highest in the European Union (Bičáková and Kalíšková, 2015). Fathers are also eligible for parental leave, however, they represent less than 2% of parents on leave (Czech Statistical Office, 2017). Fathers are now also entitled to take 7-day paternal leave until a baby is 6 weeks old. Two-parent families with children make up 49.3% of all households, with an additional 12.2% who include other family members in the household; single-parent families make up 4% (Czech Statistical Office, 2018).

According to the survey Parents 2005, in two-parent families with children under 18 years of age, employed mothers spent 3.3 hours per day on childcare and 2.9 hours on housework, whereas employed fathers spent on average 1.9 hours per day on childcare and 1.6 hours on housework. Mothers on maternity or parental leaves, on average, spent 10.6 hours a day on childcare and 6.1 on housework. In single-parent families, employed mothers did more childcare than employed fathers (2.6 vs. 1.9 hours per day), and spent more time in housework (3 vs. 2.5 hours) (Vohlídalová, 2007).

Childcare from 0 to 2 years is generally accessed in the private sector, and is attended by only 6.8% of children. Public kindergartens serve children from 3 to 5 years old. Over 85% of children in that age group attend kindergarten (OECD, 2018). However, there is no very well elaborated system of care for poor children, who are primarily Roma children, children of unemployed parents, and children from single-parent families. (Horáková, Jahoda, Kofroň, Sirovátka, & Šimíková, 2013).

"Even at 19 or 20, He Wasn't the Kind of Dad who Said, 'Oh My God, the Baby! She's Pooped Herself'"

Magda and Martin married over 20 years ago after a 2-year relationship. Magda was pregnant, but the wedding had already been planned several months before, so, unlike many other couples at that time, her pregnancy was not the reason they married (Fialová & Kučera, 1996). When the couple's first child, Nora, was born, Magda was 20 and Martin 19. Shortly after her birth, Martin performed his compulsory military service for half a year.

The life trajectories of the Svobodas were not unusual. At the start of the "new era" (i.e., after the Velvet Revolution in 1989), young people were still marrying at a relatively young age. However, the Svobodas have always differed from their peers in Martin's active involvement in caring for their young children. Martin was the first parent to bathe little Nora after they brought her home from the hospital, and when he was at home, this task remained his "speciality." After returning from military service, Martin began to be regularly involved in the day-to-day care of the child. Magda noted, "Even at 19 or 20, he wasn't the kind of dad who said, 'Oh my God, the baby! She's pooped herself,' not at all. So even then he was inclined that way. Some people are family types and some aren't. He had no problem with it back then."

Nonetheless, initially their lives were organized very traditionally, as Magda describes:

> I was on the standard 3-year maternity leave and he was going to work then. So then it was traditional, like the way it was in his family originally. He went to work; I looked after the family, cooked, cleaned, and he came and played with the child.

When Nora was 3 years old, she began attending preschool and Magda went back to work. Norbert was born when Nora was 14 years old. Magda stayed at home with him but at her employer's request after about 6 months, she started to work part-time while on parental leave, which she regarded as "ideal." "I had a computer at home and I was able to work from home." But after another 6 months, her employer urged Magda to return to her job full-time. She explains, "For me, that was such a short period. So then we had to decide what is more important and of course, for me, what was more important then, when I'd had a child after 14 years ... I decided to stay with my son. As a result, I lost that job."

During those years, Martin co-owned a hotel with a restaurant, where he worked as a manager 8 to 10 hours a day. But when he was home he always pitched in with housework and childcare. With their second child, various new "conveniences," such as disposable diapers and ready-made quality baby-food, made combining paid work and care less difficult, so the couple decided to have a third child, which turned out to be twins. Around 5 weeks before they were born, Magda was hospitalized. She describes how Martin was thrust into a primary caregiving role:

> Our daughter was there, but she had school and things. She helped out, but he took care of our son all by himself. So that was when it started, that he had to be able to manage absolutely everything – the laundry, the cooking, absolutely everything. And when the twins were born, then it just continued. It followed smoothly from there ... He got involved in everything. The only thing he couldn't do was breastfeed.

Shortly after the twins were born Martin began working from home more often, because his company was hit hard by the economic crisis. He became more intensively involved in the everyday care of the twins until eventually, from the time they were 2, he took parental leave to stay at home with them. He explains:

> The opportunity came up because the hotel where I was working began renovations, which were planned to take a year and a half. But it took longer and I was working from home during that time ... and began looking after the boys. In the meantime, things weren't working out financially well at work, so now the hotel is going down.

Magda reports that at first they alternated shifts:

> Originally I started back at just 4 hours – for a trial – and I went there in the evenings ... My husband worked outside the home; he had to see customers, clients. Now he takes care of everything from home, but then we alternated. In the morning, I was at home with the kids and he took care of his business, and in the afternoon, I went on my evening shift ... Then I changed it. I do a stable 6 hours in the morning and come home shortly after lunch.

Magda notes that over time Martin has taken increasing responsibility, "Initially I prepared the boys' lunches for my husband so that he just had to spend time with them. And in time I realized he was gradually managing it himself. I cook for him once or twice a week, the rest of the time he prepares meals for them."

"It's the Same for Both Me and My Wife. When We Can, We See to It"

Magda and Martin agree that overall, they currently share equally in caring for the children and performing the housework, although Martin does slightly more with the children the days Magda is employed. He reports: "Who has ... time or is able to ... alongside paid employment ... As for the parenting, I don't think that there's a difference between us. It's the same for both me and my wife. When we can, we see to it."

What does a typical day during the workweek in the Svoboda home look like? Magda gets up first in the morning, before 7:00 a.m., wakes up Norbert, makes him breakfast, and sees to his morning hygiene and getting him dressed. She also makes Sunar (a type of powdered milk) for the twins, but they eat later and their father helps them eat, because, as he reports, "One of the boys is a slower eater so you have to stay there with him, work with him more." At 8:00 a.m. Magda takes Norbert to a kindergarten and then goes on to her job. She works as a telephone operator for an energy company from 8:30 a.m. to 2:30 p.m. After that, Magda does some shopping before she picks Norbert up from the pre-school, and then arrives home around 4:00 p.m.

Meanwhile, Martin cares for the twins. Typically, after a morning of playing with toy trains and reading stories, at noon, Martin prepares lunch or warms up the lunch that Magda prepared the day before. After lunch, the twins sleep for around 2 hours while Martin does chores, such as cleaning up, washing dishes, and washing clothes.

The parents spend the late afternoon with the boys, playing together or attending sports practices. Afterwards, Magda prepares dinner while the children watch *Animáček*, a TV show of fairy-tale cartoons. Martin usually works on his business during this time.

In the summer, after dinner, which is usually around 7:00 p.m., the family goes outside, perhaps to do inline skating, or just to play together until the children's bedtime at 9:00 p.m. Magda gets them ready for bed and reads them a bedtime story, although Martin does it occasionally. After the children have gone to bed, Magda might prepare the meal for the next day and Martin might do additional work for his business. They also finish up the daily chores, which are split.

Magda describes their laundry and vacuuming routine:

> We do laundry almost every day. So if he does laundry in the morning, then it dries, and then I sort it. It's really half and half, because sometimes I come home and everything is already sorted. So then I put it away in the cupboards, and sometimes in the evening I'll throw something into the washing machine or I'll hang it out in the morning, but my husband does the laundry more.

She says of vacuuming:

> I do a kind of quick clean up. I just need to get a lot done, while he's very methodical and precise. So when he does something, he does it really thoroughly and unfortunately, it takes a long time. So I'm the chaotic one who does everything and not very thoroughly.

Once a week, the grandmother watches the children for 3 to 4 hours in the morning, and sometimes in the afternoon their older daughter takes care of the younger children. Martin uses this time to take care of business-related errands or meetings. On weekends, Magda reports, family work is shared:

> The weekends are really half and half, whoever happens to have time ... Our adult daughter and her boyfriend are here, so they take our older son and go somewhere with him. We're all together. Of course meals on Saturdays and

Sundays are on me, the cooking. Sometimes my husband jumps in, and makes five liters of pancakes. He's a maximalist! When he does something, then thoroughly [laughs].

Martin describes the way they manage housework as mutual assistance, "You do these basic or necessary things at home that need to be done for family life . . . The sooner it's done, then you have time together." Both parents spend as much time as possible with the children. Whereas playing with the children and coming up with activities for the family more often falls to Martin, Magda is more responsible for the mental work (Renzetti & Curran, 2003), such as choosing a preschool and after-school clubs for the children, and taking care of their health.

Magda also focuses more on the practical responsibilities of parenting:

> I can read something, play with them for a while, but I can't last that long. He thinks up games for them, thinks up things for them to do. I always have the feeling that it's silly. I shouldn't, but when I'm playing with them I'm neglecting something else that I ought to be doing. This schizophrenic feeling that I haven't got the cooking done, and now I have to play with them. I know that this [playing] is much better.

Both parents have very close relationships with their children. While the oldest son, Norbert, is equally attached to both parents, one of the twins is more a "mamma's boy" and the other more a "daddy's boy." Nevertheless, according to Magda, sometimes the boys' orientations switch, "When something's going on, then one of the twins runs to one and the other to the other one. But now that they're really fixated on him, even the mamma's boy will easily ignore me and go to his dad." The oldest child, Nora, has a very open and close relationship with both parents. Magda reports, "Unlike her girlfriends, she was always able to go to her dad even with girl problems . . . It was never that . . . 'since he's Dad I can't tell him that I've got my period.' No, she can and she knows it."

"I Definitely Accommodate the Kids More than Work"

Both parents have organized their paid work lives around family responsibilities. Martin explains, "I'm organizing, figuring out things and doing my work now so that I don't have to be at work away from the family until late at night, because four kids, three small ones, that's the kind of commitment that I can't, I don't want to tolerate that." Martin estimates that he devotes 20 or at most 25 hours a week to paid work. Although his business problems precipitated his taking parental leave, he emphasizes that it was a choice to prioritize family, "If I wanted to focus fully on my work, then the kids could go to a nursery ... The more you're with the family then in my view it's better for the family ... I definitely accommodate the kids more than work."

Magda's job takes priority now in the family, not because she is more invested in it, but because it provides the family with a more stable income. Although both parents claim to earn roughly the same income, Magda's is solely from paid employment, whereas Martin's comes from occasional business dealings, from earlier investments, as well as from the parental leave allowance.

Magda is employed part-time, 30 hours a week. Although she doesn't like the work, she accepts it as a compromise, because she doesn't want full-time employment. She had really enjoyed her previous job in a sporting union, the job she lost because she wouldn't return full-time. She had worked there from age 18, first, as an assistant secretary, then, as a general secretary. Magda recalls, "It was interesting work, it dealt with sports, with the people engaged in them, organizing competitions, trips by national teams ... interesting work with great people." Her current job is not as intrinsically interesting, but she touts its advantages, "My work doesn't affect my family that much. I don't bring my problems home. It's not like before ... 24 hours a day ... because in the evening someone might call you and want something. So I leave, close the door behind me at work, and there's peace."

Magda plans to stay in her current job for at least another year until their older son, Norbert, starts to going to elementary school and the younger boys, Petr and Pavel, are in a preschool. Then, Magda expects Martin to get a full-time job, which would enable her to work less. But, when the twins are older, Magda would like "to do some work where there is some responsibility and it's a bit interesting and varied."

"My Parents, They Did the Maximum for Me ... I Do Things the Way I Was Raised"

Martin's family background shapes his nontraditional orientation to the family, both because of the ways in which it deviated from traditionally gendered ways, and because of the emotional tenor of the family. Martin's father was involved in the family in a way that was not common for his generation (Možný, 1983). He was an active father with a direct, close relationship (i.e., one not mediated by the mother) to his two sons, albeit the activities they often shared were gendered. Martin notes:

My father did all the guy things with us. He taught us everything relating to trades, working with your hands. Mom did, I don't know, fairy tales, homework, during that first year of school. The second year it was more Dad. He was very well read; he knew history, played three musical instruments ... So he got me into playing the guitar. We had a garden. We grew fruits and vegetables. We kept animals at home.

His father was also involved in domestic chores. Martin reports, "I remember him washing the dishes ... I think that it was the same as with us. He tried." Both sons were raised to take part in housework. Their duties included vacuuming, taking out the garbage, and everyday shopping. Martin even washed the windows.

Martin remembers his family of origin also as a family with strong emotional bonds, "We loved each other. I knew that they loved me and they worked hard for me and my brother ... my parents, they did the maximum for me. ... I do things the way I was raised. To my mind it's the best way."

Martin was strongly connected to his maternal relatives growing up, especially his mother's sister's family, with whom they lived in one house. Relations between the two families were totally destroyed in the early 1990s over a property dispute that reflected changes in the importance of private property in Czech society after the Velvet Revolution (Možný, 1991). Martin, his parents, and siblings were forced to move out of the family house when his aunt's family usurped the property in Prague to profit from its high real estate value. The loss Martin suffered from the breakup of his extended family, which he blames as partially responsible for the premature death of his mother and then the death of his father, combined with the positive experience from his childhood, promote his investment in his procreative family, "In a way I lost that family, and I'd like my new family to work. There's nothing more important in my life than my family ... I have other activities and interests than my family ... but for me this comes first."

"When We Look Around Us, Everyone Is Different"

Both partners recognize that their family is "different" from others around them. Magda invokes Martin's emotional commitment to the family, as well as his feeling of responsibility for domestic work, both of which promote their equality:

My husband is kind of unique. He is kind of a domestic fowl ... He has to have all the little chicks together, then he's happy ... I can't imagine our oldest daughter moving out, he'd probably have a hard time dealing with that . . . My friends and acquaintances have always envied me for the kind of husband I have . . . So I was always proud.

Martin rejects the widespread Czech model, in which fathers "have other priorities or goals than children, or they are stuck in this fixed way of thinking that they have to make money for their children and family." He believes that family life is a joint responsibility, "If I want to have a family then I have to take care of things. And to leave everything to my wife and put my feet up, that's stupid. And it's the same the other way around, I wouldn't like that either."

Magda concurs, "He's not the kind of man where he's the head of the family. He comes home from work, sits down with a beer in front of the TV, and nothing interests him." Magda believes that Martin's focus on the family, his active involvement in childcare and housework, comes "naturally" to him, and is not the result of her putting pressure on him, "It's not that I say, 'Go do the dishes.' Sometimes I say to him, 'Our daughter will do it; it's her job.' And he says, 'Well, I can't just leave it here till this evening.' He just approaches things naturally and responsibly."

Martin's sense of responsibility for the family is reinforced by his rejection of essentialist ideas about parenting:

> I'm not generally a supporter of the view that a man can't raise a child the same as a woman can . . . That only mother can raise kids is incomprehensible to me. That mothers belong at the stove, in the kitchen, and in the home, and men should make money and go out to work, I'm not a supporter of that. I think that a man can, if he wants, raise a child in just as exemplary a way as a mother.

Martin's involvement in the family and the household has also been influenced by the collapse of his career. However, Martin willingly used that situation as an opportunity to engage more in parenting:

> I'm glad that it worked out for me to be able to be with the boys more now. I wanted that. I wasn't able to with my daughter; that was worse. . . . With the second . . . it wasn't quite enough. So now, as they say, in my golden years, I'm enjoying time with my boys.

Although the talk from Magda and Martin centers on Martin as a special kind of father, Magda's willingness to take on a breadwinner role and to avoid gatekeeping are equally important. Martin points out that their current arrangements suit her as well. Although Magda believes a parent should be home with children for the first 3 years, she admits she was unhappy being at home with her daughter for 3 years. Martin explains, "Magda couldn't stand being at home long and I wanted to be at home. It suited and suits me to be at home with the boys ... It was not just about money." Magda welcomes Martin as an equal parent. Although she believes more women than men are suited to parenting, she fully acknowledges Martin as one of the exceptions. She makes room for him to parent alongside her.

Magda and Martin have few disagreements or conflicts, and those arise only when they are tired. Their equality is underwritten by their emphasis on spending family time, coping with caring for the children and managing the housework, pooling their money, and making decisions on how the money is used, all done together, reflecting their strong mutual cohesion. Martin and Magda recognize that their neighbors and some acquaintances (but not close friends) see them as "abnormal" because they are not divorced and the gender roles in their family are "reversed." Martin remarks:

> My wife and I always joke that when we look around us everyone is different ... and we ask ourselves if there isn't something wrong with us, that they're all normal and we're the abnormal ones – always joking around. But we always conclude that it isn't true, they're all not normal and only we're normal.

Denisa and David: Equal From the Start

David and Denisa Urban are the parents of a 2½-year-old son, Cyril. Denisa works long hours in a full-time managerial position and David works for pay 4 days a week. Beginning with shared parental leave, they have consistently shared childcare, as David reports, "Parenting ... it's half and half. Some things I do, other things my wife. Whoever has the time and the mood at the given moment does whatever it is that needs to be done."

An Ordinary Day

On workdays, David wakes up first and leaves for his job at around 5:30 a.m. Denisa gets up, wakes up their son around 6:15 and makes him breakfast. She gets him washed and dressed, and then drives him to preschool for 8:00 a.m. When they arrive, she chats with him until he goes off to play with the other children. She says of her morning responsibilities, "It is also a moment when I try to enjoy my son."

Cyril is in a private nursery until his father collects him by 3:30 p.m. Then David gives Cyril some fruit or bread, and spends time with him: going for a walk, taking him to the playground, attending a special swimming course for children, or taking him to see his grandparents, who live nearby. When Cyril doesn't want to go out or in the winter when the weather is bad, David plays with him at home.

Denisa usually arrives home close to 7:00 p.m. Cyril doesn't eat much at night except for milk. David reports, "It's half and half with the milk. Whoever it is that remembers around 7 or 8 o'clock that he hasn't yet had it, that's the one who does it." Denisa notes that the evening is time for play as well, "He loves to play with cars, so we have cars everywhere now. He pulls either me or my husband to his room to play with cars."

David usually makes dinner, bathes Cyril, reads him a bedtime story, and puts him to bed by 9:00 p.m. By then David is tired and will often go to sleep with his son. However, sometimes, when Denisa isn't tired from her job, they break the regular routine and she takes over bathing and reading. Denisa sometimes does job-related work after Cyril goes to bed, but other times they all just go to sleep together in one bed.

Friday differs from the other days because Cyril goes to his grandparents' house during the day. The private nursery they use is quite expensive, so grandmother care saves them a bit of money.

Weekends are "freer" in the family. They stay in bed a bit later, and David usually makes breakfast. After the morning routines, they go out, often to visit one set of grandparents, or, in nice weather, to their cottage outside Prague.

"Sometimes He's a Momma's Boy, but I Think It's Half and Half with Us"

David and Denisa see their son's attachment to them as equal. David explains:

> Sometimes he's a momma's boy, but I think it's half and half with us. When I come to the school, recently he's started going, "My daddy! Daddy!" So it's clear that he's happy to see me. When my wife comes home in the evening and he hears her key in the door then he's off and running over to her to get a hug and a kiss.

Denisa adds:

> It is not about he goes only to me; he also comes to David to sit down, and he takes him on his knee and cuddles him ... He simply wanted Mom yesterday.

We are at home together today and he calls for daddy for the whole day. Not in the sense of crying, but he just asks where is Dad? I answer him 20 times that he is at work.

Both parents encourage their son to express his feelings. Denisa notes, "Among the first words we taught our son were, 'I like you, Cyril.' Today, we were riding and he was pleased and was shouting, 'I like Dad, Mommy.'"

The parents try to support each other's child-rearing. David says, "When one of us says 'No!' we stick to that; the other one is supportive and also says, 'No.'" Denisa also reports that they take over for each other when one of them loses patience:

> Just yesterday we decided that my husband would be lulling him to sleep and suddenly I hear them both awake an hour later. So then my husband is peevish, tired, and sometimes seethes with anger ... And I can see my son responding with more crying ... In these situations ... I pull my husband away from my son and take care of our son calmly. But then I get into the very same situation on another occasion, or just an hour later the same situation occurs again, and my husband does the same thing to me.

Denisa more often initiates and arranges their son's activities, such as selecting a preschool or a swimming club. David then does these activities with Cyril. But David also does some of the mental work of parenting, such as remembering to take Cyril for his vaccinations 3 months after a doctor's appointment.

Sick care, although shared, is not easily managed. David worries about irritating his employer if he takes time off, and when Denisa takes time off she still has to make up the work at her job. When Cyril was ill recently, first Denisa was at home with him, then David, and finally, when Cyril was recuperating, his grandmothers looked after him.

"She Doesn't Like Dusting or Vacuuming, so I Do That"

Housework is not as equally divided as childcare. Denisa acknowledges that David does more of the everyday housekeeping. He comments, "I'm just something of a nitpicker, but I don't like it when there are dishes lying around in the kitchen ... I take after my dad in this, it has to be clean. It has to be cleaned up."

They do the shopping together. The rest of their housework allocation depends on who is tired and who has time available. David explains, "She gets home later than me ... When she's more tired and wants to sit down after work, then I'll go and do something, and when I'm really tired I'll say, 'Hey, I'm not up to it,' and she'll do it."

Personal preferences also prevail. David reports, "She doesn't like dusting or vacuuming, so I do that. And cooking, when she has time then she'll bake something when I want something sweet." Normally, however, meals are David's responsibility. But Denisa points out that he doesn't have to cook very much because his mother makes them several meals a week, and their son can eat at his nursery, while they can have meals at their workplaces.

From time to time, they have had conflicts about housework, particularly when David thought Denisa was making her job more of a priority than the family. Denisa admits, "We had a discussion a few months ago that I have not been doing anything at home. So my husband was a bit depressed as he was doing everything ... So we have made an agreement that laundry and ironing should be my task."

"He Took it Over Automatically, Completely, the Whole Role"

Denisa and David met more than 8 years ago. After 3 years, they married, and within the next 3 years their son was born. Before his birth the division of labor in the family was relatively equal, which is now rather common in Czech society (Čermáková et al., 2000). Denisa said, "We did housekeeping together. It mostly was like once a week my husband got crazy and we had a cleaning Saturday. So it was mostly 50-50." They often ate in restaurants so they didn't cook much.

After Cyril was born, Denisa was at home with him first for 9 months, and then David was at home with him until he turned 2. Denisa performed more of the housework when she was at home. According to David, "She took care of most things except for the cooking because she can't cook."

But David was also involved in caring for their small son from the time of his birth:

> When I came home from work, I took him and went out with him in the pram for at least half an hour so she could get a little break ... Back then we had to change diapers every 2 or 3 hours whenever he was wet. And when he pooped you really knew it. True, at first I couldn't change his diapers. When he pooped himself I couldn't. I don't know why, but at the start I just couldn't. It really stank. And then somehow when he was around 7 months or half a year it changed and it didn't bother me anymore; I didn't mind it. So at the start that was left to her ... otherwise ... tried to help her as much as possible in the afternoon.

Moreover, from the time Cyril was 4 months old, David has been tending to him at night. Denisa invokes her not breastfeeding to explain, "My husband got up during the night instead of me. As I did not need to breastfeed, he could take care of Cyril." David notes, "He didn't cry, nothing. He was really good, even at night."

While on leave from her job because of a risky pregnancy, Denisa started to run her own business, providing accountancy services for some small companies, which she continued after Cyril was born. When he was around 5 months old, she received an opportunity to do some work from home for her employer, which she did until Cyril was 9 months old. Then she went back to her job at 80% of full time and David stayed home on parental leave. Denisa reports that they created this arrangement because "it was a desire to work and then money was certainly needed. ... I earn more than my husband, so I have the feeling that the financial side of the family is on my shoulders."

David sees it differently:

> My wife, to me it seems, she won't admit it, but she's a workaholic. She simply needs to work. Two months before she gave birth she was at home because of health concerns with her pregnancy and she was constantly bored ... And then our little boy was born and ... when she was at home with him, it was harder for her. Sometimes she'd call me to come home early, that she can't go on

Before Denisa returned to her job, there was a 2-month period during the summer holidays when both parents were home, which enabled David to learn how to look after the child by himself, and for the child to adapt as well. Denisa describes their time home together:

> We did everything as a pair. When you're alone it's more demanding. But like this, when you're both at home, that's ideal. If one isn't in the mood the other one can take over, or if one of you needs to do something, then the other can see to things. So we complement each other, there are no conflicts there.

Then, while at home on leave, David fully adopted the role of primary caregiver. Initially, Denisa was unpleasantly surprised and actually taken aback. She did not expect David to behave so maternally that she would often feel like an onlooker. Denisa comments:

> I was not quite ready for that, but he took it over automatically, completely, the whole role. ... For example, Cyril began to weep and I came to soothe him, but my husband took him from me and calmed him another way. He simply got used to it ... It was terribly obvious to him; he did it automatically. As for me, he did not think about the fact that he could be hurting me somehow. This hit me hard at the time. It was one of our first rows after we started alternating.

David also described their initial conflicts:

> My wife had things arranged one way and I had it another way. So then there'd be a conflict when I'd say something like, "I do it like this!" ... "How do you bathe him?" "I bathe him like this. He doesn't like that." My opinion was that he doesn't like the way she bathes him; he likes the way I bathe him.

Although David found his leave to entail "harder work" than when Cyril was really small, he especially enjoyed their daily walks with the baby carriage. During his leave, he assumed responsibility for Cyril's health, including visits to the doctor, just as Denisa had done during her leave. David also took over some of the organizational work while on leave, as Denisa points out:

> Until that time, when we went to do exercises with the son or something else, I had a bag prepared, had everything organized. And suddenly we went somewhere and my husband did not allow me to pack up our things ... he took over completely.

David enjoyed the break from his paid work, but he acknowledged the difficulties that arose when one person was home with the child all day:

> That really was a problem, that one person was looking after the child and by the evening was already really tired and needed someone to take over ... I was tired from all of it because you really have to watch, keep an eye on him all the time ... There were these conflicts because when the other person comes home from work they want to relax too.

Denisa reports that when David was on leave, he took over the housework as well as the childcare, "He began to do everything; he had no problems at all. He had never blamed me for anything, so ... I did minimum housework during that time I saw him doing everything well, so it really satisfied me."

Both grandmothers, who he often visited, were a great help to him. Sometimes Cyril spent part of the day with them, which gave David time to catch up on housework. They also gave him cooked food for the next few days so he didn't have to cook every day. The grandmothers' help reduced the stress on David for managing both housework and childcare at the same time, a stress that mothers often experience (Maříková, 2008; Lutherová, Maříková, & Válková, 2017).

Denisa experienced a different kind of stress. Earning three times as much money as her husband, Denisa felt the financial pressure acutely, which erupted into conflicts about money, especially when she was the only earner:

I had such a feeling I was the breadwinner of the family. For the first time … I really pulled out all the stops to earn some money. And then I got back home and saw what we spent it for. And I felt like, "We cannot go on like that. We cannot squander money."

"Her Work Definitely Takes Priority"

Disagreements and conflicts also arise between David and Denisa because the two partners balance paid work and family differently. Denisa's career is more central to her life than is David's. After 8 years working for a transnational company, Denisa has been promoted from a junior to senior auditing manager, "The pressure is so big … All meetings and discussions with clients, your subordinates and superiors, it is all up to you. The partner meets you only once for a month-long contract and everything depends on you."

Despite her previous years of experience, she had to learn "everything from the beginning." Moreover, after she was promoted over a co-worker who had previously been her superior, she had to contend with the co-worker's resentment and lack of cooperation. Denisa's enormous responsibility means that no one can cover for her now so the workload has increased immensely, "For the first time in my life I have worked around the clock this year. Four times during the contract I have not slept for two nights."

However, she increasingly feels ambivalent about the priority of work in her life:

> For the first time in my life, I am in a situation where my responsibility is so great that I realize I need to give more to my work than to my family … That's really an inner struggle that I am busy at work, which satisfied me before as I achieve good results … [Now] the job is too much for me and I say to myself that Cyril is growing up and the child begins to be more and more important.

Although others are faced with similar demands at her company, Denisa points out that they are either childless women, or men who don't feel the same guilt as she, even if they are fathers. She says, "I, specifically as a woman, cannot manage everything. The role I have now, I do not feel comfortable with it these days."

Not only is her relation to career and family an inner struggle, Denisa's overwork and her lack of emotional engagement at home have recently led to a serious conflict between David and her. Denisa has felt unable to live up to her husband's expectations of what her involvement in the family should be, "I am not strong enough. I am simply not strong enough to do more, when I go to work as I do. And I said to him, 'You have a different work; you return with a clear mind. Your hands and body are tired but your mind is clear.'"

Based on discussions with her husband, who was initially unsympathetic, and a psychotherapist, Denisa has been able to start to change. Even if, as she says, "I am not at home with them more often … I am more relaxed being at home." David has also changed his attitude, as Denisa notes, "Suddenly, he has begun to support me again and precisely the way I need to be supported. He really has the power to listen to me and not to comment without respect." Denisa still hopes to reduce her workload to spend more time with her family.

David, who is a car mechanic, maintains vehicles in a small local construction company. David says of himself, "I'm not a careerist. Whatever I've done, I've just done because I enjoy it. I actually spent a lot of time driving a bus … I enjoyed that work. For 5 or 6 years I drove around the world."

He clearly takes pride in his work. When he applied for his current job he demanded a certain wage. He told them, "'I value my work at this much and this much and either they hire me or they don't.' And they hired me." The downside of the job occurs when there is no work to do. He says, "Doing nothing is tiring, you go home just exhausted." In general, he likes his current job because the work is diverse and interesting. Nonetheless, David reports, "Her work definitely takes priority. Because even though it's interesting work, it's still manual labor and it isn't as well paid as my wife's work. When I think about what kind of wages people make, my wages aren't bad. But compared to hers they're laughable."

Although Denisa asserts, "His work does not satisfy him completely," David counters, "Every job has some drawback. But I've got it sorted in my head, I say, 'I have to stay here so that I can go pick up the little guy. They can say what they like, I'm going to do my thing.' My wages are decent so there isn't any problem."

Although Denisa and David do not always succeed completely in balancing paid work and family life, they try, and have overcome some of the conflicts that they suffered earlier. David sums up, "Because both of us are now working, we both want to be with Cyril … When we're all together, everything works fine. We both spend time with him. I don't think there are any conflicts now."

Going on Leave: "When He Announced It, They Gazed at Him Like He Had Gone Mad"

Those around the Urbans have not always been tolerant of their unconventional arrangements of care, paid work, and unpaid work. Both of them have encountered negative reactions at their workplaces. Despite David's legal right to take parental leave, Denisa reports, "When he announced it, they gazed at him like he had gone mad. They said they would not keep his place for him." Although they did ultimately hold his job during his parental leave, his employer put pressure on David to return before their son turned 3 or lose his job.

Denisa encounters a double whammy at her job. Either they see her as an uncommitted worker or as an indifferent mother. She reports, "Sometimes they say, 'You have other priorities, so you cannot perform your work well. That's clear. You have another priority.' And on the other hand, they disapprovingly say, 'You work a lot even though you have a baby.'"

Denisa has also suffered her mother's disapproval when she returned to her job. She remembers her mother's warning that their unconventional arrangements could threaten her marriage, "When Cyril came, the first insinuations came as well, like I could lose my husband if I would not take care of my son more." Nevertheless, her mother did come to appreciate David's ways, "When she saw my husband, so she said about 6 months ago that she really appreciates him for taking care of us very well. She might have been afraid he would not be able to care."

David is quite unusual among their peers. He notes that although on the weekends one sees fathers out with strollers, "During the week, when I was at home and went to the playground or went out with the stroller . . . I only met mothers. I made friends with girls – just moms." Their friends were not always understanding of their chosen arrangements. The Urbans encountered reactions like: "We admire you! but, why are you doing this?" They often argued that a man can't handle caring for a child.

The Half and Half Model: Aids and Obstacles

Denisa is far more invested in her career than is David. She has risen to a high position in her company and earns far more than he. In contrast, Denisa says David "deliberately chose a kind of work to have time for a baby," the way mothers often do (Křížková, Maříková, Hašková, &

Formánková, 2011). Right now caring for his son is David's priority. David and Denisa's relative investments in paid work undoes the gender canon that prevails in Czech society, and contributes to their balanced model of the division of housework and childcare.

David's approach toward gender in the family has helped to establish the half and half model. David grew up in a family with an unconventional division of household labor. His father did housework, and David was expected to do so as well. He recounts how his family of origin shaped his attitudes:

> Mom was in the hospital once and just our dad was looking after us. It was possible to see him cooking, cleaning, and then, even when she came home, it stayed like that. He dusted and Mom vacuumed. It was divided half and half. I just saw that it can work like that. That's why it doesn't bother me to cook, or when I have to clean up, sweep up, wipe up.

Both David's parents were employed full-time, his father as a bus driver, his mother as a nurse. His parents expected their children to be responsible for household chores and to learn to take care of themselves. David remembers, "When I was in the fifth, sixth grade, we came home and warmed up some food, or my brother warmed up the food, we ate, and then we went out. We were rather independent." As the result of this upbringing, David feels responsible for the household chores and is used to actively participating. Describing himself as a "nitpicker" who takes after his dad, David seems more concerned than Denisa with keeping a tidy, clean house, which also contributes to their undoing gendered norms of household labor.

David's strong sense of responsibility extends to caring for his child, "I think that at my age you want to have a child. We wanted him. And when I want something then I don't leave it aside ... By nature I'm like my father, with this sense of responsibility for my children, that a person has to take care of them." But more than feeling responsible, David feels entitled to share in his child's life. When they discuss who might take leave for a second child, David argues, "Why would I have no right to enjoy it? Why should I work and you can stay home for 3 years?"

Surprisingly, however, David still maintains the essentialist belief that mothers are particularly suited to care for newborn babies:

> I think that the beginning, when he was really small, I couldn't have handled that. That would have been very difficult for me, that real maternity period. When a woman carries the child for 9 months, the child bonds more with the mother. The real beginning, if the man jumps in there it would be very difficult for him at that age ... When the child is already communicating, when you can

tell that he wants something, then I think that it's possible to handle. I don't know if every man could handle it, but I think it's possible to handle it.

Denisa, for her part, has discovered through her own experience that women do not have an innately superior ability to take care of children. She says:

> I see my husband is able to provide the same care. I have always thought that it is easy to be a mother, but I feel that this ability has not been as common as usual ... In the period until his first year, when I was at home with him, ... I did not feel able to think up some fun for him and take care of him as a good mother who should know all these things.

Denisa emphatically rejects a housewife role for herself, "I would not prefer to stay home alone for a long time ... It would certainly not satisfy me, this kind of 100% care of a spouse ... to be at home for the whole day, cleaning and waiting with a warm dinner for him to return from work." Denisa also rejects the model of her own mother, an employed woman responsible for all the household work, who "loves to put the laundry in and out of the washing machine."

Denisa's rejection of these traditional and neotraditional models, her investment in her career, and her willingness to step aside and enable David to care for their child were all critical to their creation of an equally sharing family. Both partners had to be able to endure and resist the societal pressure to follow traditional gender norms.

The Urbans have been able to undo gender in family work and redefine it as shared activities. But the model practiced by the Urbans is not without its misunderstandings, disagreements, and conflicts. Their success has been fostered by their ability to communicate and to negotiate, and their willingness to spend time and emotional energy to do so. Their mutual respect and resolve to be together supports their success in working through conflicts. Denisa asserts, "I could say that our relationship, and I hope I don't jinx it, our relationship is strong."

Two Equally Sharing Czech Families

The two Czech couples grew up in different historical eras. Magda and Martin became truly equal partners after many years of parenting together, whereas David and Denisa have tried to share equally from the start. Their stories show not only that equality is possible in the Czech context, but that there is more than one path to equality. Both couples tout the rewards.

The Svobodas are happy with their family life. Martin says, "I'm content. I'm definitely happy with it ... I'm glad that it worked out for me to be able to be with the boys more now ... I chose it, this way of life; for me it's the best." It "works" for Magda as well, knowing that her children are well cared for when she is at work, "I can just clear my head, leave, and then come back with a clear head."

The Urbans are also both happy with the life they have created, sharing the care of their son. David says, "When I compare what we've gained, that's impossible to describe. When he's doing his thing here ... when you look at him, it's pure joy!" Denisa agrees, "Our son is growing up perfectly. He is marvelous, delightful."

References

Bičáková, A. & Kalíšková, K. (2015). *Od mateřství k nezaměstnanosti: postavení žen s malými dětmi na trhu práce* [From Maternity to Unemployment: Women with Young Children Returning to the Labor Market]. Prague: Národohospodářský ústav AV ČR.

Čermáková, M., Hašková, H., Křížková, A., Linková, M., Maříková, H., & Musilová, M. (2000). *Relations and Changes of Gender Differences in the Czech Society in the 90's*. Prague: Sociologický ústav Akademie věd České republiky.

Chaloupková, J. (2009). *Rodinné a pracovní dráhy mladých: holistická perspektiva* [A Holistic Perspective on the Work and Family Trajectories of Young People]. Prague: Sociologický ústav Akademie věd České republiky.

Crompton, R., Brockmann, M., & Lyonette, C. (2005). Attitudes, Women's Employment and the Domestic Division of Labour. *Work, Employment & Society, 19*(2), 213–233.

Czech Statistical Office (2017). *Focus on Women and Men – 2017*. (Table 5-7, Number of parental allowance recipients). Retrieved from: www.czso.cz/csu/czso/focus-on-women-and-men-2017.

Czech Statistical Office (2018). *Focus on Women and Men – 2018*. (Labor and earnings: Table 4-37, Gender pay gap, international comparison, and Table 4-24, Employment rates by number of children, international comparison.) (Population, families, households: Table 1-35 Private households by economic activity of head of household in 2017). Prague: Český statistický úřad. Retrieved from: www.czso.cz/csu/czso/focus-on-women-and-men-2018.

Czech Statistical Office (2019a). *Population. Czech Demographic Handbook*. (Table 1-16 Population by ethnicity by 1921–2011 censuses and Table 1-18 Population by religious belief and sex by 1921, 1930, 1950, 1991, 2001 and 2011 censuses). Prague: Český statistický úřad. Retrieved from: www.czso.cz/csu/czso/population.

Czech Statistical Office (2019b). *Rates of Employment, Unemployment, and Economic Activity – November 2018*. Prague: Český statistický úřad.

Retrieved from: www.czso.cz/csu/czso/ari/rates-of-employment-unemploy ment-and-economic-activity-november-2018.

Fialová, L. & Kučera, M. (1996). *Demografické chování obyvatelstva České republiky během přeměny společnosti po roce 1989* [Demographic Behavior in the Czech Republic During the Transformation of Society after 1989]. Prague: Sociologický ústav Akademie věd České republiky.

Horáková, M., Jahoda, R., Kofroň, P., Sirovátka, T., & Šimíková, I. (2013). *Příjmová chudoba a materiální deprivace v České republice podle indikátorů EU - vývoj v důsledku krize, fiskální konsolidace a sociální reformy.* [Income poverty and material deprivation in the Czech Republic according to EU indicators - developments as a result of the crisis, fiscal consolidation and social reforms.] Prague: Výzkumný ústav práce a sociálních věcí.

Křížková, A., Maříková, H., Hašková, H., & Formánková, L. (2011). *Pracovní dráhy žen v České republice.* [Working Paths of Women in the Czech Republic] Prague: Sociologické nakladatelství.

Lutherová, S., Maříková, H., & Válková, J. (2017). Childcare Preferences of Parents in the Czech Republic and the Slovak Republic. *Sociológia, 49*(3), 285–309.

Maříková, H. (2008). Caring Fathers and Gender (In)Equality? *Polish Sociological Review, 48*(162), 135–152.

Možný, I. (1983). *Rodina vysokoškolsky vzdělaných manželů.* [Family of Spouses with University Degrees.] Brno: Univerzita Jana Evangelisty Purkyně.

Možný, I. (1991). *Proč tak snadno. Některé důvody sametové revoluce.* [Why So Easy? Some Reasons for the Velvet Revolution.] Prague: Sociologické nakladatelství.

OECD (2018). *Family Database* (Figure PF 4.1.A, Typology of childcare, Figure PF 3.2.A Enrolment rates in early education and care services, 0–2 year olds, Figure PF 3.2.E Enrolment rates in early childhood education and care services and primary education, 3-5 year olds.) Retrieved from: www.oecd .org/els/family/database.htm#public_policy.

Renzetti, C. M. & Curran, D. J. (2003). *Ženy, muži a společnost* [Women, Men, and Society]. Prague: Karolinum.

Sekce pro lidská práva (2017). *Zpráva o stavu romské menšiny* [Report on the Situation of the Roma minority]. Prague: Úřad vlády České republiky. Retrieved from: www.vlada.cz/cz/ppov/zalezitosti-romske-komunity/dokumenty/zprava-o-stavu-romske-mensiny-za-rok-2017-168061/.

Vohlídalová, M. (2007). Trvalá nebo dočasná změna? Uspořádání genderových rolí v rodinách s pečujícími otci [A Permanent or Temporary Change? The Arrangement of Gender Roles in Families with Fathers Participating in Childcare]. In Maříková, H. (ed.) *Sociologické texty*, 7(11), 3-103. Prague: Sociologický ústav AV ČR.

20

People's Republic of China

Yifei Shen[1]
Translated by Jiayi Qian

Raised in different Chinese provinces, Kai Wang and Li Li both attended college in Shanghai, where they found jobs, met each other, dated, and married. Their daughter, Xiao Bao, was born a year after they married. In many ways, they are a typical middle-class Shanghainese family. Kai and Li both earn stable and comfortable incomes. They are dedicated to their jobs and are confident that they bring value to their employers. Kai is employed in the production and promotion of theater pieces. His job is definitely not 9 to 5. From Tuesday to Saturday, he has to work at night, usually arriving home after 10:00 p.m., and he often has to travel overnight for his job. Li is a newspaper editor in charge of a section dedicated to women. Her paid work hours are quite flexible; she can take either the morning or the afternoon shift. If she takes the morning shift, she gets to her job before 9:00 a.m. and is home before 5:00 p.m. If she takes the afternoon shift, she does not get back home until after 6:00 p.m.

A Typical Day

Kai wakes up before the alarm even goes off. He gets dressed making almost no noise at all, trying not to wake up his wife and their daughter, who sleeps in her own little bed next to their big one. After brushing his teeth and washing his face, Kai prepares breakfast for the family and

[1] Francine M. Deutsch wrote the country profile. She is grateful to Siyu Bao for her extensive help locating and translating Chinese documents and to Jiayi Qian for generously agreeing to translate the chapter. Kong Yan, Beier Yao, and Xin Gong also provided information about contemporary Chinese life.

precooks lunch for Li. At 7:45 a.m., Kai wakes up Xiao Bao by gently patting her face. Three-year-old Xiao Bao can already eat by herself, but sometimes she needs some assistance. Li insists that she eat independently, but most of the time Kai cannot help feeding her. After breakfast Kai helps her brush her teeth and wash her face. If they have some time left before Kai has to drive his daughter to kindergarten at around 8:30 a.m., Kai plays and chats with his little girl before they leave home together. After dropping his daughter off at school, which is close to where they live, Kai goes to his job.

If Li takes the morning job shift, she gets up while Kai is dressing their daughter and the family eats breakfast together. By 8:30 a.m., after cleaning up their apartment, Li is ready to go to her job. Kai and Li have hired a helper who arrives at 2:00 p.m. to do their daily cleaning, to prepare dinner for them, to pick up Xiao Bao from kindergarten at 4:00 p.m. and to play with her. Li dismisses the helper when she gets home, and feeds her daughter dinner.

Li's schedule differs when she takes the afternoon shift; she can sleep in and get up after 9:00 a.m. In that case, she starts writing articles at home and eats the lunch Kai had prepared for her, although when he is away she eats out on her way to her job. On those days, since she gets home later, the helper feeds their daughter dinner and leaves at 6:30 p.m. after washing the dinner dishes.

Regardless of Li's work shift, after dinner mother and daughter go for a walk around the neighborhood for about an hour. Back home afterwards, Xiao Bao watches TV while Li takes a shower. Then she gives Xiao Bao a shower and supervises while she puts on her pajamas and gets into bed. The little girl then has time to read to herself while Li cleans up the bathroom, hand washes her daughter's clothes, and hangs them up to dry on the balcony. At about 8:30, Li puts her daughter to sleep by reading her bedtime stories. Within half an hour, the girl is usually fast asleep.

Typically, between 9:00 and 11:00 p.m., Li uses the time to write interview summaries for the newspaper. But after 10:00 p.m., when Kai gets home, the two also often have time to talk and read. The busy day for Kai does not end here; he takes care of their daughter if she wakes up at night because, once asleep, Li does not wake up easily.

Once or twice a week, Kai can get away early and prepare a home-made dinner. On weekends, the two parents take care of their daughter, do cleaning and housework together, and go to gatherings with their friends.

The People's Republic of China is the most populous country in the world with over 1,374,000,000 people, 51.2% males and 48.8% females (National Bureau of Statistics People's Republic of China [NBSPRC], 2016). As of 2010, 91.6% of the population is Han, while the rest are ethnic minorities, comprising 56 nationalities (NBSPRC, 2013). Traditional Chinese adhere to ancestor faith and a confluence of religious beliefs composed of Confucianism, Buddhism, and Taoism. After the founding of the People's Republic of China, the government promoted atheism. While the constitution grants citizens freedom of religion, China is predominantly a secular society. In China 52% of the population is unaffiliated with any religious group, 22% adhere to folk religion, 18% are Buddhist, 5% Christian, 2% Muslim, and the remaining 1% are composed of Hindus, Jews, and unnamed others, which includes Daoists (Central Intelligence Agency, 2019). Chinese people live in diverse types of households. As of 2010, 39.8% of Chinese households consist of nuclear families. Three-generation households comprise 16.5% of the population (Hu & Peng, 2015).

Discrimination against women in the workplace is forbidden by law, but the average income of women per year is only 78% of men's (Chenglong, 2018). Women have the right to at least 90 days of paid leave for the birth of a new baby (The State Council, 2014). The regulations of different provinces give fathers parental leave for 7 to 30 days.

Among women between the ages of 25 and 34 who have children under the age of 6, 72% are employed (All-China, 2011). Based on a 2008 time-use study, men, on average, spend more hours in paid work per week than do women (*Ms* = 42 vs. 30.7), but women spend considerably more time than men on unpaid domestic labor (27.3 vs. 10.6 hours per week) (Dong & An, 2012). Among dual-earner couples with children, men spend about 45 minutes a day on housework, compared to the 106 minutes their wives spend (Liu, Tong, & Fu, 2015).

Publically subsidized preschools are financed primarily at the local level, but over half of all children enrolled in preschool are attending private preschools (Huang, Zhuang, & Zhang, 2014; PRnewswire, 2014). Preschool education isn't free and parents in cities spend a lot of money to send their children to a private kindergarten. Income is a strong predictor of children's preschool attendance (Gong, Xu, & Hong, 2015). However, in line with traditional Chinese culture, grandparents in China help a lot with childcare, especially in lower income families. Overall, 46% of seniors have taken care of their grandchildren on a regular basis (Sun & Zhang, 2013). The Chinese central government announced the goal of 85% preschool attendance by 2020 and plans to increase subsidies for preschool education, which will make it more affordable (Hu, 2018).

Childcare and Housework

The couple has a very clear division of labor: Kai is mainly responsible for cooking and for childcare in the morning, whereas Li is responsible for cleaning and for childcare in the evening. The couple is confident that they equally share responsibility for Xiao Bao's care and education. However, they found it difficult to estimate their percentage division of housework.

Kai's career requires a lot more traveling than Li's, which means that Li often finds herself with additional responsibilities. Still, Li views their division as 50/50, or as she emphasized, "balanced."

Their division of labor reflects their preferences. For example, since Li does not like cooking, everything related to the kitchen is either done by the helper or by Kai. Li reports, "He likes food and does not like the food in restaurants. He likes to invent better ways to cook a dish; for example, if he orders a fish in a restaurant ... he would buy the same fish from the market and try to cook it better himself. He is very interested in both cooking and food." Kai explains that he was forced to cook when he was in college because he lived alone and away from his family, so he gradually got used to cooking. Currently, he exchanges ideas with friends or searches online for better ways to make food for children. He sums up, "I will definitely cook for the family myself if I have the time, and it is a pity that sometimes I am too busy." "Forced" into the kitchen when he was young, now that he is a father he considers it a "pity" when he is unable to cook for the family.

According to Kai, Li generally does all the cleaning because "she has higher standards of sanitary conditions than I do. Even when I think things are quite tidy, she will start cleaning things up because she thinks the place should be in better order." Li does not even trust the part-time helper or her mother-in-law to do the cleaning. She is only satisfied when she herself does certain things, such as washing her daughter's clothes, putting clothes away at the end of the season, and arranging the apartment.

Li asserts that their abilities as well as their preferences should shape the division of labor:

> I do not think there has to be a fixed pattern in a couple's division of housework; the division should rather be based on the couple's personalities and preferences. For example, I'm less patient than Kai, and therefore when our daughter has emotional problems, Kai is usually the one to comfort her. If I had done it, I might end up arguing with her. We should take up more responsibilities that we are good at in the family.

Kai and Li have outsourced much of their domestic labor. They have paid help for housework, cooking, and childcare. Although they divide the remaining work relatively equally, with only one child and so much household help, it is a relatively small amount of labor overall.

Struggles over the Division of Labor: "I Am Equally Busy and My Job Does Not Earn Any Less than Kai's. Why Would I Have To Do All the Housework?"

Both Li and Kai reported that sharing developed "naturally." However, their story reveals the struggles that underlie their division of labor. Li has never liked cooking. Although Kai cooked occasionally since they married, they have always hired a part-time helper to clean and make simple dinners. If it came to cooking herself, Li would go out to a restaurant instead. During the early days of their marriage, Li was responsible for keeping their apartment organized, while Kai did almost no housework.

When their daughter was born, Li and Kai hired a nanny who shared the baby care and most of the housework with Li. The arrival of the baby did not much affect Kai's work life, and he did much less housework than Li. But when Li did ask him to help, he would do so, and he would also offer to cook for the family. When their daughter was 6 months old, the nanny left, and the couple hired a part-time helper. Kai's mother came to Shanghai to live with them, ostensibly to help the young couple.

Problems arose, however, with the arrival of the mother-in-law. She became the person who cooked breakfast and took over most of the childcare. Their helper did the cleaning and cooked lunch and dinner for them, leaving Kai out of the kitchen. Kai defended himself, "Well, that was because my mother had more free time than I did."

Kai explained the problems that developed:

Actually I think it's a little bit more complicated when you have your parents living with you. My wife and I have very different opinions on this particular matter. I thought that with my mother here, she could do a lot of housework and childcare, and I thought she took my place in housework sharing. In that way, I believed that I did a lot for the family nonetheless. But my wife, from a woman's perspective, did not think what my mother did can offset what I should have done.

Li was not happy living with her mother-in-law. She explains:

If I asked Kai to do anything, my mother-in-law would try to excuse him from having to do the housework by saying, "Oh no, no he's too busy, just leave it to me." I would have been OK with it if she only said that occasionally. However, what happened was that it made Kai want to simply leave any housework he could have done to his mother. He could and would have been willing to do the housework, but his mother believed housework was just women's business and also wanted me to do it. I felt offended, which also made her unhappy with me, but I am equally busy and my job does not earn any less than Kai. Why would I have to do all the housework?

As time went on, the conflicts expanded from values to habits to the way housework was done. When Kai's mother went to her hometown for Chinese New Year, neither Li nor Kai invited her back. After living with the family for more than a year, Kai's mother left Shanghai.

After his mother left, Kai started to prepare breakfast for the family and took over the responsibility for their daughter's morning routines. Li explains, "He gets up early. I told him what I wanted to eat for breakfast the next day, and he just naturally got up to cook breakfast. He knew he had no choice by then." Both of them described the transition as quite smooth once Kai's mother was out of the picture. Kai said, "When my mother was staying with us, I would not get up so early in the morning as she gets up earlier than us. The elderly seem to get up earlier anyway, and she would prepare breakfast and go grocery shopping. But once she was gone, I had to fill in."

As Kai has "filled in," there has also been more interaction between him and his daughter. Li reports:

He thought he could not play with our daughter at that time [earlier in infancy], because she was too little. He was only responding to her daily needs. Since she reached 6 months though, he has become her playmate. He did not spend as much time with her before, but they are much closer emotionally now that she is old enough to do some interactive activities.

As long as Kai is home, he is now more than happy to talk and play with their daughter.

Paid Work–Family Balance

Both Li and Kai highly value their careers. Since their daughter was born, paid work–family conflict is omnipresent, but they are both willing to compromise. Although Li is adamant that she does not want motherhood to totally determine her identity, now to make time for her daughter, she postpones her writing until late at night:

> I will not sacrifice things such as my ideals, my beliefs, hobbies and even reading just because I am a mother now. But there are a lot of things that I can sacrifice. For example, . . . now I write between 9:00 p.m. and 12:00 a.m. I could also have asked our helper to take care of my daughter between 6:00 and 9:00 p.m., but I would rather spend some time with her and do my work later at night.

Recently on top of her old responsibilities, Li was given an assignment of great interest to her. She explains how she manages:

> I work on this new task after putting my daughter to bed and I try to finish as much work as possible before Kai comes back. My boss is quite happy with what I have done so far. I think efficiency is most important. I don't claim to be busy just because I have work to do. I don't like sending Kai to do housework just because I claim to be busy with my work.

Kai has also changed a lot since he became a father. He says:

> You have to have better control of your time [when you have a kid]. My job requires a lot of traveling. Since our daughter was born, there hasn't been much change in my major responsibilities, but I would try to leave as much time as I can for my family. For example, I would try to shorten a 2-day trip by taking the first flight in the morning and flying back on the last flight at night. It is surely less laid back, but going on a business trip means you are completely away from your family. I would try to shorten them as much as possible. I have less time to rest now. I used to go to bed late and get up late too; now I still go to bed late but get up early.

Kai has also changed by not scheduling weekend meetings, leaving the theater as early as possible after shows are over, and finishing work at the office rather than bringing work home.

Li notes and appreciates the ways in which Kai has altered his work life to make more room for parenting, such as getting his team to not interrupt his weekends. "He would not help me with childcare as much before. [Now] I think the attitude he shows here is extremely important, and I am very . . . touched that he highly values his family and cares for me and our daughter."

Li and Kai discuss conflicts in their schedules, and work together to find solutions. When asked what they would do if both had to be gone for business, Kai answered, "That's very unlikely because long business trips usually don't happen all of a sudden and they don't happen too often, either. Normally, if I have anything big . . . I will let her know in advance, so that we can avoid not being at home at the same time." Li concurred, "No, that's not going to happen. I don't think there's anything that cannot be postponed. If there is a scheduling conflict, we will talk. If mine is mandatory, then you will postpone or cancel whatever you have scheduled." Li was confident that they are equally likely to compromise.

When a conflict between their job obligations is unavoidable, they rely on outside help. Li explains, "If he has to attend an award ceremony and I need to interview someone for an interview I had been trying to schedule for a long time, and he [the interviewee] could only do it that particular time, I would ask the helper to babysit our daughter. Either way we can find a solution."

Balance or Equality?

The sharing between Kai and Li is shaped by their backgrounds, the social environment they create, Li's sense of entitlement and fairness, and their commitment to having a "balanced" relationship.

Family Backgrounds

Li comes from a city known for its petroleum industry. Her father is a local government official and her mother is a teacher. Her childhood was carefree because her family had a relatively high income and her parents did not oblige her to do anything, "My parents were not at all strict with me. My dad was like, 'You can do whatever you want. If you cannot make a living on your own, stay with Mom and Dad.' I was raised in a very open-minded and happy family." Li's parents also shared housework relatively equally. Li's mother is an only child herself, and she did not like cooking, either. Li said, "My mom often says to my dad, 'Honey, peel an apple for me,' and my dad would peel an apple." Li laughed and reported that when she wanted to eat an apple,"I'll say to my husband, 'honey, I want an apple,'" suggesting that the way in which Li and Kai share housework is similar to that between Li's parents. Li believes that this is a healthy dynamic between the husband and the wife.

Kai comes from a city in Central China. He grew up in a very different kind of family environment characterized by strict discipline. If he did not meet his parents' expectations, they would beat him. It was a very traditional Chinese family: the husband earns the bread and the wife stays at home doing all the housework. Kai observed that his mother had to do too much work. Because he always thought the division of labor between his parents was unreasonable, Kai has tried not to act like his father. Moreover, Kai disagreed with his parents' child-rearing methods. He wants to provide guidance for his daughter rather than just disciplining her. Kai has rejected his upbringing in a traditional family and Li has embraced hers in a nontraditional family.

Creating an Equality-Friendly Social Context

Kai and Li have created a social environment that supports equality. They eschewed help from Kai's mother when she was undermining his participation. They don't discuss their arrangements with Kai's traditional parents. When asked about what his parents thought of his way of sharing housework, Kai replied: "They don't have any thoughts because they don't even know what I do at home now!"

In addition to avoiding criticism of their equal relationship, Li actively seeks positive egalitarian models. She intentionally socializes with couples who have "a more balanced relationship, who love each other and have a reasonable division of household labor." Li explains:

> When you hang out with them, if my husband sees that the other fathers play with their kids too while mothers are chatting together on the side, he will think that it is normal. But there are also families where fathers drop off their kids with their mothers and leave. When I join groups of mothers, I choose my friends among hundreds of them. I intentionally hang out with these families instead of those with men who do nothing at home. I want our friends to have a positive impact on my family.

Kai and Li do not have extended family in Shanghai. Having turned down Kai's mother's offers to "help," they must rely on themselves. They both invoke their strong sense of responsibility for paid work and home, and both of them are willing to rearrange their work lives to accommodate family life and each other's careers. They view each other's respective jobs and interests as equally important, and they have the same ideas when it comes to child education. Their flexible hours also help them create what they call a "balanced" division of labor.

Li has made it clear that housework and childcare should not be just her responsibility. Kai agrees that it is fair to give his wife a break in the morning:

> I usually come back home quite late. ... I rarely take care of my daughter at night. But since she is taking care of our daughter at night, she should be able

to sleep for a while in the morning. I wake up at around 7:00 a.m., no matter how late I went to bed the night before.

Communication between them is key. They negotiate and discuss scheduling conflicts until they come up with a solution. They also discuss feminism and equality and what it means with respect to how household labor should be divided. Li's feminist sensibility and awareness of gendered roles is connected to her work on woman-related publications. Li asserts: "I have to do well myself. I should not simply be known because I am someone's mother, or someone's wife. I work hard and to a large extent I want to prove to myself that I can do it. ... I'm probably not someone who just likes to follow."

Kai doesn't always agree with Li's feminist views:

> I have been constantly struggling against her ... I believe that we should follow the way labor is naturally divided between men and women. It should be natural ... The wife and the husband usually come from different backgrounds, do different jobs, grow up in different families, and therefore naturally have different understandings of many things. If they can agree on a labor division that is comfortable for both of them, that would be the best scenario.

He adds:

> You cannot say that the wife is inferior in the family simply because she does more housework; similarly the one who makes more money does not have a more superior position in the family. And that's why I think there is no point in emphasizing feminism here. ... I think the key point here is both the wife and the husband are doing as much as they can for the family.

Li concurs that the term "balance" might be better than "equality" to describe the optimal division of labor. She says:

> I think equality is a quantitative concept, but daily housework cannot be quantified easily ... I don't think it could even be sustainable if a couple does try to reach perfect equality by dividing everything 50/50 between them. Let's say if I am quite tired already and you keep saying I am supposed to do certain things, even if we did an equal share, so what?

Li has struggled to ensure Kai's participation in the stereotypically feminine tasks of the family, and expects her career to enjoy equal status. Her underlying feminism and his willingness to be fair work together to create a division of labor that they both call "balanced." Even if not entirely equal, domestic labor is shared far more than in the typical Chinese home. Li defines the balance she believes they have achieved, "Balance ... refers to a comfortable mental state, where I will do whatever I can do myself, and for anything I cannot accomplish on my own, you will offer to help. This is a happy state of the mind."

References

All-China Women's Federation, National Bureau of Statistics of China (Oct. 21, 2011). *Report on Major Results of the Third Wave Survey on the Social Status of Women in China*. Retrieved from: https://landwise.resourceequity.org/records/228.

Central Intelligence Agency (2019). China. *The World Factbook*. Retrieved from: www.cia.gov/library/publications/the-world-factbook/geos/ch.html.

Chenglong, J. (2018, March 7). Gender Pay Gap Narrows in China. *China Daily*. Retrieved from: www.chinadaily.com.cn/.

Dong, X-Y. & An, X. (2012). *Gender Patterns and Value of Unpaid Work: Findings from China's First Large-Scale Time Use Survey*. UNRISD Research Paper, 6. Retrieved from: www.unrisd.org/80256B3C005BCCF9/(httpAuxPages)/7CE1453DB093FB41C1257A8E004D6A57/$file/Dong%20and%20An.pdf.

Gong, X., Xu, D., & Han, W-J. (2015). Household Income and Preschool Attendance in China. *Child Development, 86*(1), 194–208.

Hu, Y. (Nov. 20, 2018). Preschool Education To Be More Affordable. *China Daily*. Retrieved from: www.chinadaily.com.cn/a/201811/20/WS5bf363d4a310eff303289c3e.html.

Hu, Z. & Peng, X. (2015). Household Changes in Contemporary China: An Analysis Based on the Four Recent Censuses. *The Journal of Chinese Sociology, 2* (9). Retrieved from: https://journalofchinesesociology.springeropen.com/articles?query=&volume=2&searchType=&tab=keyword.

Huang, H., Zhuang, A., & Zhang, Y. (2014). Research on the Sharing Mechanism About Financial Investment in Preschool Education: Based on the Perspective of Governance Power Adapted to Disbursement Responsibility. *Education & Economy, 3*, 21–25.

Liu, A., Tong, X., & Fu, W. (2015) Shuang xin jia ting de jia wu xing bie fen gong: Jing ji yi lai, xing bie guan nian huo qing gan biao da [Household Division of Housework for Double Income Family: Economic dependence, gender ideologies, or emotional expression?] *Chinese Journal of Sociology, 35*(2), 109–136.

National Bureau of Statistics People's Republic of China (2013). *China Statistical Yearbook 2013*. (Table 3-8: Basic Statistics on National Population: Census in 1953, 1964, 1982, 1990, 2000, 2010.) China Statistics Press. Retrieved from: www.stats.gov.cn/tjsj/ndsj/2013/indexeh.htm.

National Bureau of Statistics People's Republic of China (2016). *China Statistical Yearbook 2016*. (Table 2-1: Population and its composition). National Bureau of Statistics People's Republic of China. Retrieved from: www.stats.gov.cn/tjsj/ndsj/2016/indexch.htm.

PRNewswire (November 21, 2014). *China Pre-School Education (Kindergarten) Industry Research Report, 2014*. Retrieved from: www.prnewswire.com/news-releases/china-pre-school-education-kindergarten-industry-research-report-2014-283459641.html.

Sun, J. & Zhang, H. (2013). Zhongguo laonian ren zhaogu sun zinu de zhuangkuang ji yingxiang yinsr fenxi [An Analysis of the Situation and Influencing Factors of How Chinese Elderly Take Care of their Grandchildren]. *Population and Economics, 4*, 70–77.

The State Council People's Republic of China (2014). *Labor Law of the People's Republic of China. Ch. VII Protection for female staff and workers and juvenile workers*. Retrieved from: http://english.gov.cn/archive/laws_regulations/2014/08/23/content_281474983042473.htm.

21

Slovenia

Živa Humer and Metka Kuhar

Petra, aged 40, and Tomaž, aged 39, have been living in common-law marriage for 12 years and have two children: 10-year-old Lara and 2-year-old Lenart, as well as a cat. Three years ago they moved from their rented flat to a new, three-room modern flat, which they bought as equal owners. They now live close to the center of Ljubljana, Slovenia's capital, and near a large park and sports center.

Both have degrees in education. Petra is employed full-time at an embassy in the capital of Slovenia; Tomaž also works full-time as a special needs teacher at a public high school. Although they have no plans to change jobs, Tomaž is writing his Ph.D. dissertation and Petra would like to complete her master's thesis.

When we arrived for the interview, Tomaž greeted us with a smile, saying that Petra had called about an hour in advance of the arrival of the "lady scientists," telling him to clean up the flat and buy some snacks in the shop on the building's ground floor. He grinned quietly and said that he had carried out her "orders." However, Tomaž's role extends far beyond being Petra's assistant.

A Day in the Life

Petra, Tomaž, Lara, and Lenart start the day together. On a workday they get up around 6:30 a.m. and either Petra or Tomaž spontaneously makes tea and breakfast for the children. After breakfast, one of them prepares Lenart for kindergarten, while Lara gets ready herself. Tomaž takes Lenart to the kindergarten, and Lara goes to school on her own. Tomaž usually comes home from his job at 1:00 p.m. Lara also finishes school then and usually participates in afternoon activities, such as choir, violin, and gymnastics. Tomaž tranports her if they are far or the weather is bad. In the afternoon, Tomaž often does the dishes, quickly cleans the kitchen and bedroom, wipes dust on the shelves, and, if there is a mess, cleans the living room. He vacuums the whole flat once or twice a week. On Tuesday, he does the main household shopping. He collects Lenart from the kindergarten at 4:00 p. m. to give him time to play with his peers.

When he and Lenart arrive home, Lara is usually there already. When she was younger Tomaž prepared her a snack, but now she usually does it by herself. Tomaž always asks her, "How was school? What's new and what's for homework?" and he's available for homework help if she asks. He plays, reads stories, and draws pictures with Lenart. With Lara, he says, "We play more board games, cards, and chess. We also talk more . . . Usually Lara comes with a question and we talk about it."

Petra comes home at 5:00 p.m. If Tomaž didn't prepare lunch, she makes a quick lunch[1] for them. In spring or summer they might take turns taking the kids to the park. Petra also often takes Lara to the nearby swimming pool, while Tomaž plays at home with Lenart. During the workweek Petra prepares a light dinner and cleans up, often a dairy dish, but Tomaž generally helps. Dinner is followed by the rituals of bathing, diapering, dressing, and teeth brushing and cuddling, usually carried out by Petra. However, some evenings Petra is gone for job responsibilities so Tomaž takes over. He also takes over household chores entirely when Petra feels tired, which, according to him, is quite often.

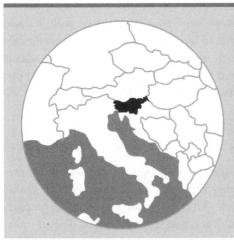

Slovenia became an independent country in 1991 with the dissolution of Yugoslavia, after having been a part of the Yugoslav socialist federal state constituted after World War II. Having slightly more than 2 million inhabitants, Slovenia is ethnically homogeneous, with a majority of Roman Catholics (57%), according to the last census in 2002. Muslims accounted for 2.4%, and

---

[1] The word *lunch* here refers to the hot meal that Slovene families often have on returning home at the end of the day. In Slovene they use the same word, *kosilo*, for this meal and the noonday meal. Much later in the evening, they then have a light supper, called *večerja*.

Orthodox Christians 2.3% of the population. A third of the population either didn't specify a religious affiliation or declared none (Central Intelligence Agency, 2019).

Of family households, 49% are couples (i.e., married, cohabiting, or same-sex partnerships) with children, 26% couples without children, and 25% are lone parent households. Approximately 23% of couples with children live in common-law marriage. Under socialism cohabitation was legally equivalent to marriage (Slovenia Statistical Office, 2019).

The employment rate for women in 2017 was 69.7%, as compared with 76.9% for men (Eurostat, 2018a). Slovene women surpass the educational levels of men (European Institute for Gender Equality [EIGE], 2018), yet the pay gap favoring men is still 7.8% (Eurostat, 2018b). Among couples with children, the full-time employment rate is 77% for women and 88% for men. Fourteen percent of women are employed part-time. The gender pay gap is greater for couples with children (EIGE, 2018).

A fully paid maternity leave for working women, starting the last month of pregnancy, is available for 105 days, of which 15 days are mandatory. Parents are then entitled to a 260-day parental leave, which can be shared between them and is compensated at 100% of salary. Additionally, fathers are entitled to paternity leave for 30 days at 100% pay (Stropnik, 2018).

Public preprimary education and care is widely available. Thirty-seven percent of children under the age of 3 are enrolled, and 91% of children between age 3 and school age are enrolled (EIGE, 2018). In addition, regular or periodic care for preschool and school-aged children, and housework help is provided by members of the extended family, usually by grandmothers. More than two-thirds of employed women and men receive a grandparent's help with childcare (Kuhar, 2011).

Despite the long tradition of full-time female employment and the promotion of gender equality (at least in the public sphere) since socialist times, the division of family labor is still highly gendered. Eighty-one percent of women, but only 28% of men spend at least an hour per day in cooking and housework (EIGE, 2018). When couples from 35 countries around the world were categorized according to how they divided paid and unpaid work, the majority of Slovene couples (58%) were classified as "second shift" couples: women worked similar hours for pay as their partners but spent at least 7 hours more per week than their partners on carework and housework. In only 16% of the couples did the men's time in domestic labor equal or exceed the woman's (DeRose et al., 2019).

Tomaž reports that recently Lenart has been waking up very early, and Tomaž has been the parent on call. He says, "We sit together in the living room. For example, this morning we woke up at 4:00 am and then we negotiated for tea, for orange ... and then he falls asleep and I read a book and made tea."

During the weekends they both cook, usually more sophisticated meals. As the more adventurous cook, Tomaž sometimes cooks Indian dishes. They might socialize with friends or visit Petra's parents. Tomaž also works in his mother's vineyard. Sometimes one will take care of both children, to give the other free time. Tomaž would either go to the mountains or works on his Ph.D., whereas Petra would spend time with her girlfriends.

Both parents nurture their children and attend to their emotional needs. Although Lenart currently prefers to be cuddled by his mother, he also sometimes wants attention from Tomaž. During the bedtime rituals, Lara calls her mother to rub her back in the bathtub, but she wants to be cuddled by both parents, and turns to both equally often with her problems. They are both concerned about her perfectionism. Tomaž explains: "If she doesn't get the best grade at school (i.e., a 5), she is stressed and afraid to tell us, for example, that she got 4. So, we started ... saying, 'It will happen that you'll get also 3 or 2. I also got it.'"

The parents also equally share sick leave. Tomaž notes that Petra doesn't entirely trust him:

> Petra ... has a habit of emphasizing which medicine the child should take, how many spoons of this and that medicine I have to give the child, and when the fever is too high and I need to give her Calpol [a medicine]. All these things I know by myself.

When both have job obligations, Tomaž's mother travels to Ljubljana, and stays with them for a couple of days. As Petra explains:

> His mother really is number one when we need help. Just recently we both had urgent matters to take care of and she came over while the kid was sick ... She is indeed a "granny on call." All I have to do is phone and she comes right away; she sleeps here, irons everything, [and] starts to clean the flat. We're really happy when someone like that is around.

Petra and Tomaž report that they hire a babysitter to spend an evening out together occasionally. Petra says, "We try to go out every fortnight. At times we can make it every week, but sometimes a whole month passes without."

Although Tomaž and Petra seem equal in their care of the children, as Tomaž explains, conflicts over how to handle things with the children often reflect their gendered perspectives, "From my perspective, Petra is too indulgent and I'm often too tough. I would play a 'father's role'; Petra would play a 'mother's role'."

Their equally shared childcare is matched by their equally shared housework. They both iron and both load and empty the dishwasher. Petra pays food expenses and Tomaž pays all other bills. He also takes care of their car maintenance and repairs. Petra takes credit for some of the mental work:

> I think and plan a lot: I'm organized – when to iron, when to wash clothes. So I'm the one who sorts out the laundry and I put it in the machine. He, on the other hand, finishes the job, takes it out, and hangs the laundry. And that works for all the things. He goes shopping, but I make him a list what to buy. Only when I'm too tired when I don't have the energy, then he does everything.

Although making the shopping list might make Petra sound like the manager, Tomaž reveals that he consults the list, but once at the market, he ignores the list and just buys what he thinks they need.

They have no explicit plan for household chores. They stress that they help one another out and do whatever is necessary. Petra explains:

> There is no specific work that he wouldn't do. He knows how to do everything from ironing to cleaning. We both do everything, but there is no schedule as you can see. We don't manage to do it all, but we don't worry about it … Sometimes I just don't care if there is some dust up there or not.

Tomaž does admit to avoiding one chore: the care of their cat; he is against having pets in a flat. "I do take care of her if there's nobody else around. I feed her, clean her litter box, but if someone else is at home, I let them know I won't do it."

Moreover, he is not as sanguine as she about the condition of the flat. Once a week there is supposed to be a big cleaning. Tomaž does the vacuuming and Petra then mops the floor; they take turns changing the bed linen, as they do with the least attractive job of cleaning the toilet. However, they often drop their agreed-upon Friday afternoon cleaning, usually, according to Tomaž, because Petra says she is too tired. Cleaning is then moved to Saturday or Sunday. Tomaž says, "That's a subject that makes our [his] blood pressure go up. When it bothers me I take a duster and start cleaning. But I don't argue like, 'You said you would dust and you haven't' … When I see what it's like and can't take it, I just clean up."

They wish they could afford to hire a house cleaner more than the several times a year that they already do, according to Petra. Petra and Tomaž have been gradually introducing their kids to household chores.

Lara takes care of her own room, vacuums the flat, and cooks vegetable soup; Lenart takes out the trash, puts his dirty clothes in the linen basket, and helps with hanging it to dry.

Balancing Paid Work and Family

Although Tomaž and Petra are both employed full-time with permanent contracts, their hours differ. The workday starts for both at 8:00 a.m., but Tomaž finishes at 1:00 p.m., while Petra is at her job until 4:30 p.m., except on Fridays when she finishes at 2:00 p.m. Tomaž enjoys frequent school holidays and is entitled to 33 days leave. He can complete class preparations at home, which allows him more flexibility than Petra, for whom paid work and family are both spatially and temporally separated. Petra only has 25 leave days per year. In addition, both his fellow teachers, most of whom are women, and the school administration at Tomaž's workplace are more forgiving than Petra's co-workers are when a sick child needs care. He describes the double standard:

> Women are more critical of other women than they are of men. When I do something they say, "Oh, that's so nice, so caring." But when a woman takes sick leave, says Petra, they'll say "What? Again?" They are more tolerant of men; they even admire you for these things.

Beyond the routine hours, Petra's job requires a lot of evenings out to attend cultural events. Tomaž takes on extra projects that are voluntary, but give them additional income, and have garnered him the highest teaching title with its higher salary. He is proud of the work he does, "I always knew that I could work well with children and students, and my confirmation can be seen in their work and respect towards me." Petra acknowledges that before he assumes a project, he always consults with her:

> Whatever he takes up, the family comes first. He'll start by arranging things at home, making provisions, organizing tasks, and then asks "Would you mind if I ..." and when, of course, we agree, only then will he start working on his project ... He doesn't take time off from the "family schedule."

Over the 8 years that Petra has been at her job, it has become increasingly demanding. Initially, she elected to work part-time (60%), which allowed for a more relaxed family life. However, because co-workers exercised their rights to go to part-time for health reasons, Petra was required to work full-time. Meanwhile, due to warnings about possible layoffs, she takes on additional projects to prove herself. She explains:

"There is a lot of pressure on me ... because of my own [feeling of] responsibility, I don't go home until everything is finished. God forbid that someone says, 'You didn't finish your work!'"

Both Tomaž and Petra love and are committed to their jobs, but Tomaž explains that his priorities changed when he became a parent: "Before, I used to live for my job; I didn't want to be absent and went to work even when ill. With Lara this changed; now she was more important." In the past Tomaž had aspired to be promoted to headmaster, but now he has no interest because he does not want the additional responsibilities and the constraints of more time at the workplace.

Creating Equality

Petra and Tomaž met when they were both employed at the same secondary school. Petra was teaching geography. They became romantically involved so Petra separated from her first husband. After the divorce came through, she moved into a rented flat with Tomaž. They had Lara, their first child, after living together for one year.

Initially, Tomaž believed that the mother would instinctively know what to do, but soon realized that parenting is not innate. He points out that neither of them knew what to do with a new infant: "We both had to learn everything and at times we panicked, got hysterical, because we didn't know a thing and had to ask our doctor for every little problem. There were quite a lot of new situations that we had to solve ourselves in one way or another."

After Lara's birth, Petra stayed at home for the entire allowed leave, the maternity leave as well as the parental leave, which could have been shared. Petra explains that she did not have a permanent employment contract when Lara was born, but had to renew her contract with the secondary school yearly. When she became pregnant, her contract was not renewed. She and Tomaž decided that she would stay at home. Tomaž made use of a collective agreement that provided a total of only 5 days of leave, but at that time, there was no state-mandated paternity leave available. He and Petra originally made plans for him to take over half of the parental leave when she got a job. Instead, however, Petra, found part-time freelance work that she was able to combine with the childcare leave.

Nonetheless, Tomaž was fully engaged in caring for Lara as a tiny infant. Home by 1:00 p. m., he changed diapers, took her to the doctor, took her for walks, as well as going shopping, and preparing meals. He adds, "Only during nights I didn't wake up much, since Petra breastfed."

When Lara was 2 years old, both Tomaž and Petra got scholarships for 3 months of study abroad. Petra went to Germany and took Lara with her. Her scholarship covered a family bonus and Tomaž arranged to join them for 2 months. While there, he took care of Lara for 4 hours per day, while Petra was studying. Petra reports, "The rest of the day we were tourists and had a great time together."

After Lenart's birth, Petra again took all of the parental leave. They didn't even discuss sharing it. She had planned to work on her master's thesis while at home, but instead, she reports, "I used time when the child was asleep for myself to treat my soul not for the master's degree." By then Slovenia had instituted paternity leave, and Tomaž took all 15 days of the paid leave, during which they all went to the seaside together.

Despite Petra's claiming the parental leave for herself, the division of labor between them became more equal after Lenart's birth. Tomaž explains:

> When Lara was born it seemed natural that Petra would get up when she cried, but with Lenart things were different and she just said, "Now it's your turn" ... With Lenart we made better agreements ... It used to be that I would tell her to go to the sauna or swimming pool to relax. Now with Lenart, she doesn't have to be told, but goes whenever she wants.

Once she went back to her job, Petra complained that she needed more time for herself:

> I felt like I didn't have any free time ... However, it happened that I was alone for a few days (Tomaž was on a business trip in Spain; the kids were with their grandparents) and I spent most of the time at home (after work) reading books, listening to music, watching movies and taking care of the flat. I admitted to myself that when I'm alone and when nobody expects anything from me, only then I feel that I have "free time."

Free time for Petra is an issue they still struggle with, partly because Lenart is demanding, and partly because of her need to fulfill what she sees as her role. Tomaž is sympathetic to Petra's conflict. On his time off, Tomaž has been taking the kids on trips for up to a week for recreational activities like skiing, or to visit relatives, giving Petra more time on her own.

Petra and Tomaž give different accounts of how they developed the division of housework. Tomaž says:

> At the beginning we had fights about it, when I saw that she was ironing and she started to iron my clothes. We realized that we'll have to discuss it and

agree about sharing; otherwise it wouldn't work. Eventually, we realized who prefers which activity; for example, she likes to iron.

Petra, however, sees the development of their division of labor as more spontaneous, "We've never sat down and discussed what either of us should do or what neither of us would like to do. That's a debate we never had."

What Helps and Hinders in Creating Equality

Tomaž's and Petra's equality has been facilitated by: the structure of their jobs; Tomaž's early socialization and Petra's resistance to hers; the care of their relationship and their constructive approach to solving problems and conflicts; and the feminist position they share. Although many in their social world tout equality, they have few models to draw on, and must weather criticism for thwarting gendered norms.

The Structure of Their Jobs

Although Tomaž takes advantage of the structure of his job to support their equality, structure alone cannot explain his involvement. Tomaž, for example, only accepts extra projects that are compatible with his family responsibilities. Likewise, he eschews the idea of becoming a director because it would add constraints. Finally, despite his aspirations to complete his Ph.D., he only works on it after the children are asleep. Tomaž explicitly chooses to limit his career aspirations so he can participate fully in family life.

Rejecting Traditional Family Norms

Tomaž and Petra both come from Christian patriarchal families. They were both baptized and received all the sacraments, but they are not practicing believers in their own family. The gendered roles of the father and mother were clearly defined in their families of origin, except that both of their mothers were employed full-time.

Tomaž's father was a tradesman and arrived home in the evening, while his mother did administrative work and came home earlier. At home, his parents embodied traditional gender-based labor. Nevertheless, Tomaž's mother taught him, as well as his sister, to perform household chores. Tomaž recounts:

[Mom] called at 1:00 p.m. from her job. I was at home and she told me to peel potatoes and cook them and so I did. I had to vacuum at home from early on. That was my daily chore. If there was any dust left, I had to do it all over; Mom was a strict supervisor … It wasn't like I was raised to be just a "boy."

Tomaž believes that Petra's family of origin is even more patriarchal, "My father-in-law is a typical old-style husband. Mom takes care of everything, including him … So I think that Petra started with the intention that she wouldn't allow such a situation."

Petra concurred that she wanted a different kind of partnership than she witnessed growing up. "When I look at my mom, I think I couldn't accept such a [patriarchal] pattern." Petra's mother's admiring view that women today have more "courage" suggests that she wasn't happy with her subordinate role. Petra reports:

I am fascinated by her saying … that we have more courage than women in the past … Not only that I had courage to divorce, but also going out alone or with girlfriends, or not to cook lunch, or to stand against your partner's will. That was unimaginable in her times and still is for her.

Petra's commitment to equality seems shaped by the cautionary tale of her mother's life, which she did not want to reproduce, "My mother had to agree with father or there was fire in the roof. Even then, I thought to myself, 'Why are they not equal?'"

Nurturing Their Partnership

The value they place on their relationship, as well as the quality of their communication contribute to their ongoing creation of equality. Their Saturday morning rituals clearly illustrate that. On weekends Petra and Tomaž often treat themselves to long breakfasts, while the children watch television and play. The importance of preserving time for themselves overrides their parenting principle that children should not watch too much TV. Although she confesses that they watch too much, Petra explains:

I think it was us who made Lenart get used to watching cartoons so that we had more time for the two of us. Now I don't mind any longer that he sits there and watches a children's show or cartoon, and we stay at the table after breakfast, sometimes for 2 hours … We finish our breakfast and then start talking, discussing things.

Petra and Tomaž are open about problems and frustrations, and face conflicts together. For example, they do not always see eye to eye on parenting because Tomaž is likely to be stricter and have less patience with the children than Petra, and because Petra often undermines his "authority." When these issues arise, they discuss and work out different ways of responding. Likewise, when Petra expressed her frustration in not having time for herself, Tomaž found ways of giving her more freedom.

Feminist Philosophy

Tomaž and Petra are consciously feminist. Besides rejecting traditional roles, their feminism is reflected in their choice to give their children different surnames. Tomaž reports:

> We gave our son Petra's surname [Horvat] and our daughter my surname [Novak], because we aren't married. That was the agreement before they were born and we stuck to it. Occasionally it causes some embarrassment, like, for instance, when I go to the kindergarten and search the list for Novak Lenart, only to realize that he is Horvat.

Tomaž's advocacy for girls' freedom shows his feminism as well:

> I'm also very critical, for example, when at the teacher's meeting female teachers mentioned that girls are wearing too short skirts, that no wonder then boys are aggressive and violent and touch them, and girls don't like that. We had a lot of conflicts. Their view was that we should organize workshops for girls to educate them, but I protested.

Mostly their feminism, however, acts implicitly in their relationship. They didn't sit down and explicitly agree that it would be 50/50. They just work things out practically as they come along, with the assumption that they are both responsible. Petra makes it clear that equality wasn't an accident; other men she had been involved with also shared the work:

> My previous boyfriends were also like that. I guess I pick that kind of people that I feel good around. Yes, I think that didn't arise out of our relationship, it is more of a special feeling that I have, special sense, so I knew that such things wouldn't be a problem.

Both of them explicitly reject essentialist ideas that the mother is naturally more suited to take care of children than the father, which made it easier for them to share all of the baby care. When asked if fathers are as capable as mothers, Petra confidently asserted, "If I would die right now, I wouldn't be worried about my kids, because they would be in good hands. I think also a man can be a single parent. There is no difference."

Elsewhere, Humer (2009) has argued that the male partner's job – his work hours and job obligations – usually in better-paid occupations, accounts for men's lesser engagement at home. Today, however, younger women are better educated than men and are catching up in the labor force (Ule & Kuhar, 2008). Petra and Tomaž surely reflect that trend. But the reason why women still perform the greater share of childcare lies in the prevailing social construct of the mother as the primary caregiver. Petra and Tomaž are able to share because they have rejected that prescription.

Nonetheless, they reveal some subtle ambivalence toward equality between mothers and fathers. For example, Petra had the prerogative to take all of the parental leave. Initially, Tomaž unconsciously believed that mothers would automatically know how to care for infants, although he was open-minded enough to soon realize that infant care had to be learned by both parents. Petra seems to gatekeep a bit, while Tomaž resists her control, such as when she gives him instructions for taking care of a sick child, although he insists he doesn't need them, or when she writes shopping lists for him that he ignores.

The Social Context

In Petra and Tomaž's social network, they are often faced with an ambivalent response to the gender equality of their arrangements. For example, despite Petra's mother's admiration of today's young women's "courage," Tomaž points out her subtle criticism of Petra's nontraditional role (e.g., she should be cooking meat for her non-vegetarian husband). Petra reports that her mother blames her when her children are ill. Among co-workers, there is a double standard for men and women who take sick leave to care for their kids. Tomaž is praised; Petra is criticized or fears criticism behind her back. Among friends, although there are some who share the way they do, Petra points out that the enthusiastic talk about equality in household labor is not always put into practice. She says, "Sometimes I hear unimaginable things. For example, she [a friend] has to make lunch every day! And then he gets angry if she doesn't! That's unimaginable to me!"

When Tomaž talks about the "new fatherhood" he starts by touting the changes, but ends up revealing that involved fathers can be the target of teasing:

> There are fewer and fewer physical jobs, increasingly more free time, and men do want these [caregiving] roles. It's no big deal any more in the sense of "Be a real man!" ... Men became more self-confident that it's nothing wrong with

taking part in care. You go out with a stroller, you do things that used to be "women's things," and you don't care if your friends tease you.

In fact, Tomaž is sometimes even exposed to mockery from part of his network of male friends, but he ignores them or responds with humor, "If I want to keep my friends, it's better that I make fun of myself than let them make fun of me, because then I may be sensitive and say 'You're not my friends.'" Tomaž's description of how he has to deal with male teasing both for parenting and for his more "feminine" interests like poetry shows his resistance to traditional male norms. But in the back of his mind, even he is thinking,"Do I look like a faggot to them?" Tomaž also points out that it is not only men who resist changing gendered roles. One obstacle to equality at home, he argues, is women's frequent wish to stay in control of the home, especially of the caregiving.

Conclusion

Despite some discouragement from friends and family, Petra and Tomaž have created an equally sharing family. Their equality is shaped by both the objective features of their employment, as well as their shared egalitarian ideology and their wishes and intentions to put that ideology into practice. Their example also shows that equality is not an achieved condition, but a process; the creation of equality is ongoing and continually worked out. The quality of Tomaž and Petra's open communication helps them put their beliefs into practice. Sometimes that means they make explicit agreements, such as giving their children different surnames, deciding how to allocate parental leave, and organizing sick leave to care for children, but often they simply improvise day by day, according to what works. Their communication helps them with simple practical things, such as how they distribute chores, and with thorny issues, such as Petra's undermining Tomaž's authority.

In summing up, Petra emphasizes their equivalence as parents, "Maybe I have a bit different approach but essentially there are no differences." Tomaž touts their satisfaction with their equitable arrangements, "It's . . . a feeling that you're not used out, unimportant – both equally frustrated, both equally satisfied."

References

Central Intelligence Agency (2019). Slovenia. *The World Factbook*. Retrieved from: www.cia.gov/library/publications/the-world-factbook/geos/si.html.

DeRose, L. F., Goldscheider, F., Javiera, R. B., Salazar-Arango, A., Cocuera, P., Corcuera, P. J. & Gas-Aixendri, M. (2019). Are Children Barriers to the Gender Revolution? International Comparisons. *European Journal of Population*. Retrieved from: https://doi.org/10.1007/s10680-018-09515-8.

European Institute for Gender Equality (2018). *Gender Equality Index 2017: Slovenia*. Retrieved from: https://eige.europa.eu/rdc/eige-publications/gender-equality-index-2017-slovenia.

Eurostat (2018a). *Employment Rate by Sex, Age, Group 20–64*. Retrieved from: https://ec.europa.eu/eurostat/tgm/refreshTableAction.do?tab=table&plugin=1&pcode=t2020_10&language=en.

Eurostat (2018b). *The Unadjusted Gender Pay Gap*. Retrieved from: https://ec.europa.eu/eurostat/statistics-explained/index.php/Gender_pay_gap_statistics#Gender_pay_gap_levels_vary_significantly_across_EU.

Humer, Ž. (2009). *Etikas krbi, spol in družina: procesi relokacije skrbi med zasebno in javno sfero. Doktorska disertacija* [Ethics of Care, Gender and Family: The Processes of the Relocation of Care Between Private and Public Spheres]. Unpublished doctoral thesis. Ljubljana: Fakulteta za družbene vede.

Kuhar, M. (2011). Skrb za otroke: Potrebe staršev predadolescentnih otrok v Sloveniji [Caring for Children: Needs of Preadolescents' Parents in Slovenia]. *Teorija in praksa, 18* (2): 473–490.

Republic of Slovenia Statistical Office (2019). *Families by Type and Average Number of Children, Slovenia 1, January 2018*. Retrieved from: www.stat.si/StatWeb/en/News/Index/7725.

Stropnik, N. (2018) Slovenia Country Note. In S. Blum, A. Koslowski, A. Macht, & P. Moss (eds.) *International Review of Leave Policies and Research 2018* (pp. 379–386). Retrieved from: www.leavenetwork.org/lp_and_r_reports/.

Ule, M. & Kuhar, M. (2008). Orientations of Young Adults in Slovenia Toward the Family Formation. *Young, 16* (2), 153–83.

22

Iceland

Ingólfur V. Gíslason

Hildur and Arnaldur, a couple in their 30s, both have academic degrees and are employed by the same international corporation in Reykjavík, the capital of Iceland. They live in a spacious flat on the outskirts of the city, with a lovely view of a small forest and a lake. They have two children, a 7-year-old son, Kristinn, and a 7-month-old daughter, Sigrún. Hildur also has a 12-year-old son, Hrafn, from a prior relationship, who lives with them, although he spends every other weekend with his biological father. Three children and full-time jobs mean they have a lot to do, which they have tried to share fairly and to tackle in a way that infringes no more upon her possibilities than his.

Two Careers Make for a Busy Schedule

When I interviewed them Arnaldur was on parental leave. Hildur had taken 2½ months of parental leave but also used vacation days to stay home for a total of 4 months. Their plan is to stretch the parental leave so that it won't be necessary for Sigrún to go to a private child minder but can go directly to kindergarten (or playschool, the Icelandic term acknowledging that children learn by playing). Ironically, they were "helped" in this plan because in their international company, Arnaldur's superior is an American, who is not thrilled by the Icelandic system of parental leave. So when Arnaldur announced his intention of taking 3 months parental leave, they negotiated an agreement that he would only be on 50% leave for 6 months rather than 3 months on 100% leave, and that he could work from home and still collect salary. So he works when his daughter is sleeping and again when the children are in bed for the night.

Iceland is ranked the most gender-equal country in the world by the World Economic Forum (2018). With a population of only 339,511 people, it is the most sparsely populated country in Europe (World Population Review, 2019). The great majority of inhabitants are white and ethnic Icelanders. Still, the last decade has seen a rapid increase in migration to Iceland so that now 10% of the population are immigrants (Statistics Iceland, 2018b). The majority of Icelanders (67%) are members of the evangelical Lutheran state church (Hagstofa Íslands, n.d.).

Iceland has very high labor market participation. In 2017, 84% of men and 77% of women, aged 16 to 74, were employed. However, 35% of women worked part-time, whereas only 14% of men did. The gender pay gap favoring men was 16% in 2016 (Statistics Iceland, 2018b).

Married and cohabiting couples with children represent 40% of the families in Iceland, 45% are couples without children, and 16% are lone parents with children (Statistics Iceland, 2018b).

Parental leave in Iceland is 9 months and divided between the parents so that the father has 3 non-transferable months, the mother the same, and there are 3 that they can divide as they like. Compensation is up to 80% of salary, but with the economic crash in 2008, a low ceiling was adopted, which reduced the number of fathers who took leave and reduced the number of days of those who did (Eydal & Gíslason, 2018). Recently, the ceiling was raised and takeup by fathers is going up, although usually the mothers take the lion's share of the leave (Fæðingarorlofssjóður, 2018).

A 2010 time-use study found that women spent on average 12.83 hours a week on domestic chores, while men spent on average 8.70 hours. The total weekly time spent working (paid and unpaid) was 54.71 hours a week for men and 47.52 hours for women. This changed, however, when children entered the equation: married, full-time working women with children spent on average 32.62 hours a week on childcare, while similarly situated men spent 18.95 hours a week. The total average workweek for those women was 90.28 hours and for the men 79.29 hours (Stefánsson &

Þórsdóttir, 2010). Although no recent time-use data exists, some evidence suggests that the gender gap in childcare may be narrowing for couples who had children after paternal leave was instituted (Arnalds, Eydal, & Gíslason, 2013).

Kindergartens are heavily subsidized by municipalities. In 2017, about 97% of children aged 3 to 5 attended preprimary school, while 95% of 2-year-olds and 47% of 1-year-olds did (Statistics Iceland, 2018a).

On a typical weekday on parental leave, Arnaldur is usually the first to wake up and lets the others sleep in a bit. Hildur has somewhat flexible hours and can vary when she gets to her job. Arnaldur fixes breakfast for the children and sees to it that the boys get off to school. After that, he says, "If I have some alone time I run upstairs and answer some emails, but otherwise I give Sigrún something to eat and put the dishes in the dishwasher or something while she is eating. Then it is just taking care of her."

He describes the previous day:

I had to go to work yesterday morning, which is unusual. I took Sigrún over to my mother with food and something to drink, and she was with her for three hours and came home around noon. Then I took over and gave her something to eat and put her to sleep, the afternoon nap. On Tuesdays and Thursdays, Kristinn is in extended stay at school at his own request ... So I work when Sigrún is sleeping. Hildur comes home between 5 and 6 usually ... then I suppose I started cooking? No, it is this complex system on Tuesdays. Kristinn practices karate, so I drive him. I got my brother to babysit her while I drove him to karate, then I came back and cooked. Hildur had been to the store and the pharmacy [because] Sigrún has a cold, and then picked Kristinn up from karate ... [on her way home]. Then I went straight to sport practice and Hildur and the kids ate together, and I came home and ate dinner when they had finished eating. Hrafn came home from his football practice that is ... from 7:30 to 8:30 on Tuesdays. We try to put Kristinn to bed between 8 and 9, and then it is just tea and watching television ... I am finishing a project at work, so I had to work late. I went to bed around one, but I didn't want to risk waking up Sigrún. She usually sleeps in her crib but because of her cold she was already in our bed. I slept on the couch last night so I wouldn't wake anyone. But then I wake up with her because Hildur is working full-time, so I wake up to give her her pacifier.

On a more typical day, Arnaldur might have 2 hours to work when Sigrún took a morning nap and another 2 hours in the afternoon. But when she was awake, according to Hildur, sometimes "he put her in this child chair in the middle of the floor behind him and then he had telephone meetings with people at his company." Hildur laughs when she contemplates her baby daughter "at a meeting."

While their division of childcare responsibilities and the paid work/family balance seems satisfying to them now, there were struggles to get to this point. Although Arnaldur took a parental leave when his first child was born, he was trying to complete a master's degree at the same time and now feels guilty that he wasn't sufficiently attentive to his new baby. Hildur recalls that time as difficult. She mentions that Arnaldur is missing from many of the photos from that period, indicating that she was taking a disproportionate amount of childcare responsibility. After he finished his degree, both of them invested long hours in their jobs, often 10 to 12 hours a day, while Arnaldur's mother, who lives in an attached house, took over a lot of the childcare.

"She is the Foreman"

Both said 50/50 when asked how they divide the household chores, but Hildur claims that she cooks more often and Arnaldur and/or the boys clean up afterwards. Arnaldur, on the other hand, thinks that he cooks just as often as she. Hildur reports that Arnaldur vacuums and cleans the house more often than she does. They employ a housecleaner who comes every other week. They straighten up the house together the night before she comes to make it easier for her to clean. The weekly grocery shopping is either done together or by Arnaldur alone. Hildur is a spontaneous buyer, whereas Arnaldur loathes going to the store when it hasn't been planned.

The only really strict division they follow, however, regards the laundry. Hildur washes and dries, and Arnaldur folds and puts the clothes away. Laundry has been a source of disagreement. Arnaldur said, "I think it is fine to be the one who folds. In that way I know that the pile is here and I can just fold when I feel like it. If someone needs something desperately, 'Just go to the pile and get it.'" Hildur has sometimes been irritated over this approach and thought that it took too long for him to get the laundry in its proper place. She has, however, changed her tactics from direct scolding, "Why is the laundry still here?" to, "There is one thing I would like you to do today, but it is ok if you don't do it till tomorrow, and that is the laundry." This strategy has helped, according to Hildur. They did try to reverse the laundry roles for one year but it didn't work out. The dirty laundry tended to pile up, so they went back to their old system.

Traditional male chores in the household are either done by Arnaldur or not at all. Neither is interested in cars so they drive old ones, rusty and dented, rarely washed, not to mention waxed. Both state that they simply see cars as a way to get quickly from one place to another and that time can be better spent on almost anything else rather than on taking care of the cars. Arnaldur does minor repairs in their apartment, like drilling and fixing, although the initiative may come from Hildur who usually initiates home maintenance and improvement as well. Arnaldur says:

> She is the foreman. We are conscious about our division of labor with something like 90% of what is done. She cooked but I cleaned up afterwards and the other way around; she washed and I folded and put away ... cleaning was always divided. We both cleaned at the same time and helped each other. ... But then taking care of the home, preventive measures and initiative, that was 99% Hildur ... I rarely see the necessity of new curtains. But it has to be decided ... and then they have to be bought and then it is my job to put them up. So if anything has to be done, she usually suggests it and then I do it. But usually I am quite happy not doing anything.

Likewise, they both agreed that Hildur had a better overview of the schedule as a whole, particularly with regard to the children. Arnaldur was very conscious of this disparity:

> Hildur has that totally ... to go to the 6 months check-up, I only remember that if I am told about it ... But making sure this is done that is most definitely Hildur ... Childproof locks and things like that, that is most certainly Hildur. I would never take the lead there ... And that they are properly dressed. I don't know if it is lack of feeling responsible or just lack of planning or just some personality thing. I rely a bit on Hildur to look after some things.

But he also regarded his behavior as problematic and has been working on it:

> I am trying. If we have to call the insurance company or we have to order something or the phone is broken or something, I am trying to do that without her having to ask me to do it ... maybe a sign of maturity ... It is humiliating not to have everything under control and to be the stupid father, so I am trying to not do it, so I call. I took Sigrún to all her check-ups ... Then we started to systematically divide ... going to school meetings. I probably went to more school visits, if anything, just to break down that myth.

Parenting Differently

Their different personalities also shape the way they shoulder parental responsibilities. Hildur is more outgoing and spontaneous while Arnaldur says of himself, "I am, of course, a complete introvert, totally ... I like being alone. I am almost anti-social, or that could be argued." Hildur, on the other hand, feels that it is important to socialize, to be with people, to connect, and to have many friends and acquaintances. Thus, Hildur is, or at least used to be, more engaged in the children's social life and their schools. Arnaldur did not see all this socializing as important, so a missed meeting or a missed outing wasn't a big deal. But recently he has realized that social life might be important for his children.

Describing her husband's relationship with the children Hildur stated, "He is very warm to them, hugs them a lot. He shows it with just playing with them and showing interest, while I ... want to teach them about life somehow." Arnaldur added, "Playing with them, talking with, checking if they feel good or bad, this comes very naturally for me ... just to understand and interpret and to be with them, that is totally 50/50."

They gravitate to different childcare responsibilities. Hildur explains:

> I take ... more of the social things, and he takes more of the sports ... When Kristinn was taking the yellow belt ... they were practicing here in the living room floor. The kids are number one you see ... and he makes them study, do the homework. That is totally Arnaldur's responsibility now that he is at home ... I just come here and ... they are mostly done with their homework.

On the whole, Arnaldur is the stricter parent. Hildur complained that all the nagging came to her, "Mom, can I do this or that? Mom, can I have this or that?" Arnaldur explained:

> I think it is because they know who is going to say "yes" ... they always ask their mother first ... If they want to be allowed to stay out longer or something like that, they go to their mother because I start asking the boring questions, "Have you done your homework? ..." "Why should you be allowed to do that, if you did this yesterday?"

Perhaps because she says, "yes," Hildur sometimes becomes the center of the family:

> I feel that everyone always comes to me ... Sometimes I feel that I can't go to the bathroom, because there is always something ... I really want to be left in peace when I am taking a bath! ... We got a cat the other day, and I am not taking care of her at all ... but she discovered that I was the main thing here ... It is the same with all the others. They will crawl into my side, stay under my blanket, on top of me, sitting on me.

Hildur was a bit perplexed about this situation given that Arnaldur is there as much as she and has always taken care of the children. She does admit, however, that she is more likely to give in to their demands, both the children's and the cat's.

The relationship is not a sunshine story of total harmony. Hildur mentions that she sometimes feels irritated that Arnaldur doesn't have the same overview as she of what has to be done for the boys, such as meetings at school and dentist appointments. But she has learned how to deal with it, "If I want him to take the boys to the dentist, then I just send him this meeting invite over Outlook, and then I let him know, 'I expect you to take them there, because I can't. I am stuck in something at work,' and then it works."

Hildur admits that Arnaldur has taken a bigger role with their schooling since Sigrún's birth because if there are early morning or evening meetings at school, it is easier for Arnaldur to participate. But Hildur expects their division to revert back once the breastfeeding period and the parental leave are over.

"This is Fun, but Very Demanding"

Both Hildur and Arnaldur find their paid work interesting and rewarding. Hildur is a project manager and supervises a development team of about 60 people:

> I know all these 60 people that are working in my project and this project matters a lot to me, and the people in the project matter a lot to me, so I think that I wouldn't want to be doing anything else, basically. You know, the day is over and I haven't eaten enough and I haven't gotten a bottle of water like I planned to do in the morning and something, so this is fun, but very demanding.

She typically puts in 45 hours a week, but sometimes as much as 60 hours if there is a crisis. When the development phase of her current project is over in a few months, she says, "I am certain that I am going to be very proud of what comes out, and then it doesn't matter that I had to ... I always come home, but sometimes I sit here with the laptop ... in the evenings. I am not going to regret this time."

Arnaldur expressed similar views, "I love my job ... [Laughs] I can't stop working, I feel that, it was fun going to work yesterday, just, you know, completely peaceful, can just sit here and hey, I don't have to take care of anything else besides what I need to do here and now." He felt that he was in exactly the right job and was not interested in climbing the career ladder:

> The work is diverse, exciting … I have gotten to that place that fits me, I am that kind of employee. I manage a small team of people; I have a super talent above me that trusts me completely and wants to do everything for me and everyone is satisfied. I am not planning to become department manager, which is not what I am looking for, to have more people … I am … where my strength is so I am at the best place. I am very happy to have fun at work.

He reports ups and downs in his paid working hours. Usually he works 8 hours a day but in some periods he has to work 10 to 12 hours. Even with the extra work, though, he goes home at the usual hour and then works after the children have gone to bed. Notably, although at home he prefers to put off laundry and shopping, he never postpones tasks for his job, "I can't remember coming to work the day after and saying I didn't finish what I was supposed to do. That I have never done at work." Nonetheless, Arnaldur does say he would like to work less so that he would have more time for sports or hobbies.

Arnaldur is also very supportive of Hildur and proud of her. "She is just talented and she is quick to climb in her career and then she is always working in some demanding job and it is difficult to have some shorter days." Hildur was well aware of his encouragement, "He supports me a lot … Sometimes, I feel like he has more ambition than I for my career. Because I sometimes lose myself in wanting to do what I think is fun and he sometimes pushes me to think, 'Don't be afraid to take any challenges.'"

When I interviewed them, Arnaldur was earning slightly more than Hildur which he felt irritated her, another indication of the importance of equality to her. Her job, in fact, sometimes takes priority because he can more easily work from home. However, for most of their careers their earnings had been very similar, sometimes she earned more and sometimes he, but there was never any great difference. He says of his recent promotion, "It was just a coincidence how this happened, who quits and who doesn't quit, so if everything would be normal then she would … get a similar salary."

Neither To Serve Nor Be Served

How have Hildur and Arnaldur moved toward their ideal of equal sharing? Hildur stated:

> When I was single, I decided I couldn't be in love with a man that expects that I should do a lot more than he, and clean up after him … And I thought that I would be single the rest of my life with one child and I thought, "Then so be

it" ... But then I met Arnaldur, and then when I got to know him better and better, I saw something in him. He lived alone and he did do all of his laundry ... He never feels that someone should serve him; he just finds that embarrassing ... I would never have moved in with him if he thought that I should clean up after him, and there was never any discussion about this when we started living together.

So Hildur was determined that she was not going to be a housekeeper and servant; their relationship should be based on equality and a fair division of labor. In Arnaldur she met someone who saw things in a similar way, as he said:

As soon as I moved out of my parents' home and started living with my friends, I knew that I wanted to have a fair system. And it is just the same in this relationship. I just feel that everyone should chip in, contribute what is fair, that is just my fundamental philosophy: equality and fairness. Of course it would have been nice to have someone folding your laundry and never talk about it, but I would just feel guilty ... I could never be the oppressor or you know, he who profits something from other people.

Both also come from families where the division of labor was not traditional. Hildur's parents were both in the labor market and shared many of the household chores. "I can remember very well my father with the dish towel in the kitchen. I never saw my mother as in some kind of service role to us all."

Arnaldur is the oldest of four brothers and grew up with a chronically depressed mother. His youngest brother is 14 years younger so it often fell to Arnaldur to take care of him and to take care of the home: cooking, cleaning, and fetching his brother from daycare. In addition, his parents were politically radical and well educated abroad and so more open-minded about gendered roles than was the norm when he was growing up.

It was good that I got to see when I was growing up that my father did a lot. He cooked a lot and, you know, he always mopped the floors, cooked ... I wasn't raised with the other idea ... There wasn't anyone who went in to our rooms and took the clothes and put them in the washing machine, and then just [took] clean laundry and put it in the dresser. That never happened.

Probably, these experiences in his own family prepared him for the role of a father, which he shouldered with ease and confidence, and brought home to him the idea that it was simply fair that everyone should chip in when facing common tasks.

Although in Iceland other couples do share 50/50, and more couples aspire to that as an ideal, Hildur and Arnaldur believe that their equality is unusual among their friends and co-workers. Hildur said, "We hardly know any couple who divides equally. I have girlfriends who [say], 'My husband would never vacuum and mop the floors ... No way that he would wash,' ... And I just [think] 'How can you stand having anyone in your home that doesn't?'"

Hildur clearly rejects the idea that caregiving is more natural for women and attributes the asymmetry in caregiving to men's resistance and their upbringing, "I know a lot of men that can perfectly well take care of this child caring part, but I also know a lot of men that can't do it because they just aren't going to do it or weren't raised like that."

Arnaldur points out that couples who have a more traditional division of labor now generally feel that they have to defend their "choice." "They always start with saying, 'She wanted to be at home with the children,' or something like that." Arnaldur was adamant, however, that in his social circle he certainly was not criticized or ridiculed for being at home. Ironically, he invokes his traditional masculinity in sports to partly account for the lack of criticism:

> No, I have never gotten any "stay-at-home housewife" bugging. It is probably because I am very confident regarding this, that you just are at home and that is normal, and that I am not a feminine man. If that would be, then maybe I would hear something like that. But I play football and everything this masculine ... so it is very difficult to tease me ... I couldn't care less and then I [would] just answer back; I would never take anything silently.

He does acknowledge encountering double standards of praise and criticism for parenting, "I hear more praise and that is also kind of irritating. It is very easy to compliment men for just doing something normal and then to yell at the women for going back to work when the child is 6 months old." Hildur also notes the double standard, "I have often been asked if I think it is okay to work these long hours away from my children ... He gets less of that kind of question. It is like he shouldn't feel guilty; I should feel guilty."

In sum, this couple came to the relationship with clear egalitarian views, in some ways shaped by their childhoods, and reinforced by their being equally invested in their careers. Consequently, both regarded equal sharing as something that *should* characterize their relationship. Still, they acknowledge that they are different and try to arrange things accordingly. If some of their arrangements seem to conform to traditional gendered roles, it is neither taken for granted nor regarded as natural. A key factor is their good communication. Everything is subject to discussion and negotiation, with the underlying principle that neither serves and neither is being served. They both see the division of family labor as a solvable issue.

Both mentioned that the Icelandic system of parental leave had been a great help in dividing tasks equally. Similarly the zeitgeist favors gender equality; politicians talk themselves hoarse on its importance. Moreover, Iceland is a fairly family-friendly society with a general willingness to provide space for family obligations. As Arnaldur said about their workplace, "Someone is always at home with a sick child, is always at this parenting meeting or something; there is a lot of tolerance regarding that."

Finally, to maintain their equality, both are willing to work on themselves. Hildur works on suppressing her gatekeeping tendencies because Arnaldur loathes being told what to do and how to do it. She reports, "If Arnaldur is, for example, baking or something, then I am never allowed to interfere." By her own admission it is hard for her to avoid criticizing instead of following in the footsteps of generations of women in her family, who she describes as "famous for interfering." She acknowledges, "I have had to mature a bit in that regard." Similarly, Arnaldur works on his tendency to leave the planning and overview to Hildur and is helped by her attempts not to order or scold but to suggest and ask.

Overall, Arnaldur and Hildur are a career-oriented couple who want to have it all: fulfilling careers, three children with parental childcare for babies, and they want to do it equally. They have their conflicts and tensions, they miss time for leisure and hobbies, but they have come close to achieving everything they want. And they have retained their senses of humor. When reflecting on the lack of equality among their peers, Arnaldur jokes, "If it really is so that we are pretty unique in this way then maybe we should have our heads examined." Likewise, when Hildur considers their lack of leisure, she wryly observes, "We take care of the children first and we realize that they won't be little forever. One day we will sit here stuck with each other, so they are prioritized before our hobbies."

References

Arnalds, A. A., Eydal, G. B., & Gíslason, I. V. (2013). Equal Rights to Paid Parental Leave and Caring Fathers – The Case of Iceland. *Stjórnmál og Stjórnsýsla, 9*(2), 323–344.

Eydal, G. B. & Gíslason, I. V. (2018) Iceland Country Note. In S. Blum, A. Koslowski, A. Macht, & P. Moss (eds.) *International Review of*

Leave Policies and Research 2018 (pp. 203–211). Retrieved from: www
.leavenetwork.org/lp_and_r_reports.

Fæðingarorlofssjóður (2018). *Nýting fæðingarorlofs* [Parental leave use]. Unpublished data from the Parental Leave Fund.

Hagstofa Íslands (n.d.). *Mannfjöldi eftir trú og lífsskoðunarfélögum 1998–2018*
[Population according to religion and world-view 1998–2018]. Retrieved
from: https://px.hagstofa.is/pxis/pxweb/is/Samfelag/Samfelag__menning__5_
trufelog/MAN10001.px.

Statistics Iceland (2018a). *Almost half of one-year-old children attend pre-primary
schools.* Retrieved from: www.statice.is/publications/news-archive/education/
pre-primary-schools-2017/.

Statistics Iceland (2018b). *Women and Men in Iceland.* Retrieved from: www
.statice.is/media/51003/women_and_men_2018_net.pdf.

Stefánsson, K. & Þórsdóttir, Þ. K. (2010). *Ánægja með fjölskyldulíf fyrir og eftir
bankahrun.* [Satisfaction with Family Life Before and After the Bank Col-
lapse]. Retrieved from: http://thjodmalastofnun.hi.is/sites/thjodmalastofnun
.hi.is/files/frettabref_thjodmalastofnunar_8_2010.pdf.

World Economic Forum (2018). *The Global Gender Gap Report* (Table 3, Global
rankings 2018). Geneva, Switzerland: World Economic Forum. Retrieved
from: www3.weforum.org/docs/WEF_GGGR_2018.pdf.

World Population Review (2019). *Iceland Population.* Retrieved from: http://
worldpopulationreview.com/countries/iceland-population/.

23

Germany

Anna Dechant, Harald Rost, and Florian Schulz[1]

Hanna and Hannes live with their 10-month-old daughter, Emma, in their own house in a city in Southern Germany. Hanna is 40 years old; Hannes is 37. Hanna is employed as a researcher at a public institute, Hannes at a bank as an IT consultant, both part-time. Hanna explains:

> So it was his wish explicitly ... discussed between us for a long time, that if we were going to have a child, then we really both wanted to look after and bring up the child ... He wouldn't like to see her only in the evenings when he comes home from work.

Hannes believes that the chance to see his child grow up is well worth his taking time off from his job for parental leave, "This is simply a unique time, and I simply wanted to use it ... That's important to me."

Although Hanna works more hours for pay per week than Hannes does (20 vs. 16, respectively), her income is slightly lower because they work in different sectors. Their combined income roughly equals that of an average university graduate in Germany, which provides them with a solid economic basis.

Equal from the Start

Hanna and Hannes started their relationship during their time at university. She studied social sciences, he computer sciences. Shortly after they

[1] The authors are listed in alphabetical order as they share equal authorship. Thanks to Antonia Schier for research assistance and to Beatrice Buchmann for proofreading. For a methodological documentation of the interview, see Schulz, Jabsen, & Rost 2008.

started dating, they began a long-distance relationship, which lasted through Hanna's taking a job in a different city, Hannes's pursuing an internship in New Zealand, and his returning to a job in yet a different German city from where Hanna was living. The first time they actually shared a place was the year they got married. There was no question that they would divide household labor equally when they were both employed, and with Hanna taking a larger share of the chores when she was unemployed or employed part-time.

With 83.6 million inhabitants, Germany is the most populous country in the European Union. Twelve percent of the population were immigrants (World Population Review, 2019). Catholic Christians make up 28.5% and Protestant Christians 26.5% of the population, while 4.9% are Muslims, 3.9% belong to other religious communities, and 36.2% have no religious affiliation (Forschungsgruppe Weltanschauungen, 2017).

Of the 41.4 million households in Germany, 21.4% are couples with children, 29% are couples without children, 6.2% are lone parent households, and 41.9% consist of single person households (Statistisches Bundesamt, 2019d).

Women's participation in the labor force is 71.5%. Almost half of the women in Germany work part-time, as compared with the EU-28 mean of 31.7%. German mothers, in particular, are likely to work part-time: 62.2% of employed mothers do so, whereas the comparable EU-28 mean is 35.8%. Like their EU-28 counterparts, only 6.2% of fathers work part-time (Eurostat, 2018). The gender pay gap is 21% (Statistisches Bundesamt, 2019c).

Employed women are entitled to go on maternity leave for 14 weeks, for a period called "*Mutterschutz*," 6 weeks before the birth of the child and 8 weeks afterwards, during which they receive their usual salary. Parental leave (*Elternzeit*), allows parents to be released from their jobs for a period of up to 3 years to care for their child. During this leave, it is possible to be employed for up to 30 hours per week. At the end of parental leave, the employer has to offer the parent a job equivalent to the one s/he had earlier. Both parents may take up to 12 months of parental leave simultaneously (Reimer, Erler, & Blum, 2018).

The division of labor is still traditional in Germany. The most recent representative time-use data for couples with children shows that men spent 2:24 hours per day on unpaid domestic labor, as compared with women's 3:49 hours (Statistisches Bundesamt, 2019e).

The expansion of institutional childcare, particularly for children under 3, has recently been a key area of German family policy. In 2017, the percentage of children in daycare was 33.1% for children under 3 and 99.4% for children between 3 and 6 years old (Statistisches Bundesamt, 2019b).

When Emma was born after 8 years of marriage, Hanna was 39 years old. Having delayed plans to become pregnant because of health problems in her mid-30s, she was older than the average first-time mother in Germany, even taking into account that women with high educational degrees tend to postpone parenthood (Statistisches Bundesamt, 2019a). Their common ideal, discussed before becoming parents, was to share paid work, household chores, and childcare equally. Originally, Hanna was planning on breastfeeding, but when that was not possible, she touted it as a great opportunity, "That meant that she [Emma] could be given the bottle by mother or father from the beginning on ... that was very beneficial to the aim we had set to both have an equal relationship to the child."

Before Emma was born, Hanna had already been working only 50% of normal work hours at the research institute. After the obligatory maternity leave of 8 weeks after childbirth, she returned to her half-time job. Hannes took parental leave[2] for 2 years and reduced his paid work hours to 40% per week when Hanna returned to her job.

Hanna and Hannes have scheduled their workdays such that one of them is at home with the child while the other one is at work. On

---

[2] In Germany, parental leave includes the right to reduce paid work hours, as well as the right to take time off entirely from paid work for at maximum 3 years. The first 2 years have to be taken after the child's birth, while the last year can be taken up to the child's 8th birthday – if the employer agrees.

Mondays and Tuesdays, Hannes is at home with Emma while Hanna is at work, and on Thursdays and Fridays it is the other way around. Hanna works every other Wednesday and Hannes takes care of Emma alone, whereas on alternate Wednesdays, when Hanna is off, they care for her together. On the weekends they share care as well.

Hannes describes a typical day at home alone with Emma:

> First and foremost, it's looking after the child: changing diapers, feeding, dressing . . . going out with the child and playing with the child, that's basically it. And next to that, you have to see what you can do in the household or which other duties you can manage . . . so, the dishwasher, hanging up another load of washing or . . . well, you don't get around to cleaning properly, shopping for something or making this or that telephone call or writing an email, and that was basically it.

Likewise, Hanna described her most recent day at home alone with Emma in similar ways. It started with feeding her, putting her in the playpen for 10 minutes to get some breakfast herself, and then changing Emma's diapers. Afterwards, when Emma was asleep, Hanna did the laundry and emptied the dishwasher. All in all, Emma was fed approximately every hour until she got a big lunch after her nap. Hanna went out shopping with her daughter, "And then I played with her; the most varied things . . . It was actually nonstop playtime till my husband came . . . at half past seven." Afterwards, she fed Emma again and then Hannes took over playing with her. That way, Hanna was able to get some housework done, finish a manuscript, write some emails, and do paperwork. Later that evening, Hannes put Emma to bed around 9:30 p. m. When she woke up one hour later, Hanna went to sleep with her. Other evenings, it could be Hannes who would take care of Emma during the night or when she woke during the night. Since Emma has been sleeping through the night ever since she was 3 months old, however, childcare at night is usually not an issue for either of them. In the evenings Hannes usually prefers spending time with childcare rather than doing household chores, and Hanna is happy to do the chores, "I think doing the domestic tasks is more relieving . . . it also is more relaxing . . . it is ok for me like it is."

There are only a few childcare tasks that are assigned specifically to one parent. For example, Hannes attends a special course for parents and children because it falls on Mondays when he takes care of Emma. He also occasionally takes Emma to the pediatrician without Hanna.

How Tasks Are Distributed

The person at home is responsible for housework. The two of them equally share laundry, vacuum-cleaning, grocery shopping, loading and unloading the dishwasher, as well as paperwork and other administrative matters. Hanna and Hannes spend almost the same amount of time doing housework, although some tasks are assigned to one or the other. Hanna does almost all the cooking and cleans the house, including the bathroom and the floors. Hannes is mainly responsible for making the beds, taking out the garbage, filling in the tax returns, performing technical tasks, and taking care of the car.

When they are both home, they discuss the distribution of tasks and decide who does what, as Hanna explains, "It's often the case ... the washing machine or the dishwasher has to be unloaded, 'Do you want to do it or do you want to look after the child?' He almost always says he'll look after the child, and I do the chores."

So preferences are important. Although he seems to tilt toward child-care and she toward doing more household tasks, the total amount of domestic work equals out.

The couple also tries to outsource as many tasks as possible. Shortly after Emma's birth, they had two cleaners who did most of the cleaning. But both of them "unfortunately quit ... and since then, many things remain undone," Hanna says with regret. Hanna and Hannes employ a gardener to reduce yard work. Every 4 weeks, Hanna's parents visit the family and help with chores that would otherwise remain undone. For example, ironing is usually done by Hanna's mother; Hanna only irons clothing herself if there is an urgent need. The couple plans to outsource more of the routine domestic chores again in the future, which would particularly relieve Hanna.

Close Relationships with Emma

Because they shared everything equally from the start, both parents believe they have the same close relationship with Emma. Hannes notes, "In many cases, if the child falls ... only the mother can pick up and comfort the child. But in our case, both of us can do that."

Despite perceiving her husband as an equal carer, however, Hanna thinks that there are some differences in the ways they interact with Emma. She points out that her husband's way of playing with Emma is more physically demanding; hers is quieter:

I think my husband is a bit more "action-oriented" ... There are also different things that we play with her ... perhaps I'm a bit quieter with her. For example, I think I sing more often with her ... I mean it's also simply a question of strength. Especially when she was younger, he carried her around more ... And also, when the child has stomach ache, there's this Ferris wheel, when you take the child and move like a Ferris wheel ... Well, that almost breaks my back!

Although Hannes is aware that Hanna thinks they have different ways with Emma, he does not see big differences in their behavior, "I play ball with her more often and such things and ... I'd say, maybe my wife takes her in her arms more or something. But I actually take her in my arms a lot too."

Hannes plans to extend the duration of his 2-year parental leave by another year so that they can continue their arrangements until Emma is 3 years old, when she will attend preschool. Until then, Hanna and Hannes believe that family care is best. Emma's grandparents are not available for childcare because they live too far away. Hanna believes that, in Germany, the staff in day nurseries are not trained adequately to care for children under 3. Hannes, however, can imagine hiring a child minder for a few hours per day as soon as Emma is 1½ or 2 years old. Hanna says it was a conscious decision to take the time to raise the child without the help of others:

I became 40 this year. Well, we waited quite a long time before having a child, and ... I think I've done so much in my life, and when I say that I'll devote one or two years to the child, for me that's somehow a thing that's completely OK at the moment.

Why They Share

From the moment the couple decided to have a child, they discussed their ideas and plans for the future and resolved to share care for their baby equally. This explicit agreement was the starting point for their equal division of paid work, housework, and childcare. When asked why it is important for them to share care for Emma equally, they named his wish to care for the child, his moderate career ambitions, her wish to be continuously employed, as well as her ideal of having him participate in childcare.

Hannes's desire to spend time with Emma and to be an attachment figure for her, along with Hanna's ideal for him to be equally involved, drove the couple's decision for him to take parental leave and reduce his paid work hours, and for Hanna to return to her part-time job quickly.

His active involvement in childcare is more important to him than projects at his job. "He's not the great career person," Hanna explains. According to her, he has always had other interests; leisure time has always been important to him. He always invested time in their relationship, as he now does in fatherhood. His lack of interest in advancing in his career was crucial for the decision to take parental leave and reduce his paid work hours. He's aware, but not worried, that he will not get an executive position while employed part-time, "That is not something that concerns me greatly, to which I aspire to, or which I'm particularly good at." Hanna plans to stay continually employed, maintaining her part-time job. Like Hannes, she has no career ambitions, and cannot even imagine full-time employment. Nonetheless, the job matters because she cannot imagine being solely responsible for household labor and childcare either:

> The idea of being at home with the child the whole week … I don't know, I don't think that would be quite my thing. I work as well and I like it, and I actually think it's good to be able to combine both of these spheres of life. I look forward to being with her and then I look forward to being at work again. Both areas simply complement each other well, and it's really, it's nice to be with her the whole day.

The Social Context

In their social environment, Hannes's brother's family is the only other example of an equally sharing family. Hannes's brother has reduced his paid work hours to 30 hours per week. There are no other role models among their friends and family. When asked about his peers, Hannes answered, "Well, amongst my acquaintances or in the neighborhood, it's at most the case that if the wife works part-time, that then somehow … grandmothers are there to look after the child or a nanny or they organize something like that, but the men are all employed full-time."

Hannes's decision to take parental leave is exceptional; at the time of Emma's birth, only about 5% of fathers in Germany chose this option. Therefore, it was often difficult for fathers like Hannes, since a career break was neither common nor acceptable for men (Rost, 2002). Hannes's decision, however, has been well accepted by his colleagues and his employer. His direct supervisor considered taking parental leave himself when his first child was born, but eventually decided not to because his salary was much higher than his wife's. Thus, he was open to Hannes's wish to reduce his work hours. Hannes reports that his colleagues do sometimes joke with "comments like, 'Yes, is it Thursday already?' when I don't turn up for work until Thursday." Hannes's colleagues are mainly female and approve of his decision, despite the additional work for them. Hannes explains, "Although I'm not there half the time ... the part-time position isn't compensated for. Instead of that, a lot of colleagues are left with the work, and they deal with it ... Well, they somehow don't get overly upset about it."

Hanna reports similar acceptance at her workplace, where she got full support from her supervisor and female as well as male co-workers, who thought it was great that she would continue on the job. She feels entitled to her choice, and asserts that she "would be irritated if there wasn't any understanding there." Their description of support by co-workers, none-theless, reveals a striking double standard. Hannes touts the support he gets for reducing his paid work hours, whereas Hanna appreciates not being criticized for continuing to work at all. Despite the positive reactions in the workplace, Hannes mentions that some men react more negatively and insinuate that they would never capitulate to a wife's preferences:

> A lot of people say, well, such a thing wouldn't be possible in their important jobs ... like that, or that's completely out of the question for them. Well, along the lines of: "I would never have let my wife order me into staying at home." Except that it isn't like that with us. ... Well, that happens sometimes. But I can really look them in the eye, because those people who "can't look after the child because of their important jobs," they can go on holiday for three weeks ... without the company going down the drain. ... It's mostly the case that ... they don't want to ... for some reason.

Hannes also suffers some negative reactions at the parent–child course he attends with Emma. He is the only father in that group. Hanna thinks that many of these courses "are based on the mother–child relationship ... Sometimes it bears that name explicitly ... and I think to myself that it's not so easy if you're a father to get into some things." Hannes reveals that he feels like an outsider in the group, although everyone is superficially friendly toward him:

> Well, now, on first impression, OK, yes, nice and friendly. What I have noticed is that when there's an arrangement for two people to meet with the children somewhere, I'm never included. Of course, I don't know if that has anything to do with the fact that I ... that they always meet on Thursdays or Fridays, well, when I have no time. But, well, there ... I'm an outsider at present – but otherwise, it's normal in the group.

Hanna and Hannes – Not a Typical German Couple

Hanna and Hannes's division of family labor deviates from the pattern that is still typical of families with young children: male breadwinners and female homemakers (Dechant & Schulz, 2014). Equality is the magic word for their lifestyle and they try to practice it from parenthood to jobs. It is their firm conviction that this way is the best for their relationship and for Emma, who has become the center of their lives. But what exactly prompted them to choose this kind of model? The egalitarian arrangement they implemented after Emma's birth can be traced back to strong ideals and values of gender equality (Dechant & Schulz, 2014).

Hanna and Hannes reflect deeply on potential outcomes of important decisions. They share common ideas and ideals on how to live together as a family. Both of them believe it is essential to develop a close relationship with Emma. Outsourcing childcare is not an option for them while Emma is so young. Hannes is not very keen on career advancement, and with an employer who was very supportive and a joint income sufficient for both of them to work part-time, Hannes was able take parental leave. Hanna could not imagine herself being a full-time mother and homemaker; she has always wanted to remain active in the labor market, which she made clear before deciding to become a mother. Hannes was not only enthusiastic about taking care of Emma, but also willing to be responsible for about half of the housework.

All in all, Hanna and Hannes are deeply satisfied with their lives. From Hanna's point of view, sharing equally means that Emma relates closely to both of them and benefits from their slightly different ways of interacting with her. Moreover, both parents experience the everyday life of being responsible for childcare and household in a similar way. Hanna explains:

> What's really good is that my husband knows what it means to be with the child the whole day ... When he comes home and everything's lying around, it's not a case of, "Why, see the child's perfectly content, what have you been doing the whole day?" Instead of that, he knows how it is if you come home and the other says, "Take the child, take the child, take the child!" ... And I think that can only be beneficial for the child, and she really has a good relationship to both parents ... Well, for her, it isn't even a question that ... Mama and Papa ... are equally there for her, and I think that's good ... I think he's a really great father. And it would be a real shame for the child ... if he didn't take the time.

Hannes is content with the current division of labor and enjoys being as responsible for Emma as Hanna is. He appreciates what he gains by spending time at home during the week. He sums up his feelings:

> It is simply a joy to play with the child and to see her grow up. And you have all the small steps, not only that the child sleeps through the night, starts to crawl

or to run, doesn't need diapers anymore, but rather small steps, like, has touched something with two fingers for the first time and not with the whole hand, has consciously watched a bird outside for the first time. Well, lots of really, really small things and that is just nice ... When the little girl laughs for the first time these are true experiences of success ... It's practically irreplaceable.

References

Dechant, A. & Schulz, F. (2014). Scenarios for the Equal Division of Paid and Unpaid Work in the Transition to Parenthood in Germany. *Comparative Population Studies, 39*(3), 615–644.

Eurostat (2018). *Employment and Activity by Sex and Age – Annual Data.* Retrieved from: http://ec.europa.eu/eurostat/web/lfs/data/database.

Forschungsgruppe Weltanschauungen in Deutschland (2017). *Religionszugehörigkeiten in Deutschland 2016* [Religious Confession in Germany 2016]. Retrieved from: https://fowid.de/meldung/religionszugehoerigkeiten-deutschland-2016.

Reimer, T., Erler, D., & Blum, S. (2018). Germany Country Note. In S. Blum, A. Koslowski, A. Macht, & P. Moss (eds.) *International Review of Leave Policies and Research 2018* (pp. 175–187). International Network on Leave Policies and Research. Retrieved from: www.leavenetwork.org/lp_and_r_reports/.

Rost, H. (2002). Where Are the New Fathers? German Families with a Non-Traditional Distribution of Professional and Family Work. *Community, Work & Family, 5*(3), 371–376.

Schulz, F., Jabsen, A., & Rost, H. (2008). *Zwischen Wunsch und Wirklichkeit – Der Alltag erwerbsorientierter Paare beim Übergang zur Elternschaft. Methodenbericht einer qualitativen Längsschnittstudie* [Between Intention and Reality – Dual-Career Couples' Everyday Life at the Transition to Parenthood. Methodological Report of a Qualitative Longitudinal Study]. Bamberg: Staatsinstitut für Familienforschung an der Universität Bamberg. Retrieved from: www.ifb.bayern.de/imperia/md/content/stmas/ifb/materialien/mat_2008_4.pdf.

Statistisches Bundesamt. (2019a). *Births.* Retrieved from: www.destatis.de/EN/Home/_node.html.

Statistisches Bundesamt (2019b). *Children in Daycare.* Retrieved from: www.destatis.de/EN/Home/_node.html.

Statistisches Bundesamt (2019c). *Gender Pay Gap by Länder from 2014 to 2018 (unadjusted).* Retrieved from www.destatis.de/EN/.

Statistisches Bundesamt (2019d). *Households and Families.* Retrieved from www.destatis.de/EN/.

Statistisches Bundesamt (2019e). *Time Use Survey.* Retrieved from: www.destatis.de/EN/Home/_node.html.

World Population Review (2019). *Germany Population 2019.* Retrieved from: http://worldpopulationreview.com/countries/germany-population/.

24

United Kingdom

Oriel Sullivan

Katherine and Dale, a well-educated middle-class couple, hold high-powered positions in the same large public-sector institution. They live in a Victorian terraced house in a city about 50 minutes from their workplace, which is out of town in the style of a science or business park. They share a commitment to gender equality in deed as well as word, rare in the UK even among their friends, and work to honor that commitment in their family lives and careers. Crucial to their equal sharing, they can take advantage of the workplace regulations of their public-sector jobs to each take a day a week off, and to use flexible hours to care for their two children, Ed, aged 2, and Matthew, aged 5. They describe these days as "daddy days" and "mummy days."

A Week in the Life

Dale and Katherine have three different sorts of days each week: the mummy and daddy days, on which one of them stays at home to care for Ed and Matthew and the other goes to his or her job; three weekdays where they both go to their jobs and the children go to a nursery on-site at their workplace; and weekend days where they are all at home. On the mummy and daddy days, the parent who is staying home is responsible for all the morning childcare tasks. The person going to work is often out of the house before the children wake up, taking the bus at 7:00 a.m. Typically, on daddy days, Katherine comes home at 5:45 p.m., while on mummy days, Dale tends to come back an hour earlier.

On shared workdays they allow themselves only half an hour to get up and out of the house together with Ed and Matthew! They all get up about 7:00 a.m., although Katherine admits Dale will often get up about 10 minutes before her. Once she's up, they split the tasks involved in getting everyone out of the house. Katherine explains, "Someone will help them brush their teeth while someone else is getting them their shoes ... Someone will be giving them breakfast." Dale adds, "I think I tend to do the breakfast more. That's quite simple, and then Katherine will come in and do the last, you know, coats on, brush teeth, out of the door." They drive together to their jobs, leaving the house at 7:30, dropping the children off at the nursery at about 8:20, collecting them again together around 4:30, and arriving home around 5:30 p.m.

The population of the United Kingdom is estimated at 66 million, 86% UK born (Office of National Statistics [ONS], 2018b). As of the last census, the most common ethnicity was white (87%), but the population also included 7% Asian/British-Asian, and 6% other ethnic groups (ONS, 2013). The majority are Christians (59%), 5% identify as Muslim, and Buddhists, Sikhs, Hindus, and Jews together comprise 4%. Over 25% of the population has no religious affiliation (ONS, 2012).[1]

Gender equality in employment and pay is guaranteed by law. Nevertheless, overall, men's employment rate (80.3%) is higher than women's (71.2%), and employed women are more likely than men to work part-time (41% versus 13%, respectively) (ONS, 2019). The gender pay gap is 8.6% for full-time workers, but jumps to 17.9% when part-time employees are included (ONS, 2018a). The overall maternal employment rate is 72%, but 64% for mothers of children under 2. Over half of employed mothers are working part-time (ONS, 2018c).

---

[1] Although the UK includes England, Wales, Scotland, and Northern Ireland, some of the statistics only pertain to part of the country. Consult reference titles for clarification.

Eligible employee mothers are entitled to 52 weeks of maternity leave of which 39 weeks are paid. The leave can be shared with eligible fathers, with the exception of 2 obligatory weeks after the birth. In addition, eligible fathers are entitled to up to 2 weeks of paid paternity leave (O'Brien & Koslowski, 2018).

Childcare for children under 15 years old is used by 75% of families in England, but more than a third of it is informal care provided by relatives and neighbors (Department of Education, 2018). In England free childcare is offered for 3- and 4-year-old children of employed parents for 30 hours per week, 38 weeks per year (lower entitlements are available in Scotland and Wales). However, only 45% of authorities report sufficient places for the 30-hour entitlement (Harding & Cottell, 2018).

In the last national time-use study (2015), women on average contributed 1:50 hours per day to housework and 40 minutes to carework, while men contributed just under 50 minutes to housework and just under 20 minutes to carework (Sullivan & Altintas, 2019).

On both daddy and mummy days, the at-home parent usually makes a trip to the drop-in daycenter (playgroup) with the children, although Dale explains that Katherine spends more time there than he:

> Katherine is much more gregarious, and so when she looks after the kids, she is much more into the swing of the daycentres 'cause it's much more a social club ... I won't be going there because I've got a big circle of mates. It's usually because it's a nice place to play and there's a jacket potato, but I see it as a stepping stone to the park or whatever the next thing is, whereas Katherine is much more likely to take them there and let them play with the other kids and then, you know, she can chat to her friends.

However, mummy and daddy days also provide an opportunity for day trips like an excursion to the Wildlife park.

On weekday evenings, Katherine says:

> They'll have half an hour telly whilst one of us makes the supper and the other will tidy up something ... we start trying to put them to bed about 7 o'clock and typically I'll brush their teeth and I'll read them a story, and then Dale will go in and do more silly things. He'll make up a story to tell them. Unfortunately, he's kind of also got into the habit of falling asleep with them.

According to Dale, the "one" making supper throughout the week is more likely to be him, although Katherine is more likely to cook the children's lunches on weekends. They agree that Dale does more tidying than Katherine, who, in his opinion, is the cause of much of what needs to be tidied up! "I smile wryly at the hypocrisy of [Katherine] sometimes saying, 'We must tidy up our toys,' whilst out of my peripheral vision I can see, you know, her bag has been dropped on the floor, her coat has been dropped on the floor."

Dale's propensity to fall asleep while telling stories to the children at night contributes to his getting more sleep than Katherine. After the children are asleep, Katherine likes to watch TV, or sometimes go out with friends. If Dale is still awake at that point, he prefers to use the computer upstairs rather than watch TV downstairs with Katherine, "I like to do something a bit more productive, like look at holidays or do some work."

Neither of them works for pay on the weekend, which provides an opportunity to be more flexible about scheduling, and for each of them to do some separate activities. Dale reports:

> We never ever had a set plan; it just sort of falls into place. If she's gone out on a Friday night to see the girls to go to a club or something like that, then I'll tend to cut her some slack and she can have the slightly longer lie in, but then I'll expect payback on Sunday morning . . . If the kids are playing up and someone needs to whisk them out of the door and go to the park, that'll be me, more often than not, but then when I come back in, often it will be Katherine that will cook the lunch and then she'll do an afternoon activity, and I'll cook the dinner, and then we will look after the kids together in the evening.

Dale regularly takes the children to the park on Saturday mornings. During this time Katherine used to try to do the hoovering before they got a house cleaner, but now it gives her a much-appreciated break. On the weekends, Dale finds time to look after his bees, while Katherine tends a vegetable garden, which Dale considers to be a leisure activity equivalent to his bee-keeping. He does admit that he is grateful for the produce!

Overall, Dale believes that Katherine has more leisure time than he, "Katherine would at least once a week, you know, she'll do something like parties." Katherine agrees that she has more leisure time overall, although she invokes her staying up later at night to explain the difference, and not because she invites people round for parties!

An Equal Division of Domestic Work?

Katherine and Dale both described their division of labor as equal with respect to childcare, but slightly in Dale's favor for housework. However, while Dale does more general tidying and cleaning, Katherine does all the clothes care. Katherine explains their division:

> I kind of tend to do the washing, I don't know why ... oh no, I know why it is: 'cause Dale always used to tumble dry [put the clothes on a drying program in the washing machine] and it drives me mad. So I always do the washing and Dale does a lot of the general tidying up and kind of things.

Dale does more of the cooking. Katherine credits Dale with being a better cook, so he tends to cook more for the adults, whereas she cooks more for the kids because, "I'm better at doing pasta and the ... more mundane kind of food."

Katherine's parents, who live nearby, however, do help them a lot. On at least 1 or 2 nights a week, one of the grandparents cooks or helps with cooking the evening meal. Dale said, "The kids like their company."

As for gardening, Dale volunteers, "I suppose Katherine does quite a bit in the garden. I don't head out to the garden. If I do then it's a disaster because I tend to just chop things down and throw things into bags, so Katherine plants things and prunes things." For the heavier work, like cutting the grass and hedges, the work that Dale would otherwise do, Katherine's father often pitches in, "We are quite lucky with Katherine's dad, so he does quite a bit so I can slack off, but if he's not about, then I would be the one that cuts the hedge and that sort of thing or mows the grass."

Katherine describes how they divide management tasks:

> For some reason, I tend to do the children stuff, so I will get their jabs [injections] done. I'm sorting out their schools; I'm sorting out the nursery side of things. Dale will do stuff like, he'll get the car insurance; he'll get the household insurance. So we both do probably equal amounts of adminy stuff, but I probably do more of the children's admin stuff, which is I don't really know why.

She speculates that this stems from when she was responsible during maternity leave for the children's inoculations, "You get like a little red book, which says what you need in different ages and I kind of, I'm the holder of the red book ... it's from when I was on maternity leave. You just got used to organizing, going to the health insurance and stuff like that." Dale agrees that Katherine does more of that and communicates more with the school, but cites visits to dentists, buying clothes, and haircuts for the children as things that he organizes.

Katherine and Dale provide an interesting example of how men's contribution to domestic work tends to be somewhat exaggerated by both members of a couple. Dale's contributions are aided by the weekly cleaner, Katherine's parents' cooking, and her father's help in the garden. Dale may get extra credit because he is more likely than she to announce what he has done around the house. Katherine says, "I tend to just do it whereas he kind of goes, 'I've done such and such.'" In addition, he expects gratitude for what he has done:

> He gets really cross with me because he feels that I'm not grateful enough. So like, I've been out with the boys and I come back and he's tidied up, he will be really cross if I don't, say, go round every room and say "fantastic job," "look what you've done."

She observes, "As a kind of strategy, I should start telling him, you know, 'Have you noticed I've put all the washing out?'" She believes that Dale's tendency to announce his efforts around the home may distort both their perceptions of the overall division of domestic tasks.

Building an Equally Sharing Family

Both Katherine and Dale had always intended to share the domestic chores and childcare. Dale explained:

> I think even before we had children in terms of work and other things, it was always gonna be an even, an equal partnership . . . then it just got extended into when we had kids . . . it's like, "We're in this together." I think we both always presumed that it should be close to 50/50. There might have been a very vague conversation before we had kids about "Are you going to be a bit of a hands-on dad?" Ehm, actually, it might have been just a statement, "You're going to be a bit of a hands-on dad!" But I know we've never really sat down and, you know, "Here's the rota," and "Here's a plan who does what."

Dale implies that initially Katherine was the main mover in their equal sharing, and that he was happy to go along with it. He added, "Katherine has always been very firm on the equality thing and quite rightly." In fact, her commitment to equality is something he really appreciates about her:

> I like the fact that she is an equal sharer. So the upside of this equality thing is if I get bored of driving, she is very happy to drive the car. The mad-sized tent that we bought is very heavy. I don't feel bad about asking her to help me carry it and she doesn't complain too much about carrying it as well, because she's quite physically strong. So I like the fact that she sort of brings that equal contribution.

Likewise, Katherine appreciates Dale's attitude toward gender equality, "I think Dale's kind of quite free in his thinking."

When asked about conflicts, both pointed to their differences in tidiness, a long-term source of tension. Katherine said:

When we first started going [out], we knew that was going to be the source of conflict between us because he's very house-proud and I'm not. So we have, over time, had a few arguments, not arguments, but it's just he had to drop his standards and I had to up my game a bit.

Dale agrees, "There is more work in total today and Katherine stepped up a bit." Katherine adds, "Now the mess is just tenfold, so it's got to the point where it freaks me out as well." She reported that employing a cleaner had helped, "You never really felt on top of it, so you'd just be a bit grouchy with each other because everything is always slightly messy, in fact, horrendously messy. I suppose it's still messy now, but ... it just helps us keep on top of it."

They manage childcare conflicts by stepping in for each other. Katherine said, "When we had our conflict it's where one or the other of us has lost their temper with the children and the other one is just going, 'Just remove yourself from this room, it'll be sorted out.'" Dale said, "I can't pretend we haven't raised the voice to the children, so sometimes Katherine has given me the look and said, 'That's a bit shouty, you know? I think daddy needs to calm it down. Why doesn't mummy take them for a bit?'"

Unlike most couples in which the birth of a child leads to a more traditional gendered division of labor, Katherine and Dale made a conscious decision to share the childcare responsibilities more equally. However, this decision was not made in advance. Katherine took her full maternity leave for Matthew's birth and then was employed part-time:

When we first had Matthew, I went part-time, 3 days, so I had 2 days off. We had a chat about it, you know, like did Dale want to have a day off with Matthew, and our work is quite flexible about stuff like that. There have been a preceding set of men having time off and Dale said, "yes," so I went up to 4 days and he dropped a day.

Despite their shared mummy and daddy days, however, infant care always remained primarily Katherine's responsibility. Dale did not move to a 4-day week until Matthew was 9 months old, and although he continued to take his day off a week during Katherine's maternity leave with Ed, she took primary responsibility for the care of baby Ed, while Dale spent time with Matthew. This may reflect their ambivalent attitudes toward biological essentialism. Katherine doesn't believe that there are inherent differences in the ability of men and women to look after children, but she does say, "I think it's really difficult for men, you know, the first 6 months. The baby is not particularly interested in them, kind of thing, but I don't think after that there's any reason why there should be any difference in parenting styles really at all."

Dale is also ambivalent. When asked whether he believes there are inherent differences in men's and women's ability to look after children, he says, "Probably fundamentally there are. It's probably driven by you know nature-nurture, probably some genetical stuff," although he adds, "No, I think a lot of it is down to culture. If people tell you enough that 'Oh no, you are not good at this,' or 'They are naturally better at it,' then you tend to fall into the trap of believing it." He remarks, "You'd think maybe the mums would naturally be better at comforting, but I don't think that's true."

Katherine's greater involvement in baby care may account for the disparity in their respective relationships with their two children, which she described:

> We're probably slightly split between the children, whereas Dale probably spends more time, probably disciplines Matthew more, whereas I'm slightly more responsible for Ed, kind of thing. You don't mean to do that, but I suppose if you've got the little baby, it's kind of a hangover from that . . . Since they are getting older it's blurred a bit more, I think. I think it's probably 50/50.

As Dale describes, both of them will do when the boys need comforting – telling testimony to an equal attachment:

> So if one of them squawks in the night, it's whoever gets there first really. Or who's least good at pretending to be asleep . . . You know, I suppose one of the tests is, if unfortunately, on the rare occasions where they have cracked themselves they'll just go to whoever is nearest, you know? There's none of this screening out. They just want the instant comfort. And obviously when we looked after them on those days on our own I don't think there have been any signs that they were distressed that mum or dad wasn't there. They occasionally nicely ask, "where's Mum?" and you say, "Mum works today."

Their only serious conflict about the children arose over bottle-feeding. Katherine said:

> Actually we did have quite a lot of conflict about feeding Matthew, 'cause I wanted to breastfeed him, and I had problems doing it for the first month, and once he got going, Dale kept trying to slip him bottled milk and I was like, "I've spent a month getting this going."

This "slipping" of bottled milk to Matthew suggests Dale's desire to be more involved in infant care. Likewise, Dale was upset about being excluded because of Ed's refusal to take the bottle:

So with Matthew, because he didn't take the breast, he was bottle and breast and that was quite nice 'cause it meant like I could take him out for walks and give Mum a break. But Ed, he wasn't doing with no bottles at all and then that meant he was tied to his Mum. He certainly couldn't go more than 40 minutes distance and then you'd have to head back. The consequence of that was that she had to be with him a lot more than she had been with Matthew.

Katherine recounts a distressing incident when she was not chosen as the preferred parent. When Ed was in nursery school, she had to go on a business trip abroad for 5 weeks. Dale covered by taking an extra day off each week, and using his flexitime. She describes what happened when she returned:

So when we go to nursery, Matthew will always run over to Dale, and Ed always used to run over to me, but when I came back from Austria he'd go to run over to Dale and that really hurt, and that was really bad. I suppose I did not mind it so much you know that Matthew was Daddy's boy 'cause I have Ed, but when, as I said, Ed was quite cross with me for leaving him, so I did find that that's probably the toughest I found it, it's the mum's like "inhale sound" you know? "They both prefer their daddy, there's something slightly wrong with me as a mother" kind of thing.

This anecdote reflects the emotional cost of equal sharing for mothers, a cost that she had to be willing to bear.

Paid Work and Family

While committed to their careers, Katherine and Dale are even more committed to their decision to share time spent with the children.

Dale, for example, points out the problem a potential promotion would create:

I've been promoted, fortunately, beyond my competence, and the next job up would be head of department and I don't know, I'm not sure I'm hugely enthusiastic about something like that because to get the head of the department job I probably would have to be prepared to go back to full-time working.

Both of them have turned down the opportunity to earn more money by increasing their paid work hours. Katherine says, "Both Dale and I, we had two increases of hours and we took one but we didn't take the other 'cause we decided, 'Right, you know, we'll take the pay cut.' So although, yeah, we wanted the money, it was kind of like, right, 'no.'"

Neither of their careers takes precedence over the other. Dale earns slightly more, and Katherine believes that he takes his career more seriously than she. However, after a year's leave to work abroad, they decided to return, even though he had been offered a promotion because it seemed that her career prospects were blocked there. Dale's job in the UK was particularly vulnerable at that time, so they discussed the possibility of him becoming a teacher if he lost his job. Dale's thinking focused on the advantages for childcare teaching would have offered, "I quite fancied going into teaching – becoming a primary school teacher – and we did think ... it would have fitted nicely with looking after the kids and I would have found that a quite enjoyable change."

Katherine took both maternity leaves in full, and would probably have continued her 3-day-a-week schedule if Dale had not wanted to take a day off. However, her career was important enough to her to take a business trip abroad when Ed was still quite young. Moreover, Katherine's initiating a discussion about them both taking a 4-day week stemmed from the discrimination she perceived when she was at her job only 3 days a week:

> I think when I was 3 days, I was definitely treated as a part-time worker, and whilst I was on maternity leave a promotion came up, which I didn't get, and I think part of the, I am sure there's, I did not do a fabulous interview, but part of the reason that I didn't get that was 'cause I was perceived as being part-time, whereas because we both work 4 days you are pretty much perceived as being full-time. You're just not there for one day.

Moving to a 4-day week was difficult for Dale, since it's more unusual for a man to request time off to care for children. He mentions two factors that helped: first, being employed within the public sector, "You have a solid base because obviously the government, public sector tends to follow the rules and regulations"; and second, that his co-workers and managers were mostly scientists:

> They are very logical, rational people, generally ... So they are amenable to the argument that sometimes what's good for the individual can also be good for the organization ... they realize that there's a benefit to them ... flexible working is the classic example.

Nonetheless, he attributes his success in being given permission to take a day off a week largely to his boss's apathy:

> So I had a fairly direct conversation with the boss and he never really gave permission, but our policies are written in such a way that it's taken as a given that the organization will let people do this up until the point someone in the line management chain can make a good case as to why it would be a disaster, and my boss's innate laziness meant he could never be bothered to write the case, and he didn't really have a case to write because it's not like I'm manning a help desk and have to be there.

When Matthew and Ed both reach school age Katherine and Dale plan to return to a 5-day workweek, but will use their flexitime to see the children off to school and pick them up.

Being Different

Among their peers, Katherine and Dale's equal sharing makes them different. Although, in theory, at least some of them believe in paternal involvement, Dale reports that only one has reduced his paid work hours. Instead, some fathers try to compensate with hands-on time on the weekends, while others "do these displacement activities where they are not quite so keen on the hands-on kiddy stuff but they will build something," and their more traditional counterparts concentrate on earning money by taking on as much overtime as possible as their paternal contribution.

Katherine finds it surprising how few couples they know are like them:

> I'm surprised by how many people have fallen ... have gone down the kind of more traditional route where the bloke works the long hours and then the woman doesn't work.

She also reports that some of their peers, presumably male, say to Dale, "Why are you doing that?" Dale's male colleagues react the same way:

> So a couple of the colleagues will go, "So why are you doing this?" and "So surely it's a bit harder work, so you could be just coming to work, you don't have to." And yeah, a few critical remarks, quizzical looks that way, and I suppose the most extreme, if there's a particular type of bloke, he would say, "This isn't proper men's work; we are not fit for it. You should be doing other things."

Dale reports that mothers tend to be impressed by his commitment to equal sharing (and grandmas particularly so), which he finds flattering. However, when women point to him as an example, he feels uncomfortable, "There's unfortunately that I get to be a point of reference to their partners, so there's 'Bob, listen to this man,' so you know I go, 'Oh God, don't do that.'"

Moreover, Dale has had to deal with some difficult social experiences in the drop-in daycenters. He has frequently been ignored and shunned by some of the mothers:

> Well very often I've been the only guy there and you do get weird looks. Some of the women are really nice and will go out of their way to have a chat because obviously you don't know any of those people ... and they come over and go, "Oh hello, how is it going?" and they will engage you in a conversation, and

then others will completely blank you and they will just go, "There's a man in the room. Oh God. There's a man, and we are all here ladies together and there's a man."

Factors Facilitating an Equally Shared Life

To explain why they differ from other couples, Dale pointed to their joint commitment to equality, and to Katherine's role in reinforcing it, "Katherine and I had always got this thing about equality, and Katherine I guess from her side, you know, made sure." Katherine gave Dale the credit, "He's probably, yeah, he's probably more unusual in that, you know, out of, even out of our peer group ... he wanted to stay home with his children."

She believes that his father had a strong influence on Dale's own nontraditional attitude to gender equality. Dale explained that his parents had a traditional division of labor: his father had a full-time job while his mother stayed at home. Nevertheless, Dale's dad showed a kind of flexibility that undercuts the idea that gender is built into the genes:

> Dad ... did quite a bit of cooking, he made curtains, which are things I can't do ... I don't think he did much of the cleaning; I don't remember him doing much washing, you know, that would fall to my mum. Mum did a lot of cooking but dad did quite a bit for those days. He was very family-orientated, very hands-on.

In conclusion, two key factors facilitate their equal lives: 1) Their shared commitment to equality, despite the ambivalence of their social environment; 2) Their both having jobs that allow them to take a day off a week. Their 4-day schedule derived in part from Dale's desire to have an equal role in looking after the kids – perhaps stemming from his father's unusual, traditionally feminine-defined talents around the home – and Katherine's having kept this desire firmly on track. It helps that they earn roughly equal salaries and have similar attitudes to their careers. Hiring a house cleaner and getting help from Katherine's parents are aids as well.

They have constructed an equal division of paid work and care within a social environment that is ambivalent about real equality. Their female friends may praise Dale, but none of their peer group is doing anything similar; when Dale takes the children to the day-centers, some mothers shun him; and despite flexible workplace regulations, Dale's boss was not all that supportive of his going on a 4-day schedule.

The factors that have helped them correspond both to the structural facilitation of men's participation in family work and to "gender consciousness" – the extent of awareness of gender issues, and the motivation to act upon them. The feminist literature identifies both of these factors as key to the continuing success of the "gender revolution." Over the last decades men have not moved into "women's work" (i.e., unpaid work) in the way that women have moved into "men's work" (i.e., employment). To account for this asymmetry, research has pointed to the institutional barriers surrounding men's employment, and the work ethos that impedes the careers of men who are perceived to put family above job. Dale appears to have negotiated this minefield successfully without damaging his own career. Other research has pointed to men's "doing gender" by not participating in traditionally "feminine" tasks, such as housework and caring. For Katherine and Dale, however, their shared commitment to equality meant that Dale equally participated in cleaning and cooking right from the start, and later evolved into a shared responsibility for childcare. It wasn't always easy, but the rewards are clear to both of them. Katherine sums up:

> I think it's very easy not to appreciate ... how hard it is staying at home with the children. When it's a great day, it's you know, it's amazingly good fun, but ... when it's not a good day, it's really tough, so I think that with Dale having done it ... he appreciates exactly what it involves ... so there's no taking it for granted. So I think it has been good for both of us ... that he's enjoyed staying with the boys, but he's also realized what hard work it can be, but it can also be lovely as well.

References

Department of Education (2018). *Provision for Children under 5 Years of Age in England, January 2018*. Retrieved from: https://assets.publishing.service.gov .uk/government/uploads/system/uploads/attachment_data/file/719273/Pro vision_for_children_under_5_2018_-_text.pdf.

Harding, C. & Cottell, J. (2018). *Childcare Survey 2018: Family and Childcare Trust*. London: Coram Family and Childcare. Retrieved from: https://www .familyandchildcaretrust.org/childcare-survey-2018.

O'Brien, M. & Koslowski, A. (2018). United Kingdom Country Note. In S. Blum, A. Koslowski, A. Macht, & P. Moss (eds.) *International Review of Leave Policies and Research 2018* (pp. 401–410). Retrieved from: www .leavenetwork.org/lp_and_r_reports/.

Office of National Statistics (2012). *Religion in England and Wales 2011*. Retrieved from: www.ons.gov.uk/peoplepopulationandcommunity/culturali dentity/religion/articles/religioninenglandandwales2011/2012-12-11.

Office of National Statistics (2013). *2011 Census: Key Statistics and Quick Statistics for Local Authorities.* (Ethnicity and country of birth). Retrieved from: www.ons.gov.uk/peoplepopulationandcommunity/populationandmigration/ populationestimates/bulletins/keystatisticsandquickstatisticsforlocalauthorities intheunitedkingdom/2013-10-11.

Office of National Statistics (2018a) *Gender Pay Gap in the UK: 2018.* Retrieved from: www.ons.gov.uk/employmentandlabourmarket/peopleinwork/earnings andworkinghours/bulletins/genderpaygapintheuk/2018.

Office of National Statistics (2018b). *Overview of the UK Population: November 2018.* Retrieved from: www.ons.gov.uk/peoplepopulationandcommunity/ populationandmigration/populationestimates/articles/overviewoftheukpopu lation/november2018.

Office of National Statistics (2018c). *Working and Workless Households in the UK July to September 2018.* (Figure 1: Employment rate of mothers with dependent children by age of youngest child, UK, July to September 2018) Retrieved from: www.ons.gov.uk/employmentandlabourmarket/people inwork/employmentandemployeetypes/bulletins/workingandworklesshouse holds/julytoseptember2018.

Office of National Statistics (2019). *UK Labour Market February 2019.* (Figure 1: Summary of UK labour market statistics for October to December 2018, seasonally adjusted) and (Figure 2: UK employment rates (aged 16–64 years), seasonally adjusted). Retrieved from: www.ons.gov.uk/employmentand labourmarket/peopleinwork/employmentandemployeetypes/bulletins/uklabour market/february2019#summary-of-latest-labour-market-statistics.

Sullivan, O. and Altintas, E. (2019) Dividing Domestic Labour and Care. In J. Gershuny & O. Sullivan (eds.) *What We Really Do with our Time: Insights from the Centre for Time Use Research* (Chapter 5). London: Penguin.

25

Portugal[1]

Karin Wall, Vanessa Cunha, and Sofia Marinho[2]

Pedro and Inês are a cohabiting Portuguese couple in their 30s. He is employed as a police officer; she administers the academic services department of a university. Pedro describes the two of them, "I am more of a laid back person; she is more active, maybe ... we get along so well because she pushes me forward and sometimes I calm her down." They have achieved an equal sharing family life rooted in togetherness, empathy, and mutual reliance. Ever since they moved in together, "it has always been sort of, fifty-fifty," according to Pedro; and when their 21-month-old toddler, Manuel, was born, their equality was only reinforced. After the 5-month parental leave (including the sharing bonus month taken by Pedro), they started alternating paid work shifts so they could share Manuel's care. Pedro works from early in the morning to mid-afternoon; Inês works an afternoon/evening shift and returns home at 9:00 or 9:30 p.m. Putting family first meant sacrificing potential rewards in the workplace, but it was a sacrifice they both were ready to make.

"We Take Turns"

On a typical workday, Pedro is on his way by 6:00 to 6:30 am, while Inês and Manuel are still asleep. Inês loves starting the day with Manuel, "Waking up in the morning, the two of us, without the alarm clock ... these are the best moments ... He is the happiest baby in the

[1] This chapter was supported by national funding from Fundação para a Ciência e a Tecnologia (UID/SOC/50013/2013).
[2] The authors are affiliated with Instituto de Ciências Sociais, Universidade de Lisboa.

world and says, 'good morning!' just like that." She takes care of him all morning, tidies up the house, makes and feeds him lunch, and leaves lunch for Pedro.

Pedro arrives home around 2:00 p.m. and Inês goes to her job. His afternoons revolve around Manuel's nap, playing, and a walk when the weather is good. Some days Manuel plays on his own, which leaves Pedro time to do housework and have some leisure. By the time Inês gets home, the baby has already had his bath and supper. Pedro waits to have dinner with Inês while she attends to Manuel. Pedro explains, "When his mother gets home the first hour belongs to her, and when I get home at lunchtime, he pays no attention to his mother, then it's my time." Inês adds, "Manuel seems to feel my absence during the afternoon, in a way that then he won't let me go, literally." For Inês, this is the most difficult time of the day:

> I just got home, just ate, I want to have that moment to watch a little TV . . . he pulls my skirt, wants to play and then at the same time . . . he is so cranky, so cranky that it doesn't work. It isn't gratifying either for him or for us. Those moments aren't good, aren't the best moments, but they are part of it.

She also gets up at night when the child cries, "Manuel hasn't allowed me a full night's sleep since the day he was born." Inês, however, does not feel resentful. She explained that their sharing is open to different ways of being and doing, "There are things Pedro does better than me and there are things I do better than him. He is a heavy sleeper, and I am not. I am super sensitive."

Portugal has a population of 10,355,493 (2018 estimate). It is predominantly Roman Catholic (81% as of the last census) and white homogeneous Mediterranean (Central Intelligence Agency, 2019). According to the 2011 census, the distribution of households was: couples with children (35%), couples without children (24%), single persons (21%), lone parents (9%), extended families (9%), and 2% were unrelated people (Wall, Cunha, & Ramos, 2014).

Portugal's family policies have been shaped by its unique history. For almost 50 years during the 20th century, Portugal had a right-wing dictatorship which was overthrown in 1974 in the April Revolution. The revolution ushered in rapid change in the domain of work, family, and gender equality policies. During the Salazar dictatorship, explicit pro-traditional family policies promoted a male-breadwinner model, emphasizing women's subordinate role and men's role as the "head of the family" and provider (Wall et al., 2017). Gender inequality and female responsibility for homemaking were written into the law (Ministério da Justiça, 1966).

After the transition to democracy, family policies promoted state responsibility to support full-time employed parents. By 2014 nearly all children aged 3 to 6 were in full-time preschool (90%) and 49% of children from birth to 2 years old were in full-time daycare in crèches (Wall, Leitão, Correia, & Ramos, 2016). Leave policies, first introduced in 1976, have become increasingly generous. Parents are entitled to 4 to 5 months of initial parental leave (at 80 to 100% of earnings), which may be divided between parents after the first 6 weeks reserved for the mother; an extra one month is available if both parents share the leave, on condition that the other partner has returned to the labor market. Twenty-nine percent of couples shared this initial parental leave in 2015. Parental leave can also be extended for 6 months (3 for each parent) compensated at 25% of earnings. In addition, fathers have a mandatory 15-day paternity leave, plus 10 optional days (Wall et al., 2017).

In 2014 the maternal employment rate was 75.7%, with less than 10% of employed mothers in part-time jobs (OECD, 2016). As of 2016, overall, 67.4% of women were employed, mostly full-time, as compared to 74.2% of men. The Portuguese Constitution of 1976 forbids gender discrimination. Yet, the gender pay gap favoring men was 17.8% (European Commission, 2017).

In families with children, women spend 18.8 hours per week on care-work, as compared to 16.4 hours spent by men. The gender gap is much greater for housework (19.8 vs. 10.9 for mothers and fathers, respectively) (Cunha & Atalaia, 2019).

When home together, cooperation and availability shapes their division. Pedro says, "If we are both home and it is necessary to change his diaper, we don't really take turns. I can do it 10 times and she can do the next 10 times, it all depends on what we are doing at that moment."

When asked about the emotional aspects of parental care, however, they both report that Inês contributes more. She says, "70% mom ... I am always hugging him, kissing him. I spoil him a lot, really. He [Pedro] probably does as well, but I am not there. Maybe, I don't know, but I think I am much more than he is."

Nonetheless, Pedro has a relationship with Manuel at least as close as his wife's. Inês explains:

> Manuel is 21 months old and we can see the relationship with his father. He never cries when I leave the house but he does when Pedro leaves – but cries out loud, "Daddy, Daddy!" ... He must have a similar perception of what his mother and father are.

Moreover, Pedro and Inês report sharing many traditionally maternal tasks equally, including providing sick care, taking Manuel to the doctor or dentist, comforting him, making decisions about him, and worrying.

"Whoever Is at Home Takes Care of It"

They contribute equally to the housework. Most day-to-day tasks are carried out by one or the other in turn. When one of them is unable to complete a planned task, the other takes over when his or her shift comes around. Pedro illustrates:

> Yesterday, I was tidying up, because I spent the whole afternoon home. I vacuumed and mopped the floor ... Usually she's more into the cleaning chores and I keep an eye on the boy. But when we are alone, whoever is at home takes care of it. Usually, I put the clothes out to dry ... We use the washing machine at night to benefit from the cheaper power rates. If she can, she will put it out to dry in the morning. If she can't do it, I will in the afternoon. We play it by ear.

Pedro's and Inês's symmetrical availability shapes the equal sharing of housework. Although Pedro used to do most of the cooking, "Now," he says, "it has been more based on availability, even more than by preferences ... Now, my partner has to prepare lunch and then I will make dinner." However, on the weekend, they treat shopping as a family outing and always do it together.

Pedro and Inês invoke their different levels of skill to explain some specialization. For example, Pedro exclusively carries out household repairs, traditionally a male domain (Wall, 2010). Likewise, Pedro is excused from ironing. "She won't let me ... because she thinks I waste too much electric power, because I am not very skilled and I can take over two minutes to iron a shirt!"

Inês also takes sole responsibility for the household finances. "That's all me. He is hopeless at it and doesn't care for it. I even do the money transfers that have to be done monthly from his account; I do them myself."

Although Pedro reports that he is "always thinking about the baby," Inês sees herself as the manager, "I'm thinking more about management, what needs doing, buying, sorting ... I tell him what needs to be purchased, and he goes out and does it."

She makes sure Pedro does his share of the work at home:

> "Pedro, you go and change the diaper ... Pedro, I did it earlier, now it's your turn." ... I make dinner, then the dishes, "Pedro, the dishes need seeing to. I am going to bed, but the dishes need sorting out." Because he said he would do it, so I have to remind him about 20 times, but even if he goes to bed at 4 in the morning he will take care of the dishes first. So there are things that are his tasks and I don't need to say a thing, but there are others that I need to spur him on because if I don't, instead of taking out the trash every day he will do it every 2 days or 3 days, but things work well and we manage.

"Where Do You Think You Are?"

Pedro and Inês met 6 years ago, when he was 25 and she 29. Inês was living alone at the time, having ended a previous 10-year relationship, while Pedro was sharing an apartment with three workmates. It was a short step from the start of the relationship to living together, "We didn't live together per se, but he would stay over and bring his backpack ... to my place and stayed there for weeks, which turned into months, and because we were good together, he ended up moving in."

Despite the atmosphere of mutual understanding between Pedro and Inês, they underwent a baptism by fire when it came to dividing up housework. Inês soon laid down the non-negotiable law. Fearing that Pedro would have "typical male habits" because, "he used to flat-share with men only," at the first sign of slovenliness, she enforced the tidiness she wanted. "I got home and there was a sock lying about and I would say to him, 'Where do you think you are?'" Pedro not only accepted Inês's leadership, but actually exceeded her expectations. She recounts:

> At first it wasn't easy because I am a tidy person and he is not ... and it annoyed me, the mess he made around our place. But I began to show I wasn't having any of it, that things couldn't be like that, and he began to tidy things up. He adapted; he began to sort his things out and surprised me because he later tidied up both his and my things, transforming himself completely into the person who did all at home. I would get home and it was spotless, just as if a maid had just left.

"Our Knowledge About Babies Was Pretty Much the Same"

Pedro recalls that he felt like a father from the first moment he saw the baby on the ultrasound. Grounded in the experience he had taking care of his nephews and nieces in adolescence, he entered parenthood believing that he was as capable of taking care of a baby as Inês. "I think that before he was born our knowledge about babies was pretty much the same." Inês admired his ability, his relaxed manner, and the pleasure he took in looking after friends' children, even the littlest ones, which inspired her to have a child together after 3 years of his patient waiting.

Manuel was born prematurely and stayed in hospital to put on weight. The nursing team taught the couple how to look after the baby. Pedro invokes this institutional support as an aid to his involvement:

> Maybe that's what made me at ease with taking care of him. He was a month in the hospital in the neonatal wing. The good thing that came out of that is that we spent almost the whole day there with him, and the nurses passed on a lot of information to us: how to change a diaper, how to bathe, and the necessary care for the baby.

Pedro took 20 days leave after the baby was born so at first, the two parents were home together. Inês confesses that she had been afraid of bathing Manuel because he was so small, "I was really scared, so Pedro bathed him. I couldn't; I didn't know how to hold him; I couldn't." Pedro was never flustered. Inês describes him:

> He wanted to do all the new things first. The first bath, the first nappy change, he did it . . . the first time to clip the baby's nails, the first of everything. The first soup, Pedro wanted to give him his first soup! I used to say, "Pedro, come on, let me do it!" . . . Pedro was a tremendous father. He was there for everything. He lived it as intensely as I did . . . I doubt that there are many fathers who live it as intensely as he did.

When Inês returned to her job, Pedro took up his share of the parental leave and stayed at home with Manuel for a month:

> Because I am a civil servant, all I had to do was hand in an application form and it got automatically accepted. It's the law that defines it as a right of ours . . . I always figured I would manage ok and I did, it actually turned out fine. I have no trouble making him fall asleep, bathing him, or dressing him, walking him on my own . . . or changing his nappy.

Although Pedro was around a lot during Inês's leave, and always very willing to look after the baby, spending the whole day alone with Manuel was different and promoted their equal sharing. Pedro says, "I think the most positive aspect was to interact with him for almost 24 hours a day."

Dividing the leave equally had originally seemed a natural choice. Inês explains:

> The initial objective ... was for me to take 2 months and Pedro the other 2 ... He wanted to stay the longest; he really did! But financially we couldn't do it ... because of the personal tax system.

Thus, they decided that she would stay at home for 4 months and that he would take the shared bonus month on his own.

During Manuel's first year, Pedro was also involved in the household chores, doing much of his wife's share. Inês credits Pedro's caring personality:

> He would protect me; he wanted me to rest ... The worst tasks, the most annoying ones, he always wanted to do them himself ... like putting the washing out to dry. "No, you stay there and I will do it." "It's 11 p.m., the dishes are in the sink. They need to go in the dishwasher." "No, let it be, I will go. Before going to bed, I will fill up the dishwasher." He likes to make others feel good ... He is very altruistic, very, so the chores, he did almost all of them.

"This Was a Decision We Made To Be Able To Spend Time with Our Son"

Pedro and Inês are both civil servants. He is a policeman; she has been employed for 10 years in the university. Both are content with their career achievements and are not looking for further advancement. Inês has reached the level she was aiming for, and Pedro's advancement would not change what he does in his job, working directly with the courts. They are content because they enjoy what they do, their careers allow them family time, and they are satisfied with their joint salary. Inês says:

> When you ask me if I'm fulfilled, I am because what I earn is more than enough for me to be happy. I am not a very ambitious person at the financial level. Neither is Pedro. Pedro is even less than I am, and I am happy with what I have ... I honestly would like to stay here forever, forever until I retire, to do what I do, which is to work with students ... I am a senior civil servant ... What would I aspire to be beyond this? To be the director? No ... nor would I like to, because ... I want to have time for my family, for my son, for my things, and I do not want to give up my free time.

Pedro is also happy with his job for the time being:

> It may be so that one day I feel like changing, or I get fed up with these tasks and I may want to try something else. But, so far, apart from the fact it suits me, I also

like it ... I have to feel fulfilled, not the least because I worked for many years in a shift-based system and now I do not ... I think it was due to my previous efforts that I managed to get to where I am now. In the meantime, Manuel was born, and it all works out really well, at least for now, while he is small.

Pedro and Inês worked out their non-overlapping job schedules by initiating changes in their jobs. Pedro gave up patrol work, which required rotating between day and night shifts, and started working a regular 36-hour-a-week Monday-to-Friday schedule. Inês arranged a continuous 6-hour day. The government departments where they are employed were open to these arrangements. Pedro's workplace was supportive of his schedule change and his leave, "My own station commander became a father when my wife became pregnant, and he also took the leave."

Likewise, Inês praises the family-friendly culture of her workplace:

The law allows us to ... opt for a 6-hour nonstop work period ... Usually this doesn't go down well, but this school is an excellent employer, and has always given us everything so that we can stay with Manuel at home.

The change, however, meant lost income. Inês explains:

When Manuel was born ... Pedro had a salary, which was 500, 600 euros more than today, because he took on some additional tasks in the police force ... So what did we do to afford this flexible work schedule? He gave it up ... When Manuel was born, I gave up working overtime, which amounted to 700 fewer euros per month, adding to Pedro's cut. It's almost a whole salary! ... It was a difficult decision for us because this was enough to afford the salary of a full-time housemaid, enough to pay the kindergarten for two children, but this was a decision we made to be able to spend time with our son.

Their decision affected Pedro's career more than Ines's because she had recently been promoted. The increase in salary almost compensated for the loss of extra income, and reinforced Inês's role as the main breadwinner. Pedro seems to be quite relaxed about it, especially because it complements his wife's responsibility for managing the family finances:

Sure, she is [the main breadwinner]! We have to acknowledge it ... because most of our family budget comes from her, doesn't it? ... I have little patience for the financial things and she ends up organizing all of it. She works with both salaries so that we can live the way we do, and try and save some for the future and keeping it all in order, leaving nothing out.

Inês concurs that her income does not threaten his masculinity, "Not in our house, that doesn't exist!" But Inês does admit that Pedro can feel "uncomfortable" because her financial superiority means she is much better placed to negotiate future career sacrifices:

> If anyone has to give up something professionally it will have to be him and not me, because we understand that if my salary carries the biggest weight, then he will have to make the biggest sacrifice ... My work has to be understood as the most important, because it is the financial cornerstone of our household.

Nonetheless, both were willing to change their shifts to accommodate the other's job demands. Such cooperation is only possible, however, because their jobs were flexible. Pedro notes, "If we had a 9 to 5, it would be impossible to do what we do ... She only has to work 6 hours a day and ... I just need to get my work done."

"Things Were Really Different Back Then"

Neither Pedro nor Inês grew up in an egalitarian family, but in their extended families of origin, communion and mutual help were important values. They both want to keep this familism alive, adding gender equality to it in their own family.

Pedro is the youngest of seven children of a traditional couple who were small farmers with little education. Their father went to work abroad for many years, and was unable to see most of his children grow up. But Pedro was a late arrival (i.e., his father was 60 when he was born) and so he benefited from his father's presence:

> Maybe my father never changed one of my diapers, but he was there for me in other ways, or tried to educate me in his way ... I remember my father teaching me things when I was little ... Things were really different back then, I think it is not even possible to make a comparison between now and 30 years ago.

Although Pedro grew up with parents who were traditionally gendered, he himself learned about childcare and housework. His parents farmed from sunrise to sunset, and relied on one of their daughters to do the housework. At age 15, Pedro's mother taught him to cook, and he took over the preparing of meals from his sister, who left to find a job. On occasion, Pedro's father would also cook if necessary, but that was his only contribution to household work. So although Pedro had no male role model to follow for equal sharing of family tasks, he did have his mother's and sister's teachings, thus demonstrating the importance of female models (Marinho, 2011). Because of his family training, when he shared a house in Lisbon with workmates, he enjoyed being the best cook in the house.

Inês is the oldest of three children. Her mother, having completed the 10th year of schooling, was a local government official in a small town, while her father was a plumber with little education. Family dynamics were more equal than in Pedro's family. Although her mother was in charge of family tasks, she encouraged her husband to share childcare and housework, and he willingly responded to her appeals for help.

> My mother did much more than my father, much more, but he did all my mother asked him to, like "hang the washing out to dry." And he would. My father cooks; he cooked often. He did a lot of the shopping; he still does it today. So it's not a sharing system like mine, but my father isn't the macho stereotype who sits watching TV and does nothing.

Inês found in Pedro the same willingness to build a companionship couple, based on communion, mutual help, understanding, and dialogue, but also gender equality, going a step further than her parents. Like her own father, Inês expected Pedro to be a "super-father":

> My mother tells that my father was a Pedro-like kind of father, really ... He changed nappies, he did everything. Even today, I still see my father as a super-father, the father who would pick me up from school, who sat me on his lap, played with me, a real super-father.

"You Don't Know What It Is To Be a Mother!"

Despite feeling "lucky" because Pedro's contributions make her life easier than it would otherwise be, at times Inês feels insecure about her identity as a mother:

> I don't think that I am not a good mother, but that I am not as good as the other mothers ... The other day I was thinking, "If I let Pedro go on that international fishing trip, I could have 3 or 4 days alone with Manuel, I could experience that, feel it." I have been told, "You don't know what it is to be a mother!" This friend of mine has three children; she's a single mother with three little children. So, in fact, I don't know what it is to be a mother compared to her. But, well, I am lucky. I wish all women were.

Inês knows that if she did not stand back and give Pedro space to parent, the sharing of tasks would not be equal, "If he was married to someone who took the initiative of doing everything herself, all the bathing, he'd probably be like other men." For her, it would not be sufficient for Pedro to take on the secondary role of "mother's helper." He must also take the initiative and, with her, create a new kind of motherhood and fatherhood.

Conclusion

Dual-earner couples with young children, both employed full-time, have prevailed in Portugal for a long time (Cunha & Atalaia, 2019). However, women have faced a double burden, since men have not been as fast to enter the private sphere of childcare and housework. Although this status quo is gradually changing, it is still far from being egalitarian (Wall, 2010; Wall et al., 2017). Inês even reports, for example, having "a friend who must take her two daughters to her parents' house if she goes out with her friends; the husband simply won't stay with them." Pedro and Inês are the exceptions.

The story of Pedro and Inês reveals the intersecting threads involved in building equality in the couple: the family-friendly workplaces and the family policies endorsing gender equality; Inês's superior career position, sense of entitlement to equality, and willingness to stand back and give up some maternal prerogatives; Pedro's early socialization into household chores and experience with childcare, as well as his willingness to limit his professional investment to care for his child; and the influence of their families of origin.

A key element has been their family-friendly job environments. Pedro's boss and colleagues were exceptionally open to his taking the leave, despite their profession, police officers, in which the gender culture tends to reinforce stereotypical masculinity. Likewise, Inês's adoption of a 6-hour day had no adverse effect on her chances of gaining promotion, as might have occurred in other contexts.

Overall, family policy in Portugal also facilitates gender equality in families. Leave policies provide a cultural sanction for women to return to their jobs after a relatively short parental leave, and encourages men to share it, establishing a conception of fatherhood that differs from traditional links between masculinity and employment, and femininity and care of babies (Wall & Escobedo, 2013). This public respect for workers' private lives, not just women's, but men's too, is thus a key element enabling a more equal paid work and family life.

Still, when children are born in Portugal, the father usually works more hours for pay or extra jobs to increase income in the case of lower-middle-class families. Or in families with higher-level skills, the father redoubles his investment in his career (Wall, 2010). But not Pedro! In contrast, he cut back on career commitments and gave up income to invest in parenthood. Although Inês's career takes precedence because of her greater earnings, she too adjusted her career and lost income as needed for their equally shared parenthood. These decisions, particularly unusual in Pedro's case, entailed a significant loss of family income. The lack of materialism is also key to their success in creating equally shared family life.

Inês's negotiating strength, which has also shaped their relationship, reflects her belief in gender equality, her sense of entitlement to obtain it, and her conviction that female influence is key to male participation. In fact, Inês's experience of equal sharing began in her previous conjugal relationship, wherein household chores were split, "It's not just the person. It's not by chance that I found two partners like this. They are this way because I also influence them."

Pedro and Inês both reject essentialist conceptions of motherhood and fatherhood. When asked whether it makes a difference in whether a man or a woman cares for children, Pedro responds, "I sincerely do not think it does, but I think that most people believe so. The only thing I didn't do for Manuel was to breastfeed him ... It makes no difference that the father does it or the mother does it." Inês adds, "They can be different, but not in the sense that the mother is more caring or a better carer than the father."

Inês's willingness to give up maternal prerogatives is another fundamental ingredient for parental equality. She made room for Pedro to take on an equal parental role beyond being the mere helper in childcare, which her father had been, encouraging him to use the caring skills he had acquired as an adolescent and young adult, accepting his autonomy in day-to-day family life.

The influence of their families of origin has had a strong impact on this couple's egalitarianism. Although he had a close relationship with his father, Pedro had no male examples of equality. He learned feminine care and meal preparation from his mother and sister, and his experience of caring for his nieces and nephews. However, skills acquired in one's own family are not always put into practice subsequently (Wall, 2010). It was crucial that Pedro encountered Inês's demand for equality, and that she wanted to find a "super-father" who would even go beyond the model of her own caring father. Inês found in Pedro the propensity to follow her leadership in building equality in household work, career, and shared parenthood. When Inês was asked what the ideal family for a child would be, she answered:

> Mine! Manuel's! At this moment, I think Manuel's. Sometimes I think, "You're such a lucky kid!" ... modesty aside ... A father that can be with his son for many hours, feed him his soup, change his diaper, bathe him ... the mother too, and they have jobs and a comfy home, nothing is missing. They have

plenty of love; they go out a lot to the countryside. The child has marvelous grandparents, uncles and aunts, cousins. I think this is an ideal family!

Pedro doesn't brag. For him, there is nothing so special about it, "I think this is normal, isn't it? At least I think it should be."

References

Central Intelligence Agency (2019). Portugal. *The World Factbook*. Retrieved from: www.cia.gov/library/publications/the-world-factbook/geos/po.html.

Cunha, V. & Atalaia, S. (2019). The Gender(ed) Division of Labour in Europe: Patterns of Practices in 18 EU Countries, *Sociologia, Problemas e Práticas*, 90, 113–137. Retrieved from: https://revistas.rcaap.pt/sociologiapp/article/view/15526/14022.

European Commission (2017). *Women in the Labour Market*. (Table 1, Employment rate, employment rate in full-time equivalents and average number of usual weekly hours of men and women 2016; Table 3, Gender pay gap). Retrieved from: https://ec.europa.eu/info/sites/info/files/european-semester_thematic-factsheet_labour-force-participation-women_en_0.pdf.

Marinho, S. (2011). *Paternidades de Hoje. Significados, práticas e negociações da parentalidade na conjugalidade e na residência alternada*. [Contemporary Fatherhood. Meaning, Practice and Negotiation of Parenting in the Couple and in Shared Residence after Divorce or Separation.] (unpublished doctoral dissertation) ICS-UL, Lisbon, Portugal. Retrieved from: http://repositorio.ul.pt/handle/10451/4940.

Ministério da Justiça (1966). *Decreto-Lei n.º 47344*. [Decree-Law No. 47344] In Diário do Governo nº 274/1966, Série I de 1966-11-25, Portugal.

OECD (2016). *Family Database*. (Chart LMF 1.3.A, Employment rates for partnered mothers and single mothers, 2014 or latest data). Retrieved from: www.oecd.org/els/soc/LMF_1_3_Maternal_employment_by_partnership_status.pdf.

Wall, K. (2010). A conciliação entre a vida profissional e a vida familiar em casais com filhos: perspectivas masculinas. [Work–Family Balance Among Couples with Children: Male Perspectives.] In K. Wall, S. Aboim, & V. Cunha (eds.), *A Vida Familiar no Masculino. Negociando velhas e novas masculinidades* (pp. 97–128). Lisbon: Comissão para a Igualdade no Trabalho e no Emprego. Retrieved from: www.cite.gov.pt/asstscite/downloads/publics/A_vida_masculino.pdf.

Wall, K., Cunha, V., Atalala, S., Rodrigues, L., Correia, R., Correia, S. V., & Rosa, R. (2017). *White Paper: Men and Gender Equality in Portugal*. Lisbon: ICS/CITE. Retrieved from: http://cite.gov.pt/asstscite/images/papelhomens/WHITE_PAPER_Men_and_Gender_Equality_In_Portugal.pdf.

Wall, K., Cunha, V., & Ramos, V. (2014). *A evolução das estruturas domésticas em Portugal, 1960–2011* [The Evolution of Domestic Structures in Portugal, 1960–2011]. In A. Delgado & K. Wall (eds.) *Famílias nos Censos 2011. Diversidade e Mudança* (pp. 43–63). Lisbon: INE/ICS. Retrieved from:

www.observatoriofamilias.ics.ul.pt/index.php/publicacoes/livros/93-familias-nos-censos-2011.

Wall, K. & Escobedo, A. (2013). Parental Leave Policies, Gender Equity and Family Well-Being in Europe: A Comparative Perspective. In A. M. Minguez (ed.), *Family Well-Being. European Perspectives* (Social Indicators Research, Vol. 49, pp. 103–129). New York: Springer.

Wall, K., Leitão, M., Correia, S. V., & Ramos, V. (2016). *Observatório das Famílias e das Políticas de Família. Relatório 2014–2015* [Observatory on Families and Family Policies. Report 2014–2015]. Lisbon: OFAP/ICS-UL. Retrieved from: www.observatoriofamilias.ics.ul.pt/images/pdf/ofap%20relatorio%202014-2015%20final.compressed.pdf.

26

Undoing Gender: Different Cultures, Similar Stories

Francine M. Deutsch and Ruth A. Gaunt

Gender is typically reproduced in families by the ongoing decisions and actions that prioritize paid work for men and care for women. The 25 equally sharing couples in *Creating Equality at Home*, who represent 22 different countries, defied social norms and undid gender in five key ways: 1) the men forged unconventional relations to paid work; 2) they embraced the "maternal" aspects of parenthood; 3) the women relinquished the position of number one parent, 4) they insisted on (at least) equal consideration for their careers; and 5) the couple shared housework.

Men and Paid Work

Hegemonic masculinity dictates that men put paid work at the center of their identity and pursuits. To fail in paid work is to fail as a man. Men typically aspire to be good breadwinners and to rise in their careers. Especially after becoming fathers, these aspirations underlie decisions in the family for men to maximize their careers by seeking and accepting promotions, working long hours, and adhering to workplace norms, even when these choices compromise their time in the family and the emotional rewards of hands-on care. Those choices exemplify how men typically do gender in the family.

In contrast, the equally sharing fathers undo gender by prioritizing care over paid work. Ivo (Croatia) explained that staying home with his daughter for 3 years did not seem like a career sacrifice because no job could be as fulfilling as the time he had with her, "Compared to Ema, my job is in 10th place, 15th, 20th." Magda (Czech Republic) said of Martin,

"If he has to choose between work and family, the family always wins. The children are in first place." She reported that although she could imagine a weekend without the children, he could not. Sam (USA) simply said of his children, "They are our lives."

In ways usually associated with mothers, these fathers put their careers on hold; they work part-time; they negotiate for family-friendly concessions from employers; and/or insist on taking advantage of family-friendly rights and benefits, even when that jeopardizes their positions at their jobs. Moreover, they acknowledge their wives as co-breadwinners, and as having equally important jobs.

In 8 of the 22 countries we studied (i.e., Austria, Croatia, the Czech Republic, Germany, Iceland, Portugal, Slovenia, and Sweden), men took some form of paternal or parental leave. Notably, Mikael (Sweden) took more leave than his wife did, as did Ivo (Croatia), who took a 3-year leave while putting his career on hold. Richard (Austria) followed Christine's 7-month leave with 2 years of reduced work hours. Likewise, David (Czech Republic) followed his wife's 9-month leave with over a year of time off, despite severe discouragement from his employer, who threatened to fire him. In some countries the leaves were shorter, but men did take them. And in several other countries, fathers had significant solo responsibility for infants without the benefit of state-mandated leave. For example, Mike (Australia) took time out of the labor force and became a "househusband" for a period after his daughter, Hayley, was born.

In 5 of the 25 *Creating Equality* couples (i.e., Australian, Czech, German, British, and Swiss), both husband and wife are employed part-time. In Germany and the UK, the men have taken advantage of government benefits to get a part-time schedule, despite whatever risks that means for their careers. Hannes (Germany), who works a 16-hour week for pay, is one of only 5% of German fathers who take advantage of the opportunity to reduce their hours. Hanna, his wife, explains, "He's not the career person." Dale (UK), who reduced his paid work hours to a 4-day week, did so despite the foot-dragging of his boss. He asserted that he wasn't interested in a promotion anyway because it would mean returning to full-time hours. In Australia, just like his wife, Joanne, Mike was able to negotiate with his employers to limit his time at his job to 30-hour schedules that meshed with hers, so they could limit outside childcare. He leveraged his reputation as a good worker to successfully arrange this family-friendly plan. Martin (Czech Republic) took advantage of some career problems to shift most of his work to home and to limit the number of hours he put into paid work.

In almost all of the cases, we can point to ways in which men have compromised their paid work. Take Gadi in Israel. He agreed to care for his infant daughter while on a postdoc, which certainly undermined the work he was doing and eventually led to his being fired. Netta, his wife, asserted, "Both of us are willing to sacrifice little for our careers. Our family life is more important." Gadi said, only slightly tongue-in-cheek, that if he couldn't take care of his daughter, he "would rather have abandoned" the postdoc.

The men who have given up opportunities or promotions include João (Brazil), a pilot who could have become a commander, but refused to pursue a career that would have meant even more time away from his family; Budi (Indonesia), who, likewise, turned down a promotion to principal; and Dale (UK) who turned down a promotion in Australia and returned to the UK because of the limited career opportunities in Australia for his wife, Katherine. Moreover, Robinson (Honduras) gave up a job so he could be with his wife and children, and Tomaž (Slovenia) has given up his aspirations to become a headmaster. When taking on extra job-related projects, he limits himself to those that don't interfere with family life, and waits until his children are asleep to work on the Ph.D. he still hopes to obtain. Sam intentionally chose a career as a teacher in the USA because it allows for a great deal of time with family. Perhaps most dramatically, Nick (USA) gave up a more lucrative career as a production manager to become a firefighter because he knew that the schedule would allow him to become a highly participant father.

Fathers were willing to press their employers for family time. Miki (Hungary) negotiated with his boss to work remotely in the Netherlands so he could be present for Mia's pregnancy, and they both attribute the baby's early connection to him to having heard his voice in utero. In his multinational corporation in Iceland, Arnaldur had to contend with an American boss who did not appreciate the parental rights that Icelanders were afforded and resisted his taking time off. Nonetheless, Arnaldur insisted on his rights and was able to successfully negotiate a longer part-time leave working at home while he cared for his baby. Likewise, Osman (Singapore) insists on his right to take time off when his child is sick, despite his boss's insinuations that his wife should be doing it.

At a superficial level, these cases are consistent with the time availability hypothesis. The equally sharing men typically have more time than other men available to do childcare and housework. However, the clear demonstration of agency by these men show that it is not an accident that they have more time available. Previous studies have shown that time available is not sufficient to produce equality in the division of household labor (e.g., Bittman et al., 2003). What our study shows is that availability can be created when men eschew the equation of masculinity and paid work. In equally sharing men, the time they have available for full involvement in family life – caring for infants on parental leave, taking care of sick children, picking children up from school, and cooking dinner – is often a direct consequence of conscious decisions made to limit paid work.

Those decisions entail both choosing a career that provides a family-friendly structure and/or taking advantage of a job's flexible structure to devote time to the family. In either case, time available is the result of conscious choices rather than the cause of sharing childcare. For example, Richard's (Austria) freelance work allows him to be home for his children, but he emphasizes that it is a choice to limit that work. He stops working at 3:00 p.m. so he can be available for childcare. Both João's job as a pilot in Brazil and Nick's job as a firefighter in the USA are structured such that they can be home several days a week, time that both of them use for childcare. Yet, neither of those jobs ensure an equally sharing husband. Puzzled by his colleagues' choices, Nick notes that other firefighters with similar schedules outsource childcare.

Men and Care

Time and tasks typically distinguish between men's and women's childcare. Mothers spend more time with children, and they do more routine and hands-on care (Craig & Mullan, 2011). The equally sharing fathers undo gender by spending far more time with their children than other men and by taking on the tasks that have typically been left to women. Additionally, they undo gender by embracing the "maternal" nurturing aspects of parenting.

Time

Even in countries as egalitarian as Sweden and Iceland, the uptake of parental leave is asymmetrical. On average, in Sweden men take approximately 3 months leave, whereas women take almost a year (Duvander & Haas, 2018). Mikael (Sweden), who has taken 8 months leave so far with his youngest child, and is planning to take another 4, is in the vanguard. The fathers in all the countries who took paternal or parental leave are groundbreakers.[1] Clearly, the fathers who take these leaves are devoting the kind of time that mothers typically devote to childcare. Likewise, those fathers who have cut back to part-time employment are responding to parenthood in the way that women often do.

Taking time *off* from paid work is not enough to produce equality in parenting; it is spending time *with* children that counts. At the time of their interviews, in 11 of the couples, fathers were spending more time per week with their children than were their wives, and in 8, mothers and fathers spent approximately an equal amount of time with the children. In the American Latinx couple, their relative time varied, with Felipe spending more than Xochitl when he was unable to get paid work. Clearly, when fathers spent more time than their wives, or worked at home, or worked different shifts than their wives, a significant amount of time with children was spent in solo care. Solo care is another indication that fathers are undoing gender, both because when men are on the front lines in solo care they have to take on all required tasks, regardless of whether or not those tasks are usually in the province of mothers, and because it frees women up for other pursuits, whether their careers or leisure activities.

Tasks

Equally sharing fathers take on the routine and hands-on jobs of caregiving: they diaper, bathe, and feed small children. They wake up with crying babies at night. They stay home to care for sick children, and they transport older children to and from school and activities. They also rush to pick up and comfort a child who has fallen, soothe their fears, and worry about children's problems in ways often seen as maternal. In some cases, the equally sharing men take on the last frontier of equality: the planning and management of childcare and housework, thinking about what needs to be done and making sure it happens.

Hands-on and Routine Care

Babies require the most hands-on care. At least 19 of the 25 fathers were or had been intensely involved in hands-on care of infants, regardless of

---

[1] Perhaps with the exception of Iceland. Arnauldur's uptake is similar to the average Icelander's, given that he used the days designated for fathers but none of the joint leave (Gíslason, 2017).

whether or not they took leave. Veronica (USA) spoke for many of the mothers when she said, "from day one he has been doing everything that I do with the exception of the breastfeeding." Take Nick (USA), the firefighter who assumed responsibility for childcare on his days off when his wife was back at her job. He spent his days feeding, diapering, and entertaining his new baby. Joanne (Australia) and Denisa (Czech Republic) didn't breastfeed, so feeding was shared between them and their husbands from the start. But despite the common belief that nursing precludes equal sharing, breastfeeding was not an impediment to many of the men. Gadi (Israel) was on night duty with his colicky daughter when his wife was on leave. Besides waking up when she needed comforting, he changed her and brought her to Netta to be nursed. In other couples, the women expressed milk to give fathers a chance to feed their babies. Moreover, two of the fathers described how they helped their wives with nursing. Osman (Singapore) helped Siti get the baby in the right position, and Nick (USA) woke up and encouraged his wife, who was struggling with breastfeeding.

Many men and women talked about the array of routine tasks fathers assumed as soon as the baby was born. David (Czech Republic) was the exception in admitting that he couldn't deal with poopy diapers for the first 7½ months. Overwhelmingly, though, these fathers did not shrink from diapering, dressing, bathing, or waking up at night with their infants. Pedro (Portugal) and Tshewang (Bhutan) bathed their children when they were newborns because their wives were afraid of the babies' fragility. Osman (Singapore) was in charge of night feedings because Siti was a light sleeper. All of these tasks entail undoing gender. As Felipe (USA) pointed out, "There are many men who don't want to change diapers because they feel like women."

Hands-on and routine care is not limited to infants. The equally sharing fathers are involved in waking children up, getting them dressed and fed, supervising their tooth brushing, and bedtime routines. Many of them either drop off or pick up their children from childcare or school. A number of the fathers do the baths or share bathing their children, and two of them (i.e., Felipe (USA) and David (Czech Republic)) insist on bathing children themselves because they are critical of the way their wives do it, and assert that the children prefer their way of bathing them. Perhaps the most dramatic example of how equally sharing fathers don't shy away from the unpleasant tasks of parenting, Richard (Austria) seems to specialize in his family for dealing with vomit.

Nurturing

Mothers cuddle and bestow affection. Mothers soothe crying babies. Mothers are attuned to their children's distress. Mothers take care of children when they are sick. These are the stereotypes that define what it means to be maternal. Equally sharing fathers do all of these things. Certainly when men report waking with their babies at night, it means that they do more than change diapers and give bottles. Middle of the night wakings require fathers to find ways to soothe and help babies get back to sleep.

These fathers also step up to comfort older children and respond to their emotional needs. For example, recall that Luka (Montenegro) was working hard to provide extra attention and affection to rectify his son, Nikola's, obvious distress over his attentions to his younger brother, Bogdan, after Nikola told him, "Daddy, you are not my dad. You are just Bogdan's dad." Mike (Australia) reports that he provides a calming influence for his son who sometimes "implodes" in the morning. A number of parents report that either of them can soothe their children when hurt or upset. In response to the question of who comforts, Hanna (Germany) says, "she needs to be hugged ... when she falls when we are walking on a path so depending on who is closer to her when this happens." Likewise, Maja (Montenegro) says, "When there is a physical trauma, they run to both of us; there isn't a difference, and we kiss, hug, and cuddle." In a few of the equally sharing families, fathers were more likely to comfort than mothers. In China, for example, despite Kai Wang's not having been much involved in infant care, now that his daughter is 3 years old, Li Li, his wife, says, "I'm less patient than Kai. Therefore, when our daughter has emotional problems, Kai is usually the one to comfort her." Xochitl (USA) is not as sanguine about her secondary role, and complains that Felipe always wants to be the one to talk to their older daughter about her feelings and to solve her problems.

Teenage and young adult children need nurturing too. Notably, Martin's (Czech Republic) now 21-year-old daughter, Nora, felt free even as a teenager to speak openly with her father about having her period, unlike friends who would never confide in their fathers that way.

In 18 of the families, the parents describe their children as having equal attachments to both of them, which, perhaps, is the best evidence of the central role fathers take in the emotional lives of their children and of their active efforts to comfort and provide affection. In some of them, one child was closer to the mother and the other to the father, and in some, attachments went back and forth. For example, Budi (Indonesia), whose son is closer to him, is more patient with him, and a bit more indulgent. "I take pity on the child. He does not want much. I don't want him to be stressed out ... I want to be available and supportive for him." In Brazil, 7-year-old Davi's closeness shifts between João and Cecília, depending on who has been spending more time with him.

Among the parents who reported on what happened when their children were ill, the majority thought sick care was shared. For example, Felipe and Xochitl (USA) both woke with their sick daughters during the night, and their father held them to provide comfort. In Singapore and Slovenia, husband and wife took turns staying home to care for a sick child. And Burak (Turkey) was much more likely than Hande to sound the alarm on illness and insist that 7-year-old Deniz see a doctor. Likewise, Ivo (Croatia) jumps to take his daughter's temperature as soon as he hears her cough and sneeze. However, in a few of the couples, mothers stayed home with sick children, either because their jobs more readily allowed for it (Montenegro), or because they believed that children needed their mothers (Hungary).

In a theoretical piece, Elliot (2016) argues that when men do care work they create a "caring masculinity" and reject hegemonic masculinity, which integrates domination as part of masculine identity. She cites numerous studies that show that when men do care work, they develop "maternal" traits, such as sensitivity and connection to the emotional life of the family. The equally sharing men's experience is entirely consistent with what Elliot means by "caring masculinity." However, we argue that "undoing gender" is a better way to conceptualize this process. Why call it masculinity simply because men are experiencing it? Caring and care work are human capacities that are available to both men and women.

Acquiring Expertise

Although participants were not explicitly asked about who had read parenting books, in four countries couples volunteered that the men had read up on parenting even before the babies were born (i.e., Croatia, Germany, Hungary, and Israel). Commonly, only mothers read the parenting books, so from the outset they develop a sense of authority and expertise to which their husbands defer. In contrast, because they had read about parenting, equally sharing men were able to start on the same footing as their wives. Thus, sometimes their wives deferred to them. For example, having read about breastfeeding, Ivo (Croatia) was able to convince his exhausted wife that she could go to sleep while he fed the baby, and could reassure her that she would be able to continue breast-feeding and that her bond with the baby wouldn't be broken. In the Israeli family, Gadi was considered the expert on parenting. Unlike Netta, who told him to just summarize and tell her what he had learned, he spent time perusing online parenting forums.

Women and Care

Women undo gender when they relinquish the exclusive primary care role for their children, when they make room for their husbands to share fully in their children's care. It is very unlikely, for example, that men would take parental leave without the blessing of their wives. Even among the equal sharers, there are few husbands who would feel entitled to share parental leave if their wives did not endorse it.

Gatekeeping refers to women's efforts to retain authority and control of the domestic sphere by discouraging their husbands' participation (Allen & Hawkins, 1999; Gaunt, 2008). The equally sharing wives, in general, are not gatekeepers. Nera (Croatia) was especially critical of women who don't allow their husbands to participate or are excessively critical when men do try to contribute to housework or childcare. She is horrified by a friend who doesn't let her husband mix formula. Recall her advice on how to correct men gently when they err, "If he heats up the milk incorrectly, you shouldn't say, 'What did you do? This is not suitable for a child!' ... say, 'It is a little too hot; cool this down a bit.'" She asserts that men want to change but they need women's help to do so. One should proudly support a husband's efforts to be equal in front of his peers, which, in their case, meant making clear that it was Ivo's choice to be home for an extended leave. She also acknowledges and defends an involved father's right to have a say in parenting decisions. "I gave him the opportunity to be Dad as I am a mom. I didn't take these rights away from him." Christine (Austria), Joanne (Australia), and Hildur (Iceland) all point out that it is necessary to stand back and accept that one's husband might not approach housekeeping exactly the way you would, but, as Joanne says, "if you want things to change, you have to give a little."

Women also undo gender when they stop trying to live up to an idealized notion of motherhood. A number of the women found it hard to be home on leave with children, and willingly ceded that role to their husbands. For example, both of the Czech women were unhappy while at home, and were happy to have their husbands take over. David describes Denisa as a "workaholic" who was terribly bored at home on leave. Martin also reports that Magda was not happy being home with their daughter. Nera (Croatia) recalls her time at home as a "catastrophe."

Other women admit that motherhood is not a completely idyllic experience and fulfilling identity. Li Li (China) opines that it is not enough for her to simply be someone's mother. Petra (Slovenia) is frustrated by not having enough time on her own. Maja (Montenegro) confesses that when her first child didn't sleep at night, she was furious "like a man" would be while her husband, Luka, was sanguine because Nikola was "just a baby." Netta (Israel), however, is the mother who most vociferously rejects an idealized motherhood identity. With humor, she describes her time alone with children as "a punishment," and freely recounts that she "couldn't stand" her infant daughter who was so filled with gas that she was "impossible" and had to be turned over every 20 minutes. Moreover, Netta was the opposite of a gatekeeper. She urged Gadi to do the reading about parenting and just summarize it for her, and she claims to be unable to do her daughter's braids; only Gadi has the skill for that. Netta not only leaves the gate wide open for Gadi, sometimes she stays on the other side. Netta also admits that when she was at her job she would forget that her daughter was sick, an indication both of her trust in Gadi's care and her rebellion against the enforced maternal worrying, designed to show others and the mother herself that she is a good mother (Walzer, 1996).

Women and Paid Work

Overwhelmingly, the equally sharing mothers have careers that are taken at least as seriously as their husbands' careers by both them and their husbands. In fact, in 8 families couples prioritize the woman's career or considered it the more important career in the family. In 13 families, both husband and wife treat the two careers as equally important, and only in 4 families do couples give the man's career priority. Even more striking, in the equally sharing families, women's incomes seem to count more than men's. When women earned more than their husbands, as they did in 9 families, the couples almost always acknowledged that the woman had the more important job. The only exception was the Turkish couple, in which Hande believed her husband's job was more important, despite her making more money. Both of them were committed to their brainchild, the publishing company, Omega, that was the focus of his career. In contrast, in the 10 cases where men made more money than their wives, couples in only 3 families considered the man's job to have greater priority. In the other 7 cases, both husbands and wives attributed equal status to the 2 jobs. Finally, although in many countries couples commonly hold down 1.5 jobs, with mothers employed part-time and fathers full-time, that pattern was never seen among the equal sharers. Either both husband and wife were employed full-time or they were both employed part-time.

When women specialize in care work and men in paid work, the compromises women make in their paid jobs often leave them under-employed, working at part-time jobs and/or flexible jobs that don't take advantage of their training and talents. That pattern was rare among the equal sharers. Overall, although they varied in their degree of career commitment and the centrality of paid work to their identities, the equally sharing women were happy with work lives that reflected their successes in realizing their ambitions.

A couple of the mothers had high-powered careers that entailed long hours. For example, Elisabet (Sweden), who is the director of transport services in a public utility in Sweden, puts in 50 to 60 hours per week, as compared to her husband, Mikael, who works a standard 40-hour week as a software engineer. She considers herself " 100% involved" in her job. Responsible for supervising numerous employees and overseeing nine sections of the organization, she is highly invested in doing the best job she can, which often means working for several hours after her children go to bed. Nera (Croatia), the mother who described her time at home as a catastrophe, does not mince words: "success" is very important to her. Denisa (Czech Republic) is an auditing manager with a multinational corporation. Although her recent promotion has led her to complain about the stress of her job and to regret time away from her child, recall that her husband, David, called her a "workaholic." He pointed out that even when she was home on leave for less than a year, she started her own business.

In those three families, the woman's job takes priority. However, the Icelandic couple, Hildur and Arnaldur, both have comparable well-paying managerial jobs in the same multinational corporation. Hildur is a project manager who supervises a creative team of 60 employees. Her enthusiasm for her career is unmistakable. She gets so involved with her work sometimes that a whole day can pass without her stopping to eat or drink. "So this is fun," she says, "but very demanding!" She is proud of her work and has no regrets about the time she puts into it. Women's choices to pursue high-powered, demanding careers defies the constraints of social disapproval and internalized images of ideal motherhood. It reflects their agency in the face of those constraints, just as men's choices to cut back on career reflect theirs.

Equally sharing mothers found ways to keep their careers from getting derailed, even when they took a more traditional route temporarily. For example, although Veronica (USA) spent 8 years at home with her children, after her first child was born she modified but did not abandon the track to get her CPA license. Licensing required her to work at an accounting firm for a year, but when the baby was born, she converted the last 6 months of the requirement to a 1-year part-time position. Sam supported her by taking over childcare on the Saturdays when she had to go to her job. Although she might have lost seniority and lowered her wages by her absence from the labor force, she was able to obtain an engaging and rewarding job in her field when she did go back to full-time employment.

Katherine (UK) suspected that she missed an opportunity for a job because she had taken advantage of her right to reduce her schedule to a 3-day week, so she suggested that instead Dale and she both adopt a 4-day week. Although technically part-time, she reasoned that missing one day a week would lead her supervisors and co-workers to consider her a full employee. And recall that when Christine (Austria) was fired from two jobs after having taken maternity leave, she did not give up. She persisted and landed on her feet in a well-paying job as an executive assistant, earning more than Richard. She is adamant that no matter how much money a husband might have earned, she would never have wanted to give up paid work. In Maja's (Montenegro) family, despite Luka's job getting priority because it is the more lucrative and inflexible job, Maja also has a professional job with a permanent contract as a psychologist in the public sector. Given her job security, she took full advantage of yearlong leaves when both of her children were born, but she also invested in her career by taking a 3-year course in family therapy while she was pregnant and on maternity leave. Magda (Czech Republic) is the one exception. Pressured to choose between coming back to her job full-time and staying home with her son, she quit the job that she loved as a general secretary in a sports union. Currently she works part-time at a much less interesting and less challenging job.

Paid work functions as a counterpoint to motherhood. Hanna (Germany), who is not ambitious and only works part-time, asserts, "It's good to be able to combine both of these spheres of life. I look forward to being with her and then I look forward to being at work again." Likewise, even Yangchen (Bhutan) and Hande (Turkey), while acknowledging the priority of their husbands' jobs, describe feeling successful and appreciated at their jobs. Hande proudly reports that every week she hears from colleagues at the publisher, "You came here, and you saved it; this place became something."

The rhetoric of some of the women sounds more traditional at first. They insist that family is much more important than their jobs. What sets these women apart from those in more traditional families who make the same claim is that putting family first is not gendered in their families. The wives' job-related compromises are matched by their husbands', whether husband and wife are both employed full-time (e.g., Israel, Singapore) or part-time (e.g., UK, Switzerland), "family first" is a motto adopted by both husband and wife. As Veronica says, "Family is more important than work to both of us." Osman (Singapore) declares, "We work to live, not live to work."

As mentioned earlier, nine of the women out-earned their husbands. Besides the valuing of their careers, they undo gender by accepting the role of breadwinner without resentment. Joanne (Australia) reports matter-of-factly that it always made more sense for her to work more than her husband because of her higher wages. Inês (Portugal) sounds proud when she says that her job takes priority in the family because she makes more money than Pedro. Hande (Turkey) is happy that she earns enough to support Burak's labor of love on Omega, their publishing company.

Felipe (USA) did earn a bit more money than Xochitl in the year before the interview, but his work as a roofer was unreliable and did not bring in enough money to cover the family's expenses. Xochitl's earnings at the dry cleaner were essential to the family's survival. Despite Felipe's comfort in undoing gender by providing stereotypically maternal care to his two daughters, he was devastated by not being the family breadwinner. Xochitl, however, was unfazed by her breadwinner role; she does not respect her husband less because her income is needed, "He feels that if he doesn't work he has no value, is worthless. He thinks that, but I don't see it that way."

What about Housework?

Housework is also an important arena for the undoing of gender. Miki (Hungary), like other equally sharing men, rejects the idea that housework is women's work, "There is no restriction that I am not going to do that because that is the kind of housework that men don't do. I wash up precisely because that will be helpful." Research on changes in the distribution of domestic labor over time show that in many countries, although men have increased their contributions to childcare, their housework hours have not changed as much (Altintas & Sullivan, 2017). Childcare may carry intrinsic rewards and may even be fun at times, but cleaning, laundry, and dishwashing are not fun. In twelve of the couples, housework is equally shared, in six the women do more than the men, and in six the men do more than the women. The Swedish couple disputes their relative shares; he thinks it is equal, but she says she does more. In nine of the families at least some of the domestic labor is outsourced. Housework is much more likely to be a source of contention than is childcare, so some middle-class couples outsource to alleviate conflict. A few families get significant help from relatives.

Even when housework is equally divided, what couples divide and the way they divide it varies enormously. In Singapore, for example, besides having a cleaner 5 hours a week, Siti and Osman eat dinner out most nights, leaving a relatively small amount of housework to share. Likewise, João and Cecília (Brazil) profit from having a maid Monday to Friday. However, like the majority of equal sharers, Nera and Ivo (Croatia) do all of the work themselves. Although they don't do much cooking because they eat their main meal midday at their jobs, the cooking they do is shared equally. While Ivo thinks of housework as no big deal, just something "normal," they are busy with tasks from laundry to shopping to changing the bed linen. "There is always something to do; you never manage to do everything!" In Netta (Israel) and Gadi's house, no one wants to do housework. She says, "We just don't do anything." He says, "We both do 60%." They each take up tasks the other can't stand. He hates loading the dishwasher. She hates hanging clothes. In some of the equal households, though, neither seems to mind the ongoing demands, and the couple seems to cooperate seamlessly, each pitching in with the job that needs to be done. Budi (Indonesia) and Tuti are a good example. Recall that they don't have specific tasks; they just focus on helping each other. As Budi reported, "While she cooks, I do laundry or clean ... If she does the laundry, I cook rice."

However, it doesn't go as smoothly in some households. In Iceland, for example, although Hildur and Arnaldur do share the housework equally, it is not without struggle. They share cooking, dishwashing, and cleaning. Hildur reports that Arnaldur does more vacuuming and mopping than she, but laundry is a sore spot. She does it and he is supposed to fold, but the laundry can sit unfolded for much longer than she likes. Different standards of tidiness also make for tensions. Richard (Austria) is messier than Christine. She can't seem to get him to clean up the stack of papers on the window sill, but tries not to let herself do more than her share of the work. They turned to paid help to reduce conflict. In Sweden, Elisabet's and Mikael's conflicting standards were resolved both by her lowering her standards and by hiring outside help. Although these conflicts appear to be gendered, with women dissatisfied with the lower standards of their husbands, conflicts in the opposite direction occurred in other families. Dale and Katherine (UK) resorted to paid help to avoid the conflicts that emerged because, as Katherine admits, Dale is more "house-proud" than she and does more of the tidying up. Felipe gets angry with Xochitl for not helping him tidy the house, but, as low-income workers, outsourcing isn't an option for them.

Relative Resources Revisited

Earning as much or more than one's husband does not seem to be a prerequisite to becoming an equally sharing couple, as might be predicted by the relative resources hypothesis. Moreover, the absolute level of women's incomes varies enormously, from Hildur and Elisabet and Denisa with lucrative management positions in Iceland, Sweden, and the Czech Republic, to Xochitl (USA), an undocumented worker in a minimum wage job. Nonetheless, when one considers the relative incomes of the equally sharing couples, in most of the cases in which men earn more, the differences between husband and wife are not large. But again, the equity in their incomes is not simply an accident. By making comparable compromises in their work lives, these couples avoid the spiral in which women's compromises result in lower wages, which, in turn, becomes the justification for their paid work taking second place in the family, and their being responsible for domestic labor (Deutsch, 1999).

Perhaps at least as important as money, however, is the way careers are treated in the family. Although under-researched in the domestic labor literature, the career commitments of women and the respect their careers get from their husbands may be as critical to sharing as their relative or absolute incomes. Dale's moving back to the UK, where Katherine was to have a better job than him, speaks to that respect, as does João's move to

Brazilia for Cecília's job, both at odds with the usual pattern of women following their husbands to promote their careers (Bielby & Bielby, 1992; Shauman, 2010).

In sum, couples undo gender every day in the decisions and actions they make about paid and unpaid work in their families. Men do so by limiting paid work, devoting time to their children, and embracing hands-on and nurturing care. Women undo gender by committing to their careers and by refusing the myths about motherhood, that mothers are irreplaceable and that motherhood is unconditionally fulfilling. Undoing gender in the family, however, is an interactive process in which men and women have linked lives (Han & Moen, 1999). Men's job decisions hinge on women's willingness to share breadwinning, and their involvement in infant care depends on women's relinquishing the prerogative of being the exclusive primary parent. Likewise, women's giving up that role depends on men's willingness to share primary care. Moreover, women's career commitments would be stymied without the respect and practical support of their husbands.

The undoing gender perspective shows that when income and time are shown to be correlates of the division of labor at home, that is not the end of the story. We have to question how it came to be that women have more time to devote to family work and that men earn more money. Doing gender underlies the decisions and actions that reduce the wages of women, augment those of men, and drive the asymmetry in the time they have to devote to domestic labor and jobs. Without underestimating the role of structural factors such as workplace discrimination and the gender pay gap, doing gender plays a significant role in producing the divergence between the lives of husbands and wives. Undoing gender creates the conditions for equality at home.

Gender Persistence

Undoing gender to create equality is a flawed, imperfect process. The families we studied, although largely successful, also show the struggle involved, and that gendered ways of doing things, and gendered reactions to change can persist. Even in these families, women are often the managers who do the mental work required to keep the family running; some still gatekeep or have to work hard not to, and some women have to wrestle with the emotional consequences of shared parenting. Some worry about men's egos when they do housework or make less money. Men who share the work compare themselves to other men and sometimes expect inordinate gratitude for their contributions.

Managing

Keeping track of the details, knowing when school registration is required, remembering to buy diapers, knowing what to put in a child's backpack for school: these describe the mental work of the household, which is still largely the province of women in about half of the equal families. Arnaldur (Iceland) refers to his wife as "the foreman." Patty (USA) calls herself "the project manager." Nera (Croatia) claims she does the management because she is more skilled, but adds, "I don't like leaving things to coincidence . . . I surely manage aspects of parenting – who will do what." Miki (Hungary) describes the dynamic between him and Mia, "She is the one . . . who does things with a far view, while I give my energy and knowledge towards realizing them." Unlike in many families where the work of management is invisible, however, the equally sharing fathers recognize the work their wives are doing. Miki, in fact, asserts, "I think that planning is a lot of work. In my profession it is also the case that the planning is a much more difficult and serious thing than the execution."

Moreover, at least a few of the equally sharing men take on aspects of the mental work of parenting. For example, Dale (UK) takes care of dentist appointments, and makes sure the children get haircuts. João (Brazil) does the clothes-buying for his son when he is abroad, and supervises the maid. Luka (Montenegro) initiates a trip to the mall when he sees that his children need clothes, decides when his children need to see the doctor, and makes the appointments. Arnaldur (Iceland) is upset about his own lack of awareness of the many details of family life that Hildur manages, from noticing the need to baby-proof the house to keeping track of school meetings. He is trying to do better by taking responsibility for some of these non-routine tasks without being asked, "It is humiliating not to have everything under control and to be the stupid father."

Management is the final frontier for couples aspiring to equality because the core prescription in the traditional image of motherhood is that "mothers are responsible for childcare." Thus, it is easier for couples to share the day-to-day hands-on aspects of parenting than the overall mental and emotional responsibility and control. Although most of the couples in the book do not maintain a manager–helper division, they have not always freed themselves fully from those core expectations.

Gatekeeping

Veronica (USA) couldn't quite let Sam take over responsibility for night feedings when her children were infants. She had to wake up, too, to see what was going on. Moreover, she clearly had the prerogative to stay home with children while he was employed. She admits that she couldn't have handled the reverse. Li Li (China) reserves certain household tasks for herself, such as washing her daughter's clothes, because she does not trust anyone else to do it, including her husband, her mother-in-law, and her paid household help. Tomaž (Slovenia) reports that Petra gives him instruction on how to give medicine when he is home with their sick child, despite his knowing exactly what to do without her help.

A few of the mothers struggle to restrain themselves from gatekeeping, particularly when they believe they can do a task better than their husbands can. Elisabet (Sweden) admits that despite her profound belief in equality, she sometimes has to fight with herself to avoid gatekeeping. Especially with regard to housework, it is sometimes difficult for her to let go, "I really have to work with myself and say, 'It's his responsibility, but it's not the same way that you like to do the dishes or ... exactly the way you like it clean.' So it's been working with myself too." Likewise, Hildur reports that she has to stifle her desire to correct Arnaldur when he is carrying out a domestic task.

Sharing Primary Parenting

When fathers and mothers share parenting, mothers sometimes have to contend with young children showing a preference for their fathers. Most of the mothers were sanguine about their children's attachments going back and forth between them, or with one child being more attached to their husbands, while the other was more attached to them. However, in a few cases, the pain of not being chosen was difficult to bear. Tuti (Indonesia) cried when her older son wanted his father to put him to sleep because she could not imitate animal sounds the way he could. Katherine (UK) was crushed when she returned from a business trip and her younger son, who had previously run to her when picked up from childcare, ran, like his older brother, to Dale, her husband. She mused, "They both prefer their daddy, there's something slightly wrong with me as a mother." Despite sharing, some mothers have not relinquished the idea that they should be number one in their children's eyes.

Even when attachment isn't an issue, it can be hard for some mothers to share the "maternal role." Inês (Portugal) playfully fought with Pedro over who would be the first parent to feed soup to the baby. But for Denisa (Czech Republic), being usurped wasn't funny. She was stunned when her husband was able to fully take over infant care when she went back to her job. She was not prepared and was deeply hurt to be shunted aside when he rushed to soothe their crying baby.

Protecting Men's Egos

A few of the women worried about whether their husbands will be damaged by not living up to hegemonic masculinity. Mia (Hungary), for example, insists that her husband, Miki, is the breadwinner, despite making more money than he. They maintained this fiction by earmarking his income for their ongoing expenses while saving her income. She explicitly says that it allows him to retain the feeling of being the breadwinner, although he states clearly in his interview that she is the "main breadwinner." (Perhaps it is she who cares that he retain the role of breadwinner.) Mia's protective behavior parallels the strategies of Ukrainian wives whose husbands can't make enough money to support their families. Wives gender the money by using their husband's money for rent or objects in their houses, such as TVs, while using their own incomes for consumables, thus rendering their money more invisible and bolstering the idea of the husband as a breadwinner (Anderson, 2017).

Hande (Turkey) is not worried about her superior income. She worries about the disproportionate share of housework that Burak has taken on. She frets that he is becoming a "housewife," and she fears that one day he will rebel. She's caught between her worries and her fatigue. She feels guilty when he seems to be doing too much, but she also says, "I don't want to kill myself just so he doesn't feel bad either."

Expecting Gratitude or Deference

Sometimes when men share the work, they feel that they deserve special credit. Deep down they may retain the gendered belief that domestic work is really their wives' responsibility. Tshewang (Bhutan) admits that if his wife criticizes him, he thinks it is unjust because he is doing so much more than other men when it is not even his responsibility. Likewise, Luka (Montenegro) sometimes complains about Maja's demands by invoking the praise he receives, "Everybody says that I am an ideal of a father and husband!" Katherine (UK) thinks that Dale expects excessive gratitude for his contributions to keeping the house tidy. She jokes that she is going to start announcing that she's hung the laundry up to match his thanks-eliciting announcements that he has tidied up a room.

Ironically, Robinson (Honduras), who presents himself as a modern feminist man, also somewhat condescendingly sees himself as Angelica's teacher. He recounts how he has informed her about equality between men and women, and has instructed her about care of the children. He does share family work equally, but seems to adopt a position of superior authority over his wife.

Undoing Gender Revisited

Undoing gender is a messy, ongoing process; equality has to be created anew every day. Despite some backsliding, the equal sharers forge ahead in this new world by daily small acts and their accompanying emotions. Masculinity and femininity become irrelevant when women act more like men and men more like women. Instead, both embrace selves that value achievement and care, the fully human selves that Freud himself invoked when he claimed that love and work were the two necessary ingredients for a psychologically healthy life (Erikson, 1950).

References

Allen, S. M. & Hawkins, A. J. (1999). Maternal Gatekeeping: Mothers Beliefs and Behaviors that Inhibit Greater Father Involvement in Family Work. *Journal of Marriage and the Family*, 61(1), 199–212.

Altintas, E. & Sullivan, O. (2017). Trends in Fathers' Contribution to Housework and Childcare under Different Welfare Policy Regimes. *Social Politics: International Studies in Gender, State & Society*, 24(1), 81–108.

Anderson, N. (2017). To Provide and Protect: Gendering Money in Ukrainian Households, *Gender and Society*, 31(3), 359–382.

Bielby, W. T. & Bielby, D. D. (1992). I Will Follow Him: Family Ties, Gender-Role Beliefs, and Reluctance to Relocate for a Better Job. *American Journal of Sociology*, 97(5), 1241–1267.

Bittman, M., England, L., Sayer, L., Folbre, N., & Mateson, G. (2003). When Does Gender Trump Money? Bargaining and Time in Household Work. *American Journal of Sociology*, 109(1), 186–214.

Craig, L. & Mullan, K. (2011). How Mothers and Fathers Share Childcare: A Cross-National Time-Use Comparison, *American Sociological Review*, 76(6), 834–861.

Deutsch, F. M. (1999). *Halving It All: How Equally Shared Parenting Works*. Cambridge, MA: Harvard University Press.

Duvander, A.-Z. & Haas, L. (2018). Sweden Country Note. In S. Blum, A. Koslowski, A. Macht, & P. Moss (eds.) *International Review of*

Leave Policies and Research (pp. 401–410). Retrieved from: www.leave network.org/fileadmin/user_upload/k_leavenetwork/country_notes/2018/FINAL .Sweden2018.pdf.

Elliot, K. (2016). Caring Masculinities: Theorizing an Emerging Concept. *Men and Masculinities, 19*(3), 240–259.

Erikson, E. H. (1950). *Childhood and Society*. New York: Norton.

Gaunt, R. (2008). Maternal Gatekeeping: Antecedents and Consequences. *Journal of Family Issues, 29*(3), 373–395.

Gíslason, I. V. (2017). Fathers on Leave Alone in Iceland: Normal Paternal Behavior? In M. Obrien & K. Wall (eds.) *Comparative Perspectives on Work-Life Balance and Gender Equality: Fathers on Leave Alone* (pp. 147–166). Retrieved from: https://link.springer.com/book/10.1007%2F978-3-319-42970-0.

Han, S-K. & Moen, P. (1999). Work and Family Over Time: A Life Course Approach. *The Annals of the American Academy of Political and Social Science, 562*, 98–110.

Shauman, K. A. (2010). Asymmetry in Family Migration: Occupational Inequality or Interspousal Comparative Advantage? *Journal of Marriage and Family, 72*(2), 375–392.

Walzer, S. (1996). Thinking About the Baby: Gender and Divisions of Infant Care. *Social Problems, 43*(2), 219–234.

27

Conclusion: The Paths to Equality

Francine M. Deutsch, Ruth A. Gaunt, and
Madison E. Richards

By their everyday decisions and actions, the equal sharers routinely defy social norms and resist conventional motherhood and fatherhood to create truly revolutionary families. Despite some flaws, they have dramatically transformed family life.

In this concluding chapter, we will consider why the equal sharers are able to resist. First, we will recount the kinds of pressures that push people toward conformity with gendered norms and propose some personality factors that enable or even promote nonconformity. Then we will review the key convictions held by equal sharers that facilitate their equality: feminism, anti-essentialism, familism, and anti-materialism. We will examine the diverse influences of their families of origin on the development of those ideas and their corresponding behaviors. In addition, we will consider government policies as facilitators of equal sharing. In the final section of the chapter, we review the rewards of equal sharing, which span the globe.

Notably, just as we highlighted in the organization of the chapters, the behaviors, attitudes, personality traits, and experiences that facilitate equality are quite similar across diverse cultures. They all operate around the world, regardless of the overall egalitarianism of a country.

Bucking the Tide

Equal sharers are nonconformists. Numerous studies have documented the power of social norms and the ubiquity of conformity. People conform because norms provide information about the "right" way to live, because violating those norms elicits social sanctions, and because conforming to a group's norms reaffirms identity. In short, "accuracy, affiliation, and maintenance of a positive self-concept were the functions of conformity" (Cialdini & Goldstein, 2004, p. 23). The puzzle we seek to solve is how equal sharers come to resist the norms surrounding them.

Their Social World

Gendered Models Prevail

Virtually all of the equal sharers live in a social world where inequality is the norm. Even in the most egalitarian countries, peers who paid only lip service to gender equality were often models. In "egalitarian" Iceland, for example, Hildur says, "We hardly know any couple that divides equally ... even though our friends are similar in education and political views." Nera (Croatia) avows that Ivo does "considerably more than other fathers ... I look at other couples around us and they are just like my dad. The husband who earns a lot of money and the wife who takes care of everything in the household." Miki (Hungary) reports, "I rather see the more traditional family model is more dominant, where the father is the breadwinner, works a lot, and when he's at home then he's resting and tired ... it's the mother who ... is responsible for raising the child." Katherine (UK) is "surprised by how many people have fallen, have gone down the kind of more traditional route where the bloke works the long hours and then the woman doesn't work." And when asked whether the younger generation might be different, Felipe (USA) demurred, "They come and the women have to warm up the food for the husband, 'I want my plate,' and the men sit down and the women get up at 5:00 a.m. to make their breakfast." Angelica (Honduras) bemoans that the problem still exists even when women are employed, "When a woman comes home she has to cook, she has to do the laundry, take care of the children while he sits around watching TV and reading the newspaper."

Five of the fathers who spend time with their children during weekdays conveyed that they are often the only men on the scene. João (Brazil) recounts, "Once I took Davi to a birthday party and I was the only father there. There were eight mothers with children and I was the only father." David (Czech Republic) recalls that when he was home on leave and he went out with the stroller, he only met mothers. Likewise, on Dale's (UK) day home with his children, he goes to a parent drop-in center where he is the only man. Nick (USA) says he's "one of the only guys who does playdates when we go to the playground during the day."

Of course, at least in some social worlds, there have been changes in fathers' roles. Ivo (Croatia) claims, "All of my friends who had children at about the same time were and still are very caring fathers who are involved in their children's lives … I doubt if any one of them would label this a woman's job." Hande (Turkey) says that in their social circle she sees men and women, for example, taking turns going to school meetings. Magda (Czech Republic) acknowledges, "Our model is a little bit different from the one that normally dominates but … the new generation is beginning to see things the way we do … When I see these young dads, they are much more involved than 20 years ago. Back then men weren't pushing prams."

But pushing prams on the weekends is far from equal sharing. Often equality is honored more in theory than in practice. Petra (Slovenia) explains:

> There are families like ours, but I think it is not a standard … In a conversation everybody speaks enthusiastically about equality … but I see it is not always like that … Sometimes I hear unimaginable things. For example, she [a girlfriend] has to make lunch every day and he gets angry if she doesn't.

In Iceland, Arnaldur reports that men now feel they have to justify unequal arrangements. The rhetoric of choice prevails, pinning inequality on their wives' desire to be home with children (Stone, 2007).

Some of the men tout new norms in paternal caring, but their caveats often belie the implication that other fathers are as involved in parenting as they are. For example, Mikael asserts, "A lot of people think the way we do in Sweden." He says his taking parental leave is "kind of normal," but then adds, "it's more normal for the mother to stay home, of course." Likewise, Dale (UK) reports that some of his "self-selected" friends are more hands-on than average, but then admits that none of them have reduced their paid work hours for childcare, and describes the "displacement activities," such as building something for their kids, that these "active" dads often substitute for interacting with them. "They are desperate to do something for the children, but they are not quite as keen to do the, 'Come on, we'll sit down and read a book; we'll play a game; you can jump on my back.'"

The equal sharers do sometimes mention friends who are similar to them. Netta (Israel) confesses that there are other egalitarian examples, but she points out that they are the exceptions, "There are lots of men who avoid doing diapering and dressing. I think that most men avoid taking the responsibility: they wait to be given tasks to do."

Judged by Gendered Norms

Whether one does gender or undoes it, one is accountable to gendered norms. People in one's social world observe and judge behavior with respect to those norms, and often react to them. To undo gender often means to disregard the judgments of friends, family, and co-workers. In a changing world sometimes the reactions are contradictory. David's (Czech Republic) decision to take parental leave was met with comments like, "We admire you! [But] why are you doing this?"

The equal sharers do get praise from some quarters, especially from women in their generation. Usually, however, it is the husbands who get praised. Ivo (Croatia) says, "All of Nera's girlfriends called me Mom [laughing] ... because it was a great idea and a good example for all of their husbands." Likewise, Dale (UK) reports, "Typically, the mothers will give you quite a thumbs up," but he is embarrassed when they hold him up as an example to their husbands. Compliments about the men are often directed to the wives. Magda (Czech Republic) remarks, "My acquaintances and friends always envied me that I have the kind of husband who helps out, so I was always proud." Angelica (Honduras) recounts, "The women congratulate us; they tell me, 'I wish I could have a husband like yours.'" However, this so-called praise is double-edged. It often comes with the implicit or explicit message that the women should be excessively grateful. Xochitl's (USA) peers tell her, "If I had a person who would help me like that, I would kiss his feet." Likewise, Maja (Montenegro) says, "I often hear that Luka is very good to me and that he is a very good father, a very good husband, and I should be grateful for that." That kind of praise can undermine equality, as evidenced when Luka invokes it to resist Maja's demands. Netta (Israel) has a humorous counter to peers' surprise about Gadi's involvement. "People always used to tell me, 'What? He helps you?' and I said, 'No way, he doesn't help me; I help him.'" Praise for men reveals a double standard that can undermine equality. Tomaž (Slovenia) receives kudos from his female colleagues for being a caring father when he takes time off to care for a sick child, but at Petra's workplace, the response is more likely to be, "Again, what's wrong this time?" Acknowledging the unfairness of double standards, Arnaldur (Iceland) is irritated by the compliments he receives for doing what he sees as "normal," when he knows that, at the same time, women are getting criticized for going back to their jobs when their child is 6 months old.

Eighteen of the couples report outright criticism for their family arrangements. Women whose husbands are taking care of the children when they go back to their jobs often suffer the criticism that they are not good mothers. Nera's (Croatia) mother tried to persuade her to stay home longer, "If you need money, I will help you. Why do you have to go to work so early? Why don't you stay at home?" Nera was particularly upset by the doctor who questioned her decision to go to back to work. "I wasn't leaving her with a stranger on the street or with a homeless person. I left her with her father." She cites the skepticism of the older generation about her husband's suitability for childcare, "What? Does he breastfeed as well?"

But it is not just the older generation that is critical. Because Inês (Portugal) shares childcare with Pedro, a friend tells her, "You don't know what it is to be a mother." Patty (USA) complains that she hears a lot of, "I chose not to have a career. And you should stay home with your kids." Hildur (Iceland) reports, "I have often been asked if I think it is okay to work these long hours away from my children and things like that; he gets fewer of those kinds of questions. It is like he shouldn't feel guilty, I should feel guilty." At her job, Denisa (Czech Republic) sometimes can't win. She is viewed critically by co-workers for leaving her child, but at the same time is suspect for having priorities other than work.

The equally sharing men get derisive messages from other men implying that they have been emasculated. Bhutanese Tshewang says, "My relatives would tell me not to be this way, that it will lessen my authority and luck (*wangten* and *lungten*), that other people will talk and make fun." Nera (Croatia) reports, "He's a henpecked person to his friends." Hannes (Germany) hears, "I would never have let my wife order me into staying home." Felipe (USA) believed that his friends talked behind his back, "She treats him like a *mandilón*." Sometimes when men deny that they are criticized, their descriptions reveal that masculinity is at issue. Arnaldur (Iceland), for example, claims that he is not criticized because he is "not a feminine man." Playing football insulates him from the charge that his domestic labor compromises his masculinity. Tomaž (Slovenia) insists that childcare tasks are no longer a threat to masculinity, "no more, be a man." Ironically, he recounts, "You go out with a stroller; you do things that used to be 'women's things' and you don't care if your friends tease you." If friends still "tease," gender is still an issue.

Several women were criticized or warned about their treatment of their husbands. Xochitl (USA) was told by her mother and sisters that she "should stop being so demanding" or she will end up divorced. Likewise, Denisa's (Czech Republic) mother warned her that she could lose her husband if she didn't do more of the care. Burak's (Turkey) sisters were outraged by Hande and Burak's division of household labor, "My sisters think I am being used." Hande's own mother tells her, "You are using this man; you are leaving it all on him." The sisters' outrage is barely concealed envy, "Our men never valued us this much."

Some of the most problematic negative reactions were elicited when men tried to take advantage of government policies to which they are entitled. Recall that when David (Czech Republic) announced he was taking parental leave, Denisa said, "They gazed at him like he was mad." He was threatened with the loss of his job. Arnaldur (Iceland) described his American boss's displeasure with the Icelandic rights of parents when he announced his intention to take parental leave. And Dale's boss in the UK dragged his feet on his request as a public employee to reduce his hours. Osman's (Singapore) supervisor gave him a hard time when he took a day off to take care of a sick child.

David took the leave anyway and didn't lose his job. Arnaldur negotiated a part-time leave for twice as long that enabled him to work from home while he cared for his baby daughter. Dale outlasted his boss's foot-dragging. And Osman said that if taking sick leave would cost him a future promotion, so be it.

Why They Resist

How are equal sharers able to resist the social pressure to organize life around gendered norms? Several factors may fortify the equal sharers to enable them to avoid conforming to gendered norms. Personality and identity, unconventional convictions, influences from families of origin, and egalitarian government policies all promote egalitarian families.

Personality and Identity

First, previous research suggests that conformity is more likely in individuals who lack self-confidence, feel insecure about their identities, or have low self-esteem (Gelfand & Harrington, 2015; Morris & Liu, 2015). Conversely, people are less likely to conform to social norms and more likely to stick to their values when they are focused on sources of self-esteem that are tied to one's intrinsic worth as a person, rather than on achievement-based self-esteem, or on the evaluations of others (Arndt et al., 2002). The equally sharing couples we studied were confident enough to follow their own beliefs and values regardless of social approval. The men's identities were not caught up in their career success or income, and the women's identities were not limited to motherhood. While mothers' low self-esteem has been shown to correlate with maternal gatekeeping (Gaunt, 2008), the equally sharing mothers had alternative sources of esteem which enabled them to relinquish having an exclusive primary care role with their children.

Second, social norms only elicit conformity when the group adhering to and advocating those norms is relevant and important (Nolan et al., 2008). Many of the equal sharers laugh off criticism from the older generation whose ideas seem outdated to them. A number of them allude to conservative people who might be critical, but distinguish them from close friends who are not. In fact, the equal sharers are sometimes in social circles in which equality is an aspirational norm, even if it is not a descriptive norm. Petra (Slovenia), for example, mentions that people in her circle talk enthusiastically about equality even if they fail to live up to it.

In two cases, parents intentionally construct a social world that would support their choices about equal sharing. Breaking old ties or creating new ones can be useful for developing a desired identity (Dingle et al., 2015). Joanne (Australia) says that they have dropped some of their old friends. Having given up income to spend more time with their children, Joanne is critical of the old group, which she sees as more materialistic. Li Li (China) says that when she chooses a group of mothers to hang out with, she picks those whose husbands are involved so it will seem "normal" to her husband. "I want our friends to have a positive impact on my family." In a few cases, the equal sharers might imagine approving reference groups, who might not be physically present but nonetheless serve as a source of implicit affirmation. For example, Tshewang (Bhutan) presumably imagines the approval of "modern" people for his involvement in domestic labor, even if they are non-existent in his life. Although speculative, one could also argue that affirmation from spouses may help inoculate equally sharing husbands and wives from criticism from sources outside their family.

Finally, some scholars have argued that people have a need for distinctiveness as well as similarity within a group (Hornsey & Jetten, 2004). This need for uniqueness may vary among individuals and may motivate some of the equal sharers (Snyder & Fromkin, 1977). For example, Ivo (Croatia) said, "I never lived according to what others do. On the contrary, I always liked doing what others don't do, this was always more appealing to me than fitting in with others, this doesn't bother me. I don't have a problem with socializing with mothers at children's birthday parties." Richard (Austria) practically revels in his role as the rare father among mothers, "Standing out, yeah, being someone special in society, I like that ... the kids are playing, you're drinking coffee, the moms and I or sometimes eight moms and two dads ... And I like that, the fact that it's unusual, that I'm doing something unusual."

Unconventional Convictions

The values themselves, of course, matter. Equal sharers held strong convictions about feminism, anti-essentialism, familism, and anti-materialism. Each of these will be discussed in turn.

Feminism and Nontraditional Gender Ideology

One of the key theories of the division of domestic labor is that nontraditional gender ideologies predict more egalitarian family work arrangements. The interviews for the research did not explicitly ask participants if they were feminists or if they held nontraditional gender ideologies, but those sentiments did come up explicitly in a number of the interviews. In addition, women's insistence on being treated as an equal partner reveals their implicit nontraditional ideologies, even if they never use the word "feminist."

Explicit Feminist Principles

When asked why she and her husband shared domestic labor, Maja (Montenegro) proclaimed, "because I am one loudmouthed feminist!" Elisabet (Sweden) also describes herself as a feminist, having discovered gender analysis at university that reflected her intuitive feelings about the unfair position of women. She says that equality is not just "a nice word" to them, that they try to put it into practice, "but it takes a lot of hard work." She describes Mikael as a feminist as well, and reports that they cooperate to give their children a nonsexist upbringing, although perhaps she would go further than he by allowing their boys to wear dresses to school. David's (Czech Republic) feminism went so far as to challenge his wife's prerogative to take exclusive advantage of parental leave. Ivo (Croatia) scoffs at traditional roles, and claims he knows no one in his generation who adheres to those roles. A man who would marry someone to clean up after him "sounds like characters from a bad novel." Gadi (Israel) explicitly says he opposes "the idea that just because you are a man or a woman, you are imprisoned in a specific role." Tomaž (Slovenia) and Petra's feminism is evident beyond their sharing of household labor. They gave their children different surnames: their son has hers, their daughter his. Tomaž has been an advocate for girls at the school where he teaches, fighting against other teachers when they exonerate boys for violent and harassing behavior toward girls by blaming the girls for wearing "too short skirts." He vehemently opposed their solution of educating girls about how to dress. Robinson (Honduras) endorses gender equality that includes the family but extends beyond it, "An equal relationship means to also respect women as they deserve in all places and under all circumstances, it can be at home, at work, or on the street."

The two Latinx men disdained *machismo* attitudes and saw their rebellion against them as providing important lessons for their children. Their attitudes are reflected in their child-rearing as well as in the roles they adopt. Robinson (Honduras) and Angelica, for example, insist that household chores, like sweeping, washing dishes, and laundry, will be done by both their daughter and sons. Robinson does not try to discourage his son from trotting around in his mother's high heels because he doesn't want to give him the wrong message about gender. Felipe (USA) encourages his daughters' interests in so-called "male" chores. Both of them hope their models will discourage their daughters from marrying *machistas*.

Interestingly, in two of the developing countries (i.e., Honduras and Bhutan), the men touted gender egalitarian ideas as a sign of their modern and educated attitudes. Robinson (Honduras) spoke at length about his feminist ideas with the academic language he learned when he was a research assistant at university:

> Social development cannot be accomplished [with] ... a patriarchal ideology in which the man has to be the breadwinner and the woman ... doing all the housework, so even though the woman is indirectly working more than the man, but who controls the goods in the house from a patriarchal ideology is only the man ... a very unequal justice, the relationships are abysmal, man at the top and woman at the bottom.

Tshewang (Bhutan) struggles trying to live up to what he sees as "modern western" values that reflect his education. He preaches about egalitarian values to his peers, which means he has to abide by them himself even when he doesn't really want to. "Given the choice," he says, "ideally I think to have the wife/mother at home while the husband is earning would be best for child-rearing." But he acknowledges, "Of course it's not good to have it like before because that would be gender exploitation."

Entitlement and Communication

Believing in equality is not enough. The equally sharing women don't just hold egalitarian principles silently, they feel entitled to equality, and insist on it. Nera (Croatia) thinks it is outrageous that anyone would believe that anything other than equality is reasonable. When reporting that Ivo took on all childcare tasks from the time their daughter was born, she asked, "How is this special? If we are both a mom and dad, how can he not do these things?" Likewise, Mia (Hungary) is flabbergasted when she observes the inequality in other families, "I didn't have a child so my partner can play for hours on the computer." When Xochitl (USA) and Felipe were guests at a cousin's house, she refused to go in the kitchen and help his wife. She protests, "Why didn't he help his wife? Because if my husband and I are guests ... Why didn't he help his wife to cook, instead humiliating my husband or me?"

For a number of the women, shared childcare and housework was a bottom line in marriage. Maja (Montenegro) claims that she didn't change her husband; she simply couldn't have married someone who wasn't like him. "While we were still dating, I saw that I could have fair relationship and fair life with this man." Hildur (Iceland) was divorced and was resigned to remaining single until she met Arnaldur, "I had decided I couldn't be in love with a man that expects that I should do a lot more than he, and clean up after him." Petra (Slovenia) explains that she and Tomaž would not be together if he didn't share. Hande (Turkey) emphatically asserted that she would never do more housework than a husband, "I can never establish that kind of marriage or relationship. I am always serving a man, everywhere is clean, magnificent house, food is being prepared, dishes ... that can't happen." Even when she was employed part-time at home and Burak was employed full-time, she waited for him to come home so they could do all the housework together.

Equally sharing women speak directly to their husbands about what they expect in marriage, often even before they are married. When Pedro (Portugal) and Inês moved in together, he had to mend his slovenly ways to meet her standards. She was not shy about stating them, and noted that he completely transformed himself, "When I got home and there was a sock lying about and I would say to him, 'Where do you think you are?' It was fast; he quickly stopped it." Maja (Montenegro) and Netta (Israel) made clear to their husbands that being a helper was not good enough. They wanted their husbands to share responsibility. Netta said to Gadi, "Listen, this house is not just mine, it's ours. The chore is not mine and the responsibility is not mine, it's also yours. Look around and take responsibility whenever you see something that needs to be done." And so it was.

Likewise, although Maja claims not to have changed her husband, she also reports:

> I remember telling him often, at the beginning of our relationship, that he shouldn't wait for somebody to clean the kitchen, but he should do that himself ... He sometimes used to say: "Maja, please, tell me what to do," and I would reply, "Why should I tell you when you know it yourself, it's the same household?"

Although Maja proclaims herself a feminist, Luka disavows feminism as a reason for his sharing. He describes himself as "just flexible." If she had wanted to have traditional roles he would have gone along with that as well. Her clear demands were key to their sharing.

Certainly, the women did not always prevail and had to make compromises, but many talked about the importance of communication in making their relationship work. Patty (USA) convinced Nick to do more housework when he was home with the kids so they would have more family time when they were all together, but he pushed back and got her to let up on her perfectionism. Veronica (USA) admitted that sometimes when she thought she was doing more than her husband, she was convinced after talking with him that she wasn't. Hildur (Iceland) learned some clear and effective ways of communicating with her husband rather than just criticizing him.

> I have started to say, "I have one project that I would like you to finish today that is the laundry, but you can also do it tomorrow." These are my expectations ... then he does it, but if I start with something like, "What is the laundry still doing here?" ... it isn't very popular.

Although housework was more likely to be a point of conflict and negotiation than childcare among these families, most of the women went into marriage expecting to share childcare. Dale (UK) attributes their equal sharing to his wife, "Katherine has always been very firm on the equality thing and quite rightly." He jokes that before they had kids she asked, "Are you going to be a bit of a hands-on dad?" He corrected himself, "Ehm, actually, it might have been just a statement, 'You're going to be a bit of a hands-on dad!'" Elisabet (Sweden) reported, "We have really talked about the ground values and the way we wanted to become parents and the way we wanted to live together." She was ambivalent about having children at all, having seen the traditional traps her friends had fallen into, but was reassured talking to Mikael when he told her he wanted to divide parental leave equally. She describes that as a "precondition" for her having had a child. Tuti (Indonesia) was concerned that her mother-in-law's involvement in childcare would undermine her authority. By using *musyawarah*, a Javanese method of airing all viewpoints, they came to a consensus. Together, they decided to hire a nanny[1] and invite Budi's mother to assist in childcare only occasionally rather than on a routine basis.

Siti (Singapore) insists that she was not going to be the kind of wife that her mother was, that she was not going to obey and serve a husband, "I want to be in a partnership for companionship and not to be a maid." Ironically, however, despite the completely egalitarian division of labor between her and Osman, they are the couple who most strongly articulates traditional gender ideology. Osman claims that he is responsible for supporting the family financially; Siti, that she is responsible for cooking her husband's dinner. Yet in reality, she doesn't cook, and they share the breadwinning. They succumb to the "myth of traditionalism" (Quek & Knudson-Martin, 2006, p. 60). Although he says it is her decision to work outside the home, Osman admits that if she thought about quitting, he would try to persuade her that her job is necessary for their family. At the same time, he does not expect her to cook after a day at work. Their lives are structured by goals that supersede their stated gender ideology. A traditionally gendered family life simply doesn't fit in Singapore with the couple's similarity in education and career and their desire to have a comfortable lifestyle. Moreover, Siti's sense of entitlement to be treated as an equal is at odds with her stated ideology. Deep down, she is a feminist, even if she protests otherwise.

Anti-essentialism

Risman (2009) rightly argued that the rejection of essentialism is a key component in the undoing of gender. The equal sharers are distinguished from more traditional couples by their belief that men and women are equally capable of caring for children. Whereas many couples who ostensibly believe in gender equality are often stymied by the feeling that men are not as capable of nurturing as women, these equal sharers are largely

---

[1] Ironically, the use of nannies and domestic workers for housework by the equal sharers contributes to the gendered nature of society. It is women who typically do this low paid work. One could argue that equal sharers sometimes create equality by taking advantage of gender discrimination against poor women.

unfettered by those essentialist beliefs (Deutsch, 1999; Gaunt, 2006). All but one of the couples who were asked if men had less ability to care for children were convinced that men could caregive well as their wives. Netta (Israel) is adamant, "Why should they be less able to care for little babies? ... no, no way!" Likewise, Xochitl (USA) said, "No, I believe that has nothing to do [with it]. This is simply *machista* mentality." Nera (Croatia) debunks the importance of biological differences between the sexes:

> Men cannot give birth or breastfeed. These are things that are not important in child upbringing. People say that a child becomes attached to the mother, but I think that a man can hug and look after a child and can develop equally good connections with their child just like a mom or a grandmother.

Her husband, Ivo, is as confident as she in his anti-essentialist views, "I don't believe in those stories in which a mother possesses natural instincts and that as soon as she gives birth, she knows what to do. This is nonsense!" Patty (USA) was adamant in refuting sex differences in the ability to care as well, "Well, they can't nurse, but other than that, NO absolutely not." In Sweden, Elisabet reflected that the differences that existed were not inborn, but socialized. Thus, it may be easier for women because they were brought up to care, but that men have the same basic human ability.

Nonetheless, some of the men and women thought there were differences between the sexes but either they didn't matter or they could be overcome. Katherine (UK) thought that mothers had a special role in the first 6 months of a baby's life, but after that there was no difference. Mia (Hungary) believed that mothers had a special bond with newborns at first, based on pregnancy and childbirth, but that fathers could develop that bond as well.

For two of the dads, becoming an involved parent shaped their anti-essentialist views. Dale (UK) said:

> I think a lot of it is down to culture. If people tell you enough that "oh no, you are not good at this" or "they are naturally better at it," then you tend to fall into the trap of believing it ... Before having kids, you'd think maybe mums would naturally be better at comforting, but I don't think that's true.

Tomaž (Slovenia) began parenthood believing that women had intuitive knowledge about infant care, but his experience with a newborn quickly disabused him. "We both had to learn everything and at times we panicked, got hysterical, because we didn't know a thing and had to ask our doctor for every little problem."

Thus, anti-essentialist views were both a cause and a consequence of equal sharing. In unequal families, essentialist beliefs discourage paternal involvement, which, in turn, reduces fathers' opportunities to become skilled and able to soothe babies, convincing them erroneously that women do have innate skill (Deutsch, 1999). In contrast to this vicious circle, when couples believed that fathers were equally suited to parenting, they facilitated paternal involvement. Their involvement created a virtuous circle in which they became as skilled as their wives, thus reinforcing their anti-essentialist views.

Familism

Familism cuts across the stories of equal sharers from diverse countries.[2] The research literature on familism grew out of a focus on the cultural values held by Latinxs who endorse close ties to the nuclear and extended family that entail loyalty, obligation, care, and prioritizing the family above the self and other relationships (Lugo Steidel & Contreras, 2003). However, these beliefs are evident among members of other ethnic groups as well, including Anglo Americans, albeit if not as prevalent as among Latinx (Campos et al., 2014). For example, an American study showed that familism was associated with husbands' contributing a greater number and a greater proportion of housework hours in Anglo families (Pinto & Coltrane, 2009). Familism in most of the research literature is defined and measured with respect to extended families, but the familism expressed widely among the equal sharers refers to their nuclear families.

Family, or at least their nuclear family, is central in the lives of equal sharers. Familism is reflected in the significance equally sharing couples assign to family life. Martin (Czech Republic) says, "There's nothing more important in my life than family. I have other interests ... lots of them, but for me this comes first." His wife, Magda, describes him as a "kind of a domestic fowl." Mia (Hungary) said of Miki, "the family has become the first thing." Xochitl (USA) asserted, "We live only for the girls." And Budi (Indonesia) explains that his identity is rooted in family, "The most important thing is spending time together with the children. I am happy when I am with my family. That's who I am." Likewise, Kai Wang (China), who resists talking about the division of labor as a feminist issue, invokes familism instead, "I think there is no point in

---

[2] Familism, of course, is not exclusive to equal sharers, in the same way that nonconformity, for example, is not exclusive to them. The familism we describe here is ungendered. Likewise, anti-materialism, nonconformity, and even entitlement can have other gendered forms, but in the case of equal sharers, their ungendered forms promote equality.

emphasizing feminism here. ... I think the key point here is both the wife and the husband are doing as much as they can for the family."

Familism is also reflected in the couples' sense of connectedness and sense of solidarity, that as parents they are working together as a loving team. Tshewang (Bhutan) describes the change he experienced when he and Yangchen became parents, "I no longer thought of her and me as separate entities but rather as "we," as one entity. João (Brazil) said, "We are a team ... I devote myself to our common goal which is our family." Magda (Czech Republic) echoed, "We are a great team." Veronica (USA) reported, "We work together toward what we believe is important for the kids, like having dinner together." Inês (Portugal) recounted that before Manuel was born, she and Pedro did everything together. They still do, but now they include their son. Likewise, Gadi (Israel) expressed that their "ideal wish is to be together with the children."

In general, *Creating Equality at Home* demonstrates the ways in which similar processes characterize equal sharers' paths in diverse countries. Nonetheless, one difference among countries that affects these processes is the distinction between individualist and collectivist cultures. In particular, Indonesia and Singapore represent collectivist cultures in which individuals are generally oriented toward their interdependence with others and are taught to identify with the goals of the group rather than the self. As Quek and Knudson-Martin (2006, p. 56) have argued, collectivist values such as "we-consciousness" and "marrying one's equal" promote couples' equality in Singapore. When collectivism in traditional societies is practiced, typically each spouse works for the common good of the family in gendered ways. Paradoxically, when gender is undone, it may be easier for husband and wife to cooperate and share family work, having been socialized into collectivist rather than individualistic norms. Budi and Tuti (Indonesia) exemplify an easy cooperative spirit that pervades everything they do for the family. Budi uses the Bahasa Indonesia term, *gotong-royong* (i.e., teamwork or cooperation) to describe their approach to family work:

> We are here in this family together and we do things together, that's our principle ... We understand that we are both very busy persons and have lots of responsibilities outside the home as well, but we also know that we need to take care of the children well and maintain the family well. These are our common goals. So we just try to focus on reaching these goals together.

Anti-materialism

When parents are employed part-time, give up promotions, or lower their aspirations for advancement, their decisions entail a financial penalty. In fact, about half of the couples voluntarily reduced their incomes, suggesting an anti-materialist ethic was at work. For some that value was explicit. Mike (Australia) reports that their decision to both work part-time means giving up luxuries, like foreign travel. His wife, Joanne, is critical of other parents who choose money over time with their children, "They might live in a really nice house; they might have two nice cars, but your children are being outsourced." Judith (Switzerland) is also critical of overly materialistic lifestyles. She seems proud of their choices when she says that they own "half a car," don't own a TV, take short vacations, don't wear designer clothes, and eat from their own garden. Inês (Portugal) points out that when she and Pedro changed their schedules and relinquished overtime income, they gave up the equivalent of an entire salary. They decided that time with their son was more important to them than money. Likewise, Netta and Gadi (Israel) are unconcerned about their lower than average income, and would not trade time for more money. Netta explains, "Both of us are people who are not very much into money and not very much into our careers."

In contrast, for Siti and Osman (Singapore), the desire to have a comfortable middle-class lifestyle was a key part of the impetus for sharing. To achieve the Singaporean dream of the five Cs (cash, credit cards, condo, car, and country club), it is essential that both of them be employed. Given their traditional ideologies, Osman is especially grateful that Siti is sharing the load of breadwinning and thus does not expect her to cook, as would be her traditional role, and is more than willing to share housework and childcare.

The Influence of Families of Origin

Socialization theories of gender development offer a simple story that children become gendered adults through parental rewards for and messages about appropriate gendered behavior, and by copying same-sex parents as models who demonstrate appropriate gendered behavior. The inverse is also hypothesized. That is, if parental expectations for children are not gendered, and if the parents themselves are nontraditional, we would expect those children to be more likely to become nontraditional adults (Bussey & Bandura, 1999).

Much of the division of labor literature ignores childhood socialization. Cunningham (2001) did show that the division of labor in the family of origin when a child is 1 year old is related to the division of labor they realize at age 31. Sons are also more likely to do female-typed chores at age 18 to 19 while still living at home, if the parents had a more egalitarian division of labor when they were 8 to 11 years old (Cordero-Coma & Esping-Andersen, 2018). The mechanisms for these findings are unclear. Are these young adults modeling parents? Had their parents been more likely to assign chores to boys? In another study, boys whose fathers were more involved in domestic chores developed more egalitarian attitudes in childhood, and those childhood attitudes were related to their adult participation in housework, but it was unclear whether their non-traditional behavior was the result of directly modeling paternal chores, or indirectly through their internalization of egalitarian values (Platt & Polavieja, 2016). The stories of the equal sharers offer some clues about the importance of families of origin, but they also show that the effects of childhood socialization are not straightforward.

The Men
As might be predicted by social cognitive developmental theory (Bussey & Bandura, 1999), 10 of the men in the global study explicitly brought up their exposure to fathers who were not stereotypically masculine. David (Czech Republic) was the only equally sharing man whose father shared household labor equally with his mother. But Osman's (Singapore) father did housecleaning; Martin's (Czech Republic) dad washed dishes; and Arnaldur's (Iceland) father cooked and mopped. Gadi (Israel) recalled of his father, "He was permanently in charge of cleaning the house. He didn't work on Friday; he would stay home and clean the house." Robinson (Honduras) remembered that his father started cooking after his grandmother had taken him to task for expecting to be waited on. João (Brazil) said, "My father was not a macho man. He was a man who was always helping with housework, helped to educate his children ... things that have helped me as a father too, as being close to my child and not let it be only with the mother."

The men's fathers challenged hegemonic masculinity in other ways as well. Dale (UK) said of his father, "He was quite arty and you know he was never a sort of blokey bloke." Pedro (Portugal) praised his father's emotional availability, "maybe he never changed diapers, but he was there for me in other ways." Luka (Montenegro) disdained his own father who was not involved in the family in any way. Instead, he adopted Maja's father and grandfather as male role models because they cherished children and put family first.

Almost as many men, eight of them, described fathers who were either absent or served as anti-models for them. Mike's (Australia) parents were divorced when he was young so he didn't have a male role model, "I didn't think that Dads didn't do this stuff." Martin's (Switzerland) father was there but did not teach him to do family work, which he hopes to teach his sons. Nick (USA) was abandoned by his father after his parents' divorce. He attributes his role in the family to that experience and vows to be a different kind of father, "I would never take off from my kids like he did ... I'll always be around." Luka (Montenegro) also spoke with bitterness about his own father:

> House duties? Nothing, nothing, total disaster. It is not even like an archetype family. It was much more drastic ... He didn't have any kind of relationship with us ... So it is not only that he didn't participate in house chores, he barely participated in our life as a father. He was present, but like he wasn't.

Richard (Austria) said of the father whose sole contribution was to bring money home, and who "never got involved in raising children at all," "I couldn't learn anything from him, except how not to do it." Burak sarcastically denigrated how his father's breadwinning role was over-valued in the family, "Mom did everything ... he didn't do anything ... but it looked like he did everything [because] he did the holy breadwinning work." Repelled by the examples of their own fathers, these fathers embraced familism and a different kind of fatherhood.

The findings of both modeling and compensatory processes echo those in a study of two generations of Israeli kibbutz fathers. Second-generation fathers who had been close to their own fathers were more involved in hands-on care of children when their fathers had either been relatively involved or relatively uninvolved compared to other men (Gaunt & Bassi, 2012).

In about half of the families, men reported significant experience with housework and/or childcare growing up. Despite the emphasis in the socialization literature on same-sex models (Bussey & Bandura, 1984), mothers and sisters were very important influences on the equally sharing men. It was usually mothers who assigned their sons household chores and taught them the relevant skills. For example, growing up, Tomaž's (Slovenia) daily job was vacuuming, and his mother called him each afternoon to assign chores that would help get the dinner prepared. His mother had strict standards; if he didn't do a job correctly, he had to do it again. Robinson's (Honduras) mother taught him to cook, do laundry, and to iron explicitly so that he would be able to help his wife. Sam (USA) credits his three older sisters with getting him used to housework, "If they had to do it, I had to do it."

Although some studies suggest that boys do more chores when their fathers participate in domestic labor (Dotti Sani, 2016), many of the equal sharers' accounts were striking because fathers in their families were excused from household labor while they were not. For example, Budi's (Indonesia) father's job was simply to earn money. Budi, on the other hand, helped his mother by ironing his father's clothes, washing his own clothes, cooking, and going to the market with her. He also had experience helping to take care of babies as young as a month old.

Although the men talked about the importance of the skills they learned for preparing them for marriage and parenthood, perhaps at least as important was the message that these tasks did not have to be gendered. Felipe's mother taught him to change diapers, so now he says that, unlike his peers, changing diapers does not make him "feel like a woman." Moreover, the time they spent with their mothers as boys may have given them a look at a world that was not always fair to women. Felipe (USA), for example, was upset that his older brothers expected his overworked single mother to wake before dawn to make breakfast for them before they went to their jobs. Although Kai Wang (China) didn't do chores, he was alienated from an authoritarian father who did no domestic labor, and he sympathized with his mother who he thought did too much work.

Finally, mothers sometimes served as the models the men could not find in their fathers. Richard (Austria) reported that he learned the most about being a parent from his mother, "she filled kids with love, me too, and her grandchildren, yeah, and I saw how she did it, I remember a lot of it." Nera (Croatia) makes a similar point about her husband, Ivo, who grew up with his mother and grandmother after his father died. She mused that perhaps they were his role models, "Perhaps [from them] he soaked up that family, affectionate way of doing things."

The Women

Although most of the equally sharing women grew up in families where their mothers were employed but also did most of the domestic labor, six of the equally sharing women reported aspects of their parents' roles that defied gendered norms. Li Li's (China) mom was an only child who didn't like housework and shared it with Li Li's father. Hildur (Iceland) remembers her dad with a dishtowel. She never imagined that those jobs should be her mother's. Inês's (Portugal) father didn't share equally, but wasn't a "macho" male. Not only did he help her mother with housework and cooking, but she describes him as a "super-father," who, like her husband, Pedro, "did everything."

The equally sharing women were as likely to witness a traditional division of domestic labor in their parents as a division that challenged gender. Hande (Turkey), who was adamant that she would not do more housework than a husband, disapproved of the "asymmetrical" contributions of her parents who both worked outside the home. When they arrived home, her father lay on the couch, drank, and read the newspaper while her mother did everything else. Patty (USA) resented her father's expectation that her mother wait on him. She'd think, "Ma, doesn't that drive you nuts?"

Women asserted that their mothers' lives provided a cautionary tale for their own. As Nera (Croatia) said, "I doubt whether I could live with a partner that is like my father in terms of job and care division. I couldn't do that." Likewise, Petra (Slovenia) was clear about her rejection of her parents' lifestyle, "I can't live like this, like our mothers did … Even then I thought to myself, 'Why are they not equal?'"

Ironically, in a few of the patriarchal families, fathers encouraged their daughters to live a different kind of life. For example, Nera's (Croatia) father strongly encouraged her to get an education so her income would put her in an equal position to her future husband. "If you are a cleaner, and he has a Ph.D., you will be in a subordinate position," he warned her. Katherine's (UK) dad took her off on kayaking adventures, while her mother stayed home cleaning the house.

The Couples

The husbands' and wives' family backgrounds fit together in interesting ways to promote equality. For example, in China, Kai Wang's rejection of the model of his patriarchal family is complemented by Li Li's imitation of her parents' equality. In Indonesia, Budi grew up with a great deal of responsibility for household chores and childcare, while Tuti was not expected to do any household work as a daughter, but rather to concentrate on education. In fact, when she went to the university her parents would come to do her laundry and bring her food. Felipe and Xochitl both recounted the pain of their fathers' absence. She wanted a different kind of husband and he wanted to be a different kind of father.

Socialization Revisited

Although contemporaneous contextual factors are certainly important in couples' division of household labor, more research is needed to investigate how experiences in their families of origin inform their division of labor. Clearly, scholarship on socialization needs to take into account the multiple paths to egalitarian sharing, including how messages from an opposite-sex parent, judgment of parents' division of labor, and the complementary needs or experiences emerging from couples' backgrounds can promote equality. Moreover, parents' attitudes toward essentialism, familism, and materialism, and the ways they shape children's views and their adult lifestyles would also be a fruitful line of investigation.

Government Policy and its Limits

Mikael has taken full advantage of Sweden's generous parental and paternal leave policies, which entitle parents to take 16 months of paid leave, as long as each parent takes a minimum of 3 months. He and Elisabet use government subsidies for household help, which cuts down on arguments over housework. Fathers in eight countries (i.e., Austria, Czech Republic, Germany, Iceland, Portugal, Slovenia, Sweden, and the UK) have received government benefits that help them share childcare. Payment schemes matter. Even among the equal sharers in this study, Pedro (Portugal) took less parental leave than planned because it didn't make sense economically. Generally, in countries where reimbursements are higher, men are more likely to take parental leave (van Belle, 2016). There is no doubt that having time with their children, either as infants when they take leave, or as older children when they use benefits to reduce their time at their jobs, allows fathers to forge close relationships with their sons and daughters, and promotes equality between them and their wives. Certainly, the availability of time off for fathers, especially when it is earmarked specifically for them rather than mothers, is one way governments can promote gender equality (van Belle, 2016).

Two caveats are in order, however. First, men have to make the decision to use parental leave when it is available. Even in egalitarian Sweden, Mikael's taking more leave than Elisabet is highly unusual, and fewer than half of fathers take any of the shared leave. In the Czech Republic less than 5% of fathers share parental leave, and in Portugal, less than 20%. Regardless of the strength of the parental leave policy, the men in our study are in the minority (van Belle, 2016). Structure in the form of government policy is not determinative. It can help families who want equality, but they have to want it!

Second, a number of the men found ways to take time off to take care of children without the use of government benefits. Nick, in the notorious USA, which is one of the only countries in the world without a paid maternity leave policy (let alone a parental paid leave policy), spent several weeks of his first summer as a father at home figuring out baby care with his wife. He saved up and used vacation time to do so. Ivo (Croatia) was between jobs and decided to wait to find another job so he could take over for Nera when she went back to work. Mike (Australia) chose to be a "househusband" for a period when his first child was born without any government subsidy.

The Rewards of Equal Sharing

Women

It is easy to see how equal sharing benefits women. An equal partner at home gives women more freedom to pursue a career and succeed. The high-powered careers of Elisabet in Sweden, Hildur in Iceland, or Denisa in the Czech Republic might not survive a household where they were doing the majority of domestic labor. In each of those cases, equally sharing husbands took over part (or even the majority) of the parental leave, enabling the women to limit the interruptions that derail careers. Although only a few women had such high-status, lucrative jobs, any career is more easily managed with an equally sharing partner. Katherine (UK), for example, thought she was taken more seriously at her job when she went from 3 to 4 days, which was possible because of Dale's willingness to reduce to a 4-day week. A number of the women noted that their husbands' caregiving enabled them to go to work with peace of mind. Women who were unhappy at home with a newborn were able to return to their jobs when they wanted to without having to rely on paid care. Denisa (Czech Republic), for example, said, "It was easier for me as I knew my son spent time with his father and not with some third person." Moreover, Hanna (Germany) appreciates the freedom she has for leisure, unlike some of her peers, whose children cling to their mothers and cannot be soothed or put to bed by their fathers, "It isn't a problem if I go out in the evening ... We don't have anything like that." Likewise, Nera (Croatia) points out that when she goes out in the evening, Ivo can handle any problem that comes up with Ema and doesn't just call her if the child starts crying.

Sharing simply makes life less burdensome for women. Moreover, for some of the women, sharing housework was a sign of respect, a noteworthy indication that they were being treated as an equal. Hildur (Sweden) and Hande (Turkey) insisted that they were not going to "serve" husbands, Siti (Singapore) that she did not want to be a maid. Siti and Petra (Slovenia) put an unequal division of domestic labor in the same category as obedience to husbands, both of which characterized their parents' relationships. In contrast, they enjoyed the respect that reflects a relationship of equals.

Men

Men are big winners. These men wanted to have significant relationships with their children, more than what a typical father experiences. Mikael (Sweden) explained, "I wanted to be as big a part of their lives as she." He views the opportunity to share "a privilege ... something I want to do." Other fathers who took parental leave also extol their experience. Ivo (Croatia) recounts, "It was great because I was able to bond with her ... this was great for me." Pedro (Portugal) is similarly enthusiastic, "I think the most positive aspect was to interact with him for almost 24 hours a day."

The time they spend with their children is important to these men. Denisa (Czech Republic) says of her husband, David, "I can see he would do everything for him [their son, Cyril] ... His work does not satisfy him completely so ... to be with the son, it is of utmost importance." With a note of wonder, Felipe (USA) reports his children's memory of the time he taught them to make tuna burgers, "The children keep in their heads all their memories, so when they grow up they will get closer to the parents who dedicated more time to them." When Gadi (Israel) was asked why they didn't hire a nanny instead of having him care for Aya while on his postdoc, he replied, "I really enjoyed taking care of her; I didn't want to stop."

The equally sharing fathers know all too well how easy it would be to miss the experiences they are having with their children. Martin (Czech Republic), the father of four children, has always been an involved, hands-on father, but it wasn't until his 4-year-old twin boys were born that he organized his business schedule to have the time to share equally, "I'm glad that it worked out for me to be able to be with the boys more now. I wanted that." He complains that he didn't have enough time with his two older children, "It wasn't quite enough. So now, in my golden years, I'm enjoying time with my boys."

Equal sharing can boost men's self-esteem. As mentioned earlier, Richard (Austria) is proud that he is living an unusual life. João (Brazil) is proud when he hears his son say to his teacher, "I like my dad; my dad is cool!" Tshewang (Bhutan), who is criticized by peers, is also proud. His wife, Yangchen's, praise affirms and motivates him:

> I feel very satisfied, especially with myself, that I am able to contribute like this, and also that she acknowledges my contribution, not to me but to others ... This makes me realize that my contribution has an impact on her and it gives me a sense of satisfaction. So I feel more encouraged to continue this way.

You can hear the pride in Nick's (USA) voice when he describes how he learned to care for his infant son on his own. At first, he was terrified, "What am I going to do with this baby?" He just kept trying different things to find out what the baby liked. Now he thinks that maybe his son is a good reader because he introduced him to Baby Einstein tapes, "He really seemed to like that."

By undoing gender, men develop their capacity for care, and change the way they view themselves. João (Brazil) asserts that developing himself to be a better father has made him grow as a human being, that "the exercise of giving" to a child generalizes "to friends, to other family members, to people who sometimes are not even relatives, but acquaintances." Martin (Switzerland) has changed his attitude toward reproductive work, which he now sees as "precious work."

The biggest payoff for their involved fatherhood is the wonder and joy parenthood can bring:

RICHARD (Austria): I'm crazy about the kids and love the time I spend with them. It's a perfect fit ... I wouldn't have it any other way.

MIKI (Hungary): I look at my child and I am filled with happiness – beautiful, clever, and my child. I cannot believe it.

MARTIN (Switzerland): I am in relationship with growing up humans ... I watch them: how they feel joy, how they get angry about something, how they get stubborn, how they get attention, become loving. That is the benefit.

HANNES (Germany): It is simply a joy to play with the child and to see her grow up ... When the little girl laughs for the first time these are true experiences of success ... It's practically irreplaceable.

DAVID (Czech Republic): When you look at him, it is pure joy!

Children

The equal sharers believe that their children benefit from having two highly involved parents. Research, mainly on fathers, confirms that positive paternal involvement is beneficial to children's development (Wilson & Prior, 2011; Lamb & Lewis, 2013). Hana (Germany) speaks for all of them when she says, "Mama and Papa ... are equally there for her, and

I think that's good ... It would be a shame for the child if he didn't take the time." In the families that have chosen part-time employment or non-overlapping schedules, father care is deemed superior to paid care. Mike (Australia) explains their job schedules as an effort to keep their children out of "childcare" as much as possible. Couples also mention that shared caregiving means they can compensate for each other. Dale (UK) explains how Katherine takes over for him if he is getting a bit "shouty." David (Czech Republic) echoes that, "If one isn't in the mood, the other one can take over."

An advantage mentioned by a few of the equal sharers is providing nontraditional role models for their children. As mentioned earlier Felipe (USA) thinks that he is showing his daughters that they don't have to marry *machistas*. Robinson (Honduras) says, "As I share I am also transmitting that message to my children so they can also acquire those types of attitudes for when they get their own family." Elisabet (Sweden) and Christine (Austria) believe that it is good for their children to see a working mother who is happy, and to see their family's lifestyle as normal.

When Inês (Portugal) contemplates an ideal family for a child, she exclaims that it is her family, "Manuel's [her son's] family!" She thinks he is "lucky," with two loving hands-on parents, a comfortable lifestyle, loving aunts, uncles, and grandparents. "Nothing is missing," she declares.

Marriage

Equal sharing can promote marital happiness. Schober (2012), for example, found that when men had a greater share of childcare tasks, their wives perceived their marriage as higher quality. The husbands' marital satisfaction was greater the higher the absolute frequency of their involvement in childcare tasks. Sharing makes communication easier because husbands and wives can understand each other's experience. As Hanna (Germany) says,

> What's really good is that my husband knows what it means to be with the child the whole day ... If a father doesn't change the child's diaper ... I can't talk with a person like that about it. But ... he knows how it is if you come home and say, "Take the child, take the child, take the child!"

Likewise, Katherine (UK) reflects, "It's very easy not to appreciate how hard it is staying at home with children. ... With Dale having done it, he appreciates exactly what it involves, so there's no taking it for granted."

Overwhelmingly, these couples are happy with the lives they've created:

TOMAŽ (Slovenia): Equally frustrated, equally satisfied.
GADI (Israel): Very satisfied. It's a lot easier to do it as a couple.
MARTIN (Czech Republic): I'm definitely happy with it. It suits me.
NETTA (Israel): For us, it works like magic.
NICK (USA): 100% satisfied.
VERONICA (USA): I think we are doing quite well.

João (Brazil) articulates how their equality follows from the strength of their marriage:

> I believe that Cecília is my soul mate and she feels that I'm her soul mate so there is this feeling of complementarity, empathy, strong friendship. We know that neither of us is walking alone, that we are really a team and that our son is part of this team along with us too.

Mia (Hungary) muses that perhaps if more people shared family work, they would be happier. In fact, the more egalitarian a couple's division of housework and childcare, the more they have been found to display marital generosity, defined as "acts of kindness, forgiveness, and expressions of affection and respect" (Wilcox & Dew, 2016, p. 98), which is associated with marital happiness both for the bestower of generosity and the recipient (Dew & Bradford, 2013). Happy marriages also promote egalitarianism (Schober, 2012). In fact, Miki (Hungary) reports that he and Mia did not have an explicit agreement to share 50/50, that it grew out of their desire to make their relationship work. The satisfaction and happiness the equal sharers express may reflect their eudaimonic approach to life, which focuses not directly on obtaining happiness but rather on the process of "living a complete human life, or the realization of valued human potentials" (Ryan, Huta, & Deci, 2008, p. 140).

Final Thoughts

The domestic labor literature is replete with studies that demonstrate that women bear a disproportionate burden of housework and childcare. Even when progress is reported, the progress is slow and doesn't convince us that we will eventually reach equality. In this context, it seems important to shout that equality is possible. As men and women reject the mandates of stereotypical masculinity and femininity, they undo gender and create equally sharing families. Although support for equality varies across the world, many of the underlying factors that facilitate equality are universal: the willingness to re-imagine paid work and family roles, and the attitudes and experiences that underwrite those re-imaginings.

The lives of equal sharers argue that explanations of inequality that focus entirely on structure miss the importance of human agency. Of course structure matters. It is certainly easier for middle-class couples like Christine and Richard (Austria) to forego potential income and set up their work lives to support equality than it is for Felipe and Xochitl (USA), who barely earn minimum wage. Yet Felipe and Xochitl do share equally. It is not an accident that, on average, Swedish couples have a more equal division of household labor than Brazilian couples do. Nonetheless, Brazilian couples like João and Cecília can equally share. In undoing gender, they challenge the gendered beliefs of the people around them as well. It is difficult to argue that men are not capable of nurturing children when one observes a father like João.

Pete Seeger (1919–2014) was an American folksinger who worked for social justice his whole life in the labor, civil rights, anti-war, and environmental movements. His words inspire us: "The key to the future of the world is finding optimistic stories and letting them be known" (Pareles, 2014). *Creating Equality at Home* does exactly that.

References

Arndt J., Schimel J., Greenberg J., & Pyszczynski T. (2002). The Intrinsic Self and Defensiveness: Evidence that Activating the Intrinsic Self Reduces Self-Handicapping and Conformity. *Personality and Social Psychology Bulletin,* 28(5), 671–683.

Bussey, K. & Bandura, A. (1984). Influence of Gender Constancy and Social Power on Sex-Linked Modeling. *Journal of Personality and Social Psychology, 47(6),* 1292–1302.

Bussey, K. & Bandura, A. (1999). Social Cognitive Theory of Gender Development and Differentiation. *Psychological Review, 106(4),* 676–713.

Campos, B., Aguilera, A., Ullman, J. B., & Dunkel Schetter, C. (2014). Familism and Psychological Health: The Intervening Role of Closeness and Social Support. *Cultural Diversity and Ethnic Minority Psychology,* 20(2), 191–201.

Cialdini R. B. & Goldstein N. J. (2004). Social Influence: Compliance and Conformity. *Annual Review of Psychology, 55,* 591–621.

Cordero-Coma, J. & Esping-Andersen, G. (2018). The Intergenerational Transmission of Gender Roles: Children's Contribution to Housework in Germany. *Journal of Marriage and Family, 80(4),* 1005–1019.

Cunningham, M. (2001). Parental Influences on the Gendered Division of Housework. *American Sociological Review, 66(2),* 184–203.

Deutsch, F. M. (1999). *Halving It All: How Equally Shared Parenting Works*. Cambridge, MA: Harvard University Press.

Dew, J. & Bradford, W. W. (2013). Generosity and the Maintenance of Marital Quality. *Journal of Marriage and Family, 75*(5), 1218–1228.

Dingle, G. A., Stark, C., Cruwys, T., & Best, D. (2015). Breaking Good: Breaking Ties with Social Groups May Be Good for Recovery from Substance Misuse. *British Journal of Social Psychology, 54*(2), 236–254.

Dotti Sani, G. M. (2016). Undoing Gender in Housework? Participation in Domestic Chores by Italian Fathers and Children of Different Ages. *Sex Roles, 74* (9–10), 411–421.

Gaunt, R. (2006). Biological Essentialism, Gender Ideologies, and Role Attitudes: What Determines Parents' Involvement in Child Care. *Sex Roles, 55*(7), 523–533.

Gaunt, R. (2008). Maternal Gatekeeping Antecedents and Consequences. *Journal of Family Issues, 29*(3), 373–395.

Gaunt, R. & Bassi, L. (2012). Modeling and Compensatory Processes Underlying Involvement in Childcare Among Kibbutz-Reared Fathers. *Journal of Family Issues, 33*(6), 823–848.

Gelfand, M. J. & Harrington, J. R. (2015). The Motivational Force of Descriptive Norms: For Whom and When Are Descriptive Norms most Predictive of Behavior? *Journal of Cross-Cultural Psychology, 46*(10), 1273–1278.

Hornsey, M. J. & Jetten, J. (2004). The Individual within the Group: Balancing the Need to Belong with the Need to Be Different. *Personality and Social Psychology Review, 8*(3), 248–264.

Lamb, M. E. & Lewis, C. (2013). Father–Child Relationships. In N. J. Cabrera & C. S. Tamis-Lemonda (eds.), *Handbook of Father Involvement* (pp. 119–134). New York: Routledge.

Lugo Steidel, A. G. & Contreras, J. M. (2003). A New Familism Scale for Use with US Hispanics. *Journal of Behavioral Sciences, 25*(3), 312–330.

Morris, M. W. & Liu, Z. (2015). Psychological Functions of Subjective Norms: Reference Groups, Moralization, Adherence and Defiance. *Journal of Cross-Cultural Psychology, 46*(10), 1279–1287.

Nolan, J. M., Schultz, P. W., Cialdini, R. B., Goldstein, N. J., & Griskevicius, V. (2008). Normative Social Influence is Under-Detected. *Personality and Social Psychology Bulletin, 34*(7), 913–923.

Pareles, J. (2014, January 28) Pete Seeger, Champion of Folk Music and Social Change, Dies at 94. *New York Times*. Retrieved from: www.nytimes.com.

Pinto K. M. & Coltrane S. (2009). Divisions of Labor in Mexican Origin and Anglo Families: Structure and Culture. *Sex Roles, 60*(7), 482–495.

Platt, L. & Polavieja, J. (2016) Saying and Doing Gender: Intergenerational Transmission of Attitudes Towards the Sexual Division of Labour. *European Sociological Review, 32*(6), 820–834.

Quek, K. M-T. & Knudson-Martin, C. (2006). A Push Toward Equality: Processes Among Dual-Career Newlywed Couples in Collectivist Culture. *Journal of Marriage and Family, 68*(1), 56–69.

Risman, B. J. (2009). From Doing to Undoing: Gender As We Know It. *Gender and Society, 23*(1), 81–84.

Ryan, R. M., Huta, V., & Deci, E. L. (2008). Living Well: A Self-Determination Theory Perspective on Eudaimonia. *Journal of Happiness Studies*, 9(1), 139–170.

Schober, P. S. (2012). Paternal Child Care and Relationship Quality: A Longitudinal Analysis of Reciprocal Associations. *Journal of Marriage and Family*, 74(2), 281–296.

Snyder, C. R. & Fromkin, H. L. (1977). Abnormality as a Positive Characteristic: The Development and Validation of a Scale Measuring Need for Uniqueness. *Journal of Abnormal Psychology*, 86(5), 518–527.

Stone, P. (2007). *Opting Out? Why Women Really Quit Careers and Head Home*. Berkeley, CA: University of California Press.

van Belle, J. (2016). *Paternity and Parental Leave Policies across the European Union*. Cambridge: Rand Corporation. Retrieved from: www.rand.org/content/dam/rand/pubs/research_reports/RR1600/RR1666/RAND_RR1666.pdf.

Wilcox, B. W. & Dew, J. (2016). The Social and Cultural Predictors of Generosity in Marriage: Gender Egalitarianism, Religiosity, and Familism. *Journal of Family Issues*, 37(1) 97–118.

Wilson, K. R. & Prior, M. R. (2011). Father Involvement and Child Well-Being. *Journal of Paediatrics and Child Health*, 47(7), 405–407.

Index

60/60 parenting, 41

abilities/expertise
  as gendered *see* essentialist views
  housework preferences and, 33, 45, 72,
    260, 273–274, 334
  influence of family of origin, 104–105,
    116, 125, 142, 339, 342, 383–384
  men's childcare expertise, 38, 114,
    173–174, 336, 352–353
  rejection of gender-based *see* anti-
    essentialism
  of Robinson (Honduras), 52–53
administrative tasks *see* management/planning
Altintas, E., 15
Anderson, N., 18
anti-essentialism, 377–379
  Austria (Richard and Christine), 231
  Czech Republic (Denisa), 267
  Czech Republic (Martin), 256
  Hungary (Mia and Miki), 143
  Iceland (Hildur and Arnaldur), 304
  Indonesia (Budi and Tuti), 102–104
  Israel (Netta and Gadi), 37–39
  Portugal (Pedro and Inês), 342
  Slovenia (Petra and Tomaž), 291–292
  Sweden (Mikael and Elisabet), 89
  USA (Nick and Patty), 176
  USA (Xochitl and Felipe), 157
anti-materialism, 34, 77, 203, 341–342,
    380–381
  see also income (as secondary to family)
arguments *see* conflict

attachment *see* emotional bonds
Australia (Mike and Joanne)
  background, 195–197
  division of everyday tasks, 197–200
  equality development, 200–201
  family–paid work balance, 201–203
  influences on equality, 203–204
  national context, 196–197
Austria (Richard and Christine)
  background, 221
  division of everyday tasks, 221–226
  equality development, 227–229
  family–paid work balance, 226–229
  influences on equality, 229–234
  national context, 222–223
autonomy hypothesis, 9

bargaining approach, 9
Baxter, Janeen, 195
Becker, G. S., 8–9
bed-time routine, 172
beliefs (unconventional), 373–381
  see also anti-essentialism; anti-
    materialism; familism; feminism;
    nontraditional gender ideology
Berk, S. F., 17
Bhutan (Yangchen and Tshewang)
  background, 121–122
  division of everyday tasks, 124–131
  equality development, 125–126
  family–paid work balance, 127–128
  influences on equality, 132
  national context, 122–123

Brazil (João and Cecília)
  background, 181
  division of everyday tasks, 181–186
  equality development, 186
  family–paid work balance, 186–188
  influences on equality, 188–192
  national context, 182–183, 188
breadwinner role
  co-breadwinners, 175–176, 210–211,
    213, 302
  and hegemonic masculinity, 18, 143–144,
    157, 338, 345, 363
  and men's self-esteem, 152, 157
  women in, 357
    Australia (Joanne), 201, 204
    Austria (Christine), 227, 229
    Czech Republic (Denisa), 262–263
    Honduras (Angelica), 49
    Hungary (Mia), 143–144
    Portugal (Inês), 338–339
    Sweden (Elisabet), 86–87, 89
    USA (Xochitl), 157
breastfeeding, 35–36, 95–96, 114, 173–174,
    324–325, 350
Buchebner-Ferstl, Sabine, 221
Buddhist practices, 126–127

California *see* Southern California
care giving *see* childcare/care giving
career opportunities
  men's rejection of, 347
    Austria (Richard), 226
    Brazil (João), 187–188
    Germany (Hannes), 313
    Honduras (Robinson), 48
    Indonesia (Budi), 101
    Montenegro (Luka), 61
    Singapore (Osman), 212
    Slovenia (Tomaž), 287, 289
    UK (Dale), 325
  as secondary to family
    Hungary (Mia and Miki), 141
    Indonesia (Budi and Tuti), 100
    Portugal (Pedro and Inês), 337–338
    Singapore (Siti and Osman), 212–213
    Switzerland (Martin and Judith), 77
  women's rejection of
    Singapore (Siti), 213
    Sweden (Elisabet), 86
caring masculinity, 352
case studies, 4–5
  see also specific countries

childcare (external)
  avoided
    Australia (Mike and Joanne), 202
    Germany (Hanna and Hannes), 312
    USA (Veronica and Sam), 167
  and changing context in Hungary, 144
  institutional
    Austria (Richard and Christine),
      231–232
    Israel (Netta and Gadi), 31, 36
  by nanny/childminder
    China (Kai and Li), 274
    Indonesia (Budi and Tuti), 101
    Singapore (Siti and Osman), 209, 212
    USA (Xochitl and Felipe), 153
  national policies *see under specific*
    countries
  by wider family
    Bhutan (Yangchen and Tshewang),
      127
    China (Kai and Li), 274–275
    cultural norms, 273, 283
    Czech Republic (Denisa and David),
      258, 262
    Czech Republic (Magda and Martin),
      252
    Iceland (Hildur and Arnaldur), 298
    Indonesia (Budi and Tuti), 101
    Singapore (Siti and Osman), 211
    Slovenia (Petra and Tomaž), 284
    Turkey (Hande and Burak), 236
    USA (Xochitl and Felipe), 151
childcare subsidy, 229
childcare/care giving
  conflict about *see* conflict
  and decision-making, 102
  equal sharing of everyday tasks
    Australia (Mike and Joanne), 198–200
    Austria (Richard and Christine),
      221–225
    Bhutan (Yangchen and Tshewang),
      126–128
    Brazil (João and Cecília), 181–184, 186
    China (Kai and Li), 271–273
    Croatia (Nera and Ivo), 107–111
    Czech Republic (Denisa and David),
      257–261
    Czech Republic (Magda and Martin),
      251–253
    Germany (Hanna and Hannes), 309–312
    Honduras (Angelica and Robinson),
      43, 45–47

Hungary (Mia and Miki), 134–138
Iceland (Hildur and Arnaldur),
      297–301
Indonesia (Budi and Tuti), 96–100
Israel (Netta and Gadi), 29–32, 41
Montenegro (Maja and Luka), 55–59,
      62–64
Portugal (Pedro and Inês), 331–334
Singapore (Siti and Osman), 209–212
Slovenia (Petra and Tomaž), 281–285
Sweden (Mikael and Elisabet), 81–82,
      85
Switzerland (Martin and Judith), 71–74
Turkey (Hande and Burak), 238–241
UK (Katherine and Dale), 317–320,
      323–325
USA (Nick and Patty), 171–174
USA (Veronica and Sam), 163–165,
      167
USA (Xochitl and Felipe), 153–155
fathers' time spent on, 11–12, 348–349
gendered division of, 367–368
   in national contexts *see under specific
      countries*
   Sweden (Mikael and Elisabet), 82–84,
      90
   Switzerland (Martin and Judith),
      72–73, 75
   USA (Veronica and Sam), 166–167
   see also cultural norms; essentialist
      views; gendered norms
help from friends, 232–233
help from wider family *see* childcare
      (external)
integration with paid work
   Australia (Mike and Joanne), 201
   Austria (Richard and Christine), 226–229
   China (Kai and Li), 276–277
   Croatia (Nera and Ivo), 112
   Czech Republic (Denisa and David),
      261–264
   Czech Republic (Magda and Martin),
      253–254
   Germany (Hanna and Hannes),
      312–313
   Hungary (Mia and Miki), 139–140
   Indonesia (Budi and Tuti), 100–101
   Israel (Netta and Gadi), 35–37
   Montenegro (Maja and Luka), 62–64
   Portugal (Pedro and Inês), 331–332,
      337–339
   Singapore (Siti and Osman), 211–212

Slovenia (Petra and Tomaž), 287–288
Switzerland (Martin and Judith), 69,
      71, 73–74
UK (Katherine and Dale), 317–318,
      323–327
USA (Nick and Patty), 174–175
USA (Veronica and Sam), 166–169
men embracing *see* men
mental work of *see* management/planning
parenting styles *see* parenting styles
rewards of equal sharing, 77, 145, 191,
      315–316, 387–391
role of fathers, 349–353
tasks *see* emotional care; feeding; night-
      time care; play/activities; sick care
theories *see* theories of domestic labor
women relinquishing control of, 38–39,
      118, 178, 256–257, 340, 342, 353–354
   see also gatekeeping; maternal identity;
      primary parenting
children, rewards of equal sharing for,
      389–390
children's surnames, 291
China (Kai and Li)
   background, 270
   division of everyday tasks,
      270–274
   equality development, 274–275
   family–paid work balance, 276–277
   influences on equality, 277–279
   national context, 272–273
Choden, Tasha, 121
cleaners *see* domestic work (outsourced)
cleaning, 33, 59–60, 62, 155, 285
co-workers, responses of, 156, 286, 292,
      313–314, 327, 369–370
Cohen, P. N., 16
collectivist cultures, 213–214, 216–217, 380
comforting *see* emotional care
communication, 376–377
   Brazil (João and Cecília), 191–192
   China (Kai and Li), 279
   Croatia (Nera and Ivo), 113–114
   Czech Republic (Denisa and David), 267
   Honduras (Angelica and Robinson), 52
   Iceland (Hildur and Arnaldur), 304
   Indonesia (Budi and Tuti), 101–102
   Singapore (Siti and Osman), 216–217
   Slovenia (Petra and Tomaž), 290–291, 293
   Switzerland (Martin and Judith), 76
   USA (Nick and Patty), 174, 176
   USA (Xochitl and Felipe), 154

conflict
  about housework, 358–359
    Austria (Richard and Christine), 225
    China (Kai and Li), 274–275
    Czech Republic (Denisa and David),
      260, 262
    Iceland (Hildur and Arnaldur), 298
    Sweden (Mikael and Elisabet), 85–86
    UK (Katherine and Dale), 323
    USA (Nick and Patty), 174
    USA (Xochitl and Felipe), 155–156
  about leisure time, 76
  about parenting
    Bhutan (Yangchen and Tshewang),
      130–131
    Czech Republic (Denisa and David),
      262
    Honduras (Angelica and Robinson),
      52–53
    Israel (Netta and Gadi), 32
    Slovenia (Petra and Tomaž), 284, 291
    UK (Katherine and Dale), 323–325
    USA (Veronica and Sam), 167
  about relationship, 154–155
  and paid work, 59, 263–264
conformity pressures, 366–371
  others' responses *see* others' responses
  see also cultural norms; nonconformity
    influences
cooking
  conflict about, 156
  outsourced, 209, 274
  preferences/abilities
    Australia (Mike and Joanne), 200
    Austria (Richard and Christine), 226
    Bhutan (Yangchen and Tshewang), 129
    China (Kai and Li), 273–274
    Czech Republic (Denisa and David),
      260
    Israel (Netta and Gadi), 33
    Montenegro (Maja and Luka), 60
    UK (Katherine and Dale), 321
  by wider family, 260, 321
  and work cultures, 17
Croatia (Nera and Ivo)
  background, 107
  division of everyday tasks, 107–111
  equality development, 111–113
  family–paid work balance, 112, 114–115
  influences on equality, 113–114, 116–118
  national context, 108–109

cultural norms
  and collectivism, 380
  and domestic labor in Bhutan, 124–125, 132
  and domestic labor in Brazil, 188
  and gender ideology in Singapore, 208,
    210–211, 213–215, 377
  impact of national context and, 16–17,
    144
  and masculinity, 18, 104, 157, 188
  and relationships in Indonesia, 105
  and shopping in Indonesia, 100
Cunha, Vanessa, 331
Czech Republic (Denisa and David)
  background, 247, 257
  division of everyday tasks, 257–260
  equality development, 260–263
  family–paid work balance, 263–264
  influences on equality, 265–267
  national context, 248–249
Czech Republic (Magda and Martin)
  background, 247–248
  division of everyday tasks, 251–253
  equality development, 249–251
  family–paid work balance, 250–251,
    253–254
  influences on equality, 254–257
  national context, 248–249

Davis, S. N., 9
daycare *see* childcare (external)
Dechant, Anna, 307
decision-making, 32, 101–102
  see also communication; conflict
deference, expectation of, 53, 363–364
demand/response model, 11
demographics, national contexts *see under*
  specific countries
Dessen, Maria Auxiliadora, 181
Deutsch, Francine M., 1, 8, 161, 345, 366
Diefenbach, H., 14
Diner, Cagla, 236
doing gender approach, 17–20, 360
  see also undoing gender
domestic labor
  division of
    equal sharing *see* equal sharing
    in family of origin *see* family of origin
    gendered *see* gendered division of
      domestic labor
    in national contexts *see under specific*
      countries

theories
  gender construction, 17–20
  gender ideology, 12–14
  national context, 14–17
  relative resources, 8–11, 14, 19,
    359–360
  time availability, 11–12, 19, 347–348
  undoing gender, 4, 20–21
  see also childcare/care giving; housework
domestic sphere
  control of *see* gatekeeping
  women relinquishing control of, 38–39,
    118, 178, 256–257, 340, 342, 353–354
    see also maternal identity; primary
    parenting
domestic work (outsourced), 358
  Brazil (João and Cecília), 184, 186
  China (Kai and Li), 271, 274
  in Honduras, 51
  Iceland (Hildur and Arnaldur), 298
  Indonesia (Budi and Tuti), 97–98, 101–102
  Sweden (Mikael and Elisabet), 90
  Turkey (Hande and Burak), 236, 245
  UK (Katherine and Dale), 323

education (preschool) *see* childcare
  (external)
Elliot, K., 352
emotional bonds/attachment, 351–352,
    362–363
  Austria (Richard and Christine), 224–225
  Bhutan (Yangchen and Tshewang), 131
  Brazil (João and Cecília), 184
  Croatia (Nera and Ivo), 110
  Czech Republic (Denisa and David), 258–259
  Czech Republic (Magda and Martin), 253
  in family of origin, 255
  Hungary (Mia and Miki), 138
  Indonesia (Budi and Tuti), 99
  Israel (Netta and Gadi), 32
  Montenegro (Maja and Luka), 58
  Portugal (Pedro and Inês), 334
  Turkey (Hande and Burak), 240
  UK (Katherine and Dale), 324–325
emotional care
  by fathers, 154, 199–200, 351
  by mothers, 72–73, 165, 172
  shared, 83, 240, 284, 324
  see also emotional bonds/attachment
employers, responses to equal sharing, 265,
    313–314, 326, 338, 371

employment hours *see* part-time
  employment; time availability
  hypothesis
employment opportunities *see* career
  opportunities
employment policies/rights, 386–387
  and employer attitudes, 212, 265, 295,
    326, 341, 347, 371
  leave for sick care, 138, 174–175, 212, 259,
    286
  see also parental leave
employment structure
  Austria (Richard), 229–230
  Brazil (João), 189
  Israel (Netta and Gadi), 40
  Portugal (Pedro and Inês), 331, 338
  Slovenia (Tomaž), 289
  Turkey (Burak), 242–243
  USA (Nick), 176–177
  see also part-time employment
entitlement to equality, 375–376
  Czech Republic (David), 266
  Hungary (Mia), 142
  Portugal (Inês), 342
  USA (Patty), 173, 176, 178
  USA (Xochitl), 158
equal sharing
  case examples *see specific countries*
  development of *see under specific countries*
  in family of origin *see* family of origin
  features of
    division of housework, 357–359
    men embracing care giving, 348–353
    men's relations to paid work, 345–348
    women relinquishing domestic control/
      identity, 353–354
    women's relations to paid work, 354–357
  influences on
    families of origin, 381–386
    government policies, 386–387
    personality and identity, 371–373
    unconventional convictions, 373–381
  responses to *see* others' responses
  rewards/impact of, 3, 77, 145, 177, 191,
    267–268, 315–316, 387–391
equality *see* gender equality
essentialist views, 14
  Brazil (João and Cecília), 184, 190
  Czech Republic (David), 266–267
  Hungary (Mia and Miki), 143
  rejection of *see* anti-essentialism

essentialist views (cont.)
  Switzerland (Martin and Judith), 72–73, 75
  UK (Katherine and Dale), 323–324
Evertsson, M., 9
expertise *see* abilities/expertise

Fahlén, S., 9
familism, 379–380
  career as secondary *see* career
    opportunities
  Czech Republic (Martin), 254
  Hungary (Mia and Miki), 141–142
  Singapore (Siti and Osman), 208, 216–218
  USA (Veronica and Sam), 161–162, 168,
    170
  see also men (embracing care giving)
family of origin
  absent fathers, 149–151, 158, 177, 200
  background of Xochitl and Felipe (USA),
    149–151
  childcare by *see* childcare (external)
  domestic help from *see* housework
  as equality role models, 382, 384
    Brazil (João and Cecília), 189–190
    China (Li), 277
    Czech Republic (Denisa and David),
      266
    Czech Republic (Martin), 254–255
    Germany (Hanna and Hannes), 313
    Honduras (Angelica and Robinson),
      50–51, 53
    Iceland (Hildur and Arnaldur), 303
    Israel (Netta and Gadi), 38, 40
    Montenegro (Maja and Luka),
      64–65
    Portugal (Inês), 340, 342
    Singapore (Osman), 215–216
    UK (Katherine and Dale), 328
  equality taught in, 383–384
    Australia (Mike and Joanne), 200
    Bhutan (Tshewang), 125
    Croatia (Nera), 116
    Hungary (Mia and Miki), 142
    Indonesia (Budi), 104–105
    Portugal (Pedro), 339, 342
    Slovenia (Tomaž), 289–290
    USA (Xochitl and Felipe), 158
  impact on parenting, 53, 116–117, 232,
    254–255
  influence of, 381–386
  responses to equal sharing, 47, 156, 245,
    265, 292, 370–371

  as traditional role models, 382–383, 385
    Bhutan (Yangchen and Tshewang), 125
    Brazil (João and Cecília), 190
    China (Kai), 277–278
    Croatia (Nera and Ivo), 116
    Czech Republic (Denisa), 267
    Hungary (Mia and Miki), 142
    Indonesia (Budi and Tuti), 104–105
    Montenegro (Maja and Luka), 64–65
    Portugal (Pedro), 339
    Singapore (Siti), 215
    Slovenia (Petra and Tomaž), 289–290
    Sweden (Mikael and Elisabet), 84
    Turkey (Hande and Burak), 245–246
    USA (Veronica and Sam), 169
fatherhood
  and hegemonic masculinity, 19, 292
  see also men (embracing care giving)
feeding, 324–325, 350
  breastfeeding, 35–36, 95–96, 114,
    173–174, 324–325, 350
feminist ideology, 373–377
  China (Kai and Li), 279
  Honduras (Robinson), 50–52
  Montenegro (Maja and Luka), 65–67
  Slovenia (Petra and Tomaž), 291–292
  Sweden (Mikael and Elisabet), 85, 90
  USA (Xochitl and Felipe), 158
  see also entitlement to equality
financial decisions, 102
financial difficulties/tensions, 49, 238, 241,
    262–263
flexibility *see* employment structure
friends
  help from, 232–233
  responses to equal sharing, 369–370, 372
    China (Kai and Li), 278
    Croatia (Nera and Ivo), 117
    Honduras (Angelica and Robinson),
      47
    Iceland (Hildur and Arnaldur), 304
    Slovenia (Petra and Tomaž), 292–293
    USA (Xochitl and Felipe), 156
  social networks, 203, 232–234, 278,
    372
full-time employment, 11–12
Fuwa, M., 13, 16

gardening, 321
gatekeeping, 13, 38, 361–362
  of equal sharing couples, 66, 166, 292,
    305

by fathers, 154
rejection of, 118, 143, 204, 256–257,
  353
Gaunt, Ruth A., 1, 8, 19, 29, 345, 366
Geist, C., 15
gender construction, 17–20, 360
  see also undoing gender
gender deviance, neutralization of, 9
gender equality
  current context, 1
  in domestic sphere *see* equal sharing
  entitlement to, 375–376
    Czech Republic (David), 266
    Hungary (Mia), 142
    Portugal (Inês), 342
    USA (Patty), 173, 176, 178
    USA (Xochitl), 158
  national contexts of, 14
  see also under specific countries
gender ideology
  and national context, 14
  see also nontraditional gender ideology;
    traditional gender ideology
gender ideology hypothesis, 12–14
gender inequality, 3
  in domestic sphere *see* gendered division
    of domestic labor
  national contexts of *see under specific
    countries*
gender-based abilities *see* anti-essentialism;
  essentialist views
gendered division of domestic labor, 2
  in family of origin *see* family of origin
    (traditional role models)
  in national contexts *see under specific
    countries*
  persistent aspects of, 360–364
    expecting gratitude, 124, 322, 363–364
    protecting men's egos, 143–144,
      244–245, 363
    see also gatekeeping; management/
      planning; primary parenting
  pressures to conform, 366–371
    see also cultural norms; others'
      responses
  resistance to *see* nonconformity influences
gendered models, 367–368
gendered norms, 369–371
  cultural influences *see* cultural norms
  others' responses *see* others' responses
  resisting *see* nonconformity influences
  see also traditional gender ideology

Germany (Hanna and Hannes)
  background, 307
  division of everyday tasks, 309–312
  equality development, 307–309
  family–paid work balance, 312–313
  influences on equality, 313–315
  national context, 308–309
Gershuny, J, 10
Gíslason, Ingólfur V., 295
gotong-royong (reciprocal assistance), 96
government policies, 386–387
  benefits/subsidies, 90, 135, 197, 229,
    386–387
  employment *see* employment policies/
    rights; parental leave
  national contexts of, 15–17
  see also under specific countries
grandparents, help from *see* childcare
  (external); housework
gratitude, expectation of, 124, 322,
  363–364
Greenstein, T. N., 9, 12
Gupta, S., 9–10

Haas, Linda, 80
Honduras (Angelica and Robinson)
  background, 43–44
  division of everyday tasks, 43, 45–47
  equality development, 47–48
  family–paid work balance, 48–49
  influences on equality, 49–53
  national context, 44–45
Hook, J. L., 15–17
household labor *see* childcare/care giving;
  domestic labor; housework
households, national contexts of *see under
  specific countries*
housewifization, 103
housework
  conflict about *see* conflict
  equal sharing of everyday tasks,
    357–359
    Australia (Mike and Joanne), 198–201
    Austria (Richard and Christine),
      225–226, 228
    Bhutan (Yangchen and Tshewang),
      125–129
    Brazil (João and Cecília), 184–186
    China (Kai and Li), 270–274
    Croatia (Nera and Ivo), 110
    Czech Republic (Denisa and David),
      259–260

housework (cont.)
    Czech Republic (Magda and Martin),
        251–253
    Germany (Hanna and Hannes), 310–311
    Honduras (Angelica and Robinson),
        43, 45–47
    Hungary (Mia and Miki), 134–139
    Iceland (Hildur and Arnaldur),
        298–299
    Indonesia (Budi and Tuti), 96–100
    Israel (Netta and Gadi), 33
    Montenegro (Maja and Luka), 59–60, 62
    Portugal (Pedro and Inês), 334–335, 337
    Singapore (Siti and Osman), 208–209,
        211
    Slovenia (Petra and Tomaž), 281–286,
        288–289
    Sweden (Mikael and Elisabet), 84
    Switzerland (Martin and Judith), 71–72
    Turkey (Hande and Burak), 238–240,
        243–244
    UK (Katherine and Dale), 319–322
    USA (Nick and Patty), 171, 173
    USA (Veronica and Sam), 164–165,
        167
    USA (Xochitl and Felipe), 155–156
  gendered division in national contexts *see
    under specific countries*
  help from wider family, 127, 262,
    274–275, 284, 311, 321
  and masculinity, 244–245
  outsourced *see* domestic work
  relative resources focus on, 10
  tasks *see* cleaning; cooking; laundry;
    tidying
  theories *see* theories of domestic labor
  women relinquishing control, 353
  see also gatekeeping
housework hours
  national contexts *see under specific
    countries*
  and time availability approach, 11–12
human capital, 10
Humer, Živa, 281
Hungary (Mia and Miki)
  background, 134
  division of everyday tasks, 134–138
  equality development, 138–140
  family–paid work balance, 140–141
  influences on equality, 141–145
  national context, 135–136, 144

Iceland (Hildur and Arnaldur)
  background, 295
  division of everyday tasks, 295–301
  equality development, 302–303
  family–paid work balance, 301–302
  influences on equality, 302–305
  national context, 296–297
identity, 371–373
  see also masculinity; maternal identity;
    personality
illness *see* sick care
immigrants (Mexican), 148–149
  case example *see* Southern California
    (Xochitl and Felipe)
income
  and anti-materialism, 34, 77, 203,
    341–342, 380–381
  difference in, 86–87, 89, 100, 127,
    143–144
  equal, 175–176, 254, 302, 359
  relative resources theory, 8–11, 359
  as secondary to family
    Australia (Mike and Joanne), 203
    Brazil (João and Cecília),
      188
    Croatia (Nera and Ivo), 115
    Israel (Netta and Gadi), 34, 41
    Portugal (Pedro and Inês), 338,
      341–342
    Switzerland (Judith and Martin), 77
    UK (Katherine and Dale), 325
    views of Siti and Osman (Singapore),
      212–213, 217–218
  women's, 354–355, 357, 359
  see also breadwinner role
Indonesia (Budi and Tuti)
  background, 93–96
  division of everyday tasks, 96–100
  equality development, 95–96
  family–paid work balance, 100–101
  influences on equality, 101–105
  national context, 94–95
interviews, 21–22
Islam, 93, 97
Israel (Netta and Gadi)
  background, 29
  division of everyday tasks, 29–33, 41
  equality development, 34–35
  family–paid work balance, 33–37
  influences on equality, 37–41
  national context, 30–31

Kamo, Y., 13
kindergarten, 223
   see also childcare (external)
knowledge *see* abilities/expertise
Knudsen, K., 14
Knudsen-Martin, Carmen, 206
kodrat (predestined obligations), 103–104
Kosakowska-Berezecka, N., 18
Kuhar, Metka, 281
Kulik, L., 13
Kusujiarti, Siti, 93

labor force, national contexts of *see under*
   specific countries
laundry
   Austria (Richard and Christine), 225–226
   Czech Republic (Magda and Martin),
      252
   Iceland (Hildur and Arnaldur), 298
   Israel (Netta and Gadi), 33
   Montenegro (Maja and Luka), 60
   UK (Katherine and Dale), 321
   USA (Xochitl and Felipe), 155–156
Luke, N., 18

McGill, B. S., 13
machismo, 51, 374
machistas, 50, 52, 153, 156–157, 374
management/planning, 361
   Brazil (João and Cecília), 184
   Croatia (Nera and Ivo), 111
   Czech Republic (Denisa and David), 259,
      262
   Czech Republic (Magda and Martin),
      253
   Honduras (Angelica and Robinson), 46
   Hungary (Mia and Miki), 138
   Iceland (Hildur and Arnaldur), 299
   Israel (Netta and Gadi), 33
   Montenegro (Maja and Luka), 59
   Portugal (Pedro and Inês), 334–335
   Slovenia (Petra and Tomaž), 285
   Sweden (Mikael and Elisabet), 83–84
   Switzerland (Martin and Judith), 73
   Turkey (Hande and Burak), 241
   UK (Katherine and Dale), 321
   USA (Nick and Patty), 172
   USA (Veronica and Sam), 164
Maříková, Hana, 247
Marinho, Sofia, 331
Márquez, Alicia, 147

marriage
   cultural differences, 94, 122
   rewards of equal sharing for, 390–391
   see also relationships
masculinity (caring), 352
masculinity (hegemonic)
   and breadwinner role, 18, 143–144, 157,
      338, 345, 363
   and cultural norms, 18, 104, 157,
      188
   and fatherhood, 19, 292
   and housework, 244–245
   and others' responses to sharing, 156,
      292, 304, 370
   and paid work, 345
   and protecting egos, 143–144, 244–245, 363
   rejected in families of origin, 189–190
   see also machismo; machistas
maternal abilities *see* anti-essentialism;
      essentialist views
maternal identity
   and cultural norms, 188
   insecurity about, 340
   rejecting idealized, 38–39, 85, 103, 112,
      276, 353–354
maternity leave
   Austria (Christine), 228–229
   Croatia (Nera), 112
   Czech Republic (Magda), 250
   Germany (Hanna), 309
   Israel (Netta), 35
   Montenegro (Maja), 62
   national contexts of *see under specific*
      countries
   Slovenia (Petra), 287–288
   see also parental leave
men
   embracing care giving, 345–346,
      348–353, 388–389
   Austria (Richard), 228, 231, 233–234
   Brazil (João), 183, 191
   China (Kai), 275
   Croatia (Ivo), 112–113, 115
   Czech Republic (David), 261–262, 268
   Czech Republic (Martin), 250,
      255–256, 268
   Germany (Hannes), 315–316
   Hungary (Miki), 139, 145
   Indonesia (Budi), 95–96
   Montenegro (Luka), 62
   Portugal (Pedro), 336–337

men (cont.)
  Switzerland (Martin), 74–75, 77
  USA (Felipe), 154, 158–159
  USA (Nick), 173–174, 177
  expectation of gratitude/deference, 53,
    124, 322, 363–364
  influenced by family of origin, 382–384
    see also family of origin
  in national labour force *see under specific
    countries*
  protecting egos of, 143–144, 244–245, 363
  relations to paid work, 19, 345–348
    Australia (Mike), 201–203
    Austria (Richard), 226, 230
    Bhutan (Tshewang), 127–128
    Brazil (João), 187–188
    China (Kai), 276
    Croatia (Ivo), 115
    Czech Republic (David), 264
    Germany (Hannes), 313
    Hungary (Miki), 140
    Iceland (Arnaldur), 301–302
    Indonesia (Budi), 101
    Portugal (Pedro), 337–338, 341
    Slovenia (Tomaž), 286–287
    Sweden (Mikael), 87–88
    Turkey (Burak), 242
    UK (Dale), 325–326
    USA (Felipe), 152, 157
    USA (Nick), 175, 178
    USA (Sam), 167–170, 178
  rewards of equal sharing for, 77, 145,
    177, 191, 315–316, 388–389
  see also masculinity
mental work *see* management/planning
Mexican immigrants, 148–149
  case example *see* Southern California
    (Xochitl and Felipe)
Montenegro (Maja and Luka)
  background, 55
  division of everyday tasks, 55–60
  equality development, 61–64
  family–paid work balance, 60–62
  influences on equality, 64–67
  national context, 56–57
Moon, S.H., 13
motherhood
  essentialist views of, 72–73, 75, 143, 184,
    190, 266–267
  gendered expectations of, 18–19
  and identity *see* maternal identity

views of Christine (Austria), 227
views of Siti (Singapore), 211
Murphy-Graham, Erin, 43
musyawarah (decision-making), 101–102

national context
  in case examples *see under specific
    countries*
  and domestic labor theories, 14–17
Nentwich, Julia C., 69
Nermo, M., 9
New England (Nick and Patty), 177–179
  background, 161
  division of everyday tasks, 171–173
  equality development, 173–174
  family–paid work balance, 174–176
  influences on equality, 176–177
  national context, 162–163
New England (Veronica and Sam), 177–179
  background, 161
  division of everyday tasks, 163–165
  equality development, 166–167
  familism of, 161–162, 170
  family–paid work balance, 166–170
  influences on equality, 169–170
  national context, 162–163
night-time care
  by fathers, 351
  Czech Republic (Denisa and David), 261
  Germany (Hanna and Hannes), 310
  Indonesia (Budi and Tuti), 99
  Israel (Netta and Gadi), 32, 35
  Portugal (Pedro and Inês), 332
  Singapore (Siti and Osman), 211
nonconformity influences
  family of origin *see* family of origin
  personality and identity, 243, 337,
    371–373
  policies *see* government policies
  unconventional convictions, 373–381
    see also anti-essentialism; anti-
      materialism; familism; feminism;
      nontraditional gender ideology
nontraditional gender ideology, 12–14,
    373–377
  Austria (Richard and Christine), 230–231
  Croatia (Nera and Ivo), 113
  Czech Republic (Denisa and David), 267
  Honduras (Angelica and Robinson),
    49–52
  Israel (Netta and Gadi), 37

Montenegro (Maja and Luka), 65–67
Portugal (Pedro and Inês), 342
Singapore (Siti and Osman), 208,
   210–211, 214–215
Sweden (Mikael and Elisabet), 85, 88–90
Switzerland (Martin and Judith), 78
Turkey (Hande and Burak), 243
UK (Katherine and Dale), 328
USA (Xochitl and Felipe), 157–158
nurseries *see* childcare (external)

others' responses (to equal sharing),
   369–372
   negative, 369–371
      Bhutan (Yangchen and Tshewang),
         125
      Croatia (Nera and Ivo), 117
      Czech Republic (Denisa and David),
         265
      Czech Republic (Magda and Martin),
         257
      Germany (Hanna and Hannes), 314
      Slovenia (Petra and Tomaž), 286,
         292–293
      Turkey (Hande and Burak), 245
      UK (Katherine and Dale), 327–328
      USA (Xochitl and Felipe), 156
   positive, 369
      Austria (Richard and Christine),
         233–234
      China (Kai and Li), 278
      Croatia (Nera and Ivo), 117
      Germany (Hanna and Hannes),
         313–314
      Honduras (Angelica and Robinson),
         47
      Iceland (Hildur and Arnaldur), 303–304
      Portugal (Pedro and Inês), 338
      UK (Katherine and Dale), 326–328
   surprise, Hungary (Mia and Miki), 145

paid work
   integration with family *see* childcare/care
      giving
   men's relations to *see* men
   national contexts of labour force *see*
      under specific countries
   women's relations to *see* women
   see also career opportunities; employment
      policies/rights; employment
      structure; income; parental leave

parental leave, 386–387
   Austria (Richard and Christine), 228–229
   Croatia (Nera), 112
   Czech Republic (Denisa and David),
      260–262, 265
   Czech Republic (Magda and Martin),
      250–251
   fathers' use of, 346, 348–349
   Germany (Hanna and Hannes), 309,
      312–314
   Hungary (Mia and Miki), 139–140
   Iceland (Hildur and Arnaldur), 295, 305
   Israel (Netta), 35
   Montenegro (Maja), 62
   national contexts of *see under specific*
      countries
   others' responses to, 265, 295, 341,
      371
   Portugal (Pedro and Inês), 336–337, 341
   Slovenia (Petra and Tomaž), 287–288
   Sweden (Mikael and Elisabet), 80, 85
parenthood
   doing gender and transition to, 18–19
   see also childcare/care giving
parenting guides, 38, 352–353
parenting styles
   case examples
      Australia (Mike and Joanne), 199–200
      Bhutan (Yangchen and Tshewang),
         130–131
      Brazil (João and Cecília), 184
      Croatia (Nera and Ivo), 111
      Czech Republic (Denisa and David),
         259
      Germany (Hanna and Hannes),
         311–312
      Honduras (Angelica and Robinson),
         52–53
      Iceland (Hildur and Arnaldur),
         299–301
      Indonesia (Budi and Tuti), 99
      Israel (Netta and Gadi), 32
      Singapore (Siti and Osman), 212
      Slovenia (Petra and Tomaž), 284, 291
      Sweden (Mikael and Elisabet), 82–83
      Switzerland (Martin and Judith), 75
      Turkey (Hande and Burak), 240–241
      UK (Katherine and Dale), 324–325
      USA (Nick and Patty), 172–173
      USA (Xochitl and Felipe), 154,
         157

parenting styles (cont.)
  conflict about *see* conflict
  nontraditional gender ideology, 157
part-time employment, 346, 355
  Australia (Mike and Joanne), 201–203
  Czech Republic (Martin), 253
  Germany (Hanna and Hannes), 307
  Slovenia (Petra), 286–287
  Swedish policy, 88
  Switzerland (Martin and Judith), 69
  UK (Katherine and Dale), 323, 326–327, 356
  USA (Veronica), 356
paternity leave, 288, 346, 348–349, 386–387
  see also parental leave
patriarchy (rejection of), 50–52
  see also nontraditional gender ideology
peers *see* co-workers; friends
personality, 83–84, 243, 337, 371–373
Pfau-Effinger, B., 16
play/activities, 31, 171, 184, 318
policies, 386–387
  benefits/subsidies, 90, 135, 197, 229,
    386–387
  employment *see* employment policies/
    rights; parental leave
  and national context, 15–17
    see also under specific countries
Portugal (Pedro and Inês)
  background, 331
  division of everyday tasks, 331–335
  equality development, 335–337
  family–paid work balance, 337–339
  influences on equality, 339–342
  national context, 332–333, 341
preschools *see* childcare (external)
preferences/abilities (housework), 33, 45,
    72, 260, 273–274, 334
primary parenting (women sharing), 362–363
  difficulties of sharing, 99, 169, 261–262,
    325, 362–363
  willingly sharing, 178, 201, 204, 256–257

Quek, Karen Mui-Teng, 206

reciprocal assistance (*gotong-royong*), 96
relationships, 375–376, 390–391
  Brazil (João and Cecília), 191–192
  Honduras (Angelica and Robinson), 47,
    50
  Hungary (Mia and Miki), 141–142
  Iceland (Hildur and Arnaldur), 301

Montenegro (Maja and Luka), 66
  Singapore (Siti and Osman), 208, 210, 217
  Slovenia (Petra and Tomaž), 290–291, 293
  Turkey (Hande and Burak), 241, 243
  USA (Veronica and Sam), 161
  USA (Xochitl and Felipe), 151, 154–155
  see also communication; marriage
relative resources approach, 8–11, 14, 19,
    359–360
religion
  in daily lives, 93, 97, 126–127
  national contexts of *see under specific
    countries*
research analysis, 22–23
research ethics, 23
research participants, 21
research protocol, 21–22
researchers, 21
resources *see* income; relative resources
    approach
responses *see* others' responses
Richards, Madison E., 366
Roder, Dolma Choden, 121
role models, 313
  see also family of origin
Rose, Judy, 195
Rost, Harald, 307
rukun (harmonious relationship), 105

Schälin, Stefanie, 69
Schulz, Florian, 307
self-employment, 226, 229
self-esteem, 152, 157, 371–372, 388–389
Shen, Yifei, 270
Shin, J., 13
sick care, 352
  Austria (Richard and Christine), 224–225
  Croatia (Nera and Ivo), 111
  Czech Republic (Denisa and David), 259
  Hungary (Mia and Miki), 138
  Singapore (Siti and Osman), 212
  Slovenia (Petra and Tomaž), 284, 286
  Switzerland (Martin and Judith), 72
  Turkey (Hande and Burak), 240
  USA (Nick and Patty), 174–175
Šikić-Mićanović, Lynette, 107
Singapore (Siti and Osman)
  background, 206–208
  division of everyday tasks, 208–210
  equality development, 210–212
  family–paid work balance, 212–213

influences on equality, 213–217
national context, 207, 214, 217
Slovenia (Petra and Tomaž)
  background, 281
  division of everyday tasks, 281–286
  equality development, 287–289
  family–paid work balance, 286–287
  influences on equality, 289–293
  national context, 282–283
social networks, 203, 232–234, 278, 372
  see also friends
socialization see family of origin
solo childcare, 349
soothing see emotional care
Southern California (Xochitl and Felipe)
  background, 147–151
  division of everyday tasks, 153–156
  equality development, 151
  family–paid work balance, 152–153
  influences on equality, 156–159
  national context, 148–149
spiritual well-being, 125
Stanley-Stevens, Leslie, 80
Stojanović, Milena Račeta, 55
Sullivan, Oriel, 10, 15, 317
Sweden (Mikael and Elisabet)
  background, 80
  division of everyday tasks, 80–86
  equality development, 84–85
  family–paid work balance, 86–88
  influences on equality, 88–91
  national context, 81
Switzerland (Martin and Judith)
  background, 69–70
  division of everyday tasks, 71–74
  equality development, 74–75
  family–paid work balance, 69, 71, 73–74
  influences on equality, 75–78
  national context, 70–71, 75–76

Takács, Judit, 134
Tazi-Preve, Mariam Irene, 221
Tennhoff, Wiebke, 69
theories of domestic labor
  gender construction, 17–20
  gender ideology, 12–14
  national context, 14–17
  relative resources, 8–11, 14, 19, 359–360
  time availability, 11–12, 19, 347–348
  undoing gender, 4, 20–21
tidying, 225

time
  devoted to children by fathers, 348–349
  see also housework hours; work hours
time availability hypothesis, 11–12, 19,
    347–348
Torres, Claudio V., 181
traditional gender ideology, 12–14
  and negative responses see others'
    responses
  in Singapore, 208, 210–211, 213–215, 377
  see also cultural norms
traditional markets, 100
trust, 50
Tsoref, H., 13
Turkey (Hande and Burak)
  background, 236–238
  division of everyday tasks, 238–241
  family–paid work balance, 242
  influences on equality, 242–246
  national context, 237–238

unconventional convictions, 373–381
  see also anti-essentialism; anti-
    materialism; familism; feminism;
    nontraditional gender ideology
undoing gender, 4, 20–21
  features of
    division of housework, 357–359
    men embracing care giving, 348–353
    men's relations to paid work, 345–348
    women relinquishing domestic control,
      353–354
    women's relations to paid work,
      354–357
  rewards of equal sharing, 387–391
  see also conformity pressures;
    nonconformity influences
United Kingdom (Katherine and Dale)
  background, 317
  division of everyday tasks, 317–322
  equality development, 322–325
  family–paid work balance, 317–318,
    325–327
  influences on equality, 327–329
  national context, 318–319
United States see New England; Southern
  California

Wærness, K., 14
Wall, Karin, 331
washing see laundry

welfare benefits/subsidies, 90, 135, 197,
    229, 386–387
welfare regimes, 15–16
West, C., 17, 20
Wolfe, C. M., 15
women
    as breadwinners *see* breadwinner role
    gatekeeping by *see* gatekeeping
    influenced by family of origin, 384–385
        see also family of origin
    in national labour force *see under specific*
        countries
    relations to paid work, 18–19, 354–357,
        359–360, 387
        Australia (Joanne), 201–202
        Austria (Christine), 226–227,
            229–231
        Bhutan (Yangchen), 127–128
        Brazil (Cecília), 186–187
        China (Li), 276
        Croatia (Nera), 112, 114–115
        Czech Republic (Denisa), 261, 263–265
        Czech Republic (Magda), 254, 256–257
        Germany (Hanna), 313
        Hungary (Mia), 140–141, 144
        Iceland (Hildur), 301
        Indonesia (Tuti), 101, 103
        Israel (Netta), 34
        Montenegro (Maja), 61, 63–64
        Portugal (Inês), 337–338, 341
        Singapore (Siti), 212–214
        Slovenia (Petra), 286–287
        Sweden (Elisabet), 86–89
        Switzerland (Judith), 77
        Turkey (Hande), 242
        UK (Katherine), 326
        USA (Patty), 175
        USA (Veronica), 166–169
        see also breadwinner role; career
            opportunities; employment policies/
            rights; employment structure;
            parental leave
    relinquishing domestic control, 38–39,
        118, 178, 256–257, 340, 342,
        353–354
    rewards of equal sharing for, 177,
        267–268, 315–316, 387–388
    sharing primary parenting, 362–363
        difficulties of sharing, 99, 169,
            261–262, 325, 362–363
        willingly sharing, 178, 201, 204,
            256–257
    see also maternal identity; motherhood
work cultures, and cooking, 17
work hours, 17, 355
    see also part-time employment
workforce, in national contexts *see under*
    specific countries

Zimmerman, D., 17, 20